Yuval Ben-Bassat is Lecturer in the Department of Middle Eastern History, University of Haifa.

Eyal Ginio is Senior Lecturer and Chair of the Department of Islamic and Middle Eastern Studies, The Hebrew University of Jerusalem.

LATE OTTOMAN PALESTINE

The Period of Young Turk Rule

Edited by
Yuval Ben-Bassat
and
Eyal Ginio

I.B. TAURIS
LONDON • NEW YORK • OXFORD • NEW DELHI • SYDNEY

BLOOMSBURY ACADEMIC
Bloomsbury Publishing Plc
50 Bedford Square, London, WC1B 3DP, UK
1385 Broadway, New York, NY 10018, USA
29 Earlsfort Terrace, Dublin 2, Ireland

BLOOMSBURY, BLOOMSBURY ACADEMIC and the Diana logo
are trademarks of Bloomsbury Publishing Plc

First published in 2011 by I. B. Tauris
This paperback edition published by Bloomsbury Academic 2021

Copyright Editorial selection and Introduction © 2011
Yuval Ben-Bassat and Eyal Ginio

Copyright Individual Chapters © 2011 Butrus Abu-Manneh, Necati Alkan, Yasemin Avcı, Yuval Ben-Bassat, Yaron Ben Naeh, Johann Büssow, Michelle U. Campos, Louis Fishman, Eyal Ginio, Abigail Jacobson, Ruth Kark, Bedross Der Matossian, Issam Nassar, Nadav Solomonovich, Mahmoud Yazbak

Yuval Ben-Bassat and Eyal Ginio have asserted their right under the Copyright, Designs and Patents Act, 1988, to be identified as Author of this work.

For legal purposes the Acknowledgements on p. vii constitute
an extension of this copyright page.

All rights reserved. No part of this publication may be reproduced or transmitted in any form or by any means, electronic or mechanical, including photocopying, recording, or any information storage or retrieval system, without prior permission in writing from the publishers.

Bloomsbury Publishing Plc does not have any control over, or responsibility for, any third-party websites referred to or in this book. All internet addresses given in this book were correct at the time of going to press. The author and publisher regret any inconvenience caused if addresses have changed or sites have ceased to exist, but can accept no responsibility for any such changes.

A catalogue record for this book is available from the British Library.

A catalog record for this book is available from the Library of Congress.

ISBN: HB: 978-1-8488-5631-8
PB: 978-0-7556-4358-5
ePDF: 978-0-85771-994-2

Library of Ottoman Studies 29

Typeset by Newgen Publishers, Chennai

To find out more about our authors and books visit
www.bloomsbury.com and sign up for our newsletters.

CONTENTS

Acknowledgements vii

Note on Transliteration ix

1 Introduction: The Case Study of Palestine during
  the Young Turk Era 1
  Yuval Ben-Bassat and Eyal Ginio

Part I   Citizenship, Election and Social Change

2 Making Citizens, Contesting Citizenship in Late
  Ottoman Palestine 17
  Michelle U. Campos

3 Elections in Late Ottoman Palestine: Early Exercises in
  Political Representation 35
  Mahmoud Yazbak

4 Children of the Revolution: Youth in Palestinian
  Public Life, 1908–14 55
  Johann Büssow

Part II   The 'Civilizing Mission' and Center-Periphery Relationships

5 Jerusalem and Jaffa in the Late Ottoman Period: The
  Concession-Hunting Struggle for Public Works Projects 81
  Yasemin Avcı

6 Understanding the 1911 Ottoman Parliament Debate on Zionism in Light of the Emergence of a 'Jewish Question' 103
Louis Fishman

7 Jerusalem under the Young Turks: A Study Based on Local Sources 125
Issam Nassar

Part III Intellectual Responses

8 Arab-Ottomanists' Reactions to the Young Turk Revolution 145
Butrus Abu-Manneh

9 Jews Writing in Arabic: Shimon Moyal, Nissim Malul and the Mixed Palestinian/Eretz Israeli Locale 165
Abigail Jacobson

10 The Young Turk Revolution of 1908 as Reflected in the Media of the Jewish Community in Palestine 183
Ruth Kark and Nadav Solomonovich

Part IV Inter- and Intra-Communal Relationships

11 Administrating the Non-Muslims and the 'Question of Jerusalem' after the Young Turk Revolution 211
Bedross Der Matossian

12 The Zionist Struggle as Reflected in the Jewish Press in Istanbul in the aftermath of the Young Turk Revolution, 1908–18 241
Yaron Ben Naeh

13 The Young Turks and the Baha'is in Palestine 259
Necati Alkan

Bibliography 279
Index 299

ACKNOWLEDGEMENTS

Many individuals and organizations contributed to this project on the Young Turk era in late Ottoman Palestine and accompanied us throughout our journey to publication.

We are grateful to the Yad Izhak Ben-Zvi Institute in Jerusalem for hosting the conference 'Centenary of the Young Turk Revolution (1908): The Young Turk Era as Experienced in Palestine', in July 2008 in honor of Professor Haim Gerber's retirement. Many of the presentations gave rise to ideas that were later developed into chapters for this book. We are grateful for the generous support for the conference provided by the Institute of Asian and African Studies at the Hebrew University of Jerusalem. Mrs. Yael Dinovitz from Yad Ben-Zvi was extremely helpful and forthcoming in helping to organize the conference and contributed to its success.

Noteworthy financial aid for the publication of this book was obtained through the efforts of several persons and institutes at the University of Haifa (the Rector, the Dean of Humanities, the Head of the Research Authority), and at the Hebrew University of Jerusalem (the Forum for Turkish Studies, the Institute of Asian and African Studies). We are thankful to all of them for allowing us to complete the publication of the book.

Mrs. Esther Singer did a fine job editing the papers, which make use of some ten different languages, unifying and standardizing them, and making them easy to read.

Finally, we would also like to thank Joanna Godfrey and Maria Marsh from I.B.Tauris Publishers who oversaw the project, and answered all our questions and concerns quickly and efficiently.

NOTE ON TRANSLITERATION

The use of Ottoman Turkish, Arabic and Persian sources in the different articles complicates the issue of transliterations in this volume. In general, when referring to sources in Ottoman Turkish, we have transliterated into modern Turkish. When referring to terms and proper names in Arabic a modified system of transliteration has been adopted that eliminates under-dots on consonants and macrons on vowels and uses just a representation of the *'ayn* and *hamza*. The editors hope that these measures will make the text easily accessible and similar words recognizable. The editors of this volume have left individual authors to make their own choices between transliterating names and terms from Arabic or Ottoman Turkish.

CHAPTER 1

INTRODUCTION: THE CASE STUDY OF PALESTINE DURING THE YOUNG TURK ERA

YUVAL BEN-BASSAT AND EYAL GINIO

In its 4 August 1325 [17 August 1909] issue, the Turkish-Arabic bi-lingual weekly *Kudüs-i Şerif / al-Quds al-Sharif* reported on a play staged in Jerusalem by the local branch of the Committee of Union and Progress (CUP).[1] Although the Turkish part of the weekly devoted several columns to the event, the section in Arabic provided its readers with minimal coverage of only a few lines. The actors were local Muslim and Greek-Orthodox children studying at the local preparatory schools. The modest entrance fees were collected to donate to the Ottoman Navy. According to the report, the children performed some 'very exemplary national plays' (*gayet-i ibret âmiz milli birer oyun icra*). People of all ages filled the *Verité* Theater at the Jaffa Gate and its surroundings to capacity, thus displaying their desire to assist the Ottoman Navy. At the end of the play, one of the schoolboys gave a speech that the journal chose to quote in full.

The speech was an appeal by the young performer to the fathers in the audience. While evoking the greatness of Ottoman seafarers from bygone generations and their ability to unite in their patriotic sentiments to successfully defend the Ottoman realms at sea, he bemoaned the incapacity of the Ottomans to face even their smallest foes during the recent period of despotism (*istibdad*) – the term used by the CUP to describe the period of Hamidian rule. Now, under the benevolent rule of the CUP, the boy continued his speech, the time had come to defend the motherland. The children were determined to make the greatest sacrifices to protect her rights. The boy claimed that his hope was to see the fathers participating fully in the effort to safeguard the motherland.

When the speaker referred to what he called the fathers' indifference to the patriotic mission of saving the homeland, he used childish language to stir the parents into action since, 'your small children are tormented every time they reflect on this reality'. The schoolboy closed his speech by declaring:

> As we heard, our neighbor, Greece, wants to detach the island of Crete from our homeland and annex it to its own domains. We have yet to see any initiative on your part to prevent such aggression that is totally devoid of any legal right! If you choose to remain passive, it is us who are ready to fulfill our defensive mission, as the Ottomans are no longer willing to relinquish any part of the motherland! [...] The Ottoman lands will always remain Ottoman![2]

This patriotic speech is emblematic of the atmosphere that the official periodical was striving to create, and is typical of its attempts to construct its authenticity and reliability. The periodical wanted to convince its readership that a unified position was shared by all the inhabitants of Jerusalem as well as elsewhere in the Ottoman Empire under the new regime. It depicted a single community, above and beyond confessional differences, that was united in its patriotic convictions and led by the young generation. This generation was not afflicted by the passivity and apathy that characterized the older generations who had come of age under the despotic rule of the ancient regime. Similar officially-supported ceremonies and celebration occurred with dazzling frequency all over the Empire. Their main goal was to popularize the messages disseminated by the new regime, which was struggling to gain legitimacy and popular support, and at the same time manipulate public opinion in its favor. Matthew Truesdell, who explored the use of public celebrations under the French Second Empire, argued that such events were a powerful instrument for 'dealing with a political system based on universal male suffrage and a society that put ever more trust in the value of popular opinions'.[3] Faced with comparable challenges and difficulties, the newly established Young Turk regime, resorted to similar techniques of which the above-mentioned play is only one modest example out of many.

The Young Turk legacy, however, is not limited to the creation of powerful images and public spectacles. In fact, it is hard to think of any other event in the late history of the Ottoman Empire that generated such high expectations for change and triggered so many political and social processes as did the Revolution of 1908. Above all, it brought the thirty-year reign of the controversial Sultan Abdülhamid II (r. 1876–1909) to an end, even though nominally he remained on the throne for almost another year, and restored the long-delayed 1876 Constitution and a parliamentary regime. The slogans and banners used at the time of the Revolution and in its immediate aftermath called for granting equal rights to all citizens of the Empire, and emphasized a belief in the commitment of the new regime to bringing progress, prosperity and modernity to all the provinces of the Empire.[4]

Many inhabitants of the Empire were eager to instigate new relationships with the Empire's political center as well as between the various ethnic and religious groups themselves. For the first time they were truly equal citizens who could elect their own representatives to the Ottoman parliament and freely express their political agendas, since the strict censorship of the media and the ban on political activity had been lifted. The policy of Ottomanism which envisioned an Empire run by a constitutional regime, whose citizens were all equal before the law, became the official state policy, at least nominally.[5]

Nevertheless, the crippling circumstances in which the Empire soon found itself, including the unilateral secession of several European provinces, the national awakening of ethnic and religious minorities, the loss of vast territories in the wars in Libya and in the Balkan Wars, and above all the onset of World War I,[6] all contributed to portraying the Young Turk Era in the historiography of the late Ottoman

Empire as a period of wars and national struggles while downplaying the civilian facets of the Young Turk rule.[7] The heterogenic nature of the Young Turk movement, whose members' common denominator was often only their wish to dethrone Abdülhamid II, and the enormous difficulties it encountered in implementing a consensual policy in the first stages after the Revolution before the CUP consolidated its hold over the Empire, contributed likewise in retrospect to this image. Hence, the decade between the Revolution and the collapse of the Ottoman Empire at the end of World War I is typically perceived as a period of desperate attempts on the part of the Young Turks, headed by the CUP, to postpone the inevitable and long-overdue collapse of the Empire. The influential Kemalist historiography as well, in its attempt to cast the events surrounding the establishment of modern Turkey as a complete break with the Ottoman past, contributed its share to the marginalization of the Revolution and its effects, and to its grim depiction.[8]

However, as recent research has shown, the decade of the Young Turk rule between 1908 and 1918 brought about some far-reaching transformations in the structure of Ottoman society, the political and legal systems, the perception of citizenship, the personal status of the Empire's citizens, the ideology the state defined as a common base for its inhabitants, as well as freedom of expression, a free press, and the right to unionize (at least until the *coup d'état* of January 1913).[9] In the words of Feroz Ahmad:

> As though in a rush to make amends for the years lost by the Hamidian generation, the Young Turks experimented with virtually every sphere of life; hardly anything was left untouched. They not only changed the political system but they also attempted to refashion society by borrowing more freely from the West than ever before.[10]

Prompted by the recent historiography of the Young Turk era and its heritage, this collective volume, which comprises twelve chapters written by scholars from different backgrounds, explores the impact of the Young Turk rule between 1908 and 1918 on the society and politics in Palestine. Palestine, a land which at the time largely corresponded to the borders of the *sancak*s of Acre and Nablus and the independent *mutasarrıflık* of Jerusalem and did not constitute a separate geopolitical and administrative entity,[11] serves here as a prism to examine and evaluate the new regime's policies. On the one hand, Palestine had several unique characteristics that differentiated it from other provinces in the Empire, such as the symbolic status of the Holy Land in international politics, the activity of various foreign governments and organizations, the heterogeneous nature of the population, and the growth of Jewish immigration and settlement activity. Moreover, the fact that a separate geo-political entity, which largely corresponded to the borders of what was generally accepted as and defined as Palestine or the Holy Land was established shortly after the termination of Ottoman rule under the British Mandate, reinforces the need to look closely at the events there during the preceding decade.[12] At the same time, due to its nature and its growing significance in Ottoman eyes, which reached its peak during World War I, Palestine can be seen as a microcosm in which many of the Young Turk policies were implemented during the decade of their rule.[13]

This volume is based on a wide variety of Ottoman sources such as Ottoman official documents, local and communal archives, the press in the various local languages, memoirs and diaries and the like. It explores the Young Turk rule in Palestine from different perspectives and provides readers with new insights into a fascinating and troubling period in the history of this land. It likewise reflects the ethnic, religious, and social diversity of Palestine's population at the time. Furthermore, it analyzes the Young Turk perceptions of Palestine as reflected in their political, economic and cultural policies as well as in their development programs for this part of the Empire. Concomitantly, it discusses the responses of the local populations to these new directives and programs originating in Istanbul and shows how the Revolution changed the lives and perceptions of the various groups living in Palestine, and how it altered their views of their own status and role within the Ottoman Empire, both vis-à-vis other communities and internally. Finally, the volume demonstrates how the various communities in Palestine perceived the Young Turk

Revolution differently according to their own particularistic agendas. These different approaches may explain the prompt disillusionment and ensuing disappointment shared by many of Palestine's inhabitants regarding the Revolution.

The chapters approach issues as varied as local politics and the emergence of civil society, political organizations, parliamentary elections, Palestinian youth in the wake of the Revolution, the role of the press, the Young Turk 'civilizing mission' in Palestine (namely efforts to achieve modernization and introduce new technologies and infrastructure), Palestine as viewed from the Empire's center including attitudes and policies towards Zionism and Arab nationalism, governance, the implementation of new legal practices and paradigms, and finally, Palestine during World War I. One of the book's main premises is that the political, social and economic transformations that characterized Palestine during the Young Turk rule had a considerable impact on later developments in Palestine,[14] including the shaping of the Jewish-Arab conflict which is widely thought to have its early political roots in the decade of Young Turk rule in Palestine.[15] Hence, in order to better grasp relationships between Jews and Arabs during the Mandate era and beyond, the decade of Young Turk rule needs to be carefully studied and reevaluated.

The first section of this volume discusses the changing notion of citizenship in the aftermath of the Revolution, the influence of the newly introduced elections, and factors of social change triggered and enhanced by the Revolution. It demonstrates that the political changes brought about by the Revolution were accompanied by far-reaching social and structural transformations. The section opens with a chapter by Michelle U. Campos, 'Making Citizens, Contesting Citizenship in Late Ottoman Palestine', in which she uses the case study of Sa'id Abu Khadra from Gaza, a young member of a family of Muslim notables, to discuss the complex identity of Palestine's Arab population in the aftermath of the Revolution and its ability to take on several identities at once. Abu Khadra, writes Campos, proved himself loyal to the Ottoman imperial project, but at the same time took issue with the direction of imperial decision-making and explicitly demanded more involvement in provincial rule for Palestine and Palestinians.

By studying the decisions and perceptions of Abu Khadra, the chapter illustrates the shifting boundaries of Ottoman citizenship in the period after 1908 and attempts by the Empire's citizens to act within its framework to achieve comprehensive reforms in various fields that would serve their interests. At the same time it highlights the factors that influenced and crystallized Palestinian notions of citizenship and politics in the period prior to World War I by looking closely at the dynamic relationship between imperial, local, ethnic, and confessional markers and modifiers of citizenship.

The transformations brought about by the Revolution in the political sphere on the local level are discussed by Mahmoud Yazbak in his chapter 'Elections in Late Ottoman Palestine: Early Exercises in Political Representation'. The Revolution made the long-delayed parliamentary regime in the Ottoman Empire a reality and several election campaigns were held for both the Ottoman parliament in Istanbul and the local councils in Palestine. The chapter examines how the old urban politics changed in light of the requirement that officials had to be elected to posts in the local administration, a process whose roots go back to the reforms in the Ottoman bureaucracy in the second half of the nineteenth century. It follows the emergence of *jam'iyyat*, 'leagues', or in fact family-run pressure groups, which acted as a proto-party system to promote the interests of the members of the families that belonged to them and ensure the interests of the members versus the local and central government. While limited in their capacity to shape local politics, these organizations were nevertheless the forerunners of political activity in the ranks of the Muslim Palestinian urban population. This chapter also shows that the founders of the *jam'iyyat* did not come from the old ruling elite, but rather from a new emerging group of merchants and entrepreneurs who envisioned the Revolution as a way to consolidate their social, economic and political status.

The Revolution as a generator of social and ideological changes is discussed by Johann Büssow in his chapter 'Children of the Revolution: Youth in Palestinian Public Life, 1908–14'. This chapter suggests that after the Revolution Palestinian intellectuals and political activists 'discovered' childhood and youth and targeted the young generation as a basis of political solidarity and as a resource for a better future. At the same time, the print media and the educational system helped promote new views of childhood and youth, thus translating the universal principles of the Revolution into local initiatives in urban Palestinian daily life.

The volume's second section deals with the Young Turks' 'civilizing mission' and various aspects of center-periphery relationships as they unfolded in the aftermath of the Revolution. It analyzes the ambitious plans the Young Turks set about to achieve, in contrast to the increasingly grim reality which prevailed in the Empire during World War I, which led people in both the center and the periphery to rethink their mutual relationships. Yasemin Avcı, in her chapter 'Jerusalem and Jaffa in the Late Ottoman Period: The Concession Hunting Struggle for Public Works Projects' sheds new light on the Young Turks' ambitious infrastructure projects in Palestine which to a large extent never materialized. The chapter stresses the need to examine the infrastructure projects and public works initiated by the Ottoman government during the Hamidian and the Young Turk eras as part of an effort to bring about modernization and centralization, especially in regions having key political and strategic importance. These efforts, in the spirit of the *Tanzimat* period, were meant to ensure the visibility of the modernizing mission of the new regime.

Louis Fishman, in his chapter 'Understanding the 1911 Ottoman Parliament Debate on Zionism in Light of the Emergence of a "Jewish Question"', discusses the issue of Zionist activity in Palestine as seen from the imperial center in Istanbul. He argues that Jewish settlement in Palestine was merely a marginal issue in Ottoman discussions on Jewish immigration to the Ottoman state. The Ottoman government and the parliament examined whether the heartland of Anatolia could serve as a suitable solution to external pressures to open up Palestine for Jewish immigration. However, Turkish politicians were afraid that a 'Jewish question' might evolve in Anatolia similar to the existing Armenian and Greek 'questions'. Hence, this debate threatened the future of the Ottoman Jewish community given the upsurge of ethnic-religious nationalism among the Turkish elite.

World War I represented both the apogee of the Young Turk involvement in Palestine as well as the Ottoman Empire's eventual retreat from this land, ending four hundred years of rule. The War caused unprecedented hardship and intensified the encounter between the new regime and the local populations by enforcing measures such as a compulsory draft, confiscation of provisions and crops, displacement of populations and the like. In his chapter, 'Jerusalem under the Young Turks: A Study Based on Local Sources', Issam Nassar discusses the hardships experienced by Jerusalem's different communities and how these molded their perceptions of the Ottoman state as well as their own communal identities.

Intellectual responses to the Revolution are discussed in the third section of this volume, which examines the complex identities of leading Jewish and Arab intellectuals and the fundamental process of reassessing their perceptions in the years following the Revolution. Butrus Abu-Manneh, in his chapter 'Arab Ottomanists' Reactions to the Young Turk Revolution', shows the extent to which the Palestinian arena, despite its unique characteristics, was enmeshed in debates taking place in the Empire in the aftermath of the Revolution. Abu-Manneh discusses the positive responses of three Arab intellectuals – two Palestinians and one Lebanese – who wrote treatises shortly after the Revolution in which they hailed this event as ending absolutist government and opening a new phase in Arab-Turkish brotherhood. In light of the skepticism expressed by many Muslims who still supported the caliphate of Sultan Abdülhamid II, one of them, an Arab *'alim* from Gaza, Sheikh 'Abdullah al-'Alami wrote in defense of the Constitution and the newly elected Parliament and argued they were compatible with *shari'a* and a guarantee of justice. Nevertheless, writes Abu-Manneh, this position soon became irrelevant, due to the spread of nationalist ideas among both Turks and Arabs.

The importance of newspapers and the media in the aftermath of the Revolution in disseminating new perceptions and ideologies is discussed by Abigail Jacobson in her chapter 'Jews Writing in Arabic: Shimon Moyal, Nissim Malul and the Mixed Palestinian / Eretz Israeli Locale'. Following the Revolution, the strict ban on free media and publication of newspapers under Abdülhamid II was lifted at once. This led to the appearance almost overnight of numerous newspapers representing various groups in the Empire,[16] and greatly contributed to enhancing ethnic communal consciousness. Despite the growing tension between the Empire's various minorities and religious groups, in Palestine the boundaries between local Sephardic Jews and Arabs during the period between the Revolution and World War I were still porous. For instance, writers such as Nissim Malul and Shimon Moyal had complex identities, which allowed them to be involved in seemingly contradictory activities, and write in newspapers representing different agendas and worldviews.

In a chapter dealing with the post Revolutionary press entitled 'The Young Turk Revolution of 1908 as Reflected in the Media of the Jewish Community in Palestine', Ruth Kark and Nadav Solomonovich focus on the dilemmas and challenges confronting the Jewish community in Palestine as reflected in the Jewish local press. The chapter discusses the ambivalent stance of the Jewish community in Palestine toward the Revolution and the internal controversies it elicited, while trying to answer questions such as how the various Jewish ethnic groups reacted to the Constitution and how the Hebrew press related to the new opportunities it embodied, such as participation in democratic processes in the Ottoman Empire.

The last section of this volume deals with inter- and intra-communal relationships in the aftermath of the Revolution. The Revolution, which initially was welcomed by the Empire's religious and ethnic minorities with great enthusiasm, soon led to escalation in tensions between various minority groups as well as within the ranks of specific groups. At the same time, it promoted reform and a process of soul- searching within the minority groups, as the papers in this section clearly indicate. In part these were the result of unfettered political activity and freedom of the press which blossomed after years of severe censorship. In the words of Hasan Kayalı 'the introduction of mass politics, a liberal press, and greater educational opportunities enhanced ethnic communal consciousness among certain groups, although they were promoted by the government with the purpose of achieving greater societal integration and administrative amalgamation'.[17]

Bedross Der Matossian, in his chapter 'Administrating the Non-Muslims and the "Question of Jerusalem" after the Young Turk Revolution', discusses the impact of the Revolution on intra-communal relations among the Empire's ethno-religious groups. He argues that more weight should be given to ecclesiastic politics at the expense of the often discussed prism of political parties when considering post-revolutionary ethnic policies in the Empire, since the former was a key factor in defining inter- and intra-ethnic policies. The chapter also examines the Revolution as a generator of reform within specific ethno-religious communities, showing that while the Young Turk Revolution advocated equality for all citizens, its reforms often served communal agendas and identities.

Yaron Ben-Naeh, in his chapter 'The Zionist Struggle as Reflected in the Jewish Press in Istanbul after the Young Turk Revolution, 1908–18', emphasizes the Revolution's role as a catalyst of reform in the Empire's Jewish establishment, and the generational struggle within this community. In addition, this chapter discusses the debate over support for the Zionist movement, which preoccupied and divided Ottoman Jewry.

Finally, Necati Alkan in his chapter 'The Young Turks and the Baha'is in Palestine', sheds new light on the complex relationships between the Empire and the Baha'i religious leadership exiled to Palestine. Although this group represented only a fraction of Palestine's population, its case was indicative of new possibilities for political activity in the Empire in the aftermath of the Revolution, as well as its relative openness to the spread of new ideas and ideologies. Particular attention is paid to post-revolutionary relationships between the Baha'i leaders and the Young Turk elite, which enabled the nascent Baha'i movement to consolidate its position in Palestine, which was later to become its world center.

Thus overall, this volume sheds new light on the last decade of Ottoman rule in Palestine, in both its Ottoman and local contexts. Palestine serves here as a prism through which Ottoman policies are examined and evaluated. As such, it explores issues as varied as center-periphery relationships, reforms and modernization, the roots of the Jewish-Arab conflict in Palestine, the early crystallization of Arab and Palestinian identities, Ottoman Jewry, Ottoman policies towards minorities, inter- and intra-communal relations in the Ottoman Empire, and late Ottoman history in general.

Notes

1. On this official periodical, see Kushner, David, 'Kuds-i Şerif/Al-Kuds al-Sharif – the official gazette of the District of Jerusalem at the end of the Ottoman period', *Cathedra* 129 (2008), pp. 67–84 [in Hebrew].
2. 'Havadis-i Mahalliya: İane-yi Bahriye', *Kudüs-i Şerif / al-Quds al-Sharīf*, 4/17, August 1909. This particular issue is kept in the private archives of Aharon Mazya (1858–1930) in the Academy of the Hebrew Language in Jerusalem. We would like to thank Ms. Smadar Barak for allowing us access to this issue.
3. Truesdell, Matthew, *Spectacular Politics: Louis-Napoleon Bonaparte, and the Fête Impériale, 1849–1870* (Oxford, 1997), pp. 3–4.
4. There are many descriptions of the euphoria that prevailed in the Empire in the immediate aftermath of the Revolution and the public celebrations which were held in major towns in the provinces. Nevertheless, this brief moment which temporarily erased past differences and tensions between the Empire's various religious and ethnic groups soon gave way to growing inter-communal ethnic and religious tensions. See Ahmad, Feroz, *Turkey: The Quest for Identity* (Oxford, 2003), p. 49. In Palestine as well there were massive public celebrations in honor of the Revolution in several towns where Muslims, Christians, and Jews, alongside Ottoman officials, celebrated the event together. Notably speeches were made in Turkish, Arabic, and Hebrew in support of equality and freedom for all the subjects of the Empire. For instance see *Habazeleth*, 38/73, 7 August 1908; *Hashqafa*, 9/93, 10 August 1908. For a unique attempt to describe the atmosphere prevailing in Jerusalem during the Young-Turk period, see Marcus, Amy D., *Jerusalem 1913: The Origins of the Arab-Israeli Conflict* (New York, 2008), pp. 59–86.
5. There is a debate among researchers whether the policy of Ottomanism was wholeheartedly adopted by the new regime or was only a tactical move dictated by their awareness that their policy was already irrelevant in light of the strong national feelings and the irredentist tendencies prevalent among many of the minorities remaining within the Empire's shrinking borders. Zürcher argues in favor of the latter and claims that although officially Ottomanism was abandoned only in 1913, in fact support for this policy by many leaders of the Revolution was only lip service. See Zürcher, Erik J., *Turkey: A Modern History* (London; New York, 2001), pp. 132–4; idem, 'Muslim nationalism: The missing link in the genesis of modern Turkey', *ha-Mizrah he-Hadash* Vol. XXXIX (1997–98), p. 67 [in Hebrew]. Other researchers such as Landau claim that the Young Turks were never inclined towards one policy, but rather adopted different policies toward different segments of the population in the Empire and beyond its borders. Thus, Ottomanism was the policy

implemented with regard to the ethnic minorities in the Empire, Pan-Islam defined policy toward the Muslim population in the Empire and abroad, and Pan-Turkism was directed to the Turkic population in Russia and Central Asia. In addition, Landau argues that the Ottomans often shifted their emphasis on various policies opportunistically according to their needs. See Landau, Y.M., 'Remarks on the attitude of the "Young Turks" to Zionism', *Zionism* IX (1984), pp. 200–201.
6. For further details, see Ahmad, Feroz, *The Making of Modern Turkey* (London, 1994), pp. 33–47.
7. Kayalı discusses at length several objective and subjective reasons for the prevalence and persistence of several misconceptions regarding the Young Turk Era and why this period has not received enough attention from researchers. See Kayalı, Hasan, *Arabs and Young Turks: Ottomanism, Arabism, and Islamism in the Ottoman Empire, 1908–1918* (Berkeley, 1997), pp. 1–6.
8. On the Kemalist view of the late Ottoman period see Ersanlı, Büşra, 'The Ottoman Empire in the historiography of the Kemalist era: A theory of fatal decline', in Adanır, Fikret and Suraiya Faroqhi (eds.), *The Ottomans and the Balkans* (Leiden, 2001), pp. 115–154; Kansu, Aykut, *The Revolution of 1908 in Turkey* (New York, 1997), pp. 4–5; Zürcher: *Turkey*, pp. 182–3.
9. Kayalı: *Arabs and Young Turks*; Zürcher: *Turkey*, pp. 97–137; Ahmad: *Turkey*, pp. 31–51; Hanioğlu, M. Şükrü, *A Brief History of the Late Ottoman Empire* (Princeton, 2008).
10. Ahmad: *The Making*, p. 31.
11. See Schölch, Alexander, *Palestine in Transformation 1856–1882: Studies in Social, Economic and Political Development* (Washington, D.C, 1993), pp. 9–17; Ben-Arieh, Yehoshua, 'Ha-Nof ha-yishuvi shel Eretz-Yisra'el 'erev ha-hityashvut ha-tziyonit' [The Settlement Landscape of Eretz-Yisra'el on the Eve of Zionist Colonization], in Kolatt, Israel (ed.), *The History of the Jewish Community in Eretz Israel since 1882* (vol. I–The Ottoman Period) (Jerusalem, 1989), p. 75 [in Hebrew]; Kushner, David, 'Ha-Dor ha-aharon le-shilton ha-'Othmanim be-Eretz Yisra'el, 1882–1914' [The Last Generation of Ottoman Rule in Eretz Israel, 1882–1914], *The History of the New Jewish Community in Eretz-Israel since 1882*, pp. 7–8 [in Hebrew].
12. In this regard, consider the words of Alexander Schölch: 'One can easily assume that in the second half of the nineteenth century the image of Palestine as a unit (as the "Holy Land" or the "Land of Israel") was more precise and more strongly formed among Europeans than it was among the local population and the Ottoman administration. But beneath the fluctuating surface of administrative boundaries, an image of the region's coherency was recognizable, at least after 1830. During the 1870s it took on contours that were clearer. To this extent, the Mandate zone of Palestine

was no artificial, colonial creation'. See Schölch: *Palestine in Transformation 1856–1882*, p. 16.

13. Ironically, Palestine is one of the regions belonging to the Ottoman Empire in which its heritage, especially in fields such as law and the land regime, survived the longest. The fact that the British Mandate incorporated Ottoman law into the legal system, for example, meant that many Ottoman laws and practices remained in place for many years. Some of them were even incorporated later into the Israeli legal system, and even today their traces can still be seen (for instance in land administration, the status of religious courts and minorities). On the contrary, in other regions of the Empire, such as the Balkans and even in Turkey itself, deliberate efforts to disengage from the Ottoman past and obliterate its influence and heritage during the early years of independence led to the eradication and replacement of many Ottoman laws and practices.

14. For an example of the Young Turk legacy in Palestine/Israel, see Eisenman, Robert, 'The Young Turk legislation, 1913–17 and its application in Palestine/Israel', in Kushner, David (ed.), *Palestine in the Late Ottoman Period: Political, Social and Economic Transformation* (Jerusalem, 1986), pp. 59–73.

15. In fact, most researchers dealing with the Jewish-Arab conflict tend to locate the roots of the political conflict in Palestine in the aftermath of the Young Turk Revolution. For instance, see Mandel, Neville J., *The Arabs and Zionism before World War I* (Berkeley, 1976); Gorny, Yosef, *Zionism and the Arabs, 1882–1948: A Study of Ideology* (Oxford, 1987); Shapira, Anita, *Land and Power: The Zionist Resort to Force, 1881–1948* (New York, 1992).

16. Kayalı, for instance, mentions 353 newspapers and journals which were published in Istanbul itself after the Revolution. See Kayalı: *Arabs and Young Turks*, p. 55; Khalidi found that in the first year after the Revolution, 35 new Arab newspapers appeared in *Bilad al-Sham* [Greater Syria] and dozens more afterwards, whereas before the Revolution most of the Arab press operated from abroad, either from Egypt or from Europe. See Khalidi, Rashid, *Palestinian Identity: The Construction of Modern National Consciousness* (New York, 1997), p. 53.

17. Kayalı: *Arabs and Young Turks*, p. 13.

PART I

CITIZENSHIP, ELECTION AND SOCIAL CHANGE

CHAPTER 2

MAKING CITIZENS, CONTESTING CITIZENSHIP IN LATE OTTOMAN PALESTINE

MICHELLE U. CAMPOS

Introduction: Revolutionary Imperial Citizenship

In the spring of 1912, Sa'id Abu Khadra, a young member of a notable Muslim family in Gaza, published one of the earliest election pamphlets in Palestinian history. While attempting to convince his fellow Palestinians to elect him to the Ottoman parliament, Abu Khadra sought to reassure his voters about the future of the Ottoman Empire and Palestine's role within it at a time of much unrest, including colonial dismemberment of the Empire in Libya, war in the Balkan provinces, and growing grumblings for Arab autonomy in *Bilad al-Sham* (Greater Syria).

> Let me inform you oh brother, that your homeland Palestine is part of great lands claimed by the Ottoman Empire, and as long as the existence of this empire is preserved, if you send me as a deputy on your behalf its stability and its prestige and the preservation of its possessions will be the first order of importance for me [...].

I will not delay in crying out in the face of the Unionists [*Ittihad ve Terakki Cemiyeti*/Committee of Union and Progress – CUP] 'you are traitors' if they deviate from the law and aim at the Turkification of the elements/groups (*tatrik al-'anasir*) of the Empire, and [likewise] I will not flinch from calling out the baseness of the Liberals (*Hürriyet ve İtilâf Fırkası*) if I discern in them the inclination for independence of the elements of the empire, whether Bulgarians, Serbs, Greeks, or Arabs. I will entreat the rest of my colleagues in the parliament in the name of religion, honor, and patriotism to be as one mass uniting this Ottoman Empire, either – God forbid – to disappear all together or – God willing – to perpetuate its existence forever and ever.[1]

In his adoption of the language and rationale of the Ottoman reforming classes and in his engagement with the institutions and promises of constitutional liberalism set in place by the 1908 Revolution, Abu Khadra proved himself loyal to the Ottoman imperial project. At the same time, he took issue with the direction of imperial decision-making and explicitly demanded more involvement in provincial rule for 'Palestine' and 'Palestinians'. In short, Abu Khadra was neither reflexively loyal to a stagnant Empire nor a separatist nationalist, but rather an engaged and empowered imperial citizen.

Abu Khadra's embrace of a rights-bearing imperial citizenship places him on the margins of conventional historiography. Until recent years, studies of the Ottoman Empire and its former provinces privileged the rise of proto-national sentiments and assumed the growing irrelevance of the Empire for its subject populations. Even though by now most scholars agree that the majority of Arabs remained loyal to the Ottoman Empire until World War I, this loyalty is too often painted in static and traditional terms, and there is a marked lack of depth regarding the evolving and varied faces of imperial identification in Arab lands.[2]

This absence in the historiography was not unique to the Ottoman Empire; the Austro-Hungarian and Russian Empires were similarly characterized as 'prisons of nations' whose decline and ultimate demise was both unidirectional and long overdue.[3] Indeed, the presumed failure of these multi-ethnic empires to successfully integrate their subject populations ideologically, politically, and socially has featured prominently among the slew of internal and external, structural and circumstantial factors of imperial collapse cited by historians and political scientists alike. Difference – between subject and ruler as well as among subject populations – was seen as a necessarily destabilizing force for imperial rule.[4]

The theoretical literature extends this assumption of difference to a sharply oppositional relationship of 'empire' and 'nation'. Not only are empires and nations depicted as mirror opposites, but in fact their opposition is seen as being constitutive. As Alan de Benoist writes, '[...] in terms of its birth and foundations, the nation has been an *anti-empire*'. In this dichotomy, empires revolved around dynastic loyalty, nations around state loyalty; empires exercised differential control, but nations distributed sovereignty uniformly; empires relied on mediating structures, whereas nations sought a direct link to the individual; empires were heterogeneous while nations were putatively homogeneous; and empires relied on vertical ties of ruler-ruled alone, whereas nations were built on horizontal ties between citizens.[5]

However, as a recent volume dedicated to a comparative study of ends of empire has argued, the objective distinctions between empire and nation are murky, at best; indeed, 'empires' often act like 'nations', and vice versa.[6] The dominant *telos* of 'empire-to-nation', and the corresponding assumption of 'subjecthood-to-citizenship', renders imperial change invisible and loyalty to empire unintelligible. As they lived, worked, and interacted with each other across the empire, imperial subjects developed diverse sentiments of belonging, both to their state and to their compatriots. While religious and proto-nationalist sentiments have received substantial scholarly attention, sentiments of belonging to empire and imperial collective identities have not yet been adequately appreciated in the historical and theoretical scholarship. Indeed, the relationship between empires and their subjects cannot be limited to inequity, coercion, and collaboration; rather, the relationship must be seen as historically contingent and dynamic, and in many cases ties of identification 'thicker' than simple cooptation were born.[7]

Re-reading empire in light of recent scholarship on public spheres, civil society, and collective identity in the fields of Chinese, Habsburg, Iranian, Russian, and Ottoman imperial studies makes it clear that late imperial rule was characterized by an increasingly modern (and highly differentiated) relationship between empire and new imperial subject-cum-citizen. In addition to the important institutional changes instigated by the Ottoman capital and ushered in during the *Tanzimat* era (1839–76), broader long-term socio-economic changes also produced a new class of educated professionals and intellectuals, an emerging popular press, and a nascent civil society – in short, all of the necessary ingredients for a new kind of imperial subject.[8] In the Ottoman Empire (as in Qing China, the Russian Empire, and Qajar Iran), revolution and constitutional patriotism played an important role in providing shared action and institutions as well as creating social solidarity and common culture horizontally *within* empire.[9]

As the case of Abu Khadra demonstrates, the struggle over an active imperial citizenship was a central component of the political culture of modernity in late Ottoman Palestine. Moving from subject (*tebaa*) to citizen (*muwatin*, Arabic / *vatandaş*, Turkish) was not only a change in juridical category, but moreover marked the decades-long substantive conceptual transformation from a passive object of imperial policies to an active partner shaping the course of imperial reform.[10] This process was accelerated rapidly after the July 1908 Ottoman Revolution, after which whether friend or foe of the new constitutional government, Ottomans articulated new and evolving expectations of their state, their own role in imperial political life, and their relationship to their fellow citizens as members of the 'Ottoman nation' (*al-umma al-'Uthmaniyya*, Arabic/ *millet-i Osmaniye*, Ottoman Turkish).[11] Through editorials and open letters in the Palestinian press, in telegrams of complaint sent to Istanbul, in the nascent institutions and civil society organizations established in the second constitutional period, Palestinian Muslims, Christians, and Jews sought to translate their embryonic ideas of politics, popular enfranchisement, and collective identity (that is to say, imperial citizenship) into the public arena. This article analyzes Abu Khadra's election pamphlet with an eye toward what it tells us about Palestinian efforts to construct an imperial citizenship that contested *status, vision* and *practice*. In it we see the tension between the articulations of liberalism, republicanism, and ethno-religious discourses about who imperial citizens were and what imperial citizens should do. It should be clear that I mean citizenship as a process rather than an event, a sphere of continuous struggle and contestation rather than a secure status or a condition of membership, whose exercise was characterized by competing ideas, contradictory practices, and uneven results.[12] In other words, the pre-war Ottoman public was preoccupied with envisioning, claiming, implementing, and contesting what it meant to be an imperial citizen, rather than plotting the Empire's demise.[13]

Voters and Citizens

One of the earliest and most tangible results of the Ottoman Revolution of 1908 was the restoration of the Ottoman constitution and the re-opening of the Ottoman parliament. Unlike the first parliament of 1877–8 whose members were appointed by the provincial councils, the new members of the revolutionary parliament would be elected by the broader (adult male, taxpaying) population.[14] The 1908 elections marked a new beginning for Ottoman civic-political life, and the opening of the parliament in December 1908 was a national holiday marked by widespread celebrations, popular anthems, poems, and plays written in honor of the new parliament, and widespread expectations that invested the parliament with the hopes for a new Empire. For new Ottoman citizens, the parliament offered a representative government for the first time in their history; discussions in the press highlighted the symbolic and practical significance of this 'operationalization of liberty'. At the same time, however, the parliamentary elections also highlighted the tensions inherent in the new Ottomanist project as the Empire's various ethnic and religious groups struggled to find their place in the body politic, balancing ethnic, religious, provincial, and imperial concerns.[15]

Press editorials and candidate platforms alike in the fall of 1908 emphasized the necessary qualities of education, honesty and experience, a reformist spirit, and a sense of public service that was demanded of the 'deputies of the nation'. Above all, the members of parliament were seen to be serving the 'public good' (*al-maslaha al-'amma*) and providing a 'holy service to the nation and the beloved homeland' (*khidma muqaddasa lil-umma wal-watan al-'aziz*).[16] This understanding of the role of the deputies to act on behalf of the will of the nation was reiterated by the newly-elected Jerusalem Member of Parliament (MP) Ruhi al-Khalidi: 'We are going to aid the Ottoman nation irrespective of her differences in religions and languages for this is the rule of law and [...] the will of the nation (*iradat al-umma*)'.[17]

For the Jerusalem and broader imperial press, which had exploded in both numbers and circulation after the Revolution, this new era demanded a new transparency and accountability of government institutions; newspapers reported regularly on parliamentary sessions in their columns 'From the Capital'. At the same time, the press provided an outlet and address for publishing complaints, admonitions, and otherwise voicing citizens' concerns. Provincial newspapers often published interviews with their local parliamentarians, or more daringly, they published 'open letters' (*kitab maftuh*) or demands to their MPs as well as to the governor, deputy governor, mayor, or other officials. For example, after a storm off the coast of Jaffa in late December 1911 destroyed over 50,000 cases of oranges destined for export, the newspaper *Filastin* published an open letter to MP Ruhi al-Khalidi about the ongoing problems with the Jaffa port, which it deemed insufficient to withstand the harsh coastal conditions and therefore was an impediment to the economic expansion of the port and the region.[18] Al-Khalidi was forced to pledge his immediate attention to the matter.

A Liberal Candidate's Vision

By the elections of 1912, the Empire was in a very different position than it had been at the height of revolutionary fervor which had framed the 1908 elections: it was territorially vulnerable on two continents, dealing with mounting complaints about the shortcomings or outright failures of the Revolution, trying to balance confessionalist demands with imperial universalism, and suppressing rebellions in various provinces. In the 1912 election, of the Jerusalem province's three standing MPs, only one, Ruhi al-Khalidi, was still running as a

Unionist; the other two MPs, Sa'id al-Husayni and Hafiz al-Sa'id, were running with the opposition party, the Entente Libérale (known in Arabic as *al-Ahrar*). In response the CUP lent its support to two other candidates: 'Uthman al-Nashashibi, a Jerusalem notable from a family that had penetrated the political and social elite within a few short generations, and Ahmed 'Arif al-Husayni, the mufti of Gaza.

Other scholars have written elsewhere on the process and outcome of this 'blatantly rigged' election in Bilad al-Sham, seeing evidence of Arab nationalism.[19] However, I argue that while the rose-colored glasses of 1908 had clearly worn off, imperial citizenship was still a very real and very fought-for notion. Our candidate, Abu Khadra, a 27-year old landowner and a Freemason, was a former delegate from Gaza to Jerusalem's Provincial Council (*al-Majlis al-'Umumi*). He was from a well-established and affluent Muslim family from Gaza that had recently sent its younger sons, Sa'id and his brother Rashid, to Jaffa.

In publishing his campaign booklet and taking his political campaign out of the *diwan* and directly to the voters, Abu Khadra aligned himself with a modern understanding of politics and a liberal understanding of citizenship in which the individual voter was the bearer of political rights, and therefore the address for Abu Khadra's appeal. While acknowledging that his campaign booklet was an unprecedented step for a local candidate, Abu Khadra informed his potential constituents that 'this is the way things are done abroad among those who understand the meaning of delegation (*al-mab'uthiyya*) and the representative system (*al-nizam al-niyabi*)'.

Abu Khadra cited his strong sense of public service as evidence that he was the perfect candidate to promote the province's interests in the capital: 'I say, "elect me O nation (*ya qawm*) to represent you in the parliament because I feel in my soul the desire and the calling to this service and I hear from within me [a voice] calling, telling me: You have within you the will (*irada*) and whoever possesses that, will be powerfully capable of serving his homeland (*watan*)"'.

Abu Khadra promised that if elected he would tirelessly work in the service of his homeland (*ashtaghil wa-ukhadim watani*) rather than sleeping in his parliamentary seat (as presumably one of the elderly incumbents was wont to do; most likely he was referring to Hafiz Bey al-Sa'id, since the historical record is silent on his parliamentary accomplishments in contrast to the other two parliamentarians). This liberal-elitist vision of representation, in which the 'best of men and the most zealous for the homeland' would fill public office, was widely shared by the Unionists.

Abu Khadra proceeded to outline his vision of modern politics and an active imperial citizenship. For one, citizenship demanded a dialogue between elected official and constituents, a dialogue based on transparency of aims, means, and results. That is, it was incumbent upon candidates to come to an understanding with the people (*umma*) in order to learn their demands and to prevent a thick veil of misunderstanding between them. Abu Khadra's pamphlet was therefore a social contract of mutual understanding between a would-be elected official and his ostensible constituents.

He turned to his would-be constituents: 'What do you promise us? I am sure you, dear voter, are thinking of this: what do you promise us the people of Palestine (*ahali Filastin*) and the residents of the province of Jerusalem?' With that, Abu Khadra outlined his ten-point plan for pushing through both imperial reform and local say in that process. Tax reform, much-needed public works like a port for Jaffa and a tramway in Jerusalem, preserving the rights of the religious endowments according to constitutional clause 111, arguing for the modification of the recently-enacted censorship laws, all demanded Abu Khadra's attention; they were also all issues that had preoccupied the Palestinian press for months and years beforehand. Indeed, Abu Khadra admiringly aligned himself with the watchdog press: 'The press is the lamp that enables the sons of the *umma* to see with its light that which circulates and that which is concealed from the actions of the government and its officials'. In return, both the Jerusalem paper *al-Munadi* and the Jaffa paper *Filastin* heartily endorsed Abu Khadra's candidacy.

Abu Khadra adopted a republican view of Ottoman citizenship that saw politics as a productive force that would protect individuals and the nation, as well as advance the 'public good' and 'public utility'. For example, when presenting his argument for the division of *musha'* (communally-owned) lands, Abu Khadra identified both private and public rationales – private ownership would encourage peasants to look after the land and develop it more productively, but more importantly, partition would defend the homeland from foreign colonists (presumably Zionists) who were able to prey on the peasants' economic needs and exploit them for rock-bottom prices. In this respect, the government was given the role of protecting the rights of peasants, landowners, and ultimately, the homeland.

Against this backdrop, Abu Khadra reiterated the fierce criticism regularly published in the Jerusalem paper *al-Munadi* attacking the record of the Jerusalem municipality, which he referred to as a 'relic of the times' out of tune with both the needs of the people and the 'spirit of the times'. The elections to the municipality were rife with corruption and fraud, in Abu Khadra's words, ruled by agents ['pimps'] who run around negotiating with each voter over his vote and each candidate over his electoral victory. Abu Khadra continued:

> It is my conviction that it is among the greatest disgraces to a living *umma*, that in the constitutional period there remains an electoral system like this at which the city's leading men blush, and which indicates the loss of the vigor and cultural nobility among a group that gives its votes to embarrassment [...] that is what causes brave and noble men to distance themselves from serving the municipalities or from entering the city council, and they are embarrassed that people will think they were elected in this manner.

For Abu Khadra, the parliamentary electoral system was also symptomatic of another 'relic of the times' – in this case the Basic Law which left intermediaries between the individual voter and the ultimate elected officials in the form of the second-tier electors. Instead Abu Khadra argued for a more direct electoral system: 'It is incumbent upon each free individual with election rights to give his vote directly to a candidate in order to say daily if the representative harms him or does not elevate his homeland: I am the one who voted and I am the one responsible with my vote'. Only in this way would both the civil rights of the individual *and* the common good [or republican vision of the nation] be preserved.

At the same time, other elements of Abu Khadra's platform also reveal the limits of this nascent Ottoman citizenship, one caught between competing notions of membership and enfranchisement. On the one hand, Abu Khadra aligned himself with the liberal universalist discourse prevalent after the 1908 Revolution, embracing his fellow Ottomans 'irrespective of their group or language'. Ottoman citizenship was, after all, both an ascribed status available to those born of Ottoman parents, irrespective of their religion or ethnicity, as well as achieved by those who underwent naturalization and received Ottoman citizenship. The Ottoman state, in this liberal vision, was to be neutral with respect to the ascriptive characteristics of its citizens. To that end, he repeatedly addressed his 'fellow citizens', 'compatriots', 'dear voter', and 'glorious citizens' without further distinction.

And yet, Abu Khadra interwove this language of modern universal citizenship with more organic, primordial language, such as his references to 'brother voter', or just 'brother'. In the revolutionary Palestinian press we hear expressions of recasting the Ottoman nation as a family, where citizens emerge as 'brothers by birth and belly' as offspring of the homeland fertilized by the constitution and patriotism in sacred communion. Certainly Abu Khadra's membership in the Masonic lodge Aurore (Shafak/Barkai) supported a civic fraternity, and the language of political kinship resonated in a kinship-based society like the Ottoman Empire. These 'dear voters, dear co-citizens, dear brothers' are universal terms which tapped into sentiments of revolutionary 'brotherhood' that built on nineteenth century Ottoman intellectuals like Namık Kemal who advocated a 'mixing of the peoples' (*imtizac-i akvam*), or Butrus al-Bustani who called for dropping religious solidarity (*'usba diniyya*) in favor of national solidarity (*'usba jinsiyya wa-wataniyya*).

However this must be understood alongside Abu Khadra's use of religious language to discuss his non-Muslim fellow citizens, where he invoked his love and respect for the 'religions of the remaining Semitic prophetic books'. By so doing, Abu Khadra linked the modern Ottoman citizen stripped of particularity or any defining attributes with a second, incongruous, notion of the *dhimmi* tolerated in an Islamic empire. While Abu Khadra fell far short of writing non-Muslims out of the Ottoman nation or body politic, it is noteworthy that their position within the Ottoman nation harkened back to their status as people of the book, rather than an unquestioned part of the civic body, a clear challenge to the liberal bases of Abu Khadra's imperial citizenship. This contradictory impulse of seeing non-Muslims as equal Ottomans while at the same time revealing lasting religious notions of hierarchy were also expressed in the Islamic modernist monthly *al-Manar* published out of Cairo, as well as in other publications of the time.

By the same token, Abu Khadra's use of homeland (*watan*) was ambiguous, sometimes referring to Jerusalem, sometimes to Palestine, at other times to the Empire as a whole. The growing criticism and calls for decentralization and cultural rights in the Arab provinces at that time were also raised by Abu Khadra, but *not* in a proto-nationalist frame. Rather, Abu Khadra cast the government's new demands on Turkish language education as 'serving the people and groups so that they would both understand each other [reinforcing bonds of civic identity] but also so that there would not be a wide gulf between the plaintiffs and the judges [protecting the legal rights of the citizen]'. At the same time, however, he accused the government's policy of 'ruling over our noble language and shaking its love in the hearts of her sons'. Abu Khadra's compromise was to demand that Turkish be optional, not mandatory, in the lower levels of school, but recognized that Ottoman Turkish would be the language of science and professionalization. This was the best way, in his mind, to 'return the virtue of mutual understanding among the groups of this Empire'. That is to say, the Arabs' demands for cultural autonomy were intended to *uphold* rather than challenge the civic Ottomanist vision. As he warned, if his prescription for reforms was ignored, 'wail for your empire, O nation, because she is in a state of death and her rulers walk toward its suicide'.

It is in this context that we can also understand Abu Khadra's later support for the Arab Congress held in Paris in June 1913. Although many scholars have made much of the proto-nationalist significance of the Congress, in fact most of the speeches and resolutions of the

Congress pushed for greater rights within the Ottoman Empire, not outside of it. Attendees at the Arab Congress did speak openly on behalf of the 'Arab nation' and the 'Syrian homeland', but they did so in the context of Arab rights in the Ottoman Empire and decentralization as the basis of political reform.[20] As the general invitation read, 'we will explain to the Ottoman state that decentralization is the rule of our life and our life is the holiest right of all our rights, and the Arabs are partners in this Empire, partners in war, partners in administration, partners in politics, but inside their lands they are partners [only] to themselves'.[21] Abu Khadra was a signatory on two telegrams of support sent to the Congress – one where he and a friend presented their demands in the framework of the 'love of reform' (*hubb al-islah*), and the second which he co-signed along with several Masonic brothers in support of a reformed Ottoman Empire.[22]

In other words, the liberal vision of Ottoman imperial citizenship as residing in the individual clashed with a communitarian understanding of citizenship that argues that individuals are situated in, embedded in, and have a strong sense of community. The battles over parliamentary quotas, provincial council representation, and language rights that took place in the last years of the Empire's existence can all be seen in the light of competing visions of imperial citizenship rather than (solely) the rise of ethnic nationalism. Furthermore, the Ottoman imperial citizenship project was also built on strong elements of republican citizenship, which sees politics as both a communal affair and as the pursuit of the common good. In the best of times, the universal, civic Ottoman nation was protected and strengthened by its members who all contributed to its welfare. To that end, universal conscription was formally adopted by the Ottoman parliament in 1909, reversing the past exemption of non-Muslims from the Ottoman military. Public discourse embraced universal conscription as sharing the burdens of defending the Empire from internal and external threats as well as providing an end to the myriad privileges (and subsequent marginalization) experienced by the non-Muslim communities of the Empire. As Shibli Nauphal, a Christian Jerusalemite declared, 'Equality is the aim of justice and its true foundation, and if the Ottoman elements will not be equal and mix their blood on the soil of the homeland in defense of it, then equality will not come about'.[23]

In addition, universal conscription was talked about as a tool of social engineering, a universalizing experience that would Ottomanize the Empire's polyglot communities. Increasingly vocal, however, was the awareness that contributions to the (imperial) public good were *not* distributed equally, and indeed, that certain individuals – and more ominously, groups – shirked their duty at the expense of the nation as a whole. The republican discourse of imperial citizenship, then, promoted rivalries around measuring each group's contribution to the Ottoman nation – in essence, of measuring Ottoman-ness itself.

And yet, rather than viewing this tension in primordialist views as evidence of the ephemeral nature or failure of the Ottomanist project, instead I will only suggest here that we look at ethnic politics as part and parcel of the imperial citizenship project. Scholars of citizenship have told us that inegalitarian and exclusionary ascriptive elements cannot be left out analytically as being simply prejudice or the triumph of primordialism. I would extend that to say that it certainly does not suggest the teleological victory of the national over the imperial- rather, ethno-religious discourses in the late Ottoman Empire are competing views of imperial citizenship in and of themselves.

Notes

Author's note: Sections of this article were first published in Campos, Michelle U, *Ottoman Brothers: Muslims, Christians, and Jews in Early 20th Century Palestine* (Stanford, CA: Stanford University Press, 2010), and are reprinted with permission.

1. *'Unsur/'anasir* (pl.) can be translated as either 'element/component', or as 'race/stock/descent'. 'Appeal', by Sa'id Abu Khadra (Jerusalem 1912, n.p.), pp. 3–4. Arab Studies Society (Orient House), Jerusalem. My thanks to its archivist, Qasim Harb, for bringing this pamphlet to my attention.
2. For a focus on the intersection of Arabism and imperial loyalty, see Dawn, Ernest C., 'The origins of Arab nationalism', in Khalidi, Rashid, Lisa Anderson, Muhammad Muslih, and Reeva S. Simon (eds.), *The Origins of Arab Nationalism* (New York, 1991), pp. 3–30; Khalidi, Rashid, 'Ottomanism and Arabism in Syria before 1914: a reassessment', in idem, pp. 50–69; Muslih,

Muhammad, *The Origins of Palestinian Nationalism* (New York, 1988); Blake, Corinne Lee, *Training Arab-Ottoman Bureaucrats: Syrian Graduates of the Mülkiye Mektebi, 1890–1920* (Unpublished Ph.D. Dissertation, Princeton University, 1991); and the contributions in Jankowski, James and Israel Gershoni (eds.), *Rethinking Nationalism in the Arab Middle East* (New York, 1997). Hasan Kayalı argues for a need to focus on the provincial 'consent' to the Ottoman imperial system rather than simply the rejection and opposition to it. See Kayalı, Hasan, *Arabs and Young Turks: Ottomanism, Arabism and Islamism in the Ottoman Empire, 1908–1918* (Berkeley, 1997), pp. 12–13. For Ottomanism as the 'status quo' see Khalidi, Rashid, 'Social factors in the rise of the Arab movement in Syria', in Arjomand, Said Amir (ed.), *From Nationalism to Revolutionary Islam* (Albany, NY, 1984), p. 54, p. 63; and Masters, Bruce, *Christians and Jews in the Ottoman Arab World: The Roots of Sectarianism* (New York, 2001), p. 179, p. 187.
3. For critiques of the nationalist literature, see the introductions of Gelvin, James L., *Divided Loyalties: Nationalism and Mass Politics in Syria at the Close of Empire* (Berkeley, 1998); Kayalı: *Arabs and Young Turks*; Todorova, Maria, *Imagining the Balkans* (New York, 1997); and Reinkowski, Maurus, 'Late Ottoman rule over Palestine: its evaluation in Arab, Turkish and Israeli histories, 1970–90', *Middle Eastern Studies* 35 (1999), pp. 66–97. Likewise, Andreas Kappeler has written that while Enlightenment scholars wrote often about the multi-ethnicity of the Russian Empire, by the nineteenth century the history of that empire was nationalized by Russian and Western scholars. See Kappeler, Andreas, *The Russian Empire: A Multiethnic History* (Harlow, England, 2001), p. 8. See also the critique in King, Jeremy, *Budweisers into Czechs and Germans: A Local History of Bohemian Politics, 1848–1948* (Princeton, 2002) for the Habsburg Empire.
4. This particular perspective is reflected in the contributions by Charles Tilly and Alexander Motyl in Barkey, Karen and Mark Von Hagen (eds.), *After Empire: Multi-Ethnic Societies and Nation-Building: The Soviet Union and the Russian, Ottoman, and Hapsburg Empires* (Boulder, 1997). For comparative studies on end of empire, see the contributions in Esherick, Joseph W., Hasan Kayalı, and Eric Van Young (eds.), *Empire to Nation: Historical Perspectives on the Making of the Modern World* (Lanham, MD, 2006); Haddad, William W. and William Ochsenwald (eds.), *Nationalism in a Non-National State: The Dissolution of the Ottoman Empire* (Columbus, OH, 1977); and Miller, Alexei and Alfred J. Rieber (eds.), *Imperial Rule* (Budapest, 2004).
5. De Benoist, Alain, 'The idea of empire', *Telos* 98–9 (1993–4), p. 91. As Benedict Anderson put it, the modern state was 'fully, flatly, and evenly operative over each square centimeter of a legally demarcated territory', whereas empires

were not due to their porous borders and differential status of center/metropolis. See Anderson, Benedict, *Imagined Communities* (London, 1991), 19–20. For a discussion of the value-laden character of this distinction throughout the twentieth century, see Lieven, Dominic, *Empire: The Russian Empire and Its Rivals* (New Haven, 2000), p. xvi.
6. See 'Introduction' in Esherick et al, *Empire to Nation*; the editors, however, also make the leap from imperial subjects to national citizens (see p. 26).
7. This understanding was eloquently expressed by Reinhold Niebuhr as the presence of 'dominion' *and* 'community' in empires as well as nations. See Niebuhr, Reinhold, *The Structure of Nations and Empires: A Study of the Recurring Patterns and Problems of the Political Order in Relation to the Unique Problems of the Nuclear Age* (New York, 1959). This flexible reading of empire was also recognized by Dominic Lieven, whose definition of empire as a 'very great power that has left its mark on the international relations of an era' allowed him to recognize both the possibility of legitimacy and popularity of the empire in the eyes of its subjects but also the possibility of an empire transforming itself into a multi-national federation or nation-state. Lieven: *Empire*, pp. xi-xii.
8. Salzmann, Ariel, 'Citizens in search of a state: The limits of political participation in the late Ottoman Empire', in Hanagan, Michael and Charles Tilly (eds.), *Extending Citizenship, Reconfiguring States* (Lanham, MD, 1999), p. 23. See also Karpat, Kemal H., *The Politicization of Islam: Reconstructing Identity, State, Faith, and Community in the Late Ottoman State* (New York, 2001); Kirli, Cengiz, *The Struggle over Space: Coffeehouses of Ottoman Istanbul, 1780–1845* (Unpublished Ph.D. Dissertation, SUNY-Binghamton, 2000); and Zandi-Sayek, Sibel, *Public Space and Urban Citizens: Ottoman Izmir in the Remaking, 1840–1890* (Unpublished Ph. D. Dissertation, University of California, Berkeley, 2001).
9. As suggested by Hannah Arendt and Jürgen Habermas, respectively. For Craig Calhoun, this Arendtian 'world-making' leads to a stronger, 'thicker' sense of peoplehood that can buttress political membership. 'In this sense', Calhoun writes, 'the nation seems more a common project, mediated by public discourse and the collective formation of culture, than simply an inheritance'. See Calhoun, Craig, 'Imagining solidarity: cosmopolitanism, constitutional patriotism, and the public sphere', *Public Culture* 14/1 (2002), pp. 147–171. See also Shabani, Omid A. Payrow, 'Who's afraid of constitutional patriotism? The binding source of citizenship in constitutional states', *Social Theory and Practice* 28/3 (2002), pp. 419–43.
10. See: Abu-Manneh, Butrus, 'The Islamic roots of the Gülhane Rescript', *Die Welt des Islams* 34/ 2 (1994), pp. 287–304; Davison, Roderic, *Reform in the Ottoman Empire, 1856–1876* (Princeton, 1963); Mardin, Şerif, *The Genesis of*

Young Ottoman Thought: A Study in the Modernization of Turkish Political Ideas (Princeton, 1962). For translations of Namık Kemal's work, see Kurzman, Charles (ed.), *Modernist Islam, 1840–1940* (New York, 2002), pp. 144–8. See also Lewis, Bernard, 'The idea of freedom in modern Islamic political thought', in Lewis, Bernard, *Islam in History: Ideas, Men and Events in the Middle East* (London, 1973), pp. 273–5.

11. I refer to 1908 as the Ottoman, rather than Young Turk, Revolution. In doing so I am underscoring the fact that the revolution was not the limited product of a small political-military elite, the so-called Young Turks, but rather was a much broader process of reshaping Ottoman political culture, the result of grass-roots mobilization, contested discourses, and vernacular political practices that took place empire-wide.

12. Thus I see citizenship as a sociological and historical question rather than simply a legal or political one. See Isin, Engin F. and Patricia K. Wood, *Citizenship and Identity* (London, 1999); Turner, Bryan S. 'Contemporary problems in the theory of citizenship', in Turner, Bryan S. (ed.), *Citizenship and Social Theory* (London, 1993), pp. 1–18; and van Steenbergen, Bart (ed.), *The Condition of Citizenship* (London, 1994). My thinking has been influenced by the insightful framework offered by Gershon Shafir and Yoav Peled treating the interplay of liberal, republican, and ethno-national citizenship discourses within a single state setting. Shafir, Gershon and Yoav Peled, *Being Israeli: The Dynamics of Multiple Citizenship* (Cambridge, 2002).

13. This active participation in Ottoman public life in the aftermath of the Revolution has been barely visible to the dominant structuralist readings of the 1908 revolution. See the critique levied in Kansu, Aykut, *The Revolution of 1908 in Turkey* (Leiden, 1997) and idem, *Politics in Post-Revolutionary Turkey, 1908–1913* (Leiden, 2000). For the distinction between structuralist and culturalist theories of revolution, see the contributions in Foran, John (ed.), *Theorizing Revolutions* (London, 1997). Other culturalist studies of 1908 include Brummet, Palmira, *Image and Imperialism in the Ottoman Revolutionary Press, 1908–1911* (Albany, NY, 2000) and Frierson, Elizabeth Brown, *Unimagined Communities: State, Press, and Gender in the Hamidian Era* (Unpublished Ph.D. Dissertation, Princeton University, 1996). For a study of the new middle classes of the Arab world in this period and after, see Watenpaugh, Keith, *Being Modern in the Middle East: Revolution, Nationalism, Colonialism, and the Arab Middle Class* (Princeton, 2006).

14. For more on the Ottoman elections see: Kayalı, Hasan, 'Elections and the electoral process in the Ottoman Empire, 1896–1919', *International Journal of Middle East Studies* 27 (1995), pp. 265–86; Khalidi, Rashid, 'The 1912 election campaign in the cities of Bilad al-Sham', *International Journal of Middle*

East Studies 16 (1984), pp. 461–74; and Yazbak, Mahmoud, 'Elections in late Ottoman Palestine: Early exercises in political representation', in this volume.
15. For more on the 1908 elections see chapter 3, Campos: *Ottoman Brothers*.
16. *Al-Ittihad al-'Uthmani*, 25 September 1908; 1 October 1908; 10 October 1908.
17. *Al-Quds*, 17 November 1908.
18. *Filastin*, 27 December 1911.
19. In particular Khalidi: 'The 1912 election campaign', and Yazbak: 'Elections in Palestine'.
20. Kawtharani, Wajih (ed.), *Watha'iq al-Mu'tamar al-'Arabi al-Awwal 1913: Kitab al-Mu'tamar wal-Murasalat al-Diblumasiyya al-Faransiyya al-Muta'aliqa bihi* [The Documents of the First Arab Conference in 1913: The Book of the Conference and the French Diplomatic Correspondence Related to it] (Beirut, 1980) [in Hebrew]. The Congress also concerned itself with the status of emigration from and immigration to Syria.
21. 'Al-Mu'tamar al-'Arabi al-awwal' [1913 booklet], republished in Ibid., p. 10.
22. Kawtharani: *Watha'iq al-Mu'tamar al-'Arabi al-Awwal*, pp. 202–210.
23. *Al-Quds*, 11 May 1909.

CHAPTER 3

ELECTIONS IN LATE OTTOMAN PALESTINE: EARLY EXERCISES IN POLITICAL REPRESENTATION

MAHMOUD YAZBAK

Elections: Early Beginnings

The Law on Provincial Administration (the *vilayet* Law) Istanbul enacted in 1864 and the amendment that followed in 1871 were part of the reforms instigated by the Sublime Porte to keep pace with global developments. Among the major changes this law brought about was a transformation in the way members of the Administrative Councils were nominated; specifically, councils were now to be made up of ex-officio members and a further number of elected members, both Muslims and non-Muslims. At the level of the *qada*, Paragraph 5 sets out in detail how its council members were elected. First an election committee consisting of the *qaimaqam*, the *qadi*, the *mufti*, the *qada* scribes and the *mukhtar*s of the non-Muslim communities was convened in the center of the *qada*. This committee then selected three times as many candidates from among the residents of the *qada* as were required to make up the council; their names were then conveyed to the *majlis al-ikhtiyariyya* (council of elders) who chose twice the number required; this list was then returned to the election committee which named the final candidates. Each village in the *qada* had one vote and the candidates chosen were those who had received the majority of the votes.[1]

In short, by allowing certain members of the public to eliminate names of candidates on lists that had been drafted by the central authorities, the Law of Provincial Administration provided the Empire's subjects with some experience in political representation, however minimal. True, the law introduced the voting principle, but agents of the central government still controlled the administrative councils. These were, of course, not popular elections. The authority to elect the candidates rested with the committee and the council of elders, and members were selected only from among the political elite. This also meant that the council in no way represented all strata of society.

The municipal councils in Palestine's main cities from the 1860s onward were also affected by Ottoman reform efforts. Unlike the administrative council, all members of the municipal councils were elected and only the mayor was nominated by the governor of the district, the *mutasarrif*, who himself was directly responsible to the governor of the province, the *wali*.[2]

According to the Municipalities Law which was introduced in 1867, only those in the town who could show they had economic resources were eligible to take part in these elections, more particularly males aged 25 or older who had paid an annual property tax of at least 50 *qurush*, and a property tax of at least 100 *qurush*.[3] In other words, these were criteria that defined the economic and social elite, a minority among the townspeople. In Nablus, for example, out of a total population of 30,000, or out of 6,216 males over 25 years old, only 304 people fulfilled these conditions; of these only 114 were eligible as candidates.[4] A similar picture emerged during the municipal elections in Jerusalem at the end of the nineteenth century where fewer than 700 Muslims and 300 Christians took part out of a total population of some 20,000.[5]

The property tax (*wirko*) department would put up lists with the names of all those eligible to vote and able to run for office in all public places in town.[6] Headed by the mayor, an election committee composed of two respected (*min mu'tabari al-ahali*) representatives of the different quarters was chosen by the *mukhtar*s and the *imam*s of the neighborhood to supervise and run the ballot. Since elections were held once every four years, voters elected double the number of members required for the municipal council: half of them served in the first session (two years) and the others in the second.[7] Because the election committee not only supervised the voting procedure but also had the power to choose which successful candidates would serve in the first session of the municipal council, various coalitions in the town put heavy pressure on the *mukhtar*s and the *imam*s to select their members and representatives.

In practice, the committee members reflected the balance of power in the town. Even though membership on the municipal council, like other local elected governmental institutions, was unremunerated it was still seen by the members themselves, the community and the officials as recognition of their prominent social status within their society.[8] Being elected to the municipal council opened doors to other governmental institutions in the locality. Thus an election process was in place in rural and urban Ottoman society by the time the Ottoman Parliament started its work for the first time in 1876.

The Parliamentary Elections

Six parliamentary elections were held in the Ottoman Empire before its demise; two of these took place during the abortive first constitutional period (1876–8). In both, provincial councils determined who would be their parliamentary deputies through informal procedures. The process proved premature since when the sultan and his cabinet found themselves confronted by deputies with challenges they had not anticipated, they dissolved parliament without much ado in February 1878.

The second constitutional period started in 1908, when the Revolutionary Young Turk regime reactivated the constitution of 1876 and the Electoral Law that had been passed in the first parliament.[9] Elections were held in 1908, 1912, 1914 and 1919, a short while after the termination of Ottoman rule in Palestine. All in all, these elections introduced the Ottoman Middle East to fundamental norms of political participation and electoral mobilization that were unprecedented.

In effect, the official vision of a representative government introduced by the Young Turks gave new life to the Ottoman constitution promulgated in December 1876 and the Electoral Law, and both remained valid until the end of the Ottoman era. The constitution provided for a parliamentary system that was composed of a nominated senate (*heyet-i âyan*) and an elected chamber of deputies (*heyet-i meb'usan*). The Electoral Law stipulated that every Ottoman male above the age of thirty with a command of Turkish, the official language of the Empire, who met the property requirements, was not employed in the service of a foreign government, and was not bankrupt or socially stigmatized in other ways (because of 'notoriety for ill deeds') had the right to be elected deputy.[10] Voting rights were restricted, again, to men over 25 years old who paid some direct taxes.

The Ottoman election process was made up of a two-stage indirect election. In the first stage, primary eligible voters elected secondary voters, one for every 500 primary voters (Art. 21). Actually, secondary voters had all the qualifications of primary voters except the tax requirement (Art. 22) and became the electors who then voted for the actual deputies.

To examine how this law and process was implemented in practice in a Palestinian *qada*, statistics can be examined from the Nablus 1912 electoral committee file, the only one of its kind to have survived from Ottoman Palestine. According to its detailed tables there were 21,372 eligible registered voters in the *qada* who were to elect 33 secondary electors. Of these, 4,607 lived in the town's six neighborhoods, and the rest lived in the *qada*'s 51 villages. An average of 32 percent of the eligible voters residing in the town participated in the elections, and 38 percent of the rural eligible voters.[11]

To facilitate the election process in Nablus, the town was divided into six electoral precincts, matching the town's neighborhood division. One balloting box was located in each neighborhood. The *sanjak*'s 108 villages were grouped into fifteen electoral precincts, matching the *qada*'s *nahiya*s (sub-districts). The center of the *nahiya*, usually the largest village in the electoral area, was chosen as the balloting center for all the villages of the *nahiya*. To exercise their right to vote, rural voters from the different villages of the *nahiya* traveled to the balloting center, often in groups.[12]

In large electoral areas that had between 750–1250 eligible primary voters, voting was two-tiered. Primary voters voted for two secondary electors from an often long list of candidates. But when there were fewer than 750 primary voters in the electoral area, they were only allowed to vote for one secondary candidate. For example, the Gharb neighborhood of Nablus had 1,001 primary eligible voters, 490 of whom showed up on balloting day and voted twice their number, i.e., 980 votes. These votes were distributed among nine secondary electoral candidates, with approximately 80 percent of the votes going to the two leading candidates. This type of voting repeated itself in the remaining neighborhoods and in the rural areas.[13]

The familial affiliations of secondary electoral candidates in the town and the rural area reflected the local political, religious and mercantile elite that administered and controlled the district and dominated the election process. That the Ottoman election process did not really allow common people to have an impact on the elections of the representatives in parliament is clearly shown by the statistics for the elections in the district of Nablus. In fact, as the towns and the rural areas were divided into electoral areas based on the traditional networks and systems of social and economic control that had prevailed for centuries, this deprived the election process of any impetus to set social change in motion.[14] Though the two stage Ottoman election system allowed common people to reach polling centers, in practice it marginalized them and maintained a considerable social gap between them and the elected deputies.

After the primary election process had been concluded, the thirty three secondary electors were invited to come to the municipality of Nablus to elect the provincial candidate for the deputyship who was to represent the *sanjak* of Nablus. As their number was small, the secondary electors could easily be influenced by the representatives of the more powerful local urban elite who were out to win the deputyship.

A similar picture emerges in the larger *mutasarrifiyya* of Jerusalem during the 1912 elections. Unlike the district of Nablus, the *mutasarrifiyya* of Jerusalem covered four *qada*s with four urban centers: Jerusalem, Jaffa, Gaza and Hebron. According to statistics culled from the local press, there were about 80,000 eligible primary voters in the *mutasarrifiyya*.[15] These were designated to elect 164 secondary electors, who elected three candidates for the parliament deputyship from a list of 22 candidates. Because candidacy for deputyship was province-wide, it allowed secondary voters from a certain *qada* to vote for candidates from other parts of the *mutasarrifiyya*. In this case, the strongest representatives of the traditional elite were likely to defeat the other candidates in the *qada*. The elected deputies, Ruhi al-Khalidi and 'Uthman al-Nashashibi, both Jerusalem residents, received fewer votes in their hometown than other candidates, but they were still able to beat their rivals in Jaffa, Hebron and Gaza due to the broad support they received in the other districts of the *mutasarrifiyya*.[16]

Local Critiques

The indirect two-stage election process came under fierce attack in the local press. As already pointed out, by choosing secondary electors who then voted for the actual deputies, the system reinforced patronage relationships and supported candidates who represented the traditional elites. Both the Palestinian newspapers *Filastin* and *al-Karmil* wrote a series of sharp editorials criticizing the way the Ottoman election system marginalized the role of the common people and continued to concentrate political power in the hands of a small group of secondary electors, who were no other than the existing elite. *Filastin* noted that:

> Our citizens (*muwatinuna*) do not stop to discuss the issues related to deputyship candidates in assemblies and newspapers, but rather who elects the deputy. Speakers expend a good deal of effort building up a consistent public opinion around their candidates, as though public opinion had any way of affecting the result of the elections or could decide who would be elected. If those who administer the election campaigns were to think seriously about the political reality, they would easily discover

that their speeches, announcements, manifests and press articles simply blow away with the wind. For a deputy to win, he needs none of this fuss, nor does this depend on public opinion. It depends upon the personal inclinations of twenty to thirty secondary electors who have the legal right to elect the deputy upon whom the progress of the whole nation then depends. Before they are about to elect them, nobody comes out and explains to primary electors how important their role actually is. In fact, it is the secondary electors – who convene for less than half an hour! – who decide who will represent the nation.[17]

Filastin thus urged every voter 'to stop voting with your eyes shut and placing your fate along with that of your family and your country in the hands of the secondary electors without any guarantee or any information as to who they will elect for the deputyship'. The writer prompts the voters in the villages and the neighborhoods 'to reach an understanding with your preferred secondary candidate, to guarantee that he will elect the deputy that you prefer and not those who satisfy his personal interests'.[18] A week before the start of the voting process, *Filastin* saw it as its duty to remind the voters how important the elections were:

> In the next five or six days you will exercise your right to vote [...] those of you who made the right choice will delight during the next four years, but those who made the wrong choice will feel sorrow throughout the long next four years. [...] We have repeatedly said that there are no ways to prevent pressures from diverting the primary elections. Our dichotomist society is replete with contradictions and paradoxes. On the one hand, there is the class who designs local policies, and on the other the class who carries out the wishes of the first. Recognition of our social weakness must not stop us from fulfilling our journalistic obligations to recommend and advise rural voters as they put their destinies in the hands of their leaders, or city dwellers who don't seem to care that they make a present of their votes to the first mediator who comes along.[19]

In an angry tone of voice the writer then exhorts his readers as follows:

> Oh, my people, close your eyes when you enter the elections center, and do not look towards those who sit there non-stop and think that by directing their glances at you they can affect your decision. Close your ears, and do not allow anybody to whisper names to you that he thinks will make you lower your head the minute you hear them. Oh, my people, when you receive your ballot slip write on it the names of your own choosing, not those that may please others. Those among you who can neither read nor write, do not show your slip to any of the local dignitaries, but hurry outside the elections center and ask someone you trust to fill it for you. Then, enter your slip yourself into the box.[20]

Al-Karmil editor Najib Nassar was even blunter in his criticism of the indirect Ottoman elections system and the ways in which the local leaders manipulated the system to serve their own interests, using the primary voters to the same end. To avoid this eventuality, Nassar suggested that the local leaders of the two rival parties, the Committee of Union and Progress (CUP) and the Entente, should decide upon and announce their preferred candidates for the deputyship before the primary elections took place. Nassar's suggestion ran counter the decision of the local leaders who preferred to announce the preferred secondary electors of each party and decide their candidate for deputy later on. Criticizing such manipulations, Nassar wrote:

> I am not willing to see our people turned into a flock, to be directed to unknown places, i.e., to elect secondary electors from among the men of the leader in every *qada*, who singles out by name the deputy that he prefers. In such cases, any deputy who owes his selection to the local leader will become his man and not the people's man [...]. These are holy rights! Nobody is allowed to manipulate them for his own interest, and dispose of the people.[21]

Self Promotion and Propaganda

As candidacy for deputyship was province-wide, candidates needed to muster and develop social and other networks in all areas of the province to get elected. Powerful candidates would embark on a tour to all main centers in the province to visit secondary elector candidates who would directly elect the deputy. Such visits served to cement old alliances and consolidate existing social, political and economic networks. They were important ways to attract secondary voters, especially in the rural areas, and to show primary voters the personal connections they enjoyed with notables and leading figures. Deputy candidates would demonstrate their support and respect by having a meal with as many invited heads of families as possible in an effort to galvanize the greatest support for themselves and the secondary electors in their constituencies. Such electoral tours were a successful public relations ploy. They invariably reached the pages of the local press. *Filastin*, for example, reported frequently on the visits of the deputy candidate from Jerusalem, Ruhi al-Khalidi. He usually timed his visits to take place on Fridays, started the tour in the town's central mosque where he participated in Friday's public prayer, met as many people as possible and then moved with a large retinue to have lunch with his supporters at the house of the local leader.[22]

Educated young candidates for Parliament who did not have such a network made use of more 'modern' campaign methods. A candidate would approach a local newspaper to publicly announce his candidacy and then publish his 'platform' that he promised to push in parliament. For example, Sa'id Abu Khadra from Gaza sent *Filastin* an announcement 'made in a new fashion that included his electoral program and personal photo'. The editor, who liked this gimmick, promised his readers to publish the announcement in full 'as it directly concerns and benefits our readers'.[23]

In his candidacy announcement Nasib al-Khatib from Jerusalem, who served as the director of the tax department in Jaffa, wrote: 'In response to a call of conscience, and [in order] to serve with love this holy *liwa* [district], I have decided to run for parliamentary elections to represent the beloved *liwa* of Jerusalem'.[24] Others used more indirect ways to promote themselves through the press. For instance, articles were delivered to the newspaper anonymously or signed by common names calling for the election of a certain candidate. For example, a certain M. al-Husayni called on *Filastin*'s readers to elect Ishak al-Budayri, who was described as 'the free nationalist, a graduate of Istanbul's School of Law. He served in Albania, Baghdad, Basra and Damascus. [...] He belongs to the elite families, and he is known for his great wisdom. If you seek to promote your nation, you must elect this young dignitary'.[25] Similarly, a certain A. al-Muwwaqit from Jerusalem wrote a letter to *Filastin* saying that:

> I heartily recommend and advise the respected citizens (*muwatinun*) to vote for Shukri Bey al-Husayni and Ishaq Abu-al-Su'ud, the most qualified and suitable personalities that could represent the *liwa* of Jerusalem in the Ottoman parliament. In addition to their steadfast nationalistic feelings, they have broad experience in national and local politics.[26]

In a more direct way, the newspaper editor saw nothing wrong in openly supporting a certain candidate, as did *Filastin* concerning the candidacy of Sa'id Abu-Khadra from Gaza:

> We call upon the electors to vote for Sa'id, not because he is a friend of ours, but more importantly, both his past and his reputation are clean [...] he will be most useful to his town. In addition to his personal abilities and his wide contacts with the higher ranks in government, his family possesses more than one third of all the lands of the *qada* of Gaza. Because of this he is very interested in promoting agriculture and the *fallah*'s livelihood.[27]

The two main parties that ran in the 1912 parliamentary elections developed different tactics to promote and assist their local candidates. Apprehensive of rising Arab national sentiment and the demand for greater decentralization, the ruling CUP sent a special envoy to central towns in Palestine to tour the area and put pressure on local leaders not to join parties with nationalistic agendas. The special envoy, Sharif Ja'far Pasha, the cousin of the Sharif of Mecca, deputy of the Hejaz, and a committed Unionist,[28] openly set about to convince Palestinian leaders not to join the opposition party, *Hürriyet ve İtilâf* (usually called *Entente Libérale*). Since he was an important public personality, the local press, the especially pro-CUP *Filastin* gave his speeches and visits extensive coverage. He paid public visits to major pro-CUP candidates, with each visit being reported in the newspaper as were some his statements. His message was that 'the central government has confidence in the Arab race [nation] and its support of the state's unity. [...] The population in the *wilaya*s of Syria, Aleppo and Jerusalem are against all moves that could harm the unity of the Empire. [...] The people in Bilad al-Sham are against Arab Nationalism'.[29] While in Jaffa, he visited the headquarters of the Jewish community where he met the chief Rabbi, who expressed his confidence in his community's support for the CUP.[30]

Al-Karmil sided with the *Hürriyet ve İtilâf* and fiercely attacked the CUP candidates in Palestine's northern districts. For instance, it accused Shaykh As'ad al-Shuqayri from Acre, a well known religious personality and CUP supporter, of allowing his campaign to be funded by the Zionist movement: 'The Shaykh is using the nation to serve the interests of the Zionist movement as well as those of the CUP. The Shaykh may be excused for his bad deeds as he considers his own interests above the nation's [...]. But our nation cannot be excused when it [is asked to] sacrifice its homeland and its interests on the Shaykh's altar'.[31]

In contrast to *Filastin*, *al-Karmil* openly came out against Istanbul's Turkification policies, which it considered responsible for 'the revolts of the Albanians and the other Macedonian peoples'.[32] As for the Zionist movement, *al-Karmil* accused the CUP of protecting and allowing it to spread in Palestine, generating a problem that would prove more complicated than the Balkan problem. The newspaper warned people 'not to elect the CUP's candidates for parliament [...] and remember how its representatives did not respect your freedom, so you must also turn your backs on it'.[33] The CUP, according to *al-Karmil*, 'aims to crush the national movement and put everybody under Turkish hegemony'.[34]

In response to *Filastin*'s coverage of the tours of the delegation of Ja'far Pasha, *al-Karmil* covered the tumultuous reception of the Entente representatives during their tour of Haifa, Nablus and Acre,[35] deliberately depicting the atmosphere to appear that CUP members were deserting to the Entente party.

Filastin, in turn, devoted a great deal of space to disproving such claims,[36] highlighting the activities of well known Palestinian intellectuals who supported the CUP, such as Khalil al-Sakakini, the head of *al-Madrasa al-Dusturiyya* of Jerusalem. On one occasion the newspaper reported that al-Sakakeni had brought together more than sixty of Jerusalem's teachers to form an Ottoman Society whose first meeting took place at the headquarters of the CUP in the city.[37]

Electoral Programs

Some electoral candidates, especially young intellectuals, used the press to inform voters how much effort they had invested in preparing future plans and electoral programs. On one occasion, a certain Nasib Affendi al-Khatib, the head of Customs of Jaffa, sent *Filastin* a letter announcing his candidacy for the next parliamentary elections, later, *Filastin* summarized six of its articles as follows:

1. To end the *musha'* system and distribute the lands among the *fallahin*. To adapt the land tax system to the land's productivity, and to improve the *fallah*'s situation by freeing him of all injustices.
2. To construct a new customs house, and build a new harbor in Jaffa to encourage commerce in the town.
3. To reform the education system and institutions in Jerusalem's *liwa*. All education taxes collected in the *liwa* of Jerusalem have to be spent locally.
4. Taxes collected in the *liwa* of Jerusalem for public works must be spent locally to help develop roads and communications in the area.
5. To spend the large revenues collected from the local pious endowments (*awqaf*) in the locality, similar to the non-Muslims' endowments.
6. To inform the people of the *liwa*, through the *Filastin* newspaper, of all the debates that will take place in parliament.[38]

Similarly, Sa'id Abu Khadra, a young candidate from Gaza, sent *Filastin* his platform. The newspaper chose to highlight only one point of the program which was devoted to Article 111 of the Constitution, encouraging the government to establish *millet* councils for each religious community. Abu Khadra claimed that the central government objected to this article 'because it knows that the moment such Councils are established each *liwa* and *wilaya* will locally administer its *waqf*. This is against the interest of the central government because the huge revenues of the *awqaf* that are collected by the central government will be distributed in the different *wilaya*s'. He promised the voters that the moment he was elected he would initiate a large coalition of parliament members to put pressure on the central government to establish local *millet* councils (*majalis milliyya*)[39] to administer the *wilaya*'s *awqaf* and the revenues it derived from them. *Filastin*'s editor saw this program as the most important step forward for the Ottomans in general and the Arabs in particular. He concluded, 'we hope that if Sa'id Affendi Abu-Khadra is elected he will not forget his promise to us'.[40]

Against Jerusalem's Hegemony

As we saw, candidacy for deputy was province-wide, allowing secondary voters from a certain *sanjak* to vote for candidates from other parts of the province. The constitution stipulated that candidates for deputy had to be 'from the people' of the particular province of their candidacy (Art. 72), providing for a degree of decentralization.[41] In practice, the province-wide elections enabled the most powerful families in the *sanjaq/liwa* to control the election process, and marginalized not only the rural leadership but also the less powerful urban elites. The 1912 parliamentary elections in Palestine provide a good illustration of this process. By making the capital of the *qada* the election center where the secondary voters from the rural area were summoned to cast their votes, the rural leadership was put at a disadvantage and the urban candidates for parliament had an edge.

A list of secondary electoral candidates elected in the different quarters of Nablus in 1912 clearly reflected the newly emerging power groups in the town and *qada*. Representatives of the big merchant (*tujjar*) families received more votes than any of the candidates from the families of the traditional elite. However, members of the old political elite families, such as the Tuqans, 'Abd-al-Hadis and Nimrs, who had moved into the soap industry and mercantile enterprises succeeded in generating a good deal of influence in the parliamentary elections, and preserved their family's power.[42] In fact, all Nabulsi candidates for secondary electors were part of town's 'club' of the mercantile elite and the soap industry.[43] Similarly, all winners came from the same social group. The diversified network of connections that members of this social group had developed in the rural area allowed them to easily impact and control the patterns of voting in this area as well. Thus, when the representatives of the rural area were summoned to Nablus to elect one or two candidates for parliament, it was clear where their votes would go.

However, in an effort to consolidate its political hegemony in the town and in its rural areas, the new mercantile elite created a new form of power base called *jam'iyyat*, or leagues.[44] A *jam'iyya* was a league of families or social groups who had common interests and who worked to ensure the election of their candidates to the local administrative institutions and parliament. The *al-Jam'iyya al-'Abasiyya,* led by Shaykh 'Abbas al-Khammash, who was also in the soap business, succeeded in controlling the politics of the town for two full decades. One of their most obvious successes was the election, in 1908, of Shaykh Ahmad Khammash to the Ottoman parliament.[45] In 1912, the rival *Jam'iyya* of al-Hammadiyya, headed by the big merchant Tawfiq Hammad, defeated the 'Abasiyya and was able to send two of its members, Tawfiq Hammad and Haydar Tuqan, to the Ottoman parliament.[46]

In fact, the two-stage parliamentary elections enforced the hegemony of the urban elite over the rural leadership. Only representatives of Palestine's urban elite families were elected to the Ottoman parliament. More precisely, during the six different elections for parliament that took place in Palestine, only candidates from Jerusalem, Gaza, Jaffa, Nablus and Acre were elected.

However, as the *mutasarrifiyya* of Jerusalem included several *qada*s and various urban centers, competition for parliamentary elections produced new types of social and political struggles between the different urban centers of the *mutasarrifiyya*. The political hegemony of Jerusalem as it emerged from 1872 onward when the town became the capital of a separate *sanjaq* directly attached to the Ministry of Interior in Istanbul, greatly contributed to the spread of the political hegemony of Jerusalem's traditional elite through parliamentary elections over other urban centers in the *sanjaq*.[47] This trend started in 1877, when Yusuf Diya' al-Khalidi was the only elected deputy from Palestine. Jerusalem's political hegemony became even clearer in 1908, when in the parliamentary elections of that year two of the *sanjaq*'s three deputies came from Jerusalem. They were Ruhi al-Khalidi and Sa'id al-Husayni, members of established traditional elite families. The third was Hafiz al-Sa'id, a member of an old elite family from Jaffa. During the 1912 campaign, the CUP supported the elite candidates from Jerusalem, and ignored Jaffa and other urban centers in the *sanjaq*. The CUP's attitude irritated Jaffa's elite, and 'Isa al-'Isa, the editor of *Filastin* joined the fray and sparked a fierce fight against the hegemony of Jerusalem's elite. On 17th April 1912 he wrote:

> We regret to express our disagreement with the CUP concerning the parliamentary elections in our *liwa* [of Jerusalem]. We do not accept the damage done to our town [Jaffa] [in order to] please some families from other towns. No, before we became Unionists we were born Jaffans. [...] What matters to the CUP is that our parliamentary representatives belong to the party, but we are concerned that they should not come from one town alone. Towns of the *liwa* must not be enslaved by one town that [can claim] no uniqueness over the others. [...] We need our representatives to be unionists, but not to be ordered whom to chose [...] but, if these conditions are not respected, then we will conclude there is no difference between the Unionists and the others. Dear Khalid Bey [the head of the CUP in the *liwa* of Jerusalem], please, tell us what guilt and misdeeds have the people of Jaffa [done], to make you deny them their right to nominate a candidate from among themselves, and made you give Jerusalem

all the power. [...] You have ignored the Unionists of Jaffa who actually have taught all other towns.

As his criticism failed to make the party change its attitude, *Filastin*'s voice became even more strident. Three days later, al-'Isa wrote:

> Oh, Jaffa and Gaza, the two great cities ignored and humiliated by the regional leadership of the CUP, who look at your inhabitants as though you were insects, I am dedicating these words to you. [...] Let us ask, are the Jerusalem members of the CUP party preferred over others, what makes them unique? Have they supremacy over others? Is their city superior to yours?
>
> The *liwa* of Jerusalem has 165 secondary electors, more than half of these come from the Gaza and Jaffa districts. Why are you willing to bestow your votes like a present to the others, like the voters in Hebron have done?
>
> The general leadership of the CUP party in Jerusalem have only supported the Jerusalem candidates to represent the *mutasarrifiyya*, and the party's central authorities accepted it, thinking that the rest of the *mutasarrifiyya*'s inhabitants are useless, and good only for fishing and for humble jobs.
>
> How can you bear this humiliation? Why do you not protect your downtrodden rights? Why are you ready to give your votes to others, but withhold them from your town's candidates? Oh, secondary voters of Gaza and Jaffa, form a coalition and vote for your local candidates. To summarize, Oh, voters of Jaffa and Gaza make a coalition to choose your three representatives to parliament; one from Jerusalem, one from Gaza and another from Jaffa. If you do this, you can preserve your rights, but if you prefer Jerusalem's candidates over those of your town, you will humiliate yourself and your descendents.[48]

Filastin's critical attitude annoyed the CUP and its candidates, and they put pressure on al-'Isa, who, so it seems, had acquiesced: 'The editorial of this issue was supposed to deal with the elections, but I promised not to write on this issue again, and I'll not break my oath'.[49]

Jaffa's candidates, as they did not have the support of the party authorities, lost the elections. Three parliamentary representatives were elected from the *liwa* of Jerusalem: Ruhi al-Khalidi and 'Uthman al-Nashashibi, belonging to Jerusalem's old elite, and Ahmad 'Arif al-Husayni from Gaza, an ex-mufti representing the two branches of the large Husayni family in Gaza and Jerusalem.

The election to parliament of these three candidates began a stable tendency that would become clearer in the following years, under the British Mandate, when Jerusalem's elite would entirely dominate the politics of Palestine. In other words, the 1912 parliamentary elections already singled out Jerusalem as the 'political capital' of Palestine until 1948.

Notes

1. *Al-Dustur* [Constitution], translated by Nawfal, Nawfal (Beirut, 1301 [1883/4], vol. 1, p. 389 [in Arabic]. For a full discussion of new local and regional administrative institutions at the level of the *qada*, see Yazbak, Mahmoud, *Haifa in the Late Ottoman Period, 1864–1914: A Muslim Town in Transition* (Leiden, 1998), especially chapter two.
2. For a detailed study of municipal elections, see Yazbak, Mahmoud, 'The municipality of a Muslim town: Nablus 1868–1914', *Archiv Orientalni: Quarterly Journal of African and Asian Studies* 67 (1999), pp. 33–60.
3. For the amendments inserted in the Vilayet Law in 1871 and the municipal regulations of 1877, see *al-Dustur*, vol. 1, section 7, article 111, p. 418; vol. 2, pp. 410, 433, 440–443. See also, Municipality of Nablus, Municipal Archives of Nablus, division 4, book 3, no. 64 (hereafter, MAN).
4. MAN, d. 6, b.1, p. 14; Ihsan al-Nimr, *Ta'rikh Jabal Nablus wal-Balqa* [The History of Jabal Nabus and al-Balqa] (Nablus, undated), vol. 3, p. 30.
5. Gerber, Haim, *Ottoman Rule in Jerusalem, 1890–1914* (Berlin, 1985), p. 61.
6. MAN, d. 4, b. 1, no. 364.
7. MAN, d.6, b. 2, miscellaneous, 9 Nisan, 1330 M/22 April 1914.
8. Al-Najah University Archives, Nablus, *Records* of *Majlis al-Shura of Nablus*, vol. 1, case no. 80.
9. Kayalı, Hasan, 'Elections and the electoral process in the Ottoman Empire, 1876–1919', *International Journal of Middle East Studies* 27 (1995), p. 267.
10. Ibid., p. 266; for an Arabic translation of the Electoral Law see *al-Muqtabas*, 28 December 1908.
11. Based upon calculations from an official notebook from the 1912 parliamentary Elections in the *qada* of Nablus. Abu-Dis Archives, 24\1,1\328\14,

Parliamentary elections held in Nablus and its district in 1328\1329 M. (1912\1913).
12. Abu Dis Archives, 24\1,1\328\14, Population census in preparation for parliamentary elections in the *qada* of Nablus.
13. Abu Dis Archives, 24\1,1\328\14, Results of parliamentary elections in Nablus, p. 36.
14. For a detailed study of the political, social and commercial networks in the district of Nablus, see Doumani, Beshara, *Rediscovering Palestine: Merchants and Peasants in Jabal Nablus, 1700–1900* (Berkeley and Los Angeles, 1995), especially, chapter four.
15. *Filastin*, issue 110, 10 February 1912; issue 128, 17 April 1912; issue 122, 23 March 1912; issue 131, 27 April 1912; issue 133, 30 April 1912.
16. Ibid., issue 128, 17 April 1912; issue 133, 30 April 1912.
17. Ibid., issue 115, 15 February 1912.
18. Ibid.
19. *Filastin*, issue no. 127, 13 April 1912.
20. Ibid.
21. *Al-Karmil*, 10 September 1912.
22. For a description of such tours, see *Filastin*, issue 117, 22 February 1912; *al-Karmil*, 11 October 1912.
23. *Filastin*, issue 121, 20 March 1912.
24. Ibid., issue 110, 10 February 1912.
25. Ibid., issue 120, 16 March 1912.
26. Ibid., issue 112, 17 February 1912 (for similar propaganda see also *al-Karmil*, 26 October 1912).
27. Ibid., issue 127, 13 April 1912.
28. Khalidi, Rashid, 'The 1912 election campaign in the cities of Bilad al-Sham', *International Journal of Middle East Studies* 16 (1984), p. 467.
29. *Filastin*, issue 123, 27 March 1912; issue 131, 26 April 1912.
30. Ibid., issue 124, 30 March 1912.
31. Ibid., 6 September 1912.
32. *Al-Karmil*, 27 Sep. 1912.
33. Ibid., 1 October 1912.
34. Ibid., 8 August 1912.
35. Ibid., 15 October 1912.
36. See for example, *al-Karmil*, 26 October 1912, and *Filastin*, 24 February 1912.
37. *Filastin*, issue 110, 10 February 1912.
38. Ibid., issue 113, 21 February 1912.
39. According to Abu Khadra's suggestion, the local *millet* councils were to act as religious communal councils for each religious community in each *wilaya*.

40. Ibid., issue 124, 30 March 1912.
41. Kayalı: 'Elections and the electoral process', p. 269.
42. For an in-depth study of the social changes in Jabal Nablus in the late Ottoman period, see Doumani: *Rediscovering Palestine*, especially chapter 5.
43. For a full list of the candidates, see Abu Dis Archives, 24\1,1\328\14.
44. Yazbak, Mahmoud, 'Nabulsi ulama in the late Ottoman period, 1864–1914', *International Journal of Middle East Studies* 29 (1997), p. 83.
45. Ibid., p. 84.
46. Abu Dis Archives, 24\1,1\328\14.
47. For a detailed study of the rise of Jerusalem in the late Ottoman era see, Abu-Manneh Butrus, 'Jerusalem in the Tanzimat period, the new Ottoman administration and the notables', *Die Welt des Islams* 30 (1999), pp. 1–44.
48. Ibid., issue 129, 20 April 1912.
49. Ibid., issue 130, 23 April 1912.

CHAPTER 4

CHILDREN OF THE REVOLUTION: YOUTH IN PALESTINIAN PUBLIC LIFE, 1908-14

JOHANN BÜSSOW*

In most general accounts of modern Palestinian history, the impact of the Young Turk Revolution on Palestinian society has been assessed as marginal.[1] However, recent research has demonstrated that the Revolution was an important catalyst for societal and ideological transformation in Palestine. In a political situation which allowed for greater freedom of speech and which provided new opportunities for political participation, a variety of social categories became potential bases for political mobilization; primarily confession, nation, and class.[2] Palestinian intellectuals and political activists, I argue, also targeted the young generations as a potential core for political solidarity and as a resource for a better future. Based on contemporary Arabic press articles, diaries, and autobiographies, this chapter highlights an important and often overlooked area in which the ideas of the Revolution were translated into local initiatives in Palestine and more generally in the Middle East. The chapter first provides an overview of social and cultural trends indicative of a change in the perception of youth in Palestine around 1900. It then discusses cases in which the new sensibility to youth became politicized. Finally, it presents two institutions, the print media and schools, which promoted new concepts of childhood and youth. Interest in childhood, youth, and education – a worldwide phenomenon that had left its mark in Palestine much earlier – arguably underwent substantial quantitative as well as qualitative change after the Revolution.

Before presenting the evidence for new discourses and practices regarding children and youth, some methodological problems must be addressed. The changing relations between the generations have been alluded to in the historical literature on late Ottoman Palestine, but to date have not been dealt with systematically. In fact, attitudes towards age and generations have rarely been considered by historians of Muslim and Middle Eastern societies.[3] Second, due to the easing of Ottoman censorship in 1908, there are a considerable number of printed sources from the Young Turk period in comparison to a scarcity of sources from the preceding decades. The sources from the Young Turk period, in particular Arabic newspapers and magazines, shed light on aspects which remained in the dark for the preceding decades. Hence it is often difficult to decide whether a given social phenomenon described in these sources is specific to the Young Turk period or whether it is a continuation of earlier patterns. Finally, biographical and autobiographical texts covering this period were mostly written after World War I. To preclude projecting later ideas onto the late Ottoman period, I cite only such concepts which have parallels in strictly contemporary texts such as newspaper articles or diary entries.

A Heightened Sensibility for Generations and Life Stages in Late Ottoman Palestine

Around 1900, a growing number of Palestinians started to keep diaries, some of which were later adapted as memoirs or autobiographies.[4] These texts often reveal an intense preoccupation with age. An instructive example is the autobiography of the Palestinian lawyer, politician and ethnographer 'Umar al-Salih al-Barghuthi (1894–1965) which was published under the title of 'Stages' (*al-Marahil*).[5] In his book, al-Barghuthi presents his life in seven 'stages'. He starts with the stage of childhood (*al-tufula*, age 1 to about 10) which corresponds to his education and upbringing in his native village of Dayr Ghassana, some 40 kilometers north of Jerusalem. This is followed by the stages of puberty (*al-murahaqa*, roughly age 10 to 15) during which the author attended several schools in Jerusalem, adolescence (*al-futuwwa*, age 15 to 20) which corresponds to the time in which he attended a boarding school in Beirut and became politically active in his native village, and youth (*al-shabab*, 20 to 25) which coincides with World War I. The remaining three stages are manhood (*al-rujula*, 25–40), maturity (or 'age of grey hair', *al-kuhula*, starting at 40 and lasting until around the late forties or mid-fifties) and old age (or 'age of the white haired', *al-shaykhukha*, beginning about age 50).

The concept of seven stages in human life probably draws on antique theories which were adapted into Arabic literature,[6] although it still needs to be investigated how widespread they were in Palestine during the nineteenth and early twentieth centuries. Scattered evidence from other sources suggests that this pattern could have been well established in late Ottoman Palestine. A newspaper article of 1911 for instance remarks that boys had to adopt the dress of adults at the age of fifteen, i.e. exactly at the age which al-Barghuthi refers to as the transition between puberty and adolescence.[7] In addition, the rise of mass schooling and military conscription most likely added to the common experience of life stages.

Mass schooling according to European models stimulated interest in childhood and youth within the Ottoman population. To begin with, it was a new experience for pupils to be strictly separated by age groups. As the memoirs of contemporaries tell us, this experience was even more intense for those enrolled in boarding schools. Here, a new social milieu was forming outside the common forms of family and everyday sociability.[8] Moreover, education in Palestine was marked by intense competition between different schools supported by the state, local communities or trans-regional religious institutions. Many of these schools had specific pedagogical orientations and thus sharpened awareness that the time spent in school was a decisive period in one's life which was also crucial to one's future career.

Again, al-Barghuthi's autobiography provides a good example.[9] The author began his education in a traditional Islamic primary school (*kuttab*) in his native village, Dayr Ghassana, where he was instructed together with other boys from the village. The only teacher, who was referred to as *shaykh*, enforced discipline in the classroom mainly by physical punishment with the bastinado (*falaka*). Shortly after al-Barghuthi finished the *kuttab* at the age of nine, the governor of Jerusalem advised his father to send his son to the Ottoman 'Tribal School' (*Aşiret Mektebi*) in Istanbul.[10] However, after a personal examination of the boy, the governor decided that al-Barghuthi was still too young and inexperienced in Ottoman Turkish and told him to attend the Jewish *Alliance Israélite Universelle* (AIU) School in Jerusalem.[11] The fact that the highest representative of the Ottoman government in Jerusalem recommended a foreign school seems surprising, but it only underlines the high prestige of these institutions, even in the eyes of Ottoman administrators. Al-Barghuthi's father agreed, and so the child was sent to Jerusalem for his higher education. Al-Barghuthi's memories of the AIU school are very favorable. He praises the healthy conditions, the discipline, and the systematic curriculum and recalls that attending this school made him feel as though he had been 'transplanted from a barbaric age to the era of modern culture and civilization'.[12]

Al-Barghuthi writes that in 1905, at the age of eleven, he convinced his father to send him to the francophone *Frères* School, a foundation run by the Roman Catholic *Institute of the Brothers of the Christian Schools* (*Frères des Écoles Chrétiennes*).[13] Indirectly he explains this new self-assuredness as resulting from his personal development during the age of puberty.[14] His father complied with his wish. In comparison to the AIU, al-Barghuthi's judgment of this school was negative. He recalls that there were no specialized teachers, and all subjects were taught by only one teacher who imposed a strict regime of mutual denunciation, punishment, and rewards. Speaking French was mandatory on the school grounds and strictly enforced by the beadle. Everyone was forced to take part in the school services or suffer the penalties which, according to al-Barghuthi, made Jewish and Muslim pupils only more determined to escape. After a while he recalls to have longed to return to the AIU.

The transition from one educational system and from one language to another also caused other problems. Religiously observant friends urged al-Barghuthi's father not to neglect his son's Islamic education. The father then arranged for a *shaykh* to meet with the boy twice a week to give him private lessons in Arabic, Qur'anic recitation and Islamic ritual duties. During the holidays he took daily lessons with an *Azhar* graduate who instructed him in Islamic law, theology and logic. The result, al-Barghuthi recalls, was mental confusion (*fawda*), as he discovered more and more contradictions between modern science and Islamic teachings.[15]

In 1906, after one unhappy school year at the *Frères* School, a friend of the family, the Islamic scholar Raghib al-Khalidi, convinced al-Barghuthi's father to send him to the English St. George's School which had a good reputation in Muslim circles.[16] Al-Khalidi himself sent his three sons to this school which was located in Jerusalem's wealthy Shaykh Jarrah suburb. Al-Barghuthi remained there a year and a half. He found this school very competitive – for instance, pupils were seated in the classroom according to their performance with the best students sitting in the first row – but also as characterized by more cooperative relations between teachers and pupils than the *Frères* School.

Al-Barghuthi graduated from St. George's in 1907. Now, in the stage of adolescence, he asked his father to send him to law school in the United States.[17] To his regret, his father decided that an Ottoman education would be more beneficial to his future career. It was decided that al-Barghuthi would study for some years at the *Sultaniye* High School (*Mekteb-i Sultani*) of Beirut in order to prepare him for studying law at Istanbul's newly founded Imperial University (*Darülfünun-i Şahane*).[18] School life at the prestigious *Sultaniye* reminded al-Barghuthi of the hated *Frères* School. Discipline was taken to the extreme. Students were only addressed by their identification numbers which were stitched on the collar of their school uniform. They were permitted to leave the school grounds only on Fridays. On other days the policemen of Beirut could easily identify them by their uniforms and sent truancy reports to the school headmaster containing the identification number of every student they observed in the city.[19]

Nevertheless, al-Barghuthi and his friends developed a number of tricks to slip out of the school grounds at night. He and his classmates, he recalls, spent nights 'watching films, enjoying sexual pleasures with a girl or similar things'.[20] Upon graduation he returned home with the clear intention of continuing his education in Beirut and Istanbul. However, his hopes for a career in the service of the Empire were dashed by an accident during the same summer which forced him to remain in his native village. Thus, as he remarks, just about the time of the Revolution he 'entered the battle of village life' without feeling fully prepared.[21] What followed was a stormy phase of political activity which was, at least in part, an expression of revolt against paternal authority and a personal adaptation of the revolutionary Zeitgeist. This episode in al-Barghuthi's biography will be discussed further below.

Al-Barghuthi's repeated moves to different schools and cities were not unusual for the sons of Palestine's Muslim elite around the turn of the century. Out of a sample of nine prominent personalities from late Ottoman Jerusalem, three attended non-Muslim schools and five studied in schools outside their hometown. On average, they attended more than three different educational institutions.[22] Moreover, al-Barghuthi's criticism of the authoritarian spirit that reigned in many of the contemporary schools can also be found in numerous other Arabic autobiographies and memoirs.[23]

Military service was another important and rapidly expanding state institution that is to be considered in this context. General conscription in the Ottoman Empire was introduced by army regulations in 1843.[24] However, it was not until the 1870s that conscription was enforced all over Palestine. According to law, all Muslim men between the ages of twenty and forty had to serve at least five years in regular (*nizami*) army units. Afterwards they did two years of active reserve duty (*ihtiyat*) and seven years of inactive reserve (*redif*), and finally they spent eight years in the militia (*mustahfiz*). The time period for conscription into *nizami* units (ages 20–40) thus exactly fit al-Barghuthi's definition of the two life stages of youth and manhood.

The men obligated to serve in their age group were chosen by drawing lots. Until the end of the Hamidian era, conscripts could buy their way out at each call up for the duration of one year, at a cost of 50

Ottoman Pounds. Military service was feared, and until 1875, the inhabitants of Jerusalem nurtured hopes that they might escape military service or exemption payments altogether, because it was argued that like the 'holy cities' of Mecca and Medina, Jerusalem's entire population should be exempt.[25] By 1891, despite local opposition, the conscription system in the district of Jerusalem was consolidated, and it became a reservoir for recruits who were employed in battles in virtually every corner of the Empire. Thus, while the region of Palestine enjoyed several peaceful decades, a sizable number of its youthful male population was constantly involved in the Empire's wars. Ottoman conscription registers document that towards the end of the Hamidian period almost every village and hamlet in Palestine had been subjected to conscription.[26] In these registers, young men were listed by year of birth. Accordingly, a growing number of Palestinians must have felt that age mattered and needed to be documented. In the wake of the Revolution, the heightened sensibility to life stages and generations manifested itself in public debates.

Youth as the Target of Individual Civilizing Missions and as a Resource for Political Activism

As François Georgeon highlights in his biography of Sultan Abdülhamid II, alongside some liberally-minded administrators and intellectuals of the older generation, young military officers and graduates of the college of public administration (*Mülkiye*) played a major part in the Revolution of 1908.[27] In other words, most Young Turks were young indeed. But the term 'youth' carried yet another meaning. The Revolutionaries were inspired by the global trend for 'young' movements (cf. Young Italy, Young America, and Young Judaea, but also cultural trends such as *Art Nouveau / Jugendstil*). More recently, Georgeon has suggested that the shared experience of the *Tanzimat* reforms and the Revolution inspired a new consciousness of generations (*nesil*) among Ottoman intellectuals. This consciousness found prominent expression in the title of Halid Ziya's novel *The Last Generation* (*Nesl-i Âhir*) and in the *Club of the New Generation* (*Nesl-i Cedid Kulübü*) founded by Prince Sabahaddin in Istanbul.[28]

In Palestine there was an exponential growth in the numbers of school and university graduates who had a heightened sensibility for generational differences. In the years before 1908, many ambitious young Palestinians waited for a chance to make their ideas heard and to become 'a public man' (Hebrew: *ish tziburi*) as one of them, the Sephardi Jewish entrepreneur Yosef Eliyahu Chelouche (1870–1934), later put it.[29] For many of them, this chance came with the Revolution of 1908.

In terms of the ages of the main actors in the Revolution in Palestine, we find a picture similar to that sketched by Georgeon for Young Turk circles in Istanbul and Salonica. Those who first dared to speak out publicly in favor of the Revolution were mature persons, often with a record of liberal intellectual activity. They were led by two members of Jerusalem's most prominent Muslim families, Raghib al-Khalidi (born about 1860) and Husayn Salim al-Husayni (roughly the same generation).[30] Yet most activists who subsequently invoked the Revolution in support of their political and cultural activities were younger people. They had received a modern education and shared similar resentment toward the established leaders in government as well as in *millet* organizations. Their common enemy was termed 'despotism' (*istibdad*, used both in Ottoman Turkish and in Arabic). The charge of *istibdad* was leveled against a number of authoritarian father-figures. An obvious addressee was Sultan Abdülhamid II who in post-Revolutionary rhetoric was styled as the very embodiment of despotism. One of Jerusalem's leading intellectuals of the period, Khalil al-Sakakini (1878–1953), extended the notion of despotism beyond the realm of the central government by stating in his diary that 'we rid ourselves of the despotism of the government, but we are still under the domination of the communal leaders'.[31] Not only the spheres of government and *millet* administration were scrutinized; some came to see despotism as a pervasive phenomenon that also permeated family relations, and especially the relations between fathers and sons.

An anecdote about Is'af al-Nashashibi (1885–1949), the son of the prominent landowner and local politician 'Uthman al-Nashashibi, provides a colorful example of rebellion against a dominant father. A gifted pupil, Is'af received his higher education at the Greek Orthodox

Patriarchate School in Beirut. Concurrently, he studied Islamic subjects with local Muslim scholars.[32] Back in Jerusalem, Is'af al-Nashashibi established strong ties with some of the leading Christian Arab intellectuals of his generation such as Khalil al-Sakakini and the editor of the newspaper *Filastin*, Yusuf al-'Isa (d. 1948).[33] About the same time he lost interest in the career as a businessman his father had envisaged for him. Al-Sakakini notes in his diary that Is'af's reluctance to join the family business sparked a conflict between father and son. What in earlier times might have been a private family matter now became a *cause celèbre*. Al-Sakakini writes:

> He [the father] discovered that he [his son Is'af] had devoted himself to literature (*adab*), an art that does not enrich anyone or make him fat. On the same day, he learned that his son had sold a piece of land in Jaffa. This made him furious, and he called the police to search for him and arrest him. Eventually he spotted him at the Jaffa Gate, but the boy ran away. The father and the police followed him and caught him at the New Market (Suq al-Jadid). People started gathering. We, the friends of the boy, came to the place of the incident in the hope of either saving the boy or calming down the father – but to no avail. The boy yelled: 'Fight 'Uthman, pride of your country!' The father took up his sort of language, asking me: 'Sakakini, is this the end of those who read Shumayyil's *Introduction*?!' By this he meant the Introduction to Shumayyil's book on Darwinism.[34]

Shibli Shumayyil (1850–1917) was one of the popularizers of the ideas of Charles Darwin in the Arab World. Describing this scene, al-Sakakini, who had read widely in European literature, may have had Turgenev's novel *Fathers and Sons* in mind, with its description of the cleavage between younger and older generations in mid-nineteenth century Russia which was attributed to the influence of nihilism. Even before 1908, a process of integration had taken place in which a young generation of Christians, Muslims and (some) Jews established a transcommunal identity of being Arab literati (Arabic: *udaba*, sg. *adib*) revolting against the conservatism of their parents.

In the period after 1908, this shared consciousness was suddenly articulated in a fairly radical fashion. Sentiments criticizing 'despotic' family structures resonate in a long article by another graduate of a Russian school, Iskandar al-Khuri al-Baytjali (1890–1973)[35] which appeared in the cultural journal *al-Nafa'is al-'Asriyya* {Modern Treasures} in 1912. Al-Baytjali describes young people in Palestine whose parents denied them the right to education. He calls them 'the martyrs of the twentieth century' and continues: 'O reader, do you know what the martyrdom of the twentieth century is? Woe betide the families which cause such souls to be sacrificed on the altar of traditions!'[36]

In 1911, an editorial in the newspaper *Filastin* on the occasion of the Ottoman national holiday (*'id al-umma*) on July 24 carried this sentiment further into a more political and even militant direction. In an appeal to the 'new generation' of pupils in Palestinian schools (*al-nash' al-jadid*), the author called on his young compatriots not to believe the claims of the old and still powerful elites that *they* had brought about the Revolution. Instead, Palestine's youth should actively participate in local politics and help 'cleanse the earth' (*tunazzif al-ard*) of those 'turncoats' who were trying to dominate 'the age of the constitution' as they had dominated the previous 'age of despotism'.[37]

The autobiography of 'Umar al-Salih al-Barghuthi mirrors this sentiment. At the same time, it provides an illustration of political activism which took a political turn towards militant Arab nationalism. Al-Barghuthi writes that after his educational career had been interrupted by an accident at the age of fourteen, he experimented with educational and political projects which were all targeted at the young generation in his native village of Dayr Ghassana. First, he organized an informal club (*nadwa*) of young men in which he delivered 'lectures in the natural and social sciences in order to plant the seeds of the scientific way of thinking in some souls'.[38] Secondly, he began to organize the first girls' school in Dayr Ghassana. Here he managed to enlist the support of a Western female missionary teacher from a school in one of the neighboring villages. The classrooms were located in part of the al-Barghuthi family seat. When operational, 80 girls were taught by two teachers who were also lodged on the Barghuthi family's premises.[39]

Subsequently, inspired by the new ideological trend of Arab nationalism, al-Barghuthi began to organize a secret paramilitary youth group whose members were recruited from Dayr Ghassana and the villages around it. He writes that he founded his organization in explicit opposition to the old style of political leadership (*zu'ama*) along the lines of his father Shaykh Mahmud al-Salih, which was based on tradition and reverence for the elders. Thus, this form of political activity was a revolt both against the Ottoman government and against his father. Al-Barghuthi's organization was called 'The Arab Association' (*al-Jam'iyya al-'Arabiyya*) and had its own flag in the colors of the Arab nationalists: white, black, green, and red. It had four principles:

(1) Members had to be under thirty years of age.
(2) They needed to own a rifle or a revolver.
(3) A new member needed two members of the association as guarantors and was to swear an oath of allegiance to the association, its leader, and its flag.
(4) Every member had to commit himself to absolute loyalty and solidarity to the leader and to his comrades.

According to al-Barghuthi, the new association soon numbered several hundred members. The description of its actions resembles that of young men's associations in earlier periods of Arab history which were commonly referred to as *futuwwa* (Arabic: youth or adolescence).[40] The author indeed suggests this parallel as the corresponding chapter in his autobiography is entitled *Adolescence (Futuwwa)*. Al-Barghuthi's group extorted 'taxes' of their own; local opponents were robbed or put under arrest. Their activity reached its peak when the young men marched *en bloc* during the Islamic Nabi Salih pilgrimage festival,[41] brandishing flags and weapons and singing patriotic songs. In retrospect, al-Barghuthi describes with an overtone of amusement how this experience filled him with excessive pride and made him identify with heroic figures such as Saladin, Muhammad 'Ali, or even the prophet Muhammad.[42] However, the twofold revolt against government and paternal authority ended in a double defeat. First, the display of force at the pilgrimage aroused the suspicions of the governor of Jerusalem who shut down the association and passed orders to supervise the activities of the unruly young man. Secondly, much to his dismay, his father forced him to marry a cousin who had not received a modern education and who after the marriage apparently did everything to keep her husband within the confines of a traditional way of life.[43]

Al-Barghuthi's secret organization was indeed a case of a 'young' movement. He writes that his personal motto during these years was 'struggle and pleasure' (*al-ijtihad wal-istimta'*).[44] The implicit hedonism in this motto is reminiscent of the writings of Khalil al-Sakakini whom al-Barghuthi met regularly during the year 1914.[45] In any event, al-Barghuthi's autobiography provides unusual insights into an individual's 'civilizing mission' in the Palestinian countryside during the Young Turk era. The prestige of a modern education empowered the adolescent and even emboldened him to rebel against the authority of his father and the governor.

Parallel to these individual voices and initiatives targeting youth, there were two institutions in Palestine which thrived during the Young Turk period and helped ascribe a political meaning to the notion of generation: the print media and schools.

Youth in the Post-Revolutionary Palestinian Print Media and Schools

Topics related to childhood and youth occupied a prominent place in the Palestinian newspapers and journals that started to appear after the abrogation of the Hamidian censorship regime in 1908. A plethora of articles and essays in Arabic, Hebrew, German, and other languages highlight the importance of childhood, youth, and education in subsequent years. Here I focus mainly on the Arabic press.

In public debates, children and youth served as metaphors for the renewal of society but were also referred to in more concrete terms as the future bearers of the Revolution's motto 'unity and progress' (*ittihad ve terakki*) and as assets in which society should invest. It is important to note that Palestinian journalists themselves often established a direct link between the Revolution and their call to direct greater attention to the young population. A case in point is an anonymous moralizing piece in the Arabic literary journal *al-Nafa'is al-'Asriyya*, which was founded in 1908 in Jerusalem by the Greek Orthodox Palestinian writer Khalil Baydas (1874–1949).[46] Entitled *al-Awlad wal-Hurriyya* [Children and Freedom], the author calls upon the fathers in his society to educate their children to prepare them for the 'age of freedom' (Arabic: *al-hurriyya*).[47]

This article spells out paradigmatically how Palestinian civil society activists appropriated the slogans of the Revolution and applied them to their own goals. According to the author, freedom is a value which is the very essence of a fully human existence but it makes high demands on the individual. Freedom requires order (*nizam*), otherwise it could simply create a disoriented 'mass of people' (*jumhur*) which would be easy to manipulate. A free man – it is worth noting here that the author refers only to the male segment of the population – was characterized by the ability to make his own law (*shari'a*) and to guide himself (*qiyadat nafsihi*).

These virtues, the author continues, must be instilled by the father. One should not believe in the common misapprehension that children are able to develop these faculties by themselves as they grow up. Rather, they depend on adults who serve as role models and who demonstrate the value of self-reliance. These moralizing statements reveal the anxieties of post-revolutionary anarchy. More importantly, they did not remain on a theoretical level but were translated into a number of practical initiatives in the field of educational reform. Again, these initiatives were tightly aligned with the press. Journalists worked to disseminate what they perceived as positive examples of modern education, and it may well be that they were actively encouraged to do so by some of these educational institutions. In some cases there was even a direct overlap between the two institutions. Khalil al-Sakakini for instance was active both as an educator and a journalist, and from 1911 onwards, the journal *al-Nafa'is* was printed in the printing house of the Syrian Orphanage in Jerusalem. Not surprisingly, the orphanage, its school and their founder, the German Protestant Johann Ludwig Schneller (1820–96), received broad coverage in the pages of the journal.[48]

In the 1880s, the Ottoman government began to perceive schools as key institutions for the future of the Empire.[49] In Palestine, the building of state schools was especially encouraged to counter the influence of private missionary establishments. Although contemporary statistics should always be handled with care, it is safe to say that by the end of the Hamidian period more than 10 per cent of the school-age population (defined by the authorities as children aged 7–11) in the District of Jerusalem went to state schools and acquired at least basic literacy in Arabic.[50] Including the private schools it might have been 30 per cent.[51] In addition, more than five hundred young men of each age group went to Ottoman *rüşdiye* and *i'dadi* schools and thus acquired a *lycée* knowledge of Ottoman Turkish, French, arithmetic and other subjects which qualified them for a post in the Ottoman civil service – and of course to matriculate at the Jerusalem teachers' college and become teachers in turn.[52]

Thus, in quantitative terms at least, the Hamidian educational policy was relatively successful. By the end of the period, there must have been several tens of thousands of people in Palestine, men and women, who could read at least official notices and were able to understand the Arabic part of the government gazette *al-Quds al-Sharif*.[53] Government service could now rely on a cadre of young men with a solid general education and the ability to converse with foreigners in French. Tevfik Bey, who served as governor of Jerusalem between 1897 and 1901, greeted this development with enthusiasm and hoped that the government schools' graduates would be loyal 'machines' in the service of the central government and the palace.[54]

It is questionable, however, whether the latter objective was met. As Benjamin Fortna summarizes in his comparative study of similar educational endeavors in countries such as Russia or China, 'the emergence and spread of higher mass-education produced unanticipated consequences' and, even worse for the reigning statesmen, 'public education and the production of a new educated elite reinforced the spread of revolutionary ideas and the emergence of a politically conscious counter-elite'.[55] The same could be felt in Palestine in the years preceding the Revolution. For many among the educated young generation it must have been utterly frustrating to have acquired access to the exciting world of the new print media, especially the popular Egyptian newspapers and journals, but be denied the right to any journalistic activity at home, or to have acquired organizational skills and be denied the right to organize cultural clubs, charitable associations, or private schools.[56]

We have already seen that after 1908 the existing state and community schools were often portrayed as expressions of an authoritarian *ancien régime* mentality. Wasif al-Jawhariyya took up catchwords of the Young Turk era when he later recalled the drastic disciplinary measures at the German Protestant School in Jerusalem: 'Thus was the injustice and despotism (*al-zulm wal-istibdad*) in education during this period'.[57] In an article in *Filastin*, the teacher and writer Bulus Shahada compared English, French, and Ottoman school books and came to the conclusion that the Ottoman Turkish books were 'children of the era of Abdülhamid', full of 'megalomania, vainglory, and hypocrisy'. Shahada concluded: 'One should shut them away [...] in order to prevent them from misguiding the minds of adolescents'.[58]

After 1908, several new private schools experimenting with new educational approaches entered the scene. Their concepts and their practical performance were subjects of lively discussion in the local newspapers. Again, the keywords 'freedom' (*hurriyya*) and 'constitution' (*dustur*) figure prominently. The goals of educational reform that were discussed included educating the female population,[59] raising the standard of vocational training,[60] reviving Islamic and Jewish religious learning in Jerusalem,[61] and strengthening the local languages, be it Arabic or Hebrew.[62]

The press portrayed a variety of new schools that were regarded as models of educational reform. Among those most frequently discussed were three boys' schools: The Muslim *Rawdat al-Ma'arif* [Garden of Learning] school that was founded 1908 in the Haram al-Sharif complex of Jerusalem, the American Christian *Friends* school in Ramallah (founded in 1889),[63] and the Constitutional School in Jerusalem (*al-Madrasa al-Dusturiyya*). The latter was founded in 1909 by a group of young Christian and Muslim intellectuals including Khalil al-Sakakini, 'Ali Jarallah, Jamil al-Khalidi, and Aftim Mushabbak.⁶⁴

As its name suggests, the Constitutional School aimed to embody all the hopes that had been placed in renewed education in the post-Revolutionary period. It took up a number of reformist educational concepts that had recently been developed in Europe and America, among them an integrated kindergarten (*bustan atfal*), as well as an emphasis on sports and on arts and crafts in the curriculum. Its most unusual feature, however, was that it was a multi-confessional school in which Muslims, Jews, and Christians studied together without one confessional group dominating the other. This fact made the school indeed stand out in the wider educational landscape of Palestine and the wider region. The school's short history is also highly indicative of the general impact as well as of the shortcomings of initiatives by Palestine's young civil society activists. On one hand, al-Sakakini garnered support from the municipality, several leading Ottoman administrators, and local notables in and outside Jerusalem. On the other hand, the school was in a precarious financial situation and was several times threatened by closure. The outbreak of World War I put a definitive end to the project.⁶⁵

In addition to their educational activities, schools served as venues for public events such as award ceremonies, sports events, plays and exhibitions. These events received extensive coverage in the press and were discussed by local intellectuals. During the Young Turk period, schools emerged as one of the most important places for public speeches and ceremonies. They provided government officials as well as local dignitaries with the opportunity to present themselves to a well-educated urban public. The public, in turn, must have shared a feeling of constituting a vanguard of social progress in their region.

The school celebrations of the Constitutional School received exceptional coverage in the pages of the newspaper *Filastin*. With their emphasis on order, achievement and aesthetics, some of these articles convey a utopian hope that these schools might form the nucleus of a new society. In this vein, Is'af al-Nashashibi wrote about a celebration at the Constitutional School:⁶⁶ 'I saw in this success and progress of the pupils [...] something that promised a glorious future for Jerusalem [...].

This school, with its commitment to the constitution and to patriotism, is an [...] encouragement to pioneers'.

The schools' well-choreographed celebrations were means of self-representation, not arenas for public debate. In at least one case, however, they led to an exercise in free speech. In 1911 the newspaper reported an award ceremony at Jerusalem's state Secondary School (*al-Maktab al-I'dadi*) which was held in the presence of the governor, the leading members of the local government and the most important Islamic dignitaries. In a speech during the celebration, the local director of education (*mudir al-ma'arif*) demanded a reform of primary education in the District of Jerusalem. According to the article, this speech in turn motivated a Muslim *shaykh*, probably a preacher, to give an improvised speech in which he directly criticized the local government. The governor is reported to have reacted quite coolly, admonishing the *shaykh* that this was 'not a battlefield' and that if he had complaints he should keep to the customary means of petitioning.[67]

Another social practice that developed especially in and around Christian schools was sports. *Filastin* provided extensive and sympathetic coverage of public sports events in Jerusalem, Jaffa and Beirut. Among these events were football matches in Jerusalem that mostly involved students of local Christian schools and that were followed by hundreds and sometimes even thousands of spectators. Palestine's first Arab football team was founded in 1908 at the Anglican St. George's School in Jerusalem, two years after a Jewish football team had been founded in Jaffa.[68] In 1909, this team defeated the Syrian Protestant College in Beirut.[69] Other important institutions in the nascent sports life in Palestine were the 'Sports Club' (*Cercle Sportif / al-Muntada al-Riyadi*) which was founded in 1911[70] and the sports day of Jerusalem's St. George's School which was held for the first time in 1913.[71]

The journalists also discussed the social and cultural implications of sports. In September of 1911, *Filastin* described a football match (*sibaq futbol*) in Jerusalem in which a British team including the British consul and several physicians and teachers played against local teachers and students. The anonymous author of the article uses the occasion to make two general observations on sports in his society. Firstly, he notes, sports were beginning to be taken seriously and to be distinguished from 'useless children's games devoid of order'. Secondly, the attitude towards movement had changed. Previously children were urged to sit still, and at the age of fifteen they had to stop playing and to adopt the manners of adults. When children have to stop playing, the author remarks, they become 'stiff, weak, and deprived of energy'. At present, however, sports and physical activity were encouraged. The author continues: 'Man (*al-insan*) needs to be broad shouldered, mobile and strong in order to persist in the battle of time (*ma'rakat al-zaman*)'. The 'battle of time' is reminiscent of the term 'battle of village life' which al-Barghuthi used to describe the challenges of adulthood.[72]

These metaphors[73] could take on real meaning. For instance, the curriculum of Khalil al-Sakakini's Constitutional School included paramilitary training.[74] The author further remarked that the growing popularity of sports had already changed dress styles among adolescents and young men. Whereas previously a boy had to wear adult clothes at the age of fifteen, now members of the 'new generation' could be seen wearing short pants even past the age of sixteen.[75] Obviously, the new importance of youth after the Revolution resulted in the cultivation of a new youthful *habitus* which modified the traditional concept of a sharp dividing line between youth and adulthood. Youth was presented as a phase of life with positive connotations which was desirable to begin earlier and to end later than in the traditional models of life stages.

The new ideal was the youthful, fearless, and strong human being, which was almost invariably equated with the masculine gender. Manliness (*rujula*) often served as shorthand for these virtues. The authors writing in *Filastin* found such manliness chiefly in the British schools. Thus, Yusuf al-'Isa praises the students of Jerusalem's St. George's School: 'It produces pupils with a strong constitution with their head held high. Talk to them and you will have the impression of talking to a man, not to a boy'. Comparing the Anglican bishop to the much-criticized local clerics, 'Isa remarked: 'The progress of the peoples is brought about by such men, and these are the deeds that characterize true men'.[76]

Conclusion

Sultan Abdülhamid II was reported to have commented on the developments after the Revolution that 'freedom' under the revolutionaries resembled 'a horse in the hands of a child'.[77] It is not surprising that the Sultan chose such an image, since inter-generational conflict was an important aspect of the revolutionary events after 1908. While for conservative critics of the Revolution the image of the child might have represented irresponsibility, for many revolutionaries children were a symbol of hope for a better future.

Even before 1908 there was heightened public concern regarding the importance of childhood and youth in Palestine. The Young Turk Revolution, however, created the opportunity for this trend to express itself publicly. Literally in the first days after the Revolution, ambitious young people entered the scene. They felt united by a sense of being part of a new generation, and they shared a special commitment to children and youth, i.e. the next generations, whom they viewed as their natural allies. During the following months and years, institutions such as newspapers, schools, sports clubs and public ceremonies endowed this commitment with more lasting forms. From the beginning, Palestinian youth were also targeted as potential recruits for political causes, whether Ottomanism or Arab nationalism.

Youth was a common denominator which united members of different confessional communities in Palestine. However, it was also an ambivalent concept that was interpreted in various ways. Protest against communal leaders or Is'af al-Nashashibi's revolt against his father were celebrated as a bold revolt in the name of hedonism and liberalism against the 'despotism' of the older generation. At the same time, the examples of al-Barghuthi's short-lived *futuwwa* movement or that of paramilitary training in the *Madrasa Dusturiyya* show that the discourse about youth could also include authoritarian and militant tendencies.

Many of the young activists in these institutions rose to political prominence in Mandatory Palestine. How exactly this specific heritage of the Revolution lived on under the changing political circumstances after 1918 remains a question for future study.

Notes

*Collaborative Research Centre 586, *Difference and Integration*, Universities of Halle-Wittenberg and Leipzig, Germany. I would like to thank Orit Bashkin for her helpful remarks on an earlier version of this chapter.

1. For example Khalidi, Rashid, *Palestinian Identity: The Construction of Modern National Consciousness* (New York, 1997); Manna', 'Adil, *Tarikh Filastin fi Awakhir al-'Ahd al-'Uthmani, 1700–1918: Qira'a Jadida* [History of Palestine at the End of the Ottoman Period: A New Reading] (Beirut, 1999); Krämer, Gudrun, *A History of Palestine: From the Ottoman Conquest to the Founding of the State of Israel* (Princeton, 2008); a different view is suggested in Pappé, Ilan, *History of Modern Palestine: One Land, Two Peoples* (Cambridge, 2004).
2. See Khalidi: *Palestinian Identity*; Campos, Michelle, *A 'Shared Homeland' and Its Boundaries: Empire, Citizenship, and the Origins of Sectarianism in Late Ottoman Palestine, 1908–13* (Unpublished Ph.D. Dissertation: Stanford University, 2003), pp. 119–136, 172–6.
3. Georgeon, François and Klaus Kreiser (eds.), *Enfance et jeunesse dans le monde musulman / Childhood and Youth in the Muslim World* (Paris, 2007); Berger, Lutz, *Gesellschaft und Individuum in Damaskus, 1550–1791* (Würzburg, 2007), pp. 213–220. See also the thematic issue on 'Jerusalem Childhoods', *Jerusalem Quarterly* 37 (2009).
4. For example al-Jawhariyya, Wasif, *Al-Quds al-'Uthmaniyya fil-Mudhakkirat al-Jawhariyya* [Ottoman Jerusalem in the Jawhariyya Memoirs], vol. 1, edited by Tamari, Salim and Issam Nassar (Jerusalem, 2003); al-Sakakini, Khalil, *The Diaries of Khalil Sakakini: New York, Sultana, Jerusalem, 1907–1912*, Volume I, edited by Musallam, Akram (Jerusalem, 2003) [in Arabic]; Tamari, Salim (ed.), *'Amal al-Jarad: Al-Harb al-'Uzma wa-Mahw al-Madi al-'Uthmani min Filastin: Yawmiyyat Jundi Maqdisi 'Uthmani, 1915–1916* [The Year of the Locust: Diary of an Ottoman Soldier from Jerusalem], (Beirut, 2008).
5. See Tamari, Salim 'The last feudal lord in Palestine', *Jerusalem Quarterly*, 16 (2002), pp. 27–42.
6. The corresponding terms in antique Latin literature are *infans, puer, adolescens, iuvenis, vir, senior, senex*. Binder, Gerhard, 'Age(s)', in Cancik, Hubert and Helmuth Schneider (eds.), *Brill's New Pauly*, Antiquity volumes, online edition 2009; European medieval models of life are discussed in Ariès, Philippe, *Geschichte der Kindheit*, third edition, translated by Neubaur, Caroline and Karin Kersten (Munich and Vienna, 1976), pp. 69–91.
7. *Filastin*, 16 December 1911, p. 1.
8. Georgeon, François, *Abdulhamid II: Le sultan calife* (Paris, 2003), p. 327. Cf. Aries: *Geschichte der Kindheit*, pp. 47f.

9. For the following see al-Barghuthi, 'Umar al-Salih, *Al-Marahil* [Stages] (Amman/Beirut, 2001), pp. 81–3.
10. See Rogan, Eugene, 'Aşiret Mektebi: Abdülhamid IIs school for tribes, 1892–1907', *International Journal of Middle East Studies* 28 (1996), pp. 83–107; Deringil, Selim, *The Well-Protected Domains: Ideology and the Legitimation of Power in the Ottoman Empire, 1876–1909* (London, 1998), pp. 101–104.
11. On the AIU schools in the Ottoman Empire see Aron Rodrigue, *French Jews, Turkish Jews: The Alliance Israélite Universelle and the Politics of Jewish Schooling in Turkey, 1860–1925* (Bloomington, 1990).
12. Al-Barghuthi: *Marahil*, p. 85.
13. On the *Frères* schools in the Ottoman Empire see Ange Michel, *Les Frères des Écoles Chrétiennes en Turquie, 1841–2003* (Istanbul, 2004).
14. Ibid., pp. 95–97.
15. Ibid., pp. 98–101.
16. Ibid., pp. 103–17. On St. George's School see also Furlonge, Geoffrey, *Palestine is My Country: The Story of Musa Alami* (London, 1969), pp. 33f.; Nashashibi, Nasser Eddin, *Jerusalem's Other Voice: Ragheb Nashashibi and Moderation in Palestinian Politics, 1920–1948* (Exeter, 1990), p. 4.
17. For the following see Barghuthi: *Marahil*, pp. 117–26; cf. Hanssen, Jens, *Fin de Siècle Beirut: The Making of a Provincial Capital* (Oxford, 2005), pp. 171–80.
18. See Shaw, Stanford and Ezel Kural Shaw, *History of the Ottoman Empire and Modern Turkey*, vol. 2: *Reform, Revolution and Republic: The Rise of Modern Turkey, 1808–1975* (Cambridge, 1977), pp. 109f., 250f., 387.
19. Ibid., p. 125.
20. Ibid., pp. 124f.
21. Ibid., p. 104
22. Büssow, Johann, *Hamidian Palestine: Politics and Society in the District of Jerusalem, 1872–1908*, (Unpublished Ph.D. Dissertation: Free University, Berlin, 2008), p. 330.
23. For example al-Jawhariyya, *Mudhakkirat*; Schumann, Christoph, *Radikalnationalismus in Syrien und Libanon: Politische Sozialisation und Elitenbildung, 1930–1958* (Hamburg, 2001).
24. Zürcher, Erik Jan, 'The Ottoman conscription system in theory and practice 1844–1918', in idem (ed.), *Arming the State: Military Conscription in the Middle East and Central Asia 1775–1925* (London and New York, 1999), pp. 79–94.
25. Başbakanlık Osmanlı Arşivi (BOA), İ.MM, 15 Muharrem 1287 / 17 April 1870; *Die Warte*, 15 July 1875, cited in Carmel, Alex *Palästina-Chronik*, vol. 1: *Deutsche Zeitungsberichte vom Krimkrieg bis zur ersten jüdischen Einwanderungswelle, 1853–1882* (Ulm, 1978), p. 203.

26. On Ottoman military conscription registers preserved in the Israel State Archives see Pagis, Jonathan, *Ottoman Population Censuses in Palestine, 1875–1918* (Jerusalem, 1997) [in Hebrew]; cf. Büssow: *Hamidian Palestine*: pp. 472–6.
27. Georgeon: *Abdulhamid II*, p. 327; idem: 'Enfance et jeunesse', pp. 148f.
28. Ibid., pp. 152f.
29. Yosef Eliyahu Chelouche, *Parashat Hayay* [The Story of My Life] (Tel Aviv, 1931), p. 105 [in Hebrew]. For general information on the Chelouche family see the article 'Chelouche' in *Encyclopedia Judaica*.
30. Al-Barghuthi, 'Umar al-Salih and Khalil Tutah, *Tarikh Filastin* [The History of Palestine] (Jerusalem, 1923), p. 242; cf. Barghuthi, *Marahil*, p. 110; cf. Manna', 'Adil, *A'lam Filastin fi Awakhir al-'Ahd al-'Uthmani* [The Notables of Palestine during the Late Ottoman Period], second edition (Beirut, 1995), p. 124.
31. Al-Sakakini: *The Diaries of Khalil Sakakini*, p. 302.
32. Al-Hawwari, 'Irfan Sa'id Abu Hamad, *A'lam min Ard al-Salam* [Notables from the Land of Peace] (Haifa, 1979).
33. Al-Sakakini: *The Diaries of Khalil Sakakini*, pp. 287, 301, 305.
34. Cited in al-'Awdat, Ya'qub, *A'lam al-Fikr wal-Adab fi Filastin* [Prominent Figures of Thought and Literature in Palestine] (Jerusalem, 1976), p. 626f; cf. Hourani, Albert, *Arabic Thought in the Liberal Age, 1798–1939*, second edition (Cambridge, 1983), pp. 248–53.
35. On Baytjali see Hawwari: *A'lam*, pp. 87f.
36. Al-Baytjali, Iskandar al-Khuri, 'Al-Shuhada fil-qarn al-'ishrin' [Martyrs of the twentieth century], *al-Nafa'is al-'Asriyya* 4 (1912), pp. 68–78.
37. *Filastin*, 22 July 1911.
38. Al-Barghuthi: *Marahil*, p. 138.
39. Ibid., p. 139.
40. Irwin, Robert, 'Futuwwa: Chivalry and gangsterism in medieval Cairo', *Muqarnas* 21 (2004), pp. 161–70.
41. During the late Ottoman period, the pilgrimage festival of *Nabi Salih* (The Prophet Salih) was celebrated at the same time as the Christian Easter week and the Islamic *Nabi Musa* (The Prophet Moses) pilgrimage in Jerusalem. On the festival see Barghuthi: *Marahil*, p. 76–8 and Aubin-Boltanski, Emma, 'La réinvention du *mawsim* de Nabî Sâlih: Les territoires palestiniens (1997–2000)', *Archives de sciences sociales des religions* 123 (2003), pp. 103–120. On the *Nabi Salih* shrine northwest of Ramallah, one of three locations in Palestine in which the Prophet was venerated, see al-Ju'beh, Nazmi, 'Maqam Nabi Salih', in Sharif, Walid et al., *Pilger, Sufis und Gelehrte: Islamische Kunst im Westjordanland und Gazastreifen* (Tübingen, 2004), pp. 154–55.

42. Al-Barghuthi: *Marahil*, pp. 145f.
43. Ibid., p. 149.
44. Ibid., p. 127.
45. Ibid., p. 158.
46. Tamari, Salim, 'Le café des manants: Khalil Sakakini, prince de l'oisiveté de Jérusalem', *Revue des Etudes Palestiniennes*, 90 (2004), pp. 78–87.
46. On the journal see Abu Hanna, Hanna, *Tala'i' al-Nahda fi Filastin: Khariju al-Madaris al-Rusiyya, 1862–1914* [The Pioneers of the Revival of Arabic Language and Culture in Palestine: the Graduates of the Russian Schools], (Beirut, 2005), pp. 62–5.
47. Anon., 'Al-Awlad wal-hurriyya', *al-Nafa'is al-'Asriyya* 3 (1911), pp. 69–71.
48. Anon., 'Schneller, Munshi' Dar al-Aytam al-Suriyya fil-Quds al-Sharif wal-Ma'ruf bi-Abi al-Aytam', (Schneller, Founder of the Syrian Orphanage in Jerusalem, Known as the Father of Orphans) *al-Nafa'is* 4 (1912), pp. 505–516.
49. Somel, S. Akşin, *The Modernization of Public Education in the Ottoman Empire 1839–1908, Islamization, Autocracy and Discipline* (Leiden, 2001). Fortna, Benjamin, *Imperial Classroom: Islam, the State, and Education in the Late Ottoman Empire* (Oxford, 2002).
50. Cf. Ayalon, Ami, *Reading Palestine: Printing and Literacy, 1900–1948* (Austin, 2004), pp. 21; 163, n.14. Somel: *The Modernization of Public Education*, Appendix.
51. Ayalon: *Reading Palestine*, p. 22.
52. Cuinet, Vital, *Syrie, Liban et Palestine: Géographie administrative, statistique, descriptive et raisonnée* (Paris, 1896), p. 564.
53. *Kudüs-i Şerif / al-Quds al-Sharif* was a bilingual newspaper in Ottoman Turkish and Arabic founded in 1903. Yehoshua, Ya'akov, *Al-Sahafa al-'Arabiyya fi Filastin fil-'Ahd al-'Uthmani, 1908–1918* [The Arabic Press in Palestine during the Ottoman Period, 1908–1918] (Jerusalem, 1974), pp. 33–9.
54. Tevfik Bey, Mehmed, *Bir Devlet Adamının Mehmet Tevfik Bey'in (Biren) II. Abdülhamid, Meşrutiyet ve Mütareke Devri Hatıraları* [The Memoirs of the Statesman Mehmed Tevfik Bey (Biren) Concerning the Period of Abdülhamid II, the Constitution, and the Armistice], edited by Hürmen, Fatma Rezan, 2 vols. (Istanbul, 1993), vol. 1, p. 140 [in Turkish].
55. Fortna, Benjamin, 'Education and autobiography at the end of the Ottoman Empire', *Die Welt des Islams* 41/1 (2001), p. 2.
56. Shahada, Bulus, 'Al-Madaris fi Filastin' [The Schools of Palestine], *Filastin*, 10 July 1911, p. 2; al-Khalidi, Raghib, 'Al-Kulliyat al-Islamiyya', *Filastin*, 19 July 1911, p. 1; 22 July 1911, p. 1.
57. Jawhariyya: *Mudhakkirat*, p. 22.

58. *Filastin*, 15 July 1911, p. 2. On Bulus Shahada see al-Hawwari: *A'lam*, pp. 111f.
59. For example *Filastin*, 15 July 1911, p. 3; 16 November 1912, p. 2; 12 July 1913, p. 3; Eberhard, Nochmals, 'Jugendpflege', *Altneuland* 3/5 (1906), pp. 129–140.
60. For example the resolutions of the Provincial Council (*Meclis-i Umumi*) of Jerusalem, analyzed in Gerber, Haim, *Ottoman Rule in Jerusalem, 1890–1914* (Berlin, 1985), pp. 140f.
61. *Filastin*, 8 March 1913, p. 3; Strohmeier, Martin, *Al-Kulliya al-Salahiya in Jerusalem: Arabismus, Osmanismus und Panislamismus im Ersten Weltkrieg* (Stuttgart, 1991), pp. 16–18. On the Sephardi *Talmud-Torah* school of Jerusalem see *ha-Herut*, 15 September 1912, p. 4; 22 March 1913.
62. *Filastin*, 15 July 1911, p. 1; Loewe, Heinrich, 'Die Stadtschule in Palaestina', *Altneuland* 2/3 (1905), pp. 65–73; and idem, 'Die Dorfschule in Palaestina', ibid., 1/3, pp. 71–76; Rektor Jugendpflege, Eberhard, 'Schul- und Erziehungsverhaeltnisse in Jerusalem', ibid., 2, XI/XII, pp. 321–349; and idem, 'Nochmals Jugendpflege', ibid., 3/5, pp. 129–140.
63. *Filastin*, 12 July 1913, p. 3.
64. Ibid., 2 September 1911, p. 3.
65. Ibid., 30 March 1912, p. 2; 14 August 1912, p. 3; 31 August 1912, p. 3; 14 May 1913, p. 2.
66. Ibid., 2 August 1911, p. 1.
67. Ibid., 19 July 1911, p. 3.
68. According to the official website of Maccabi Tel Aviv, its football team was founded in 1906 as 'Maccabi Harishon Le-Zion Yaffo'. See http://www.maccabi-tlv.co.il/Data.asp?id=2&lang=en
69. Ibid., 16 December 1911, p. 1; 3 January 1912, p. 2; 13 April 1912, p. 4.
70. Ibid., 1 November 1911, p. 3; 219, p. 1. See also Khalidi, Issam, 'Body and ideology: Early athletics in Palestine (1900–1948)', *Jerusalem Quarterly* 27 (2006), pp. 44–58.
71. *Filastin*, 9 July 1913, p. 3.
72. Al-Barghuthi: *Marahil*, p. 104.
73. The source for this expression might be Charles Dickens' novel *The Battle of Life*, first published in 1846. 'The Battle of Life' is also the original subtitle of the diaries of Sami 'Amr. See 'Amr, Sami, *A Young Palestinian's Diary, 1941–1945: The Life of Sami 'Amr*, edited and translated by Katz, Kimberly (Austin, 2009).
74. *Filastin*, 2 September 1911, p. 3.
75. Ibid., 16 December 1911, p. 1.
76. Ibid., 9 July 1913, p. 3.
77. *Filastin*, 24 January 1912, p. 4.

PART II

THE 'CIVILIZING MISSION' AND CENTER-PERIPHERY RELATIONSHIPS

CHAPTER 5

JERUSALEM AND JAFFA IN THE LATE OTTOMAN PERIOD: THE CONCESSION-HUNTING* STRUGGLE FOR PUBLIC WORKS PROJECTS

YASEMIN AVCI**

Introduction

'*Continuity*' is always a key to understanding revolutions, because change, especially if it is imposed from above, has a contradictory and subtle nature. As continuity and change are closely intertwined in any developmental process, it would be probably wrong to see these two concepts as mutually exclusive. The Young Turk Revolution of 1908 is regarded as a crucial turning point in the history of the Ottoman Empire. The immediate aims of the Revolution were the destruction of the authoritarian regime of Abdülhamid II (1876–1909) and the restoration of a constitutional, parliamentary government. For this reason the two periods are usually considered as opposing eras. Evidence suggests that the new regime, however, was in fact a continuation of the long process of reforms that had started with the inauguration of the *Tanzimat* decree of 1839 and continued in the reign of Abdülhamid II.

Generally speaking, in the field of provincial administration the main goal of the *Tanzimat* reforms was to restructure a centralized state and enforce state authority over all sectors of the population. To achieve these goals, public works, the communication infrastructure, schools and the urban infrastructures all needed to be developed, because they all were considered part of the modernization process which was perceived as a survival strategy.

After their rise to power, the Young Turks continued to support many of the dominant trends of the *Tanzimat* period, most noticeably the emphasis on centralization as a way of preserving and consolidating the Empire. In order to ensure the visibility of the new regime's modernizing mission, it attempted to carry out public works projects, especially in regions with strategic political importance, like Palestine. These projects also showed their desire for recognition and a search for legitimacy through a show of continuity, technological capacity and modernity. The Young Turks, like their predecessors, were aware that investment in urban infrastructure was an integral part of the emergence of popular sovereignty. Moreover, these public works projects were designed to block the growing influence of the European powers. These projects thus created new types of rivalry between the Ottoman government and the European powers in their attempts to dominate local politics in cities with political and economic importance.

In this chapter, I deal with the public works scheme developed during the period of Ottoman reforms to foster the urban development of two cities in Palestine, Jerusalem and Jaffa, and also to consolidate Ottoman rule over this contested land. The construction of an electric tramway system, the supply of electric light and drinking water, the extension of the Hejaz railway line to connect Haifa with Jerusalem, the improvements of docking and customs facilities at the port of Jaffa, and the drawing up of a city plan for Jerusalem were all included in this scheme. Although the concessions for these projects were actually granted to individuals or companies, the schemes mostly remained on paper. Nevertheless, these plans deserve serious consideration as clear indicators of the dilemmas or problems of much of Ottoman urban policy as regards modern urbanization. Public works projects thus shed light on the Young Turks' decision-making processes in urban affairs. In addition, these schemes strikingly illustrate the special attention devoted to these two cities by the new government of the Young Turks, just as in the past.[1] The main source of this study is the Ottoman documents obtained both from the Prime-ministerial Ottoman Archive in Istanbul (the Başbakanlık Osmanlı Arşivi) and the Israel State Archives in Jerusalem; however in order to avoid possible bias I have also referred to an external source, the British consular state archives in London (Public Records Office).

The Imperialistic Dimension of the Concession-Hunting Struggle: the Cases of Jerusalem and Jaffa

The 1850s marked the beginning of a critical phase in the history of the Ottoman Empire's relations with the European Powers. Due to factors related to the military and political weakness of the Ottoman state, European influence took on ever-increasing importance in determining the fate of the Empire and its transformations. In the age of reforms, the critical financial situation of the Ottoman state, which became patently clear after the first foreign loan contracted in 1854, facilitated the penetration of foreign interests and influences in economic and political fields.[2] The capital-starved government had to make use of foreign capital and grant concessions to build and run all types of economic enterprises in the Empire. As the economic vassalage of the government to its foreign creditors continued, the foreign concessionaries enjoyed considerable freedom of movement and activity, which benefitted their firms and governments rather than the Ottoman state.

Granting concessions to encourage the development of certain economic sectors such as manufacturing, trading or banking can be seen as a determinant of a liberal economy which was in fact advocated by many circles of Ottoman intellectuals and statesmen during the nineteenth century. The liberal tendency of the Young Turk regime, however, was to be changed with the beginning of the World War I. In 1914, the Ottoman government abolished capitulations unilaterally, enacted new legal regulations to control foreign companies, and tried to nationalize certain railways, such as İzmir-Kasaba and Mudanya

Railways and railways in Syrian lands; hence thus the term 'national economy' began to be used more frequently.[3]

The bulk of the foreign capital which entered the Empire in the second half of the nineteenth century appears to have concentrated mainly on the financing of public services rather than on the production sectors.[4] This process was the reverse of what had happened in other countries, where manufacturing and trade encouraged the public services sector.[5] In fact, the concession-hunting struggle in the Ottoman Empire had an imperialistic dimension, because the investment pattern was determined not only by the foreign investors' profit motives, but also by the European powers' political interests. The clearest evidence of this imperialistic tendency was the nature of the railway network in the Ottoman Empire. As is well known, most of the Ottoman railways were constructed through foreign investment. Since they were designed to serve the economic and political interests of the investors' country,[6] many lines in fact lacked rational network connections, or the rail gauge of many lines was below the usual standard:[7]

> Within the Ottoman Empire, because of the nature of the concessions to foreign companies, railroads resulted in an increase of foreign economic control over the state and the separation of the Empire into economic spheres along the tracts of the railroads controlled by different European companies.[8]

Another factor behind the concession-hunting struggle was undoubtedly the Ottoman government's military and administrative considerations and its determination to bring about modernity. Its goal of achieving the integrity and unification of imperial territories necessitated the modernization of urban infrastructures and the improvement of public services. However, due to the appalling lack of local capital and managerial skills, this could only be managed through foreign capital investment.

To launch the country's economic development, the *Tanzimat* statesmen realized they had to look abroad for assistance. And indeed they did not lack bids from Europeans anxious to make capital investments in the country. However, they suspected that the motive behind these proposals for extensive public projects such as railroads and highways, ports or water supply projects was to advance the economic and political interests of foreign governments at the expense of the Ottoman state. Thus, granting a concession usually took a long time, and the authorities frequently changed their mind and cancelled the negotiations just before signing the contract. In the period of Abdülhamid II, the sultan's autocratic preoccupations led to a policy of more supervisory control from the palace in granting concessions. As discussed below, the sultan preferred granting concessions to companies under the direction of an Ottoman citizen and not to foreign investors. Similarly, the Young Turks, though they promoted liberal political and economic policies until 1914, usually tried to regularize the question of foreign investment and economic activities. They regarded the creation of concessionary enterprises owned by foreign shareholders as a loss of national sovereignty. Most of their endeavors, however, were obstructed by further financial entanglements and political problems in the Empire.[9]

Water Supply Projects: The Fiercest Rivalry

As happened in many Ottoman cities of political and economic importance, the attempt to build an appropriate modern urban infrastructure in the developing cities of Jaffa and Jerusalem gave rise to a furious struggle for concessions, which was political rather than economic. Probably the fiercest rivalry that occurred between different political groups in Jerusalem was for water projects. Throughout the ages, including in the nineteenth century, Jerusalem's water supply has always been extremely problematic. In the middle of the nineteenth century the city's water supply was provided by a complex system consisting of domestic and community cisterns, public pools and the local springs. This system caused severe competition not only between the communities who wanted to achieve autonomy and control over water reserves, but also between the city and the surrounding countryside.[10] Nevertheless in the final quarter of the nineteenth century there was a shaky equilibrium satisfying all the needs of the inhabitants. When the relative stability of the population changed and rose dramatically, water crises became very frequent.[11]

The first proposal to construct water works was made by an English engineer named John Irwine Witty, who published the results of his survey in 1864.[12] A year later another proposal was submitted by Lady Bourdett-Coutts, a British philanthropist, who, however, failed to reach an agreement with the municipal authorities regarding the management of the works.[13] At that time the Jerusalem Municipality had just commenced its activities. Initially it concentrated on the cleanliness of the city. The municipality only took on greater authority after the promulgation of the Provincial Municipality Law in 1877,[14] when it expanded the scope of its activities to improve the infrastructure and the conditions of urban life. On the other hand, the Jerusalem Municipality, as an administrative body, had to act in concert with other governmental bodies in the Jerusalem Province (in practice, provincial authorities closely supervised its activities). Little was undertaken without informing them and almost every municipal resolution required the approval of the administrative council or the district governor (*mutasarrıf*). Moreover, in some cases, the approval of the central government was also necessary, especially when projects involving large sums of money were concerned. Apart from strict governmental control over the municipal administration, the Jerusalem Municipality was also dependent on the attitude of the consuls and the heads of the foreign communities (the large population of foreign residents, who lived mainly in the quarters outside the city walls, was represented by their foreign consulates).[15]

In 1894, on the initiative of the Jerusalem Municipality, a project was formulated to insure the city with an adequate supply by bringing water from the main springs at 'Arub, about a two and a half hour ride from the city. Frangia Bey, the chief engineer nominated by the Ministry of Public Works in Istanbul, completed the necessary survey. In his report dated 1894, he stressed that 'the inadequacy of water has been the most important issue affecting the Holy City for more than ten years, as the days go by, the needs become more pressing, more urgent'.[16] A year after his report, the acting British consul in Jerusalem informed the Foreign Office that a scheme had been presented by a French syndicate to supply Jerusalem with water by diverting the sources of 'Arub, and a favorable report on the subject had been sent to Istanbul. However, nothing came of this plan because the required capital, which Frangia Bey estimated at 80,000 Turkish liras, could not be raised. In 1897 the municipality had to be contented with the cleaning of Solomon's Pools and the repair of the pipes.[17] In 1901, a year of extreme drought, a sum of 6,000 liras from the *waqf* revenues was used to lay pipes to Solomon's Pools. These measures helped to relieve the most acute needs of the city to some extent.[18]

Following the droughts of 1905 and 1907, new plans were presented to respond to a renewed demand on the part of the municipality. This revival of interest was partly due to the publication of Frangia's report in 1908, as well as another one in 1909 by Max Magnus, a German engineer and the director of the Carl Franke Institute of Bremen. In his report, Magnus raised doubts as to the feasibility of Frangia's project, and argued in favor of deviating the spring at 'Ayn Farah, located some thirteen kilometers north of Jerusalem.[19] Between 1909 and 1910 not only Germans, but also a French company, an Italian-Belgian firm, and even the Palestine office of the Zionist Organization took part in this concession-hunting struggle. The head of the Zionist Organization, Dr. Arthur Ruppin, offered to cooperate with the German firm of Carl Franke to build Magnus's project. In order to outbid their competitors, he was ready to mobilize Jewish capital and establish an Ottoman company that would apply for the concession. However, in 1909, without the cooperation of the Zionists, an advance contract was signed between the Jerusalem Municipality and Carl Franke to utilize the springs of 'Ayn Favar and 'Ayn Farah.

In the contract, the firm was authorized to operate the business for a period of thirty years, after which the concession would revert to the municipality. As municipalities were not authorized to grant concessions, the contract had to be confirmed by the central government. In the contract it was stated that if the central government failed to accept the concession within six months, the issue would be regarded as annulled.[20] And indeed as was expected, the contract was cancelled. Some sources claim that the main cause for this failure was the pressure on the local and central governments to transfer the concession to an Ottoman company in which Jewish institutions would participate.[21] On the other hand, the acting British consul in Jerusalem,

James Morgan, stated that the German firm withdrew from the negotiations, because the terms of the concession were found to be too onerous.[22]

Despite the fierce rivalry for concessions, in fact, the water works projects were not expected to generate large profits.[23] As local springs of 'Arub or 'Ayn Farah were located below the mean altitude of Jerusalem, these water works necessitated a central electric installation to operate steam pumps, which greatly increased the necessary initial investment. Thus, the interest of foreign firms and religious organizations in securing the concession was not economical but primarily political. The mere act of making a proposal to undertake the business meant having a say in matters related to the prosperity of Jerusalem, while strengthening their influence over the public life of the Holy City by dominating its infrastructure.

In 1909 the Central government issued an imperial decree (*irade-i seniye*) that authorized the Jerusalem Municipality to raise revenue for water works. It instructed the cession of skins and guts of animals slaughtered in Jerusalem to the Municipality. The revenue derived from their sale would be used to cover at least in part the expenses of providing the city with a proper water supply. The deputies of Jerusalem in the Ottoman Parliament, Ruhi al-Khalidi and Sa'id al-Husayni presented guarantees to the Central government that the inhabitants of Jerusalem would be willing to participate in this campaign.[24] Nonetheless, foreign subjects and the protégés of the European powers rejected this solution on the grounds that the Ottoman authorities did not have the right to impose an additional tax without the consent of the embassies concerned.[25] The embassies usually did not cooperate with the municipal authorities as regards urban administration. They were reluctant to pay taxes and force their subjects to obey the new municipal regulations.[26] Some of the consuls regarded the activities of the municipal authority as an infringement on their rights.[27] Thus, foreign inhabitants of the city imposed real restrictions on the scope of municipal authority.

The developing port city of Jaffa constituted another arena for a furious concession-hunting struggle. During the second half of nineteenth century, Jaffa grew from a small township to the most important coastal city in Palestine. This extraordinary revival was linked to the integration of the Empire into the world economy and the inevitable growth of its trade with Europe. By the twentieth century, of all the ports in the Eastern Mediterranean, only Beirut exceeded Jaffa in the volume of imports and exports.[28] The development of Jaffa was also a result of the town's becoming a economic and communications hub, while Jerusalem had also grown for religious and political reasons. The reorganization of the Jerusalem Province (*kudüs mutasarrıflığı*), following the Provincial Law of 1871, as a district administrative area reporting directly to the Ministry of Interior in Istanbul, was another factor that enhanced the economic importance of Jaffa.[29] In the following years the city of Jaffa, just like the other urban centers in the province, received increased attention from the Ottoman administration.

The Ottoman government had attempted to promote the development of Jaffa as early as 1891.[30] This project dealt with the irrigation of the orange groves in the plains surrounding Jaffa and supplying it with drinking water from the 'Awja River [ha-Yarkon] which flows into the sea a few kilometers to the north of Jaffa. In 1893 a report on the proposed scheme was drawn up by Frangia Efendi, the local government engineer.[31] In 1894, Joseph Navon, an Ottoman citizen from the prominent Sephardi families of Navon and Amzalak, applied to the Central government to secure the concession. His name can also be found in the Ottoman archival documents as the bidder for the construction of a Jaffa-Jerusalem railway line in 1888, although he sold his concession to a French company in 1890 due to funding problems.[32] Navon endeavored for three years from 1894 to 1897 to secure the tender for the Jaffa water work concession through pressure and connections with Diryese Paşa, the Secretary in the Yıldız Palace (*mabeyn başkatibi*).[33] As far as can be determined from the Ottoman archival documents, apart from Joseph Navon, a Lebanese citizen named Philippe Efendi, a French merchant, and Meir Dizengoff, a prominent Jewish activist who later became the mayor of Tel Aviv, were among the other promoters. However, the central government did not grant the concession until 1916.[34] In that year the bidder was again Euripide Mavromatis, who won the concessions for the construction and operation of water works in Jerusalem, in addition to the electric tramway and electric lighting in Jaffa.[35] Unfortunately the Jaffa scheme was to share the same fate as that of Jerusalem.

Physical Means of Urban Development: Transportation, Communication, Electric Lighting and Seaports

The idea that the physical modes of urban development such as roads, railways, tramways, seaports and the telegraph promote the integration of a territory with the imperial center was surely one of the principles of *Tanzimat* modernization. The new technologies adopted from Europe not only improved the urban infrastructure in certain cities, but they were also used by the central government all over the Empire to enhance its control over its own population. Thus both the *Tanzimat* statesmen and the Young Turk regime were enthusiastic about these projects, and the inadequacy of capital to meet investment needs forced them to welcome foreign companies. This is why opposition within governmental and intellectual circles to the flow of foreign capital into Ottoman Empire was not overly strong until the outbreak of the First World War. The Young Turk government also took necessary steps to encourage foreign investments by issuing regulations.[36]

In June 1910, when a new law concerning concessions related to public welfare was passed, the municipalities took priority over the other administrative bodies in the province in examining proposals for technical works. However, the contract signed between the municipal authorities and the promoter was still subject to final confirmation from the central government.[37] In 1910, the Jerusalem Municipality, in cooperation with the central government, devised a more complex scheme. The 1910 scheme, apart from the delivery to Jerusalem of water from ʿAyn Farah and ʿAyn Favar, also included the construction of electric lighting, electric tramways in Jerusalem and between Jerusalem and neighboring Bethlehem, the repair of the old sewers in the old city of Jerusalem, the construction of new sewers in the neighborhoods outside the city walls, and the construction and operation of a telephone system in the cities of Jerusalem, Jaffa and Bethlehem. This scheme was based on the assumption that obtaining the concession for this overall scheme would help to turn the water supply works for Jerusalem into a profitable investment.[38]

The Jerusalem Municipality announced in the local newspapers that bids for the planned public works projects could be addressed either directly to the Ministry of Public Works or to the Municipality of Jerusalem.[39] In order to encourage entrepreneurs, the Ministry of Public Works also printed a pamphlet that listed the specifications for the Jerusalem tramway and electric lighting schemes in French.[40] The most striking feature of this pamphlet is the stipulation that the concessionaire would be required to set up an Ottoman limited liability company which would have to use Turkish in its reports to the authorities and the public. It was also stipulated that all disagreements and law suits that might arise between the Municipality and the company would be settled by the Ottoman courts, which would have jurisdiction. In addition, for a period of five years from the date of the imperial decree sanctioning the contract, the concessionaire would be given priority for five years to secure the same type of concession in the city of Jaffa.

In fact, the first known plan to build an electrically powered public transportation system between Jerusalem and Bethlehem was proposed in 1907. The idea was put forward by the French company that operated the Jaffa-Jerusalem Railway. However, the Municipality was unable to pay the sum of 300 Turkish liras necessary for the preliminary survey, and the idea was abandoned for three years.[41] The 1910 scheme envisioned four tram lines, and the total length of lines was to be about 15 km.[42] All lines would run from the Jaffa Gate; the first line to the street of St. John (about 2.6 km), the second line to the Schneller School (2 km), the third line to Sheikh Jarrah Mosque (2.2 km), and the fourth line to Bethlehem (9.5km).[43]

As regards the telephone, recent studies show that the new regime tried to develop telephone communication as well. The prohibition against the installation of residential telephones imposed by Abdülhamid II in 1886 was abolished in 1908. Until 1910 the Ministry of Post and Telegraph tried to maintain its monopoly over all telephone communication and all applications for concessions were rejected.[44] Thus it is no coincidence that the local government planned to install telephone lines after 1910.

Between 1910 and 1914 there is no evidence of any further steps taken to begin work. In January 1914 an agreement regarding the construction and operation of an electric tramway system, the supply of electric lights and power and drinking water to the city of Jerusalem was signed between the Mayor of Jerusalem, Husayn Salim Hashim Efendi and Euripide Mavromatis, an Ottoman citizen living in Istanbul.[45] However, the onset of the World War I prevented him from beginning the work.[46] Thus the story of water supply to Jerusalem at the end of the Ottoman period is obviously a chronicle of delays and failures. However, the British Mandate government kept the original Ottoman plans, and implemented the 'Arub project later.

Apart from the Jerusalem Municipality's public program of 1910, another municipal infrastructure plan was developed by the Palestine Chamber of Commerce. This was a business league founded by the *Mutasarrıf* of Jerusalem Suphi Bey in 1909, with the aim of promoting the industrial, commercial and agricultural development of Palestine. Municipal minutes indicate that the Palestine Chamber of Commerce was also in touch with the Jerusalem Municipality in examining the main projects.[47] Its president was a native merchant, Hacı Yusuf Efendi, and it was composed of eighteen members, among whom were merchants, bankers and engineers of different nationalities.[48] The initiative was to draw up a general urban plan for Jerusalem.[49] However, due to the lack of available sources, we do not know the details or the outcome of this attempt.

Another project which was also interrupted by the war was the construction of a railway line to connect Jerusalem via Nablus with the Haifa railway, which had already been connected in 1905 with the Hejaz railway from Daraa junction. It was planned by the chief engineer of the Hejaz railway, Meissner Paşa, and in 1907 the Ottoman government granted the concession to the Ottoman Commission of the Hamidiye-Hejaz Railway. It was expected that the line would allow the transfer of troops in case of need and facilitate the export of agricultural products from Nablus and Jenin, which up to then were sent from Jaffa Port.⁵⁰ Another aim was to increase the number of Muslim pilgrims visiting Jerusalem. However, the Ottoman Company could not start work until 1912. By 1913 only a seventeen kilometer branch of the line was built from 'Afule to Jenin. Some sources argue that the failure was caused by French pressure on Istanbul, since the French were unwilling to have rivals to their railway business in Palestine, a region regarded traditionally as being within France's sphere of influence.⁵¹

The most challenging problem to Ottoman rule in Jaffa was the modernization of the port's infrastructure. Due to the shallow depth and the long reef beds, Jaffa port was only suitable for small sailing ships and small boats. All larger ships had to anchor in open sea and employ small boats to bring the cargo and passengers to shore. In the mid-1860s some renovations were made including the building of a lighthouse, the construction of a landing, and the repair of the customs house.⁵² However, by the last quarter of the nineteenth century, as trade through the port had grown tremendously, large-scale developments were required for the safe anchorage of ships coming from all over the world. From 1860s onwards many different proposals to modernize the port's infrastructure came from foreign circles, including from German, French, Austrian, American and British engineers. Local consuls also recognized the potential for the development of shipping trade through efficient transport from Jaffa.⁵³ Thus, the construction of a modern harbor at Jaffa became another example of imperialistic rivalry to dominate the urban infrastructure. In August 1878, a French company managed to secure the concession to build a port in Jaffa. However it could not raise the necessary fifteen million Francs to implement the project.⁵⁴

The Ottoman government preferred to act on its own. In 1880, Hasan Fehmi Paşa, the Minister of Public Works, proposed the construction of a breakwater, about one kilometer long, which would enable large ships to anchor in Jaffa. As an investment of four million Francs was required, this project could not be implemented either. In 1886, the Director of Customs in Beirut was ordered to submit a report on possible ways to develop the port into a modern deep-water facility.⁵⁵ The building of a new customs house in 1888 was part in this scheme.⁵⁶ In 1892, an Ottoman citizen named Tellioğlu Atnaş Efendi applied to the central government to undertake the work. Derviş Paşa and Şakir Paşa, from the Palace Secretariat, recommended him to the Ministry of Public Works as an honorable Ottoman merchant capable of managing the project, but nothing came of this attempt.⁵⁷

The major public health initiative undertaken by the government at Jaffa was the construction of a disinfecting station in 1905. It enabled passengers to undergo disinfection without being obliged to proceed to Beirut for that purpose.⁵⁸ As a result, the prevention of certain epidemics, such as cholera and malaria which previously were very common, did improve to some extent.⁵⁹ Another inconvenience at the port was the lack of a life boat station. Landing in Jaffa in the winter and spring, when stormy weather was common, was often risky and even led to accidents with casualties. In 1906 the Ministry of Public Health began to consider the necessity of establishing a life boat station (*tahlisiye şubesi*), but the proposal was rejected by an imperial *irade* issued on the grounds that at that time the Jaffa port was not suitable for large ships.⁶⁰

In the early twentieth century, the existing landing facilities were still far from meeting the commercial requirements of the growing port. As imports to Jaffa continued to increase, the most urgent need was the extension of the customs house. Trade in Jaffa was hampered by long delays and the Jaffa merchants had trouble clearing their goods through customs.⁶¹ In 1905 the chief civil engineer of the Jerusalem province, Kindanyan Bey, was asked to inspect the customs house and to give his opinion as to the way it could be repaired and enlarged. In his report he presented three different options, including estimates on the costs of building a new customs house with the desired improvements.⁶² Finally in 1907, the government decided to build a roof over the open space at the entrance to the customs house to provide sufficient facilities for carrying out customs operations until a new building was built. A strong wooden pier was also built for the landing of passengers and their luggage, and a winch with a four- ton capacity was installed. The acting British vice-Consul Falanga observed that all 'the work was executed in twelve days which was considered a very short time and this was thanks to the energy displayed by the authorities and the Director of the Customs'.[63] The *Mutasarrıf* of Jerusalem received a telegram from Istanbul expressing the Sultan's high appreciation, and the *Kaymakam* of Jaffa and the Director of the customs house were honored with a silver medal for the promptness and energy with which the work was carried out.[64] According to the reports of the British vice-consul, after these improvements were made all transactions were carried out very satisfactorily according to newly imposed principles. However, the customs house building was still too small for the growing traffic of Jaffa trade.[65]

From 1908 onwards the Ottoman governments became more serious in their intention to build a new customs house in Jaffa. The Ministry of the Interior ordered the municipality of Jaffa to survey the site and to estimate the building costs.[66] A complete plan with estimates was drawn up by an engineer sent from Istanbul. The scheme consisted of building a new customs house opposite the existing one between the rocks and the shore.

The project would cover 34,000 square meters of filled in land for the building and its dependencies. The cost of the whole work was estimated at 50,000 liras.[67] Later on in order to finance the project an additional tax was imposed on orange exports, but it met with opposition from traders and the representatives of the shipping companies.[68] Despite considering large-scale development plans, the government could not raise the required money to modernize the Port of Jaffa. Just before the outbreak of the War, the Minister of Finance wrote to the Minister of the Interior about the need for an overall modernization of Jaffa Port, and his disappointment that no work on the project had been done:

> Despite the increasing importance of Jaffa as a commercial city, the communication hub for Jerusalem, a city subjected to imperialistic rivalry, the point of transit for visitors coming from all over the world, and as a port producing an annual revenue of about 100,000 liras, the quay and the customs accommodation

are totally inadequate. In particular the dilapidated state of the customs house visible to friends and foes is at odds with the honor and dignity of the Ottoman state. [...]. We should ensure that all means are undertaken to improve the infrastructure of the harbor in a way appropriate to the high dignity of the state.[69]

Conclusion

In the age of Ottoman reforms, both Jerusalem and Jaffa underwent an intense process of change. The increase in built-up areas, the tremendous rise in the population and visible economic growth are among the best indicators of that development. During that period, Jerusalem was transformed physically and conceptually from a religious city to a major political-administrative center, and Jaffa, a tiny and backward city on the coast of Palestine, became the main port of the country. From the late 1880s onwards the Ottoman central government paid close attention to improving the infrastructure and facilities in the cities of Jaffa and Jerusalem. The various plans indicate increasing State involvement in public services. The establishment of municipalities signaled the actual beginning of that involvement. However at first, the municipality did not have broader decision making powers over the modernization of the urban infrastructure. In the *Tanzimat* period the Council of Ministers (*meclis-i vükelâ*) generally examined the proposals and granted the concessions. During the reign of Abdülhamid II, the Sultan and the Palace Secretaries exerted a decisive influence on concession grants and on the investment patterns of foreign capital. It was only with the promulgation of the Second Constitution, that the local governor, the administrative bodies of local government, and especially the municipalities, became more active in dealing with matters concerning public works concessions. However, as the final confirmation was in the hands of the central government, securing a concession still meant winning the power struggle in Istanbul, and confronting the various parties, some of which supported French or English interests, while others advocated German political influence in the Ottoman Empire.

By focusing on public works schemes, I have tried to explore how these projects mirrored the political struggles between the Ottoman administrators and the European powers. From the Ottoman point of view, the plans for public works developed by the Europeans or independent religious institutions were seen as somewhat indirect territorial claim-making, at least on a symbolic level. On the other hand, the Europeans regarded the Ottoman administration as incapable of carrying out any technical project and as reluctant to grant concessions, due to the fear of later political complications by favoring the English over French, German or Russian interests. This fear helps account for the skepticism of the Ottoman government towards proposals put forward by foreigners, and preferred to grant concessions to Ottoman citizens. This policy was especially evident in cities such as Jerusalem and Jaffa which were exposed to imperialistic rivalry for political influence.

Notes

* The term 'concession-hunting' is borrowed from Shahvar, Soli, 'Concession-hunting in the age of reforms: British companies and the search for government guarantees; telegraph concessions through Ottoman territories 1855-58', *Middle Eastern Studies* 38/4 (2002), pp. 169–193.

** Pamukkale University, Faculty of Arts and Sciences, Department of History, Denizli-Turkey. Archival research in the Public Records Office (London) for this study was made possible through a grant from the Turkish Academy of Sciences (Türkiye Bilimler Akademisi-TUBA). I wish to express my gratitude for their financial support.

1. Jerusalem, as the third holiest city in Islam, always occupied an important position in the Ottoman imperial perception. In some Ottoman archival documents, the name of Jerusalem was included in the concept of 'Haremeyn', a term generally used for the privileged cities of Mecca and Medina. The imperial patronage of Kanuni Sultan Süleyman in the development of Jerusalem through infrastructure works, such as the repair of the city walls and ensuring an adequate water supply system, is well known. The Jerusalemites occasionally received shares from the allocation of pious endowments established for the benefit of the cities of Mecca and Medina. For instance, the inhabitants living in the quarters within the city walls, just like that of Mecca and Medina, were exempt from certain

taxes. From 1841 onwards, however, the *Sancak* of Jerusalem had a different importance. New developments that occurred in the last quarter of the nineteenth century caused the government to deal with new difficulties in controlling the Jerusalem province effectively. The cities of Jerusalem and Jaffa became the most crucial cities in Palestine, because of increased foreign interests manifested by missionary activities and Jewish immigration starting in the 1880s. For further details see Avcı, Yasemin, *Değişim Sürecinde Bir Osmanlı Kenti: Kudüs 1890–1914* [*An Ottoman City in Transition: Jerusalem 1890–1914*] (Ankara, 2004), pp. 67–91 [in Turkish]; idem, 'Jerusalem in the age of the Ottoman reforms: the urban identity and institutional change', *Arab Historical Review for Ottoman Studies* 40 (December 2009), pp. 9–21.
2. Eldem, Edhem, 'Ottoman financial integration with Europe: foreign loans, the Ottoman Bank and the Ottoman public dept', *European Review* 13/3 (2005), pp. 431–3.
3. For further details see Toprak, Zafer, *Türkiye'de Ekonomi ve Toplum (1908–1950), Milli İktisat-Milli Burjuvazi* [*Economy and Society in Turkey (1908–1950): National Economy-National Bourgeoisie*] (Istanbul, 1995) [in Turkish].
4. Okyar, Osman, 'The role of the state in the economic life of the nineteenth-century Ottoman Empire', *Asian and African Studies* 14 (1980), p. 156.
5. Hershlag, Zvi Yehuda, *Introduction to Modern Economic History of the Middle East* (Leiden, 1997), p. 52.
6. Şen, Leyla, 'Merkez-çevre ilişkilerinin önemli bir dinamiği olarak Osmanlı İmparatorluğu'nda ulaşım sistemleri' [Transportation systems in the Ottoman Empire, as dynamics of center-periphery relations] *Kebikeç-İnsan Bilimleri İçin Kaynak Araştırma Dergisi* 11 (2001), p. 96 [in Turkish].
7. The standard gauge (1.4 meter) was mostly used throughout the Ottoman Empire, but in order to cut down on costs, the 1.05-meter narrow gauge was also used in many railroads, such as the Jaffa-Jerusalem Railway, the Damascus-Beirut Railway, the Mudanya-Bursa Railway and the main branch of the Hejaz Railway. See Bonine, Michael E., 'The introduction of railroads in the Eastern Mediterranean: economic and social impacts', in Philipp, Thomas and Birgit Schäbler (eds.), *The Syrian Land: Processes of Integration and Fragmentation: Bilad al-Sham from the 18th to the 20th Century* (Stuttgart, 1998), p. 60–63.
8. Ibid., p. 62.
9. 'On the eve of the World War I in 1913, foreign investment in the Ottoman Empire –Egypt and investments in the Ottoman Public Dept totalled 1.686 million francs or 70 million pounds sterling'. See Hershlag: *Introduction to Modern Economic History*, p. 53.

10. See Singer, Amy, *Palestinian Peasants and Ottoman Officials: Rural Administration around Sixteenth-century Jerusalem* (Cambridge, 1994), pp. 103–104.
11. 'The population of Jerusalem went from 10,000 inhabitants in about 1850 to 70,000 at about 1910, which increased basic water requirements from 300 cubic meters per day to more than 2000'. Lemire, Vincent, 'Water in Jerusalem at the end of the Ottoman period (1850–1920): technical and political networks', *Bulletin du Centre de recherche français de Jérusalem* 7 (Autumn 2000), p. 145.
12. See Whitty, John Irwine, *The Water Supply of Jerusalem, Ancient and Modern* (London, 1864).
13. Public Record Office, Foreign Office (hereafter, FO) 78/4644B, J. McGregor-Foreign Office, 29 January 1895.
14. The Western-style municipality was one of the new institutions introduced as part of the general reform program of the *Tanzimat*. Preparations for the establishment of municipal councils in provincial towns were made, first, by the promulgation of the *Vilayet* Law in 1864. Although the Law of 1864 recognized 'every village as a municipality', as patterned after the French Commune system, it did not include any articles on the establishment of municipalities in the provincial towns. It was the ensuing amendments in the *Vilayet* Law, inserted in 1871, which initiated a more integrated approach to the administration of the provincial towns by calling for the creation of municipal councils. This law has a separate section, Chapter 7, including eighteen articles that provide many details on municipal administration. The text of the provincial administration law of 1871 appears in Ottoman in *Düstur*, vol. I, pp. 625–51.
15. Avcı: *Değişim Sürecinde Bir Osmanlı Kenti*, pp. 169–71.
16. The text of the project developed by Frangia Bey was published in 1908. It was identical to the one he proposed to the Municipality in 1894. An abridged version of his project was also published in 1912. See Frangia, G., *Projet: Sur l'adduction des eaux d'Arroub* (Constantinople, 1912).
17. *Başbakanlık Osmanlı Arşivi* (hereafter, *BOA*), İrade Evkaf, 9, 24 Rebiülahir 1315 [21 September 1897].
18. FO, 195/2255, no. 26, E.C. Blech-N. R. O'Conor, 30 July 1907.
19. Lemire: 'Water in Jerusalem', p. 140.
20. Jeusalem Municipality Archives (hereafter JMA), Water Supply, c. 614.
21. Eliav, Mordecai, *Britain and the Holy Land (1838–1914)* (Jerusalem, 1997), p. 363.
22. FO, 195/2255, no. 26, E. C. Blech-N. R. O'Conor, 30 July 1907.
23. FO, 195/2351, no. 3, J. Morgan-Foreign Secretary, 11 August 1910.
24. BOA, İrade Dahiliye, 1, 6 Ramazan 1327 [21 September 1909].

25. FO, 195/2351, no. 12, H. E. Satow-G. Lowther, 4 March 1910.
26. Avcı: *Değisim Sürecinde Bir Osmanlı Kenti*, pp. 172–4.
27. For instance, in 1906, 'Ali Ekrem Bey, the governor of Jerusalem province, reported to the Grand Vizier that the Russian Consulate had stopped its nationals from paying any municipal fines, arguing that a judicial authority had not confirmed them. The other consulates, following the example of the Russians, also took the residents under their protection and postponed paying their municipal taxes. As a result, municipal fines took fairly long to collect. Israel State Archives, 'Ali Ekrem Bey Collection, Division 83, no. 23, 1906.
28. In 1910, for example, the tonnage of steamships cleared at Jaffa was 1,115 compared to 1,701 in Beirut. See Gilbar, Gad G., 'The growing economic involvement of Palestine with the West, 1865–1914', in Kushner, David (ed.), *Palestine in the Late Ottoman Period: Political, Social and Economic Transformation* (Leiden, 1986), p. 201.
29. Kark, Ruth, 'The rise and decline of coastal towns in Palestine', in Gilbar, Gad G., (ed.), *Ottoman Palestine 1800–1914* (Leiden, 1990), p. 77.
30. BOA, Yıldız Mütenevvi Maruzat Evrakı, 56/27, 10 Rebiülahir 1309 [12 November 1891].
31. FO, 78/4498, no. 13, J. Dickson-Foreign Office, 17 July 1893.
32. Avcı: *Değişim Sürecinde Bir Osmanlı Kenti*, p. 188.
33. BOA, Meclıs-i Vükela Kataloğu, 90/76, 29 Receb 1314 [3 February 1897].
34. BOA, Dahiliye Nezareti İdare Kataloğu, 191/11, 24 Rebiülahir 1332 [22 March 1914].
35. BOA, Dahiliye Nezareti Umur-ı Mahalliye ve Vilayat Müdürlüğü Kataloğu, 74/10, 16 Şaban 1334 [17 June 1916].
36. Toprak: *Türkiye'de Ekonomi ve Toplum*, pp. 64–5.
37. Tümertekin, Sıddık, *Türkiye'de Belediyeler: Tarihi Gelişim ve Bugünkü Durum* [The Municipalities in Turkey; Historical Development and Present Stiuation], (Istanbul, 1946), p. 129.
38. For the specifications of the schemes for the Jerusalem telephone, sewer and water supply see FO, 195/2351, no. 58, J. Morgan-G. Lowther, 3 October 1910.
39. FO, 195/2351, no. 66, J. Morgan-G. Lowther, 18 November 1910.
40. Ministère des Travaux Publics, *Concession de distribution publique d'énergie électrique et des tramways électriques dans la ville de Jérusalem et ses faubourgs* (Istanbul, 1911). BOA, Dahiliye Nezareti İdare Kataloğu, 88/8, 17 Ramazan 1332 [10 August 1914].
41. FO, 195/2255, no. 53, E. C. Blech-N. R. O'Conor, 22 October 1907.

42. For the specifications of the schemes for the Jerusalem tramway and electric lighting see FO, 195/2351, no. 63, James Morgan-G. Lowther, 5 November 1910.
43. FO, 195/2351, no. 3, J. Morgan-Foreign Secretary, 11 August 1910.
44. Tekeli, İlhan and Selim İlkin, 'The public works program and the development of technology in the Ottoman Empire in the second half of the nineteenth century', *Turcica* 28 (1996), p. 219.
45. JMA, Water Supply, c. 614. BOA, Dahiliye Nezareti İdare Kataloğu, 88/8, 17 Ramazan 1332 [10 August 1914].
46. Borchard, Edwin M., 'The Mavromattis concessions cases', *The American Journal of International Law* 19/4 (October 1925), p. 728.
47. JMA, the Minutes of Jerusalem Municipality, vol. XIII, 1324–1325 [1909–1910].
48. *Bulletin de la Chambre de Commerce d'Industrie et d'Agriculture de Palestine* 1/1 (Jerusalem, 1909), pp. 1–3.
49. FO, 195/2321, no. 54, E. C. Blech-G. Lowther, 24 June 1909.
50. BOA, Yıldız Mütenevvi Maruzat Evrakı, 295/143, 27 Muharrem 1325 [13 March 1907]; Dahiliye Nezareti İdare Kataloğu, 4–1/38, 6 Zilhicce 1329 [28 November 1911].
51. Özyüksel, Murat, *Hicaz Demiryolu* (Hejaz Railway), (Istanbul, 2000), pp. 212–13.
52. FO, 195/800, A. J. Khayat-Foreign Office, 12 November 1864.
53. For further details see Kark, Ruth, *Jaffa: A City in Evolution 1799–1917* (Jerusalem, 1990), pp. 235–8.
54. Schölch, Alexander, *Palestine in Transformation 1856–1882, Studies in Social, Economic and Political Development* (Washington D.C., p. 137.
55. BOA, Dahiliye Nezareti Mektubi Kalemi, 1371/166, 13 Ramazan 1304 [11 October 1886].
56. BOA, Yıldız Mütenevvi Maruzat Evrakı, 35/79, 7 Cumadiyül'evvel 1306 [21 June 1888].
57. Ibid., 65/17, 6 Muharrem 1310 [31 July 1892].
58. FO, 195/2199, no. 25, J. Dickson-N. R. O'Conor, 7 July 1905.
59. Kark: *Jaffa*, pp. 215–16.
60. FO, 195/2199, no. 44, J. Dickson-N. R. O'Conor, 19 October 1905. BOA, Yıldız Sadaret Hususi Kataloğu, 498/93(1), 23 Zilhicce 1328 [19 February 1906].
61. FO, 195/2175, no. 23, J. Falanga-N. R. O'Conor, 26 July 1904.
62. FO, 195/2199, no. 1, J. Falanga-W. Townley Esquire, 6 February 1905.
63. FO, 195/2255, J. Falanga-N. R. O'Conor, 15 April 1907.
64. Ibid., no. 11, J. Falanga-N. R. O'Conor, 13 May 1907.
65. Ibid., J. Falanga-N. R. O'Conor, 10 July 1907.

66. BOA, Dahiliye Nezareti İdare Kataloğu, 74/19, 2 Cumadiyül'evvel 1329 [31 May 1911].
67. FO, 195/2287, J. Falanga-G. Lowther, 31 December 1908.
68. BOA, Dahiliye Nezareti İdare Kataloğu, 40–2/23, 16 Zilhicce 1331 [15 November 1913].
69. BOA, Dahiliye Nezareti İdare Kataloğu, 59/72, 24 Cumadiyül'evvel 1332 [20 May 1914].

CHAPTER 6

UNDERSTANDING THE 1911 OTTOMAN PARLIAMENT DEBATE ON ZIONISM IN LIGHT OF THE EMERGENCE OF A 'JEWISH QUESTION'

LOUIS FISHMAN

The Ottoman Parliament was, to a great extent, a microcosmic reflection of the Ottoman society at large. Its chambers included Turkish and Arab Muslims, Armenians and Greeks from Istanbul and the Anatolian lands as well as Jews from Turkish and Arab regions of the Empire, among others. All of the members were Ottoman citizens, who with the ushering in of the Young Turk Revolution, rejoiced in the hope that the oppressive regime of Sultan Abdülhamid II would be replaced by a just government supporting the ideals of the French Revolution *'Liberté, égalité, fraternité'*.[1] However, a look at the 1911 Ottoman parliament debate on Zionism will demonstrate to what extent the Committee of Union and Progress failed to implement these principles. Far from being united, the parliament was divided between the different ethnic and religious groups, and the debate stands as chilling testimony to future internal violent conflicts.

This debate has only been interpreted in the local context of 'Jews versus Arabs'. It is astonishing that so little attention was paid to the debate in Parliament following Neville Mandel's account in his pioneering work on Zionism during the Ottoman period.[2] What is clear is that this debate provides one of the most vivid examples of how Zionism was perceived in different ways among different Ottoman (Muslim and non-Muslim) parliamentarians. Furthermore, the tensions between the different ethnic and religious groups made discussing the issue of Zionism all the more difficult and led some of the non-Muslims to question whether the Muslims criticizing Zionism were not actually driven by a Turkish Muslim chauvinism. When placed in the context of Istanbul's politics clearly a great deal more can be extracted from this debate that can help shed light on the prevalence of anti-Semitism in Istanbul, and the general lack of understanding of Zionism at the time. Thus a new approach is needed to this debate and the broader issues it raised.

For the Palestinians, Zionism was a tangible problem, one that was taking its toll on their daily lives. It was removed from anti-Semitic sentiments, and was not based on the typical ethnic conflicts common to reality in Ottoman Istanbul. For this reason, the Palestinian's unique situation of having to demonstrate a two-tiered approach to Jewish communities (accepting the local Jewish community and rejecting the immigrant community) was incomprehensible to some parliamentarians who could not differentiate between 'foreign' and 'local' Jews. In fact, it is only possible to fully understand the debate once placed in the context of the Ottoman Empire at large, where a 'Jewish' question emerged following the 1908 Young Turk Revolution. Thus the debate over Zionism had to do as much with Jewish migration to Ottoman Iraq and other regions in the Empire as it had to do with Palestine.

The Jewish Question and the Project of Jewish Immigration to Ottoman Iraq

Over the last two decades, Ottoman historians have taken great strides in rethinking the role of non-Muslims and their place in politics and society. When the Ottoman parliament was reinstated in 1908 after the Young Turk Revolution, these non-Muslim communities joined their Muslim counterparts as members of the Committee of Union and Progress (CUP) to form a solid block in the parliament. However, within a few years of the Revolution, tensions between the different ethnic and religious groups came to the fore, with factionalism overpowering unity, and chaos taking hold.

While most scholars for obvious reasons have focused on the emerging 'Armenian' and 'Greek' questions within the Ottoman lands, a few scholars have investigated the possibility that parallel to these Christian communities, there was also a 'Jewish' question. Unlike the Armenians, who faced massacres in 1894–5, and renewed ones in 1909, or the Greeks, whose nationalist movement introduced a whole string of defeats and land losses to the Sublime Porte, the Jews posed no such obvious threats. Thus there is a need to reconsider not only internal Jewish-Muslim relations, but also to recontextualize the Jewish community within the context of the other non-Muslim communities to grasp the changes the Jewish community of Istanbul went through in the years following the 1908 Young Turk Revolution. Like other groups, the Jewish community was also experiencing a transition in terms of identity, nationalism, and loyalty to the state. Examining the late Ottoman period can also provide the necessary foundation for understanding the tribulations of the Jewish community during the first few decades of the modern Turkish state.

For Ottoman Muslims in Istanbul, the strengthening of Zionist ideology among the local Jewish communities triggered the warning that similar to the other non-Muslim communities, the Jews in Palestine were leaning toward nationalist-separatist sentiments, which posed a great danger to the future of the Ottoman State. Following the Young Turk Revolution, new expressions of a European type of anti-Semitism were on the rise, forcing the Jewish community to reassess their future in Ottoman lands.[3] Importantly, Jews in the Ottoman lands adopting a Zionist ideology differed from their European Zionist counterparts; for them, Zionism was a cultural form of nationalism, an emerging identity which did not clash with their loyalty to the Ottoman state and which did not require moving to the far-off lands of Ottoman Palestine.

This preliminary research will focus on two main sources which demonstrate the need to reassess the status of the Jewish community: an exchange of letters between Ebüziyye Tevfik and Moiz Kohen, as they appeared in the Istanbul newspaper *Tasvir-i Efkar*, and the above mentioned 1911 debate over Zionism in the Ottoman parliament. The Young Turk Revolution provided the Ottoman Jewish community with the needed platform to integrate into the Ottoman political system and to become full-fledged citizens. However, their 'special' status in the CUP as the 'preferred' non-Muslim community gradually came to an end by 1911, and the Jews, similar to other non-Muslim communities, lost their new- found political and social status. The phenomenon of how Jews were accepted – or not accepted can be documented in the ongoing debates over Zionism, which when taken in the context of Istanbul's political elite had only a distant relationship to the actual issue of Jewish migration to Palestine. Rather it was also related to an ongoing debate concerning the mass-transfer of Jews from the Russian Empire to Ottoman Iraq; certainly, combating such a plan was the legitimate right of the opposition. However, the fact that opponents of such a plan justified their opposition based on anti-Semitic rhetoric placed Jewish politicians on the offensive. It is important to note that the Ottoman Jews supporting mass migration were among the most influential Jews of the period – Moiz Kohen and Nissim Russo – and were close to the political elite. These Ottoman loyalists believed that there was no contradiction between their loyalty to their Ottoman homeland and Zionism. However, in stark contrast to the Zionist Organization, they believed that Zionism was not bound by borders, and that any mass migration of Jews to the Ottoman Lands was within the realm of Zionism. Explaining his type of Zionism, Moiz Kohen said the following in a letter to the editor of Salonica's influential Judeo-Spanish newspaper, *La Epoka*: 'Zionism was a movement of Jewish immigration to Turkey and preferably to Palestine, which holds a certain historical attraction for the Jews'.[4] According to Kohen, 'in my articles, published in *Tasvir-i Efkar*, in *Zaman*, and in *Yeni Asir*, etc., I have always favored, with great insistence, this immigration – from an Ottoman as well as from a Jewish point of view – since I am convinced that it can greatly contribute to the progress of the country and guarantee the security of thousands of our unfortunate coreligionists'.[5]

The fact that Jewish immigration to the Empire at large was questioned testifies to a shift from the former policies of Sultan Abdülhamid II who allowed Jewish communities to sprout up throughout Anatolia during his reign, where no less than seven Jewish farming communities were established by the Jewish Colonization Association (JCA).[6] It was in this spirit that in the spring of 1909 the JCA embarked on a comprehensive plan for the settlement of millions of Jews in the Ottoman province of Iraq. In fact, the *New York Times* termed on these new attempts to settle Jews here as a 'new phase of Zionism';[7] furthermore, it was this plan that Moiz Kohen introduced to the Ottoman press, one that made the front page of *Tasvir-i Efkar*.

As the editor of *Tasvir-i Efkar*, and a member of parliament from 1908, Ebüziyye Tevfik had earned the reputation of being anti-Semitic ever since the publication of an inflammatory pamphlet entitled *Memleket-i İsrailiye* [The Israelite [Jewish] Kingdom] during the period of Sultan Abdülhamid II, and was one of the first Ottomans to brandish the specter of a Jewish-Freemason alliance, which would endanger the Ottoman state.[8] Tevfik's thoughts cannot be disregarded as representing a single individual stating his personal views. He was one of the most prolific figures of the Young Ottoman period and retained his status during the Young Turk period until his death in 1913.[9] As we will see below, Tevfik had no qualms about presenting anti-Semitic arguments to prevent Jewish immigration to the Ottoman Empire.

In an article for *Tasvir-i Efkar*, Moiz Kohen made clear why he supported mass immigration of Jews to Iraq,[10] and addressed Ebüziyye Tevfik's concerns that the Jewish migrants might pose a new ethnic question to the state on a par with 'the Bulgarian independence, the Bosnia-Herzegovinan uprising, [and] the events in Crete'. Clearly, Tevfik was correct in questioning whether in fact the Ottomans were importing a new ethnic conflict; however he concluded that he was confident 'the Children of Israel [if they would challenge the State] would remain trembling and wretched in the face of an Ottoman attack'.[11]

According to Tevfik, the main problem of allowing such a huge number of Jews to immigrate was the imminent economic danger. He stated that 'Perhaps the greatest danger from among what we have discussed is material; the outcomes and details of such an economic struggle which will spread like a great deluge [...]', and that 'we are confident those Jews which will be transferred [to Iraq] will not work in agriculture but rather be those who watch their accounts carefully even though they appear to be simple and pure individuals, and they will bring disasters and calamity – such as the Plague of Locusts – [which] will spread over all the Ottoman Lands'.[12]

Tevfik's anti-Semitic rhetoric should not be seen as a 'lone voice' since it is clear that by 1911 conspiracy theories linking the Jews with the eventual overthrow of Sultan Abdülhamid II began to undermine the very essence of the CUP government.[13] Furthermore, the conspiracy theories provide ample evidence that indeed for some Ottomans, a 'Jewish' question had emerged. While previous scholars have highlighted the spread of negative stereotypes to Jews, it needs to be placed in the framework of the emergence of a 'Jewish Question', which coincided with the emergence of other ethnic questions prevalent in the Empire. Eli Kedourie first documented this opposition in his article entitled *Young Turks, Freemasons, and Jews*, basing his findings on the letters of the British ambassador in Istanbul, Gerard Lowther which were dispatched to London on 29 May 1910.[14] According to Lowther, Jewish Freemasons had infiltrated the Young Turks and at their head was the Jewish deputy from Salonica, Emanuel Karasso,[15] furthermore Salonica's large *Dönme* population was working hand in hand with the Jews and together they had secretly taken over the Young Turk movement. In addition to the internal threat of Freemasons, there was also an external one, since Karasso was collaborating with Jewish Freemasons in Italy. Another threat was constituted by the appointment of Jewish ambassadors by the United States (Oscar Strauss) and the Italian Consul General (Primo Levi) in Salonica. Significantly, Lowther accused Oscar Strauss (the Jewish US ambassador) of promoting the Jewish immigration scheme to Mesopotamia (previously mentioned as Iraq), viewing it as an extension of Zionism which was aimed towards the 'practically exclusive economic capture of Turkey and new enterprises in that country',[16] because '[the Jew] seems to have entangled the pre-economic-minded Turk in his toils and as Turkey happens to strive to maintain a position of exclusive influence and utilize it for the furtherance of his ideals, viz. the ultimate creation of an autonomous Jewish state in Palestine or Babylonia as explained by Israel Zangwill [...]'.[17]

Conspiracy theories involving a Jewish plot to secretly take control of the Ottoman State continued to simmer and resurfaced in the spring of 1911, parallel to the debate on Zionism in the Ottoman parliament; a crucial point that has been overlooked. For example, on 3 March 1911, the opposition accused the minister of Finance, Cavid Bey, a *Dönme*, of showing undue preference to Jewish capitalists and their agents, some of whom were suspected of favoring Zionism. Even Karraso Efendi was approached by a Muslim deputy from Amasya who stated 'if you come in crowds, there will be no room for us'.[18] Finally, after pressure on the CUP, the Jewish contingent in the Parliament and other influential Jews began to distance themselves from the party. For example, in October, Karasso Efendi finally resigned, realizing that he was doing more harm than good within the CUP party ranks.

Moiz Kohen, in his diary, discusses his growing dismay with opponents of Zionism and how the tension had reached unbearable levels by the spring of 1911.[19] While this unpublished diary provides few details on Kohen's personal thoughts, he touches several times on the issue of Zionism, Jewish immigration to the Empire, and the rise of anti-Semitism. In mid-March he commented that '[...] the question of Zionism continues to worry me, one can clearly see that anti-Semitism has already started to take root in Turkey as a result of this stupid movement'.[20] In addition to his concerns regarding Jewish Ottomanism and the Jewish question in general, he was also a devoted Freemason, and was worried that other Freemasons would question his loyalty to them since he was constantly working for Jews, and had even joined the local *B'nai Brith* organization, making his fellow masons suspicious.[21] This led him to the conclusion that he was '[...] inclined to retire from the activities ministered until now for the exclusive interests of the Israelites, as a real Mason I need to work for the good of humanity in general and not only for the Masonic lodges. We can also work for the good of the *patrie*, meaning for the good of all my citizens'.[22] And on his participation in BB [the *B'nai Brith*]:[23] '[...] this may help create a bad reputation for me in the eyes of the Turks who might consider me a Jewish nationalist although I am (actually) a fierce enemy of Jewish nationalism'.[24]

It crucial to point out that Kohen understood that the Ottoman Jews were experiencing a similar struggle as the Armenians and that they could work together to achieve mutual goals. Therefore, he discussed these issues with an Armenian priest, and pondered on the idea of writing a book on the questions the different nationalities faced in the Ottoman state.[25] More importantly, Moiz Kohen's April entries into his diary serve as a general metaphor for the situation the Jews were confronted with in Istanbul. Similar to the other non-Muslim groups that welcomed the CUP, new forces arose during the post-Young Turk Revolution that highlighted the predicament of having to chose between communal loyalties and that of the state. Kohen's disillusionment with the Turkish Muslim population is crucial to understanding that Ottoman Jews possessed divided loyalties, at least in the eyes of the majority. While Kohen stressed that he would continue his 'efforts dedicated to the good of the *patrie* and to the Ottoman nation',[26] he also declared that he was 'unjustly suspected by the Turks and Jews'.[27] Concerning the Turkish Muslim population, he mentions with great disappointment that his 'opinion about the spirit of tolerance of the Turks has started to be shaken as a result of the publications of the Roumeli', an influential Istanbul newspaper that was attacking Zionism.[28] It is impossible not to end with the following quote, in which he leaves the group which 'despises Jews' unnamed, but from the context it is possible to speculate that he is speaking about Turks in general:[29]

> I observe that the [blank] despise the Jews. It is hidden disregards which can suddenly burst. I persist in my idea that it is not a cause from which we [Jews] should distance ourselves; on the contrary this should push us to get closer and closer, because scorn and misunderstanding often come from the lack of knowing one another. When people know each other well they [will] like each other and have mutual respect.

Although it is not possible to trace the rise of anti-Semitism in Ottoman Istanbul, it can be seen that the dynamics behind anti-Zionism in Istanbul were radically different from what was observed in Palestine A twenty-four page pamphlet in Turkish entitled *Siyonizm Tehlikeleri* [The Dangers of Zionism], published in Istanbul in 1913, shows once again those supporting anti-Zionism were in essence anti-Semitic.[30] In fact, it was basically a repetition of previous claims that the driving force behind the CUP party were 'Jews, the Zionists, and the Freemasons'.[31]

The 1911 Ottoman Parliamentary Debate on Zionism

This was the backdrop for the 1911 Ottoman parliament debate Zionism, which was raised by two Palestinian representatives from Jerusalem: Ruhi al-Khalidi and Sa'id al-Husayni. With Jewish figures in Istanbul retreating from the public sphere, and the lack of understanding among parliament members of what Zionism really was, the Palestinian representatives were forced to stress that the debate was only about Jewish immigration to Palestine, and that it was not directed against Jews in general, whether in Palestine or other regions of the Empire. In other words, the Palestinians had to take a two-tiered approach: on one hand voicing their opposition to immigration of Jews to Palestine but on the other hand stressing the fact they were not anti-Semitic but merely anti-Zionist; a distinction blurred among some of the Istanbul Muslim Ottoman elite.[32] Furthermore, with ethnic tensions on the rise, any debate on Zionism easily ignited the different ethnic groups' claims of discrimination and racism.

This helps clarify why the two Palestinian parliamentarians, Ruhi al-Khalidi and Sa'id al-Husayni, were so quick to refute claims that they were anti-Semitic especially in light of the fact that there were no real accusations of the sort expressed in parliament. In fact, Sa'id al-Husayni went out of his way to present the Jews in a positive light, attesting to the fact that:[33]

> The Jews are a hard-working, intelligent, and economical nation. Above all, they are most progressive in agriculture, and in crafts. It is undeniable that in the Jerusalem district that both they and the local population have benefited from the scientific,

agricultural, and industrial offices, which they have created and established. For this reason, the Jews wanting to immigrate from other countries to the Ottoman Land should be allowed to do so, but on condition that they accept Ottoman citizenship, and go to other districts (*vilayet*) outside of Palestine, as I said before, the ones in Palestine have reached a sufficient number. [In fact] there is no danger in accepting and registering various [Jewish] immigrants according to the limit the district is able to receive. On the contrary, I call the attention of the Minister of Interior to the above-mentioned positive effects [of Jewish migration].

Sa'id al-Husayni's views regarding Jewish immigration deserve special attention because of the sharp contrast they present to those expressed by more polarizing figures such as Ebüziyye Tevfik. As we have already seen, Tevfik vehemently objected to all Jewish immigration on the basis that the Jews would bring corruption and mayhem with them. Sa'id al-Husayni, on the other hand, expressed a generally positive view of the Jewish community in Palestine, even though he favored a moratorium on further immigration to Palestine.

Above all, the two parliamentarians were genuinely concerned that they should not be categorized as anti-Semitic both because Jews made up a large part of their constituency and because anti-Semitism was an ideology that clashed with their own cosmopolitan worldview. Both Ruhi al-Khalidi and Sa'id al-Husayni were quite familiar with the Jewish community in Palestine; both of them periodically attended the AIU schools, and both had a basic knowledge of Hebrew.[34] Furthermore, al-Khalidi was a Freemason, and as such undoubtedly contrasted with the outspoken, extreme anti-Zionists in Istanbul such as Ebüziyye Tevfik, who linked Freemasonry with Zionism as a threat to the stability of the Ottoman State.

In addition, the Jews in Parliament were members of the same party as al-Khalidi and al-Husayni (the CUP). As a result, the two certainly realized how sensitive the subject of Jewish immigration could be, not only because of the presence of Jewish parliamentarians, but also because numerous ethnicities and religious groups were represented in their parliamentary grouping. However, regardless of their intentions, we will see that al-Khalidi had opened a Pandora's Box by introducing the question of Jewish immigration to the floor. Upon the response of the Jewish parliamentarian from Izmir, Nissim Matzliah, the Parliament rapidly escalated into chaos.

Neville Mandel mentions nothing about the very serious reaction al-Khalidi provoked from Nissim Matzliah, stating that Matzliah 'did not want to take a stand on the Zionist issue, because he was a Jew [...]'. In fact, according to the Ottoman parliamentary report, the exact opposite occurred: Matzliah took al-Khalidi to task for mentioning the Torah (*tevrat*) during his speech about the history of Zionism, even though it was not discussed in any derogatory way. First, however, Matzliah stressed that he wished to clarify a few points concerning Zionism and stated that 'if Zionism is indeed harmful to the State (*hükümet*), then without question my loyalty lies with the State'.

However, Matzliah took offense with al-Khalidi's references to the Torah, stating, 'what is the sin of the local and foreign Jews living in this region as a result of such things being written in the Torah'. In other words, as a Jew, Matzliah felt it only natural that Jews would immigrate to Palestine. As we will see below, this is a similar stance as the one taken by an Armenian parliamentarian towards Jewish migration to Palestine. Matzliah answered sharply stating: 'If he wishes, let him burn the Torah. Let's have the Torah burnt for the State! I suppose Ruhi Bey is a Muslim, I am also a believer. In order to be a believer, the Torah's *ahkam* [legal provisions] were superseded following the dignified and honorable revealing of the Glorious Quran; this is my belief'. Ruhi Bey was quick to defend himself, explaining that this was only done to 'exemplify the foundation of Zionism'. Angrily Matzliah answered back that 'you have gone so far in your presentation as to speak of things which no one in the government has ever heard of before [...] by claiming the existence of an Israelite [Jewish] government (*hukümet-i israiltye*) in Ottoman lands'. With shouts of discontent arising from the floor, Tevfik stepped in exclaiming that the formation of a Jewish government 'is the secret goal. Undoubtedly you are also aware of this!' In closing, Matzliah reiterated the need to fully investigate the matter but concluded confidently that 'I am obliged to present to this session that Ottoman Jews are very devoted to the

State, and I believe they will be found to be patriotic lovers of their nation (*hammiyetli vatanperverler*)'. And, in relation to the foreign Jews: 'We firmly believe that the Jews look upon the Ottoman State with the best intentions (*rahat yüzü görmüşler*)'.

Finally, echoing Ruhi al-Khalidi's earlier statement, Matzliah concluded that 'the oppression and hostility that the European Jews have experienced [...] humanity cannot [even] bear. I believe that this intelligent nation will live here in comfort and will not betray it. [In fact], this nation will be better served and no one will be able to find a friend better than the Jews'. What is remarkable about this statement is how similar it is to Moiz Kohen's previously discussed article. Clearly, even if the Jews were not Zionists, they found it hard to even consider the fact that their European counterpart immigrants would rebel against the Ottoman State, or for that fact harbor any harmful intentions.

Following Nissim Matzliah, the floor was turned over to an Armenian who expressed his suspicions that the question of Zionism was actually the workings of Muslim chauvinism. In my opinion, this is one of the more fascinating explanations of how a non-Muslim Ottoman perceived Jewish immigration to Palestine and its possible implications regarding the status of non-Muslims in the Empire. This Armenian parliamentarian, Vartkes Efendi from Erzerum, provides a chilling prophecy of what the Armenian people would endure in the Ottoman State by first tackling the Jewish question:

> Gentleman, why is Russia driving the Jews out? Perhaps over there they [the Jews] want to establish a kingdom (*padişahlık*) as well? Why in Austria, Germany, and England are they rising up against the Jews? Perhaps over there, also is another Land of Palestine? Over which they [perhaps] want to establish a kingdom? The Ottoman State has never attacked the Jews why should they begin now? (Calls of: 'This is wrong!') Please, this is not wrong! When we say [such] things [about Jews] here, if the primitive people outside see a Jew next to them, they will say this is a traitor! How is this so? They said this first about the Armenians! I am saying the people shouldn't learn a lesson from these words and find an excuse to act against them [the

Jews]. Once upon a time when people complained to the government about the activities of the Armenian nationalists (*ermeni komitecilieri*) the Armenians would say in response 'what can we do? This nationalist idea (*komitelerin fikri*) has been spread as propaganda throughout the Armenian population, we cannot stop it, it circulates by itself'. Now, aren't we faced with exactly the same situation? (Calls of: 'this is different!') It is the same! Gentlemen, I am speaking as an Armenian. I am afraid that what has happened to me will happen to the Jews (calls of: 'That is the problem!'). And I say this from an Ottoman perspective; not an Armenian one, or a Jewish one. [Simply] the Jews are in the Land of Palestine, and the Armenians, in the mountains of Anatolia. They are so far apart from one another that I have no reason to do them any special favors.

Vartkes Efendi continued, in answer to Ruhi al-Khalidi, that he did not attribute such bad characteristics to the Jerusalem representatives. Finishing his point, however, he revealed his fear that the violence against Jews could even spill over and reach the Armenians 'if tomorrow in the Land of Palestine, or anywhere else, a riot should occur, they will behead more Armenians than anyone else!'. This inflamed one of the Muslim parliament members, who blurted out 'wrong, wrong! The Turks are not that savage!' to which, Vartkes replied 'I saw the person who beheaded my father. You did not see this! Please, I know whether it was a savage act or not'. In response, the Muslim yelled that this was during the period of Abdülhamid, at which point Vartkes quickly returned to the main topic, Zionism. Finally, before moving on to the question of the current violence directed at the Armenians, Vartkes reiterated that he wanted the government to assess the situation in Palestine, to understand the whole picture. Following this, Vartkes continued his talk and focused completely on the Armenian question, which continued to keep the Parliament up in arms.

The parliamentary debate continued and, following the debate relating to the Armenians, new tensions were aired concerning discrimination against the Greek population in the public sector.[35] Only after this debate and other related ones, did the issue of Zionism once again reach the floor, which in turn led to a broader issue that the Ottomans were facing: the growing Arab question. Leading the discussion was the parliamentarian representing the Province of Syria, Shukri al-'Asali. The role of Shukri al-'Asali was especially important since Northern Palestine was under his jurisdiction, and, unlike the Jerusalem parlimentarians, he was not Palestinian.

Shukri al-'Asali was in some senses the most effective speaker, focusing concretely on how Zionists were able to achieve dominance. The first interesting point he touched on was that some Jews actually did adopt Ottoman citizenship, but retained their former citizenship – a choice that proved helpful if they ran into legal issues, where they simply used their former passports, and denied the existence of their Ottoman citizenship. Similar to Ruhi al-Khalidi, he also stressed that the Jewish community in Palestine was completely autonomous, not even using Ottoman courts, or other services. According to Al-'Asali, they were slowly taking over villages and regions to such an extent that they were administrating them on their own: 'Three quarters of the district of Tiberias, half of the district of Safad [...] half of Haifa, above all Jaffa (the district) has totally been filled with Jews, and such is the case with Jerusalem', he commented, adding that this was possible since 'they have *martins* and other such illegal weapons in their homes'.[36] Following this a Greek parliamentarian questioned him on his remarks about Tiberias, pointing out that there were also local [Ottoman] Jews in Tiberias. Al-'Asali explained that this was true for the city but not for the villages, which were completely filled with foreigners. Continuing about the proliferation of weapons, he stated the following:

> At first when they arrived, they employed local guards, at that time they were not brave; but slowly, they became brave and their bureaucrats (*memurlar*) started to smuggle hundreds of weapons, and passed out *martins*. I know this very well. Following this, they began to employ their own guards, and it is has reached such a stage that this year [...] they came from their villages to the village of Yemha, where they raided the village's property (*eşyasını gaspedip gitmişlerdi*).

He went on to explain that they met secretly without letting either Muslims or Christians into their clubs, and there they sang their national anthem, and on holidays, they raised their Zionist flag in place of the Ottoman flag. He further went on to explain the effectiveness of the Zionist postal service. However, his words did not seem to capture the interest of the parliament; Shukri al-'Asali started to address what practical steps could be taken to protect Palestine from the Zionists. Here, he reported to the parliament that Salah al-Din al-Ayyubi's fortress had been sold to Zionists.[37] Al-'Asali was finally cut short by Ibrahim Efendi, who steered the debate back to the Jews.

Ibrahim Efendi challenged Shukri al-'Asali on a number of points – providing us with a unique perspective on how other Muslim Ottomans perceived the Jewish community as a whole, which would have implications as to how they perceived the Jewish *yishuv* in Palestine. First he was quick to point out that the 'Jewish question' (*yahudi meselesi*) was not at all new in the parliament because it had been debated 15 times.[38] He further stated, similar to what Ebüziyye Tevfik mentioned in his article, that he did not see the Jewish community (in Palestine) as a serious threat since the Ottoman army numbered over 'one million soldiers'. He continued '100,000 Jews (including their wives and children) came to Jerusalem, and they are not going to conquer Iraq and Syria', debunking the idea that the Jews were interested in founding a state not only in Palestine, but also in Syria and Iraq.

Ibrahim Efendi continued, stating that Jews who were not Ottoman citizens should not be seen as a threat. He pointed out that foreigners were found throughout the Empire and that 'Beirut's commerce was in the hands of foreigners, [and] Salonica's trade was in the hands of foreigners'. Moreover, 'foreigners have not revolted, they have worked for years, for centuries [here], they have studied in the Commerce Schools, they have taught in these schools [...]. Let us open our eyes, we too want to advance our country, we also want to be human [...]'. After acknowledging that foreign citizens had played a positive role in the development of the Empire, he moved the discussion on to a consideration of the state budget.

As if this debate had not gone far enough, the last group to raise concerns about their future in the Empire was the Arabs, led by Khalid al-Barazi Efendi, also from Syria. Perhaps realizing what a controversy this might cause, al-Barazi first demanded that he be allowed to have 'freedom of speech' (*hürriyet-i kelam*) and threatened that if anyone cut him off he would simply leave. For our purposes, it is important to place the Arabs' frustration within the overarching context of the Empire, especially in light of what we have seen in this debate. Alienation in the Arab population was growing at an alarming rate, and Zionism only exacerbated this. As we will see, though, Zionism was just one of the questions they were facing in their growing divide with Ottoman Istanbul and their Turkish compatriots.

Khalid al-Barazi first stated that 'if someone from another race (*anasir*) is suspicious of the loyalty of the Arab people, I would totally reject (*kemal-i şiddetle red*) and disapprove of this with all my being'.[39] Although it would be erroneous to read too deeply into this statement, it is important to emphasize that some Ottoman citizens were suspicious of the Arabs of the Empire and their growing separatist views. He continued by stressing the importance the Arabs placed on Islam and that in the end 'this state is an Islamic one', and that anyone who questions the law (*hak*) and justice of the Sultan (*emir ül-müminin*) is in essence a rebel.[40] Focusing on the inequalities between the Arabs and Turks, he reminded the chamber that this discussion had been previously addressed by Shukri al-'Asali, and noted that there were no Arabs among the Ministers and the governors, and that Arabs only made up one percent of the upper echelons of the bureaucracy. Unlike the oppressive times of Abdülhamid II, the government was now committed to equality (even though this had yet to be concretized). According to al-Barazi, the Arabs lagged seriously behind the other ethnic groups in terms of their knowledge of Turkish; yet Arabic had special status since it was the Holy Language of the Quran. He stressed that he did not want only Arabs to fill the government positions in their regions, but demanded that the Ottoman administration at least learn Arabic, and went so far as to point out that even the British sent bureaucrats that knew the local language to their colonies (Egypt, India, and the Sudan) – an assertion which one member of parliament disputed.[41] The debate continued, reaching no real conclusion, and focused more specifically on the Ottoman State's problems in Yemen.

This very long parliamentary debate illustrates the problems the Ottoman State was facing just three years before the start of World War I. Crucially however, this debate sheds light on what a chaotic state the Parliament fell into once they began discussing Zionism. In this multi-ethnic/religious atmosphere, there was not one singular perception of Zionism, and that the Palestinians and Syrian representatives were losing an uphill battle. It is evident that Zionism, for many members of the parliament, especially the non-Muslims, was seen through their own reality, as a question of the future status of the non-Muslims, and to some extent, the non-Turkish elements of the Empire. In other words, in the parliamentary debate, Zionism and Jewish immigration were treated more as a 'Jewish' question, and the Palestinian population was never taken into consideration. This debate was thus an ominous warning of what would occur to the Ottoman non-Muslims, especially the Armenians, during World War I.

Conclusion

This chapter has placed the issue of Zionism into an 'Ottoman' and 'Istanbuli' context. What emerges is that the debate over Zionism in the Sublime Porte was only tangentially connected to what actually was happening in Palestine. Rather, Ottoman perceptions (Muslim or non-Muslim) of Zionism were multifaceted and resulted from perceptions of different realities.

In the first section of this chapter, I have argued that a 'Jewish' question emerged. Moiz Kohen's writings show that the Jewish community understood this predicament. While I do not claim that anti-Semitism was widespread in the capital, clearly Ebüziyye Tevfik's writings demonstrate that it was prevalent. It should come as no surprise that the mainstream Muslim Turkish elite began to question the Jewish communities' loyalty to the State. The growing Turkish nationalism and the simple fact that all of the non-Muslim communities reassessed their role in the State following the Young Turk Revolution, at a time when their loyalty to the state was being challenged, contributed to this development.

This is the context in which the Ottoman parliament debate on Zionism needs to be grasped. Without an understanding of the interethnic dynamics of the post-Young Turk Regime and the fact that a 'Jewish' question had emerged in some circles, it is impossible to engage with this Ottoman debate. For the Palestinians, this situation was detrimental since many parliament members (both Muslim and non-Muslim) could not comprehend the Palestinians' concerns and fears, and did not see that the Jewish community posed any threat whatsoever. On the other hand the Palestinians were also in a predicament since they did not see eye to eye with the Ottoman Turkish elite who were against Zionism. This was due to the very fact that this opposition was grounded in anti-Semitic rhetoric that fomented fears of Jewish conspiracies, in addition to the fact that both Jerusalem representatives were members of the ruling CUP party.

Finally, the chapter provides us with ample evidence that the tensions the Jewish community would face in the early years of the Turkish republic date back to the Young Turk era. In essence, like the other non-Muslim communities, Jewish participation in the political sphere would end even before World War I, never to return in the modern Turkish Republic.

Notes

1. Interestingly, these ideals were stamped on Ottoman coins post 1908; however, the word 'equality' was replaced with 'justice'.
2. Mandel, Neville J., *The Arabs and Zionism before World War I* (Berkeley, 1976).
3. In fact, much of the current rhetoric linking the Turkish Republic and the Young Turk Revolution to a Jewish-Mason-Dönme conspiracy can be traced back to the years prior to World War I.
4. Kohen, Moiz, 'An Explanation', in Landau, Jacob M., *Tekinalp: Turkish Patriot 1883–1961* (Leiden, 1984), p. 55 (a translation of an article which appeared on 20 December 1910 in *La Epoka* on p. 271).
5. Ibid., p. 55.
6. The JCA was a philanthropic organization founded by the Baron Maurice de Hirsch in 1891 with the sole purpose of relocating Jews who lived in countries where they were persecuted or were living in poor economic conditions. Thus, most of their energies were devoted to relocating Russian Jews to the

Americas and Palestine. In Anatolia, it established agricultural communities near the cities of Eskişehir (Mamure), Istanbul (Mesila Hadasha), Silivri (Fethiköy), Akhisar (Or Yehuda), and Balıkesir (Tekfur Çiftlik). For more on the Jewish settlements during this period, see Bora, Siren H., 'Alliance Israélite Universelle'in Osmanli Yahudi cemaatini tarım sektöründe kalkındırma çalışmaları ve Izmir yakınlarında kurulan bir çiftlik okul: "Or Yehuda"' [Development Efforts in the Agricultural Sector by the Ottoman Jewish Society Alliance Israélite Universelle and the Agricultural School Established Near Izmir: 'Or Yehuda'], *Çağdaş Türkiye Tarihi Araştırmaları Dergisi* 1/3 (1993), pp. 387–400; I was able to see photographs of the graves of the former Jewish residents, which can be found on the outskirts of the adjacent Turkish village. What is evident from the grave stones is that this group of Jews was also undergoing a Hebrew revolution, since some of the stones have Modern Hebrew passages.
7. *The New York Times*, 7 June 1909, p. 7.
8. Lewis, Bernard, *The Emergence of Modern Turkey* (London, 1961), p. 208n.
9. For more on Ebüziyye Tevfik see Gür, Alim, *Ebüzziya Tevfik Hayatı: Dil, Edebiyat, Basın, Yayın ve Matbaacılığa Katkıları* [The Life of Ebüzziya Tevfik: Language, Literature, Press, Publication, and Printing: Supplements] (Istanbul, 1998).
10. *Tasvir-i Efkar*, 16 October 1909.
11. Ibid.
12. Ibid.
13. For more on the history of the role the Freemasons in the development of the Committee of Union and Progress, see Hanioğlu Şükrü M., 'Notes on the Young Turks and the Freemasons', *Middle Eastern Studies* 25 (1989), pp. 186–94 and Jacob M. Landau, *Exploring Ottoman and Turkish History* (London, 2004).
14. Kedourie, Elie, 'Young Turks, Freemasons and Jews', *Middle Eastern Studies*, Vol. 7/1 (1971), pp. 94–103.
15. Hanioğlu: 'Jews in the Young Turk Movement', p. 523.
16. Kedourie: 'Young Turks, Freemasons and Jews', pp. 94–5.
17. Ibid., p. 92.
18. This is not to say that there were no members of the CUP that did not support this plan. The *Times* correspondent briefly mentions that since the Jewish immigrants 'would take kindly to agricultural pursuits in their new home and supply the want labor, which must otherwise be the greatest bar to the early realization of any schemes for Mesopotamian development, they dream also of the creation, in one of the Arab centers, of a force which

will in some degree be a counterpoise to the numerical superiority of the Arabs'.
19. Unfortunately, I only possess part of his unpublished diary spanning from May 1907 to June 1911.
20. Ibid., entry 12 March 1911.
21. The *B'nai Brith* during this period was in the midst of establishing its first lodge in the Ottoman State. For a history of the *B'nai Brith* in the Ottoman Empire, see Bali, Rifat, 'Bir Yahudi dayanışma ve yardımlaşma kurumu: B'nai B'rith XI. bölge büyük locası tarihçesi ve yayın organı HaMenora dergisi' [A Jewish Support and Assistance Foundation: The History of *B'nai Brith*'s 16th division Grand Lodge and its Organ of Publication HaMenora], *Müteferrika* vol. 8–9 (Spring-Summer 1996), pp. 41–60.
22. Kohen: Unpublished diaries, entry 12 March 1911.
23. Moiz Kohen abbreviated *B'nai Brith* to BB. Nevertheless this calls for caution since it is not absolutely certain that he is talking about the *B'nai Brith* here and in other places.
24. Kohen, Unpublished diaries, entry 29 March 1911.
25. Ibid., entry 3 April 1911, and 5 April 1911.
26. Ibid., entry, 6 April 1911.
27. Ibid., entry, 9 April 1911.
28. Ibid., entry 10 April 1914.
29. Ibid., entry 16 April 1911.
30. Mahsin, A., *Siyonizm Tehelikeleri* [The Dangers of Zionism] (Istanbul, 1329 [1911]). In fact, the anti-Semitic literature that is widespread in Turkey today is almost an exact replica of what is found in this pamphlet.
31. Hanioğlu, 'Notes on the Young Turks and the Freemasons', p. 519.
32. Meclis-i Meb'usan Zabit Cerideleri [Proceedings of the Ottoman Parliament], 3 Mayıs 1327 (16 May 1911), p. 556 [in Ottoman Turkish].
33. Ibid., p. 557.
34. Khalidi, Rashid, *Palestinian Identity: The Construction of Modern National Consciousness* (New York, 1997), pp. 69, 77.
35. Meclis-i Meb'usan Zabit Cerideleri, p. 566.
36. Ibid., p 572.
37. Ibid., p. 574.
38. Ibid. It would be interesting to survey the parliament reports as a whole to check whether there were common themes linking the different debates. Apparently he was also referring to the debates that were held concerning Iraq.
39. Ibid., p. 575.
40. Ibid.

41. It is striking that when they talk about Arabs they for the most part call them simply 'son of Arab', and not Arab, which contrasts with the Kurds, Armenians, and Jews. While beyond the scope of this chapter, it is interesting to mention that when they talked about the Kurds, they mentioned that they used Turkish among themselves to correspond.

CHAPTER 7

JERUSALEM UNDER THE YOUNG TURKS: A STUDY BASED ON LOCAL SOURCES

ISSAM NASSAR

Introduction

The period of the Young Turks in Palestine has hitherto not been adequately studied. The majority of published works on this period are devoted to Zionist activities and Jewish relations to Palestine's Arab population, or events relating to the Empire, particularly with regards to its European territories. This is partly due to what I would define as an obsession with Zionism and the Palestine-Israel conflict as well as to the limited access to official documentation from that period in the Ottoman records in Istanbul. However, in the recent decades, a number of dairies, journals and memoirs from Palestine from that period have become available. They, to some extent, fill in the gap relating to primary sources from that time.

In this chapter, I examine the social and political events that occurred in Palestine and Jerusalem in particular during the last years of Ottoman rule in which the Young Turks were in power. The question that this study tackles is to what extend did the rise of the Young Turks to power influence the emergence and rise of sense of local identity and perhaps a larger sense of Arab nationalism in the Ottoman district of Jerusalem?

To study Palestine during World War I, one has to take a number of elements into account. The first is the nature of the Ottoman system itself and its rule over Palestine and Syria. The second is life in Palestine at the time of the War in terms of the population, Jewish immigration and the presence of foreign nationals there, particularly in Jerusalem, including the presence or absence of the diplomatic corps in the city and the region. Third, there is the question of the global situation that produced the Great War and the entry of the Ottomans on the side of Germany and Austro-Hungry, a topic which is beyond the scope of the current study.

In this chapter, I draw primarily on largely understudied sources such as memoirs, and personal and family papers from that period. This corpus includes the papers and letters of Khalil al-Sakakni in which he provides insights into the enlightened elites in Jerusalem before, during and after the War. Al-Sakakini was an educator and intellectual in Jerusalem who frequented meetings and social gatherings with leading figures in the city during that time. Similarly, the diary of an Ottoman solider from the city, Ihsan Turjman, who was an acquaintance of al-Sakakini sheds light on the thoughts of an average conscript in Jerusalem regarding the War, the administration and the Ottoman Turks. Wasif Jawharieh, a musician from Jerusalem relates details of social life during the War years of notable and ordinary Jerusalemites at the time. These sources, and others, show that the people of Palestine were fairly ambivalent in their attitude toward their rulers. We also find great hopes for change from the despotic rule of Sultan Abdülhamid, mixed with resentment at attempts to 'Turkify' the state.

Setting the Frame

Palestine, and the rest of Bilad al-Sham, fell under the control of the Ottomans in the second decade of the sixteenth century. During the Ottoman centuries, a political and administrative tradition gradually took hold in the region, which in many cases intersected and represented a continuation of the regime of the Mamluks who ruled Bilad al-Sham from the mid thirteenth century until 1516–7. The Ottoman administrative system rested largely on the power and prestige of the Empire's armies. In fact, some of the most powerful rulers of the sultanate arose from their ranks. This is partly due, as historian Naim Turfan pointed out, to the fact that the state itself was built up by *ghazi*s and fighters who later on assumed positions of power within the Empire.[1] This fact might account for why the Arab lands of the Empire were well integrated into the Ottoman imperial system, but not their Arab residents, as they were absent from high government positions for the entire four centuries of Ottoman rule. Out of the 215 grand viziers in the history of the sultanate, not a single one of them was Arab – although three were possibly of Arab origin.[2] This is a significant point, especially in light of the fact that only 78 of them were Turks whereas many others came from the ranks of other ethnic or national communities in the Empire.[3] This might also, although partly, explain Arab animosity towards the Turks, particularly in the last two decades of the Empire.

Still, this does not adequately explain why Muslim Arabs from Bilad al-Sham did not occupy high offices in the ranks of the state, or why those offices they did hold tended most often to be in the ranks of the judicial *shari'a* institutions. For long periods of time Jews and Christian Arabs were part of the *millet* system where they had rights and duties and were under the control of their religious hierarchy. This fact in itself might account for some of the special ties they had with their respective communities of faith abroad. In the local sphere, Arabs of all religions served in the administrations of their cities, towns, villages and communities.

Therefore, it is perhaps logical to conclude that the *Tanzimat* reforms of the nineteenth century possibly had a negative effect on the status of the Arab officials in the Empire. The *Hatt-ı Hümayun* issued in February 1856, for example, decreed 'the equality of all religions in the Empire' and granted 'Ottoman citizens equal access to educational institutions and equal treatment before the law'.[4] The *millet* system was abrogated and it was replaced by the authority of the government. Arabs who played a significant role in the life of the Empire were now marginalized as a result of the declining position of the religious establishments. It is worth recalling in this context that the Young Turk Revolution in 1908 was partly motivated by the reinstatement of the Ottoman Constitution, itself a product of the *Tanzimat* period, which confirmed the reforms discussed here. The fact that some of these reforms were not successfully implemented in Palestine, or in some cases were employed far before they became laws, as Doumani suggested in regards to the 1858 Ottoman Land Code, does not undermine this point.[5]

Furthermore, the Revolution itself, although it resulted in a general liberalization or relaxation of repressive policies previously in place and promised major reforms, did not represent an attempt to seriously challenge the existing Ottoman system. The Committee of Union and Progress (CUP), itself was not essentially a progressive movement despite its overthrow of the Hamidian regime and its slogans such as 'liberty', 'equality', 'fraternity', and 'justice'.[6] Even though the new leaders proclaimed 'equality of all Ottoman subjects without distinction of religion or race', the fact remains that most of these promises were never implemented or seemingly carried out.[7] The period of freedom of the press, assembly and forming parties came to an abrupt end even before the Ottoman sultanate officially entered the Great War.

The War Reflected in Local Sources

In an entry written on 15 September, 1914, about a month and a half before the Ottomans officially entered the War, Khalil al-Sakakini commented on the ban on newspapers in Palestine saying that 'people do not read these days, other than the telegrams they get, as most local newspapers have been stopped and the Egyptian ones are banned by the government'.[8]

Is it possible that al-Sakakini's apparent frustration regarding 'people not reading' was a reflection of the new political trend emerging in Palestine regarding self identity and Ottoman rule especially in light of the debates that relate literary activity to ethnic or national identity?[9] The answer takes us back a few years before the War, when an incident in Jerusalem started what appeared to be the first signs of an emerging Arab mobilization in Palestine and the desire to challenge the central authorities in Istanbul. Upon the discovery by the *waqf* authorities in 1911 that an English archeological team was carrying out excavations in the Haram al-Sharif area, the Jerusalem Muslim elites mobilized to stop it. The wrath of the *a'yan*, or notables, was directed against the central authorities in Istanbul as well as the local Ottoman rulers of the city especially when it became clear that the excavating team had the approval of the authorities in Istanbul. It did not take long for the protest to be joined by the Muslim elites in other cities in Palestine. Nablus notables from the families of Tuqan, Tamimi, Nabulsi, Hammad and Abdu sent letters to the Ottoman parliament and the Muslim Higher Court in Istanbul protesting work in the Haram. The governor sent a report to the authorities in Beirut protesting the excavations:[10]

> The protest by the notables is significant particularly in light of the fact that it came only three years after the Arab regions enthusiastically celebrated the arrival of the Young Turks to power. A description of such celebrations is found in the memoirs of Wasif Jawharieh where he illustrated how Jerusalem celebrated the arrival of the news of the success of the Young Turks' coup in 1908: The Ottoman coup took place on 11 July 1908 at the *Asitane*;[11] the government showed great joy, but not as great as that of the Arabs in the country. [...] the leaders of the army from the Committee of Union and Progress lead by Niyazi, Enver, Jamal and others, were victorious in removing the despot 'Abd al Hamid who ruled for more than 33 years through injustice and despotism. [...] I remember Jerusalem's night was like daylight with every house lit by candles.[12]

Jawharieh described in a detailed and favorable tone how Damascus Gate was ornamented and how the authorities erected four victory arches in the area between the gate and Notre Dame de France to the west. In his memoirs, we also find a description of what he considered to be the impact of the coup on Jerusalem. Describing how the Revolution affected the economic situation in the city he wrote: 'As a result of the Ottoman coup and the granting of freedoms to the masses so they could improve their social and political rights, in particular the Arab regions [...] the standard of living rose and the will to learn increased'.[13]

In fact, this viewpoint appears to dominate the section in Jawharieh's memoirs that deals with the pre-War period. It does not appear that the changes in government and the struggle between the political orientations within the CUP had any effect on his view, and in fact, he does not even mention them. However, a few years later, Jawharieh's apparent excitement seems to have faded away when he complains in 1914 about the taxes demanded by the government as its troops entered the Great War. Recalling the dire economic situation in Jerusalem, he wrote:

> For a long time now, the Turkish government increased its demands from the public with various excuses and on different occasions like support to arm the troops, support to strengthen the army, and support for the Ottoman Red Crescent society [...] the situation is dire and it is simply not possible to keep up with these demands and with taxes. At the same time, no one could dare to refuse the demands of the authorities. This was the time of injustice and despotism.[14]

Such injustice could explain the peculiar behavior of Jawharieh's neighbor Mikhael who hung pictures of Sultans, Abdülhamid and Muhammad Rashad, in his toilet. Mikhael would often go to the toilet to hit the pictures with his shoe, declaring 'you are wearing us out with your taxes'.[15] Having the pictures of Abdülhamid who was removed by the Young Turks, and Rashad who was appointed by them, is rather significant and is confirmed by Jawharieh's description of the period as 'the time of despotism' as we saw above. Coming from the person who praised the coup as putting an end to Hamidian despotism, Jawharieh's lumping together of both eras appears to be an indicator of a new development in ways in which the Arabs looked at their Turkish rulers.

Such a complaint about the economic situation was not limited to Jawharieh, but is also found in the diary of Ihasam Turjman. In an entry in his journal dated 10 July, 1916 Turjman wrote that:

> Jerusalem has not seen worse days. Bread and flour supplies have almost totally dried up [...]. Every day I pass the bakeries on my way to work and I see a large number of women going home

empty-handed. For several days the municipality has distributed some kind of black bread to the poor, the likes of which I have never seen. People used to fight over the limited supplies, sometimes waiting till midnight. Now, even that bread is no longer available.[16]

Turkish–Arab Relations

Despite such displays of disapproval, the relations between the Turks and Arabs did not reach a dead-end before at least a year into the War. There is little evidence that the Arabs entertained the idea of separation from the Empire, despite their substantial grievances against its government. A situation of cooperation and negotiation between the CUP and the emerging Arab nationalist movement appears to have existed before the War started.[17] In fact, on a few occasions, the CUP chose to support representatives of the emerging Arabism movement at the expense of their party interests. One example is the 1914 parliamentary election when they supported Arab candidates who ran against their own party candidates. In Acre for example, the authorities arrested supporters of Sheikh Asʿad al-Shuqayri, the Unionist candidate, to enable his Arab nationalist competitor ʿAbdel Fattah al-Saʿdi to win. In Nablus, the Unionist Haydar Tuqan was made to lose the elections in favor of the opposing candidates.[18] Nevertheless, such acts should be viewed essentially as attempts by a few individuals in the leadership to safeguard the Empire, rather than a principled endeavor to see the Arabs as equals. The fact is that the CUP was stolen by a small group of people even after membership surged (by 1908 it had 83 branches throughout the Empire with a total membership of 850,000).[19]

While many must have joined the party out of conviction, a large number joined for various other reasons including pressure, personal or economic interests or simply curiosity. Khalil al-Sakakini, for example, was visited by a sheik in his home on 25 September, 1908, who asked him to join the committee. Al-Sakakini asked him questions and for a few days to think it over. Several days later, he pledged in a secret ceremony to uphold the constitution and the orders of the

CUP.[20] Nothing in the rest of al-Sakakini's diary indicates that he was ever active in the Committee. In fact, he clearly became an advocate of Arab and Syrian nationalisms in no time after the ceremony.

Despite promises of equality in the Empire by the Unionists and the conciliatory tune of the Arab nationalists, it is clear that the leaders of the CUP did not trust anyone but Turks. Four years before the beginning of the War, Talat Bey, Pasha later on, had already made it clear at a meeting of the local branch of the CUP in Salonica in 1910, that 'there can be no question of equality, until we succeeded in our task of Ottomanizing the Empire'.[21] Although Talat was referring to the failure to incorporate non-Muslims in the Balkans and Greece (or what he called *ghiaur*), his statement applied to all non-Turks in the Empire since his premise was that of Ottomanizing. At a time when all the people of the empire were already Ottoman citizens, especially after the re-instatement of the constitution, Ottomanizing could only mean Turkifying of non-Turks in the empire including Arabs, Armenians and others in this case.

The leaders of the Young Turks embraced the ideology of *Pan-Turanianism*, particularly after the defeats in Tripoli and the Balkans. As Zeine Zeine has argued, 'the shock of [the] disaster' of war losses between 1911 and 1913 resulted in a wider spread of 'a genuine desire for national regeneration among all educated Turks'.[22] Therefore, the claim could be made that anti-Arab sentiment was already visible among the Turks on the eve of the WWI. But a rise of a separatist movement in the Arab regions was not as apparent. Rather, Arab leaders and parties were calling for a decentralized Ottoman state composed of two nations, one Arab and one Turkish.

At the same time, within the ranks of the CUP, talk of an 'Arab Question' started to become public, not to mention broad references among British officials after the Ottomans entered the War. Only ten days after the sultanate entered the War, Enver Pasha, the Minister of War, told Jamal Pasha that 'the news from Syria points to a general disturbance in the country and great activity on the part of the revolutionary Arabs'.[23] This is why Enver instructed Jamal Pasha to take command of the 4th Army, which led the latter to arrive shortly afterwards in Syria where he soon implemented ruthless policies against his

Arab subjects. Jamal's insistence on carrying on with the executions of Arab political leaders first in Beirut in August 1915, and in Damascus in 1916, sent a clear message that he was not going to tolerate any Arab nationalist sentiment. Similar executions took place in various other cities in Syria, Lebanon and Palestine, including in Jerusalem on several occasions.

Based on the impression one gets from his memoirs it is clear that Jamal Pasha, though publically advocating Turkish – Arab cooperation and partnership, harbored anti-Arab feelings. This is especially obvious in his treatment of those sentenced to death and his Arab subjects, as well as his attitude toward Emir Faisal and his father the Sharif Hussein of Mecca. Arabs in his book are often referred to as treacherous and as traitors, and he also discusses the literary hypocrisy of the Arabs in general.[24]

By the same token, advocates of Arabism were also changing their tone and policies, and inching gradually more towards separation from the Turks. The mood among the Arabs was changing and the ruthless policies of Jamal Pasha must have played a pivotal role in the attitudinal change among the inhabitants of Palestine in particular. Nevertheless, it cannot be said that they had given up completely on the Empire until more than a couple of years into the War. What is clear in this case, however, is that the people of Palestine were organically connected to the peoples of Syria and Lebanon and their positions followed suit with those of the intellectuals and leaders in those places.

The Identity of the Jerusalemites

Ihsan al-Turjman, a local conscript in the Ottoman army stationed in Jerusalem, gives us an insight into this issue when he records the following in his diary on 5 September, 1915:

> What does this barbaric state want from us? [Do they want] to liberate Egypt on our backs? They promised us and other fellow Arabs that we would be partners in this government, and that they are seeking to advance the interests and conditions of the

Arab nation. But what have we actually seen from these promises? Had they treated us as equals, I would not have hesitated to give my blood and my life – but as things stand I hold a drop of my blood to be more precious than the entire Turkish state.[25]

This account clearly suggests that the general mood in Jerusalem, and by extension in Palestine and Syria, was anti-Turkish. This is only one person's view, but considering the circles in which Turjman was moving, his views were probably more representative than not. He was close to the mayor of Jerusalem Hussein al-Husseini, and regular visitor to the house of Khalil al-Sakakini and his circle of friends. A similar attitude of the locals towards the War and the authorities in Istanbul was also reiterated in the dairy of the Spanish consul in Jerusalem at the time, Antonio de la Cierva y Lewita. In an entry dated 16 February, 1915, de la Cierva noted that 'the Arabs are angered at the Turks as they have sent them to die'.[26] The dairy entry then turns to what de la Cierva thought was a weak national consciousness among the Arabs at the time, stating that they are not 'able to resist the oppressors', and lamenting that the Arabs 'have no awareness of the spirit of nationalism'.[27] But his claim was actually proven wrong in light of the events that unfolded in the next few months.

One example that could serve to challenge the Spanish Consul's claim relates to the establishment of the Ottoman Red Crescent society in Jerusalem in 1915. Following the authorities' quick dismissal of Hussein al-Husseini from his position as mayor, along with the other members of the city council, al-Husseini moved to establish the Jerusalem branch of the society. It is very possible that such a move was designed to act as a parallel institutional power to the new council. By contrast to the newly appointed council members, most of whom were Turks and all of whom were Muslims, the board of the society's chapter was native and inter-communal. Along with al-Husseini who became its head, its members came from the ranks of Jerusalem's prominent families and included Jews and Christians and did not include any Turks. In fact, it is perhaps more important to highlight 'prominence' over religious affiliation. The board of the society consisted of five other members, two prominent native Jews, two prominent Christians and one Muslim. In a sense, the society was more about local representation and communal solidarity than about doing what the Ottomans required. As Jacobson suggested, the composition of the board was a sign for a sort of post Ottoman alternative that al-Husseini was starting to advocate.[28] His alternative, unfortunately, did not have a continued impact. Jacobson pointed out that this was possibly the last national or communal committee or organization on which Jews served voluntarily along with Muslims and Christians in support of a national government.[29]

Far from being a pioneer in interrelations among the different religious groups in the city, al-Husseini maintained the state of coexistence that was already prevalent in Jerusalem at the time. The best evidence for the religious mix in the fabric of Jerusalem comes, once again, from the memoirs of Jawharieh. Throughout his memoirs from the period before and after the Young Turk Revolution, Jawharieh describes to his reader how rich and multi-religious life was in Jerusalem. From his depiction of the ritual practices of every religious group and the role members of other religions played in such rituals, he paints a picture of a mosaic in which inter-communal solidarity was a prime feature. For example, as a Greek Orthodox Christian, he appears to have attended every celebration in the city, be it Muslim, Christian or Jewish. Describing the Ramadan night festivities in Jerusalem during his childhood, around the turn of the 20th century, Jawharieh wrote:

> Often, my brothers and I would participate in the Zikr celebrations in the shrine of Sheikh Rihan – in the Sa'diya quarter of the Old City – next to our house, and we would participate in the chanting with the amateurs and the professionals. Then late at night, we would visit our neighbors, Sheikh Muhammad al-Saleh, among them [...] and others, and spend the nights enchanted by music, particularly when I would take my musical instrument (al-Tanbourah) and would sing accompanied by my brother Tawfik. We would eat, drink and enjoy the sweets and would be very happy.[30]

Similarly, he described the annual Jewish celebrations in the city in which 'the Christian and Muslim Jerusalemite Arabs used to participate'. The celebration took place in the *Sheikh Jarrah* area north of the Old City and constituted a visitation to what Jews believe to be the tomb of Simon the Just.

> Twice a year they used to visit the tombs and spend the entire day in the shade of the olive trees. Most were Eastern [*mizrahi*] Jews who kept their traditions, in particular, those among them who were Palestinian Jews. Musical string groups and choirs were always present. I remember Haim, the oud player, and Zaki from Allepo who used to play the *daffy* (tambourine) and sing the *Mowashahat of Andalusia* [...] with the Jewish public in the celebrations.[31]

The fluidity that existed between the communities was reflected in the new local educational practices in the city such as the *Dusturiyya*, or constitutional school that was set up by al-Sakakini along with 'Ali Jarallah, Aftim Mushabbak and Jamil al-Khalidi in the aftermath of the Revolution. The policy of the school was to reject physical/corporal punishment typical to the missionary schools in the city at the time. In an entry recorded on Sunday 1 January 1911 al-Sakakini wrote:

> A year and a half had passed since my new school was established [...]. The *Dusturiyya School* stands out in a number of ways:
>
> 1) It brings together students from different religious and denominational backgrounds [...].
> 2) The school functions on the principle that the pupils are honorable and not subservient, and need assistance to grow in pride, not the opposite, and in need of emotional growth and freedom to be creative.[32]

Jawharieh and his brother Tawfiq attended the *Dusturiyya* School after their father took them out of the German Lutheran School (*al-Dabagha*), following a violent assault on Wasif by one of the teachers. Jawharieh described the education he received in his new school, listing the topics that he had to study. These included 'grammar, literature, mathematics, English, French, Turkish, physical education and *Qur'anic* studies for Christians', i.e., the *Qur'an* for non-Muslims.³³

Such a secular yet multicultural spirit is exemplified by the life of Jawharieh himself. He grow up in a religiously mixed neighborhood in the Old City of Jerusalem, learned to love and appreciate the *adhan*, or Muslim call for prayer, and grew up to become a musician playing in a group composed of musicians from all religious orientations. His own name was given to him to honor a leading Arab figure, Wasif Bey al-'Azem, from Damascus. At the same time, after his conscription into the Ottoman Naval service in the Dead Sea during the War, he also befriended many Turkish officers and was fond of telling about his adventures with them. In a way, Jawharieh embodied the various identities prevalent, or emerging, at the time; i.e., Ottoman, Arab, Palestinian, Jerusalemite and Christian-Arab. Yet, the concept of 'Ottoman identity' appears to have gradually diminished as the War progressed. This feeling emerges clearly from the entry in his memoirs regarding the War and the Ottoman involvement in it: 'The Arab people of the Empire were under the threat of annihilation at the hands of Ahmed Jamal the blood-shedder who rules our lands now and who is killing its devoted children'.³⁴

While Jawharieh's statement indicates a strong sense of Arab identity as well as strong opposition to Jamal Pasha's policies, it also suggests that a local patriotism was emerging since the term 'Arab people' could also have meant the natives of Palestine. It is comparable to the attitude that appears to have been behind the structure that former mayor al-Husseini had in mind when forming the board of the Red Crescent Society. Jacobson described this attitude as that of a 'local patriot' who 'combined a dedication to the city of Jerusalem as an urban locale and for its residents, of all religious beliefs'.³⁵

The idea of a 'local patriot' is evident in the writings of Khalil al-Sakakini. In an entry in his notebook written shortly before his arrest by the Ottomans and his later imprisonment in Damascus, dated 3 December 1917, just a few days before the British forces entered Jerusalem, he wrote:

> I am, I am simply a human being, nothing else. I do not belong to political parties or religious factions. I consider myself a patriot wherever I am, and strive to improve my surroundings whether they are American, British, Ottoman or African, whether they are Christian, Muslim or pagan. I only work to serve knowledge, and knowledge has no homeland.
>
> What is a patriot?
>
> If being a patriot means to be sound of body, strong, active, enlightened, moral, affable and kind, then I am a patriot. But if patriotism means favoring one school over another and showing one's brother hostility if he is from a different school or country, then I am no patriot.[36]

The Ottoman officials reinstated al-Husseini to his position as mayor before the British forces took over Jerusalem and he delivered the message of surrender to them. Why did the Turkish officials choose not to deliver the letter themselves and negotiate an honorable withdrawal of their forces? The fact that the surrender resulted from a meeting to which the army's leaders in the region called local notables from the various religions in the city might be significant, as it implies that the Turks recognized that the local patriots were in charge of the city. This is a unique event in the history of the city. The entry of General Allenby into the city on 11 December 1917 appears to have amounted to a national celebration. It was not because of the British and what they had in mind for Palestine, but rather that the population of the city was happy to see an end to Ottoman rule and to conscription. Jawharieh describes his family's preparations for Christmas that year with the following:

> Truthfully, it was a joyous holiday for all our family because the British had come and the Arab people were rid of the nightmare of the tyrant Turks. We all had great hope for a better future, especially after what we had suffered from war, famine,

and disease, in particular, typhus, which had spread all over the country. Thank God for saving our youth from the damned army service.[37]

At least for the time being, a sense of relief appears to have touched everyone in the city regardless of their religious affiliations or ideological orientation.

Conclusion

The diaries, papers and memoirs discussed in this chapter clearly provide insights into how the people of Jerusalem, and Palestine by extension, felt about the Young Turks. They enhance our understanding of the period and the later developments concerning Arab Palestinian demands on the British for an independent Palestine. The Young Turk rule in Palestine helped advance Arab nationalism in the country. Communal solidarity could be seen as an indicator of the rise of a local nationalism particular to Palestine. The War years saw the city and its affairs 'negotiated' between its people and their rulers for the first time in decades. With most foreign consuls out of the picture, in particular those who often meddled in the affairs of the city, be it the Russians, the French or the British, as well as a halt to Zionist immigration into Palestine, the people of the city came to the forefront and started to take matters in their own hands. In fact, with the policy of deporting citizens of the enemy countries, many Jewish immigrants were forced to leave. Native Jews were also more than ever in charge of the affairs of their community, unlike later times when the Zionist immigrants would play that role.

The initial rise of the Young Turks to power no doubt empowered the people of Palestine who appeared to have high hopes for change. But this situation quickly led to resentment because the aspirations of the non-Turks were not fulfilled and the Empire rapidly became engaged in the War. There is evidence that the ambivalence displayed by the authors of these diaries towards their new Ottoman rulers was more widespread than what some commonly claim.

Notes

1. See Turfan, Naim M., *Rise of the Young Turks: Politics, the Military and Ottoman Collapse* (London, 2000), pp. 3–14.
2. Kayalı, Hasan, *Arabs and Young Turks: Ottomanism, Arabism, and Islamism in the Ottoman Empire, 1908–1918* (Berkeley, 1997), p. 20. For a complete list of the names and origins of the grand viziers in the Empire see http://en.wikipedia.org/wiki/List_of_Ottoman_Grand_Viziers (July 8, 2010).
3. Kayali: *Arabs and Young Turks*, pp. 17–20.
4. Smith, Charles, *Palestine and the Arab-Israeli Conflict: A History with Documents*, Seventh Edition, (Bedford/St. Martins, 2009), p. 49.
5. Doumani argues that sales transactions of the *miri*, or state lands, took place as early as the 1830s. See Doumani, Beshara, 'Rediscovering Ottoman Palestine: Writing Palestinians into history', *Journal of Palestine Studies* vol. 21/2 (Winter 1992), p. 12.
6. Hanioğlu M. Şükrü, *A Brief History of the Late Ottoman Empire* (Princeton and Oxford, 2008), p. 150.
7. Zeine, Zeine N., *The Emergence of Arab Nationalism* (Beirut, 1966), p. 83.
8. Al-Sakakini, Khalil, *The Diaries of Khalil Sakakini: Orthodox Renaissance, World War I, Exile to Damascus*, Volume II, edited by Musallam, Akram (Jerusalem, 2004), p. 97 [in Arabic].
9. Kayali, who is critical of granting such significance to language, discusses the debate among historians of that period regarding the role of literary societies such as *al-Ikha* [Arab-Ottoman Brotherhood Society], *al-Muntada al-Adabi* [The Arab Literary Club] and *Türk Derneği* [the Turkish Society) among others. See Kayali: *Arabs and Young Turks*, pp. 88–96.
10. Fishman, Louis, 'The 1911 Haram al-Sharif incident: Palestinian notables versus the Ottoman administration', *Journal of Palestine Studies* vol. 33/34 (Spring 2005), pp. 13–14.
11. *Asitane* is short for *Asitane-i Aliye*, commonly translated as Sublime Porte. It refers to the Ottoman government house in Istanbul that was also the place of residence of the sultan, known as Topkapı Palace.
12. Jawharieh, Wasif, *Al-Quds al-'Uthmaniyya fil-Mudhakarat al-Jawharieh* [Ottoman Jerusalem in the Memoirs of al-Jawhareih], Book One, edited by Tamari, Salim and Issam Nassar (Jerusalem, 2003), p. 107 [in Arabic].
13. Ibid., p. 136.
14. Ibid., p. 105
15. Jawharieh: *Al-Quds al-'Uthmaniyya*, p. 104.
16. Tamari, Salim, *The Year of the Locust* (Berkeley: University of California Press, forthcoming).

17. Tibawi, A. L., *A Modern History of Syria Including Lebanon and Palestine* (London, 1969), p. 201.
18. Kayalı: *Arabs and Young Turks*, p. 175.
19. Hanioğlu: *A Brief History of the Late Ottoman* Empire, p. 160.
20. Al-Sakakni, Khalil, *The Diaries of Khalil Sakakini: New York, Sultana, Jerusalem, 1907–1912*, Volume I, edited by Musallam, Akram (Jerusalem, 2003) [in Arabic], pp. 308, 320–21.
21. Ibid., p. 87.
22. Zeine: *The Emergence of Arab Nationalism*, p. 113.
23. Ibid., p. 127
24. Djemal Pasha, *Memoirs of a Turkish Statesman, 1913–1919,* (New York, 1922), pp. 197–237.
25. Tamari: *The Year of the Locust.*
26. Mazza, Roberto, 'Antonio de la Cierva Lewita: The Spanish consul in Jerusalem 1914–1920', *Jerusalem Quarterly* no. 40 (Winter 2009/10), p. 38.
27. Ibid., p. 38.
28. Jacobson, Abigail, 'Alternative voices in late Ottoman Palestine: A historical note', *Jerusalem Quarterly File* no. 21 (August 2004), p. 47.
29. Ibid., p. 47.
30. Jawharieh: *Al-Quds al-'Uthmaniyya*, p. 77.
31. Ibid., p. 74.
32. Al-Sakakni: *The Diairies of Khalil Sakakini*, Volume I, p. 347.
33. Gelvin, James L., *The Modern Middle East: A History*, 2nd ed. (New York and Oxford, 2005), p. 103.
34. Jawharieh: *Al-Quds al-'Uthmaniyya*, p. 198.
35. Jacobson: 'Alternative voices', p. 47.
36. Al-Sakakini, *The Diairies of Khalil Sakakini*, Volume II, p. 97.
37. Jawharieh: *Al-Quds al-'Uthmaniyya*, p. 280.

PART III

INTELLECTUAL RESPONSES

CHAPTER 8

ARAB-OTTOMANISTS' REACTIONS TO THE YOUNG TURK REVOLUTION

BUTRUS ABU-MANNEH

Prologue

This chapter is not a prelude to the Arab movement after the Young Turk Revolution. Rather, it is about certain Arab intellectuals who, like many others, were extremely resentful of the despotism of Sultan Abdülhamid II (r. 1876–1909) and his policies. They applauded the Revolution and the restoration of the Constitution while cherishing high hopes of the new government in Istanbul led by the Committee of Union and Progress. These intellectuals were strong believers in the continuation of the Ottoman Empire and in the ideal of Ottomanism. In their view, the implementation of such an ideal would lead to the integration of all the Ottoman subjects into a political community of citizens who would enjoy equal rights and obligations. In their belief such a development would give the Empire a new lease on life and the power needed to face external threats and internal challenges. But, as is known, shortly after the Revolution, beginning with the Young Turks, nationalistic tendencies were given priority over other feelings and beliefs, thus dispelling these views and aspirations.

The following discussion casts light on these intellectuals and provides a brief account of their beliefs. It shows that such views of compromise and accommodation which they called for in their writings soon after the Revolution attracted fewer adherents as time went by, and were consequently left behind and neglected.

Arabs, Turks and the Ideal of Ottomanism

The last phase of the Arab-Turkish relations in the Ottoman Empire ended with much disappointment and disillusion on the part of the Arabs with the policies of the Young Turks led by the CUP. But this rift was not what Arab intellectuals and leaders of public opinion aspired to soon after the Revolution or expected to happen.

As early as the beginning of the second phase of the *Tanzimat* period (1856–76) certain leading statesmen at the Sublime Porte demonstrated an interest in transforming the political system of the state from an Ottoman-Muslim system based on confessional communities to a Western system based on equal citizens. The first measure in this direction was taken by the proclamation of the Reform Edict in February 1856 which granted non-Muslims legal and political equality with their Muslim compatriots. According to Davison 'the whole edict implied the removal of millet barriers and the substitution of a common citizenship for all the peoples of the Empire. But complete equality, egalitarian Ottomanism was yet to come'.[1] Sometime later, several further measures were undertaken. In 1868 for instance, in a speech by Sultan Abdülaziz which inaugurated the Council of State and the Judicial Council, all the citizens were described as the 'children of the same fatherland'.[2] Similarly, in January 1869 the Nationality Law was promulgated which officially changed the status of all the inhabitants of the state from subjects of the Sultan (*re'aya*) to citizens, though Davison suggests that 'Ali Paşa's real reason was to limit the abuses of the Capitulations.[3] However, in a sense, it actually supplemented the edict of 1856. These measures formed the basis of the ideal of 'Ottomanism' (*Osmanlılık*) which classified all the Empire's subjects as Ottoman citizens. Understandably, it was a legal and political rather than an ethnic identity and devoid of any religious content.

One of the early exponents of this ideal was the *Basiret* [The Insight] newspaper whose publisher and editor Basiretçi 'Ali Efendi apparently enjoyed good relations with statesmen at the Porte in the early phase of its publication.[4] Founded in January 1870 in Istanbul, it devoted a number of articles to the promotion of the ideal of Ottomanism. In an article published in July 1870,[5] over a year before the death of 'Ali Paşa, under the title of 'Osmanlılık sıfatı' [The Ottoman Traits] we find the following definition of this ideal: 'It is natural that all those who dwell within the borders of the *Vatan* [...] fall under the attribute of Ottomanism [and that ...] the connotation of "Ottoman" does not distinguish between religious or ethnic belonging'. In another issue which appeared about three weeks later under the title 'İttihad-ı Osmanı' [The Ottoman Union], *Basiret* called for this ideal again and emphasized its benefits for the Empire: 'If all the communities (*millets*) that live in the Ottoman land unite in an Ottoman union they would be able to stand in face of such a big country as Russia [...]'.[6] In other words, it was a call for Ottoman unity as a means of protecting the integrity of the Empire and defending it, which suggests that this ideal and its promotion may have reflected a political trend at the Porte elaborated in the second phase of the *Tanzimat*.

After the death of 'Ali Paşa in September 1871, his followers from among the new generation of bureaucrats/reformers took this view several steps further. They finally succeeded in making it part of the Constitution which they took a major role in drafting and which was promulgated towards the end of 1876.[7] In Article 8 this concept of equal citizens who share a common territory as a fatherland and who on the whole, are subject to the same law was confirmed. The article states that 'all those who are subjects of the Ottoman State, whatever their religion or confession, are classified as Ottomans without any distinction'.[8] One of the early manifestations of this ideal was the elections and the convening of Parliament in 1877–8 in which all the provinces of the Empire were represented.

The ideal of Ottomanism was received with much satisfaction by Syrian litterateurs at the time. Ahmad Faris [al-Shidyaq] the founder and editor of the weekly *al-Jawa'ib* in Istanbul (1861), gave full support in his paper to the actions and policies of 'Ali and Fu'ad Paşas and after them to their followers.⁹ So did Khalil al-Khuri the founder and editor of *Hadiqat al-Akhbar* that appeared weekly in Beirut from 1858.¹⁰ Similarly, Butrus al-Bustani added his voice to the above in his biweekly *al-Jinan* that appeared in Beirut in 1870 and in his other papers.¹¹ Equally so did Farah Anton in his monthly *al-Jami'a* which was first published as *al-Jami'a al-'Uthmaniyya*, 'one of the most important purposes of which [was] serving the Ottoman fatherland [...] and especially [the idea of] pan-Ottomanism'.¹² With the help of these and other publications, the ideal of Ottomanism gained wide acceptance in the Arab provinces not only among non-Muslims but among Muslims as well. This reality was also reflected on the cultural level as we shall see below.

But the growth of such an Ottoman community of equal citizens who inhabited a common fatherland was not given the chance and enough time to evolve and come to maturity due primarily to Hamidian policies. Sultan Abdülhamid II, as is known, dissolved the Parliament and suspended the Constitution, both of which were amongst the most appropriate means for the achievement of such a goal. Moreover, a political community existed in a fatherland to which each and all its members owed allegiance. But the Sultan fell back on traditional political values such as cultivating his image as Caliph and emphasizing the Islamic character of the state. This policy was designed to elicit allegiance to his person at the expense of allegiance to the fatherland. Moreover, the concept of the equality of all citizens inherent to the ideals of Ottomanism was undermined as a result of such policies.¹³ Such measures enabled Sultan Abdülhamid II to rule in an absolute manner for over three decades. But the spread of the attribute of Ottomanism as a common denominator among all his subjects, which should have been given priority over all other identities, slowed down and suffered a retreat. In other words Sultan Abdülhamid perhaps succeeded in preserving the traditional prerogatives of the sultanate but this success was achieved at the expense of the evolution and consolidation of a coherent Ottoman political community toward which 'Ali, Fu'ad, Midhat and other statesmen at the Porte were striving. The repercussions of the Hamidian policy are beyond the scope of this chapter, but they are referred to here in order to better capture the reactions of Arab intellectuals to the fall of the Hamidian regime and the restoration of the Constitution and Parliament, the themes of this paper.

In addition to the negative effects of the Hamidian policy, the ideal of Ottomanism suffered another blow. The modernization of the administration concomitantly involved a tightening of the system of centralization. This system was run by an ever- increasing and powerful bureaucracy, mostly of Turkish origin. Moreover, the official language became exclusively Ottoman-Turkish, but the new officials hardly knew any other language except Turkish. These measures of modernization took place at the expense of the share in provincial affairs which local notables enjoyed, as did the *'ulema* through the *shar'i* court.[14] In the case of the Arab provinces both groups used Arabic and scarcely knew Turkish. During the Hamidian period, however, some effort was undertaken to incorporate non-Turks trained at the high schools in Istanbul into the system, but apparently this effort was insufficient and did not change the basic fact that the local role decreased while the central role was reinforced. In other words, the concept of Ottomanism did not match the developments on the ground. As a result, the issues of centralization and participation in the government, as well as the language question were to surface once again during the Young Turk period and form the substance of the grievances of rising Arab nationalist feelings.

Nevertheless, the Arabs, generally speaking, continued to believe in the ideal of Ottomanism not only because it provided them with the basis of equality with the Turks but also because they, like many other Ottomans, believed in the absolute necessity of preserving the Empire, both as the last bastion of Islam as well as a barrier in face of foreign pressure, especially French ambitions as regards Syria.[15] As such, it was the best guarantee for their future and the future of their lands.

This genuine attitude towards the Ottoman Empire is reflected at the cultural level. Even before the Young Turk Revolution, there was a growing interest among the Arabs in the history of the Empire and in learning the Ottoman-Turkish language. Many publications on these subjects appeared in Cairo, Beirut and (after the Revolution) also in Damascus. They were a sign that many young Arabs had started to be culturally oriented towards Istanbul, a theme which is not widely known and merits a separate study.

The authors of these books were motivated by the desire to disseminate 'the history of the state to which we belong and are boastful of its glorious deeds'.[16] Many other authors contributed to this effort by writing either concise histories for schools or longer surveys for the general reader.[17] Although earlier Arab historians had taken an interest in the history of the Ottomans this had never been on such a wide scale.

Simultaneously, the interest in learning Ottoman-Turkish grew as well. Several textbooks for teaching the language at schools and for Arab youth were published in Beirut in the last few decades of the nineteenth century. One of the first of these authors was Lewis Sabunji (1838–1928). In his early life he taught Ottoman Turkish at high schools in Beirut. For pedagogical purposes, he translated the *Kavaid-i Osmaniye* [The Grammar of Ottoman Turkish] of Fu'ad and Cevdet Paşas into Arabic. He wrote that he was motivated by his feeling of a growing tendency among Arab youth 'to study the Ottoman language'.[18] Similarly, Yusuf Husni, the teacher of Ottoman at the Sultaniyya high school in Beirut referred to what motivated him to write his grammar book of the Ottoman language. He notes that he decided to write it 'when I noticed that the desire for learning the Ottoman language is widespread in the Syrian districts and its learners are increasing'.[19] It is 'the official language' wrote the school's principal, Mustafa Halki, in a letter to the author, and added that it is greatly needed for understanding the new laws and regulations of the state and for higher education.[20]

To conclude, on the eve of the Young Turk Revolution and soon afterwards, despite policies that were not conducive for the ideal of Ottomanism to reach maturity and take its true course, we find the Arabs, on the whole, believing in it and in the possibility of cooperation on equal terms with the Turks. These Arabs were strong believers in the continuation of the Ottoman Empire and cherished high expectations of the end of despotism and the restoration of Constitutional government. They hoped these developments would usher in freedom of expression and an era of equality. This message was conveyed in the treatises written immediately after the Revolution.

The Arab Immediate Reaction to the Young Turk Revolution

Despite the broad discontent with the rule of Sultan Abdülhamid II among many strata of the inhabitants of the Empire, it was the CUP, composed predominantly of Turks, who succeeded through its middle ranking officers, especially from the Third Army posted in Macedonia, in engineering the Revolution and forcing the Sultan to restore the Constitution and Parliament. Even though the Revolution was not equally received and certain traditional classes were reserved about it,[21] there is strong evidence that it generated a wave of euphoria among the young and educated classes all over the Ottoman lands, not the least in the Arab provinces.[22] Many young men from among the Arab litterateurs, especially from among the exiles in Egypt or Paris, joined the Committee or as it had come to be called: The Party of Union and Progress. Many Arab students in Istanbul joined as well, and soon after the Revolution the Arabs apparently put their faith in the Young Turks in their hopes for a better future.

This feeling of euphoria and willingness to cooperate with the Young Turks among the Arabs was reflected in several publications which appeared soon after the Revolution. Interestingly, Arab historians who discussed the reaction of the Arabs to the Young Turks' policies, such as George Antonius or Zeine N. Zeine, did not refer to any of these publications despite the fact that they expressed the immediate attitude of many Arabs towards the Revolution and the end of the despotic regime.

The Rise of Expectations and the Aspiration for Ottomanism

Soon after the Revolution several Arab intellectuals and journalists, including three Palestinians, Salim Qub'ayn, M. Ruhi al-Khalidi, and Sheikh 'Abdullah al-'Alami, wrote treatises or long essays in praise of the Constitution and freedom which appeared within months after the event. These provide us with a view of the political thinking of these intellectuals and their expectations from the new era.

The first to appear was a short book called *al-Dustur wal-Ahrar* [The Constitution and the Freemen] written by 'The Liberal Ottoman,' as the author, Salim Qub'ayn, described himself.[23] This booklet of sixty-four pages was published in Cairo in August 1908 barely a month after the Revolution.

Qub'ayn's booklet was followed by a book written by Sulaiman al-Bustani named *'Ibra wa-Dhikra aw al-Dawla al-'Uthmaniyya qabla al-Dustur wa-Ba'dahu* [A Lesson and Remembrance or the Ottoman State before the Constitution and after it]. It was published in October 1908 in Cairo as well where the author was residing when the Revolution took place.[24] It was followed by several other publications in addition to many newspaper articles, among which was a long essay by Ruhi al-Khalidi of Jerusalem which appeared in two installments in *al-Hilal* in Cairo in November and December 1908 under the title 'Asbab al-Inqilab al-'Uthmani wa-Turkiyya al-Fatah' [The Reasons of the Ottoman Revolution and Young Turkey]. Simultaneously it was serialized in *al-Manar* in three installments in the issues of volume eleven that appeared at the end of October, November and December 1908.[25] Another treatise was written by Sheikh 'Abdullah al-'Alami of Gaza which he called: *A'zam Tidhkar lil-'Uthmaniyyin al-Ahrar aw al-Hurriyya wal-Musawa wal-Mab'uthan min Ta'alim al-Qur'an* [The Most Significant Commemoration for the Free Ottomans or Freedom, Equality and the Parliament are from the Precepts of the Qur'an].[26] The fifth piece was a book written by a journalist from Aleppo called 'Abdulmasih al-Antaki entitled *Ghayat al-Amani fil-Dustur al-'Uthmani* [The Utmost Aspirations of the Ottoman Constitution]. In it he collected articles from newspapers related to the restoration of the Constitution from the outbreak of the Revolution until the deposition of Sultan Abdülhamid II in April 1909.[27] Antaki left his city Aleppo and immigrated to Cairo to escape the oppression of the authorities. As he tells us, when his 'teacher' 'Abdulrahman al-Kawakibi also escaped to Cairo in 1899, he associated with him there.[28]

These five books and treatises appeared in Cairo, except for the book by 'Alami which was published in Beirut at the very end of 1326/1908. Of these authors, 'Alami was the odd man out. Whereas the others were a diplomat and a historian, a poet and a writer, and two journalists, 'Alami was an *'alim* and a graduate of *al-Azhar*. Nevertheless, they were still all Ottomanists in the sense that they believed in the necessity of the continued existence of the Ottoman Empire and in the equality of all its citizens as well as in the cooperation of all the ethnic groups that inhabited it in running the affairs of the state. What undermined the cooperation and thus the Ottomanist ideal in their eyes was the rise of tyranny and of oppression during the Hamidian era aggravated by the seizing of the real power in the state by the *Mabeyn* [the Secretariat at the Palace which coordinated the contacts between the Sultan and the Sublime Porte].[29]

Salim Qub'ayn of Nazareth was a graduate of the Russian Seminar in his town. He immigrated to Cairo in 1897 escaping the Hamidian oppression. His book is perhaps the least important of these publications. Of journalistic value, it opens with an introduction applauding liberty followed by entries about what he called 'the heroes of the Constitution' starting with a short entry on Sultan Abdülhamid II, who was still on the throne, until April 1909, praising him for restoring it. After that he presents short accounts of Midhat Paşa 'the father of the Constitution [...]',[30] followed by short biographies of Sa'id and Kamil Paşas, two prominent grand viziers of the Hamidian period, and ends with the makers of the Revolution.

Bustani and Khalidi on the other hand, appear to have been members of the Young Turk movement already before the Revolution,[31] and were elected to the Parliament, the *Meclis-i Meb'usan*, which was convened towards the end of 1908. The first represented Beirut and the second Jerusalem. Both were strong believers in the ideal of Ottomanism.

Bustani's book appeared shortly after the Revolution. Not surprisingly it was dedicated to the memory of Midhat Paşa. Sulaiman al-Bustani received his education at *al-Madrasa al-Wataniyya* which was established and directed by his elder kinsman Butrus al-Bustani in Beirut in 1863 and which inspired its students with the ideal of

Ottomanism. After graduation he worked at the newspapers which his kinsman founded in Beirut along with the latter's son Salim and in the later 1870s he helped them edit the Encyclopedia *Da'irat al-Ma'arif*. Having been a poet, he translated into Arabic verse the *Iliad* of Homer, for which he learned ancient Greek. Where necessary he consulted experts on Homer from among the Greek scholars in Istanbul.[32] The translation appeared in Cairo in 1904 with a long introduction by him and immediately placed Bustani among the leading Arab literati of the time.[33]

As mentioned, Sulaiman al-Bustani was brought up on the ideal of Ottomanism. These Arab Ottomanists believed that equality and cooperation between Turks and Arabs and a Constitutional regime were the best guarantee for their future and the future of their countries. As mentioned above, in the early 1870s, in their periodical *al-Jinan* and their other publications the Bustanis, both father and sons, wrote repeatedly in favor of this ideal. For Sulaiman al-Bustani, it remained his political conviction throughout his life. He even went further than his cousins in defending it, as his treatise *'Ibra wa-Dhikra* shows. After the Revolution and the publication of his book he returned to Beirut and was elected as a representative of the city to the Ottoman Parliament.

Like Bustani, Ruhi al-Khalidi was also of Ottomanist convictions. His father Yasin, was the *Başkatib* (chief clerk) of the *shar'i* court of Jerusalem and his uncle Yusuf Ziya was the first mayor of the city and its representative in the first Ottoman Parliament of 1877–8. Like Butrus al-Bustani, the Khalidis were also affiliated with Mehmed Rashid Pasha, the Governor General of the Province of Syria between 1866 and 1871, and through him to the later *Tanzimat* statesmen.[34] Ruhi al-Khalidi acquired his higher education at the *Mülkiye* College in Istanbul, whose graduates were groomed for the civil service. But unwilling to have such a career he ended up in Paris where he first studied Political Science and then at the Sorbonne, Oriental Studies. While still in Paris he was appointed as the Ottoman Consul General at Bordeaux in 1898 where he served for the next ten years. Following the Revolution he was elected as one of the representatives of Jerusalem to Parliament, a position he held until his death in 1913.

In their writings Bustani, Khalidi and Qub'ayn did not directly attack the Sultan who was still the head of the state at the time. Instead they directed their criticism at the *Mabeyn*. Khalidi regarded the usurping of power by the *Mabeyn* as the turning point in the retrogression of the state. According to him the change for worse took place when General Ahmed Cevad Paşa assumed the Grand Vizierate (September 1891- June 1895). At the age of forty, young and inexperienced in governmental affairs he could not withstand the pressure exerted upon him by the *Mabeyn*. As a result, he wrote, 'the center of the government passed to Yıldız Palace and the council of ministers was practically deprived of its powers and the ministers turned simply into executives'. 'The *Mabeyn* became a small but powerful government within a large but weak one'. Most of these officials, he added, were not only corrupt but 'ignorant and stupid',[35] and were responsible for the maladies of the state. Sulaiman al-Bustani agreed with him, and also attributed the corruption in the state and the oppression to the coterie of the *Mabeyn*.[36] In addition, he blamed the secret police (*Hafiye*) who were part of the apparatus of oppression.[37]

While Khalidi, as a historian, analyzed the background of the Revolution starting with the *Tanzimat*, Bustani made the point to provide his readers with the feeling of hope and high expectations in the new era. In his words, with the restoration of the Constitution, 'justice has taken the place of oppression, security has prevailed after fear, and hope replaced despair'.[38] He was sure that equality among all the citizens of the Empire would be the guiding principle of the coming age.[39]

Bustani, moreover, was of the belief that despotism caused the ebbing of national feeling (*wataniyya*). Nevertheless, having been a strong believer in the ideal of Ottomanism he reassured his readers that 'we are still a living nation'.[40] What binds the ethnic elements (*'anasir*) in the Empire together is 'the common interests', and if, in addition, the official language (i.e. Ottoman-Turkish) was disseminated and education expanded, the syllabus unified and the teaching of the history and geography of the Ottoman lands emphasized, then fraternity among all the citizens would be guaranteed.[41] Thus, despite the differences among them, within twenty five years they would become 'one nation' (*umma wahida*).⁴² Indeed, Bustani regarded ethnic and religious fanaticism as the worst enemies of the Empire. Thus, he wrote in another paragraph of his book: 'The best means to diminish ethnic fanaticism is to make learning Turkish compulsory' (in all schools).⁴³ Similarly, 'the best means to reduce religious fanaticism is to conscript the Christians into the army like the Muslims'.⁴⁴ No wonder that high-ranking Turkish officials described Sulaiman al-Bustani as 'the most loyal non-Turk to Turkey [sic.!]'.⁴⁵

In brief, these are the views of leading Arab intellectuals at the time concerning the new era. The Sultan was not seen as responsible for the corruption and tyranny of the Hamidian era but rather the coterie of the *Mabeyn* and the secret service who kept him constantly in fear of the liberals and the enemies of his sultanate and who committed many oppressive acts in his name. The remedy, in the eyes of these intellectuals, was the application of the ideal of Ottomanism.

The Constitution and the *Shari'a*

However, a debate arose among Muslims whether the Constitution was compatible with the *shari'a*, a point examined by both Khalidi and Bustani. For the former, despotism (*istibdad*) was the source of all evil and the cause of backwardness and decline. Despotism, he wrote, 'is of Asian origin and foreign to Islam'.⁴⁶ He continued that Islam introduced 'the first system of laws that vehemently opposed *istibdad* [...] and provided security for the members of the '*umma* and for the *dhimmis* for their property, life and honor'.⁴⁷ Bustani, on the other hand, quoted the incumbent *Şeyh-ül Islam*, Mehmed Cemal'üddin Efendi, who, when was asked by the Sultan to issue a *fetva* [legal opinion] against the insurgents answered: On the contrary 'grant them the Constitution because it is compatible with the honored *shari'a*'.⁴⁸ Bustani emphasized that the highest *shar'i* authority in the state, was also of the opinion that there was no contradiction between the Constitution and the *shari'a*.

The author whose central argument was precisely this point was Sheikh 'Abdullah Salah al-'Alami of Gaza, a descendent of a notable family in the city. From a short biography written by his son

Dr. 'Abdulhalim we learn that he studied at *al-Azhar* for seven years and upon his return in the mid 1880s, started teaching at the central mosque in the city. The method of his teaching, we are told, was to encourage his students to express their views freely within the bounds of rational thinking and the *shari'a*. It attracted many students to his classes and led his son to claim that he laid the foundations for the city's cultural revival and that he was 'the *mujaddid* of the views of *Salaf al-Umma al-Salih*'.[49] In another biography written by Sheikh 'Uthman al-Tabba', a contemporary *'alim* from Gaza, 'Alami is described as 'having been fond of reading [...] modern and foreign books'.[50] We do not know whether he knew any other language except Arabic, but his son informs us that his father specialized in *tafsir* (Qur'an exegesis) and 'in refuting the views of the missionaries' and that for this reason 'he studied the Bible and the Gospel'.[51] At any rate, perhaps due to his having had *salafi* tendencies or to the fact that his courses attracted many students, al-'Alami was shunned by certain *'ulema* of Gaza, some of whom were his own teachers. At a certain stage, he was forced to leave the city and went back to al-Azhar. After a year he made his peace with his teachers and returned to Gaza. A little later we find him opening a drugstore to earn his living though apparently not for long. Finally, he left the city in 1902 and immigrated to Beirut where he taught Arabic at the Vocational School (*Maktab al-Sana'i*). He was still there when the Revolution broke out and the Constitution was restored.

Al-'Alami wrote his book *A'zam Tidhkar* soon after the Revolution. He printed and published it in Beirut at the very end of 1908, later than the publication of Bustani's and Khalidi's books. In a book review by M. Kurd 'Ali in the Damascene monthly *al-Muqtabas*, it was stated that 'its author wrote it when he realized that many of the common people (*al-'amma*) expressed doubts whether the Parliament or liberty are compatible with the *shari'a*'.[52] *Al-Muqtataf* which also presented a review of the book stated that 'it is an important book in which its author proved [...] that liberty and the councils of *shura* are in accord with the *shari'a*'. 'Alami, continued the reviewer, tried to prove his views by quoting twelve verses from the Qur'an.[53] On the other hand strangely enough, there is no reference to the book in *al-Manar* despite the fact that the theme of the book was relevant to its topic.

Two main themes discussed by 'Alami in the book interest us here. The first was Ottomanism and the second the compatibility of the Constitution with the *shari'a*. Like the other authors discussed above, 'Alami was a strong believer in Ottomanism, the components of which in his view were absolute equality, unity and brotherhood between all Ottoman citizens. In the new age, he argued, there should be no differentiation between citizens. In his eyes, to say that a Turk is distinguished in any way from an Arab or a Muslim from a non-Muslim is unacceptable. They are all Ottomans no matter which ethnic group or religious community they belonged to: 'Equality has become their motto as we learn from the verses of the honored Qur'an'.[54] Moreover, by 'uniting the Ottoman *umma* [sic!] its significance is enhanced and its existence safeguarded'.[55] Moreover, he called for the cooperation of all Ottoman citizens in the service of the homeland (*watan*) and the state, non-Muslims included as long as 'they did not come out against us or demonstrate hostility towards us'.[56] All Ottomans are 'brethren' in the service of the state and the homeland. 'We are all brethrens in citizenship and in enjoying [the protection of] the Constitution'.[57] Only unity, fraternity and equality would guarantee the future of our country and state.[58] Finally, he praised the CUP for overturning the despotic government and changing it into a constitutional one.[59] Such statements coming from an *'alim* show to what extent 'Alami was enlightened and ahead of his time.

'Alami tells us, moreover, that he wrote his treatise because many common people wondered whether the Parliament was in accordance with the *shari'a*. In his answer he cites twelve verses from the Quran to prove that it was so,[60] and added that authority in Islam 'is bound by the religious law and by the *shura*'.[61] Even the Messenger of God was required to resort to consultation as the Qur'an commands (*wa-shawirhum fil-amr*).[62] He concluded that consultation and the convening of the *Mab'usan* Assembly were an absolute necessity. They derive their legitimacy from the Qur'an and do not contradict the *shari'a*.[63]

In other words, 'Alami was totally against despotism. Like Ruhi al-Khalidi, he was of the belief that it was the cause of much evil.[64] In his own words: 'We were prevented from freedom of expression and freedom of thought. The lower officials were our overlords before the higher ones'.[65] In Islam he added 'rulers should not have absolute power [...] but should be subject to the *shari'a* or to laws based on the *shari'a*'.[66] Our freedom, he concluded, which was guaranteed by *Qur'anic* law was denied to us formerly, but now we have regained it through the Constitution.[67]

Such views of Sheikh 'Abdullah al-'Alami were undoubtedly received with favor among the literati. But his views along with commentaries which he used to write for a weekly in Beirut made him unpopular among certain circles in the city.[68] For this reason he preferred to return to Gaza where he was appointed deputy Mayor of the city and later an inspector in the Department of Education. Finally, just before the British occupied Gaza in 1917 he left for Damascus and lived there until his death in 1936.

Conclusion

The treatises examined in this chapter illustrate what certain Arab thinkers advocated soon after the Young Turk Revolution. They were strong believers in the Ottomanist ideal which in their eyes was the best guarantee for preserving the unity of the Empire. Indeed, in the circumstances it was the best political alternative for their lands. Nevertheless these publications have been neglected by historians exploring the relations between the Arabs and the Young Turks and the rise of the Arab national movement after the Revolution such as George Antonius, Zeine N. Zeine or others who wrote in Arabic. Indeed, the ideas and principles advocated in these treatises proved soon afterwards to be an illusion. Instead of the euphoria there came frustration, instead of Ottomanism there came Turkish nationalism, and the hope for equality and fraternity faded away. Thus these treatises were soon irrelevant and had no place in the narrative of the Arab national movement which emerged soon after and which was the theme of these Arab historians mentioned above. At any rate, these treatises represented a trend of political and social thought which testifies to the immediate reaction of Arab Ottomanists to the restoration of the Constitution and the Parliament in the Empire.

Notes

1. Davison, Roderic H., *Reform in the Ottoman Empire 1856–1876* (Princeton, 1963), p. 56.
2. Ibid., p. 243.
3. Ibid., p. 263.
4. Yerlikaya, İlhan, *Basiret Gazetesi* [The Newspaper Basiret] (Van, 1994), pp. 149, 153 [in Turkish].
5. 'Osmalılık sıfatı' [Ottoman Traits], *Basiret* 117, 12 Rebiyülahir, 1287 [12 July 1870] [in Turkish].
6. 'İttihad-i Osmanı' [The Ottoman Union], *Basiret,* issue no.130, 29 Rebiyülahir 1287 [29 July 1870]; Yerlikaya: *Basiret Gazetesi*, pp. 109–113, 168–170.
7. Davison: *Reform in the Ottoman Empire,* pp. 361–4; See also Somel, Selcuk Akşin, 'Osmanlı reform çağında osmanlıcılık düşüncesi (1839–1913)' [Ottomanism Thought in the Ottoman Reform Period], in Alkan, Mehmet O. (ed.), *Tanzimat ve Meşrutiyet'in Birikimi* [The Formation of the Reforms and the Constitution] (Istanbul, 2001), pp. 88–116 [in Turkish]; Özcan, Azmi, 'Osmanlıcılık' [Ottomanism], *TDV Islam Ansiklopedisi*, vol. 33 (2007), pp. 485–7 [in Turkish].
8. 'Devlet-i Osmaniyye tabiiyetinde bulunan efradin cumlesine herhangi din ve mezhebte olursa olsun bila istisna osmanlı tabir olunur'; see also Somel, 'Osmanlı reform', p. 105 ff.; and Doganalp-Votzi, Heidemarie, 'The state and its subjects according to the 1876 Ottoman Constitution: Some lexicographic aspects', in Kieser, Hans-Lukas (ed.), *Aspects of the Political Language in Turkey, 19th-20th Century* (Istanbul, 2002), p. 61, p. 69.
9. Al-Maqdisi, Anis, *Al-Ittijahat al-Adabiyya fil-'Alam al-'Arabi al-Hadith* [The Literary Currents in the Modern Arab World], third edition, (Beirut, 1963), pp. 20–21 [in Arabic]; al-Sulh, 'Imad, *Ahmad Faris al-Shidyaq: Atharuhu wa-'Asruhu* [Ahmad Faris al-Shidyaq: His Work and His Period] (Beirut, 1980) pp. 235–6 [in Arabic].
10. On Khalil Khuri and *Hadiqat al-Akhbar*, see Bawardi, Basilius, 'First steps in writing Arabic narrative fiction: The case of Hadiqat al-Akhbar', *Die Welt des Islam* vol. 48 (2008), pp. 170–195; Zachs, Fruma, *The Making of a Syrian Identity: Intellectuals and Merchants in Nineteenth Century Beirut* (Brill, 2005), pp. 228–9.

11. Abu-Manneh, Butrus, 'The Christians between Ottomanism and Syrian Nationalism: The ideas of Butrus al-Bustani', *International Journal of Middle East Studies* vol. 11 (1980), pp. 287–304.
12. Jeha, Michel, *Farah Anton* (Beirut, 1998) pp. 40–41 (a quotation from the preamble of the first issue of *al-Jami'a al-'Uthmaniyya* published in Alexandriya on 15 March 1899) [in Arabic]; Reid, D. M., *The Odyssey of Farah Anton* (Minneapolis and Chicago, 1975), pp. 101–103.
13. Findley, Carter V., *Ottoman Civil Officialdom a Social History* (Princeton, 1989), pp. 266, 269, 281; Findley uses the phrase 'undermining Tanzimat egalitarianism'.
14. Abu-Manneh, Butrus, 'The later Tanzimat and the Ottoman legacy in the Near Eastern successor states', in Mansour, Camille and Leila Fawaz (eds.), *Transformed Landscape Essays {...} in Honour of Walid Khalidi* (Cairo, 2009), pp. 61–81.
15. Maqdisi: *Al-Ittijahat al-Adabiyya*, p. 119; Arsalan, Shakib, *Sira Dhatiyya* [Autobiography] (Beirut, 1969), pp. 69–70, 106–7 [in Arabic]; Kayali, Hasan, *The Arabs and the Young Turks*, p. 70 (Berkeley, 1997); Tauber, Eliezer, *The Emergence of the Arab Movements* (London, 1993), pp. 121–2; *al-Manar*, XI (1909), p. 937.
16. Al-Hanbali, Shakir, *Al-Ta'rikh al-'Uthmani al-Musawwar* [The Illustrated Ottoman History] (Damascus, 1331/[1913]), p. 2 [in Arabic].
17. For instance, see the works of: Ibrahim al-Ahdab, Haqqi al-Azm, 'Abd al-Qadir al-Dana, Muhammad Hilal, Ibrahim Hilmi, Husein Labib, Muhammad Fareed and others.
18. Sabunji, Lewis, *Al-Mir'a al-Saniyya fil-Qawa'id al-'Uthmaniyya* [The Exalted Mirror in Ottoman Grammar] (Beirut, 1867), p. 3 [in Arabic].
19. Husni, Yusuf, *Al-Idahat al-Jallyya fi Qawa'id al-Lugha al-'Uthmaniyya* [Plain Clarifications of the Rules of the Ottoman Language] (Beirut, second impression, 1885), pp. 3, 9–10 [in Arabic].
20. See the letter by Mustafa Halki, the school's principal to the author, pp. 9–10.
21. Kedourie, Elie, 'The impact of the Young Turk Revolution in the Arabic speaking provinces of the Ottoman Empire', in Kedourie, Elie, *Arabic Political Memoirs and other Studies* (London, 1974), pp. 124–61, see pp. 129ff.
22. Al-Husri, Sati', *Al-Bilad al-'Arabiyya wal-Dawla al-'Uthmaniyya* [The Arab Lands and the Ottoman Empire] (Beirut, 1965), pp.109, 126 [in Arabic]; Barru, Tawfiq, *Al-Arab wal-Turk fil-'Ahd al-Dusturi al-'Uthmani 1908–1914* [The Arabs and Turks during the Ottoman Constitution Period, 1908–1914] (Damascus, 1991), pp. 81–3 [in Arabic].
23. On Salim Qub'ayn see Abu Hanna, Hanna, *Tala'i' al-Nahda fi Filastin: Khirriju al-Madaris al-Rusiyya 1862–1914* [The Pioneers of the Revival of

Arabic Language and Culture in Palestine: The Graduates of the Russian Schools], (Beirut, 2005), pp. 147–8 [in Arabic]; al-'Awdat, Ya'aqub, *Min A'lam al-Fikr wal-Adab fi Filastin* [Prominent Figures of Thought and Literature in Palestine], Third Impression (Jerusalem, 1992), pp. 512–4 [in Arabic].

24. On Sulaiman al-Bustani see al-Bustani, Fu'ad Afram, 'Sulaiman al-Bustani [...]', *al-Mashriq*, XXIII (1925), pp. 778–91, 824–43, 908–925; Baz, Gorgi Niqola, 'Sulaiman al-Bustani' in de Tarrazi, Filip (ed.), *Ta'rikh al-Sahafa al-'Arabiyya* [The History of Arab Press] , vol. 2, (Beirut, 1913), pp. 159–68 [in Arabic]; Hourani, Albert, 'Sulayman al-Bustani (1856–1925)', in Seikaly, Samir, R. Baalbaki, and P. Dodd (eds.), *Quest for Understanding: Arabic and Islamic Studies in Memory of Malcolm H. Kerr* (Beirut, 1991), pp. 43–57.

25. On Ruhi al-Khalidi see al-Asad, Nasir al-Din, *Ruhi al-Khalidi Ra'id al-Bahth al-Ta'rikhi al-Hadith fi Filastin* [Ruhi al-Khalidi the Pioneer of Modern Historical Research in Palestine] (Cairo, 1970), see pp. 35–64 [in Arabic]. See also Khalidi, Rashid, *Palestinian Identity: The Construction of a Modern National Consciousness*, 2nd ed., (New York, 2009), pp. 76–87.

26. On Sheikh 'Abdullah al-'Alami see a short biography by his son 'Abdulhalim al-'Alami in al-'Alami, 'Abdullah, *Salasil al-Munazara al-Islamiyya al-Nasraniyya* [The Series of Islamic – Christian Disputation] (Damascus, 1390/1970–71), pp. a-d [in Arabic]; al-Tabba', 'Uthman, *Ithaf al-A'izza fi Ta'rikh Ghazza* [Presenting the Notables in the History of Gaza], edited by Abu-Hashim, 'Abdullatif Z. (Gaza, 1999), vol.4, pp. 400–405 [in Arabic].

27. On 'Abdulmasih al-Antaki see al-Kayyali, Sami, *Al-Adab al-'Arabi al-Mu'asir fi Suriyya 1850–1950* [The Contemporary Arab Literature in Syria 1850–1950] (Cairo, 1968), pp. 181–6 [in Arabic]; *al-Mashriq*, XXV (1927), p. 116; See also Sarkis, Yusuf I., *Mu'jam al-Matbu'at al-'Arabiyya wal-Mu'arraba* [Lexicon of Arab and Arabized Printed [Books]] (Cairo, 1928). p. 493 [in Arabic].

28. Kayyali: *Al-Adab al-'Arabi*, p. 182.

29. The *Mabeyn* was an office in the Palace that coordinated the connection between the Sultan and the Sublime Porte. See Pakalın, Mehmed Z., *Osmanlı Tarih Deyimleri ve Terimleri Sözlüğü* [Dictionary of Ottoman Historical Idioms and Terms] (Istanbul, 1946–53), vol. 2, pp. 375–7 [in Turkish].

30. Qub'ayn, Salim, *Al-Dustur wal-Ahrar* [The Constitution and the Liberals] (Cairo, 1908), pp. 26–34.

31. *Al-Hilal*, XVII (1908), p. 67; al-Asad: *Ruhi al-Khalidi*, p. 59.

32. Al-Bustani, Sulaiman, *Iliyadhat Humirus* [The Iliad of Homer] (Cairo, 1904), pp. 70–72 [in Arabic]; Hourani: 'Suleyman al-Bustani', p. 48.

33. Maqdisi: *Al-Ittijahat al-Adabiyya,* pp. 372–3.

34. On Yusuf Ziya al-Khalidi see Schölch, Alexander, *Palestine in Transformation, 1856–1882: Studies in Social, Economic and Political Development* (Washington, 1993), pp. 241–52.
35. *al-Hilal*, XVII (December, 1908), pp. 150–57.
36. Al-Bustani, Sulaiman, *'Ibra wa-Dhikra, aw al-Dawla al-'Uthmaniyya Qabla al-Dustur wa-Ba'dahu* [A Lesson and Remembrance, or the Ottoman State before the Constitution and after it] (Cairo, 1908), pp. 19, 64 [in Arabic].
37. Ibid., pp. 64, 83–9.
38. Ibid., p. 82.
39. Ibid., p. 98.
40. Ibid., p. 197.
41. Ibid., pp. 38–9, 98; *al-Mashriq*, XXIII (1925) pp. 910–11; Zaydan, G. in *al-Hilal*, XVII (1908), p. 816.
42. al-Bustani: *'Ibra wa-Dhikra*, pp. 200–201.
43. Ibid., pp. 98, 200; Barru: *al-Arab wal-Turk*, p. 77; Hourani: 'Suleyman al-Bustani', p. 52; on the other hand his compatriot Rashid Rida the publisher and editor of *al-Manar* called for Arabic to be the common language of the Ottoman Empire as it is the language of Islam. See *al-Manar* I, pp. 769–71; III, p. 194.
44. al-Bustani, *'Ibra wa Dhikra*, pp. 98, 200; Barru: *al-Arab wal-Turk*, p. 77.
45. According to Fu'ad Afram al-Bustani in *al-Mashriq*, XXIII (1925), p. 919.
46. *al-Hilal*, XVII (1908), p. 69.
47. Ibid., pp. 69, 76.
48. Al-Bustani: *'Ibra wa-Dhikra*, pp. 99–100; a similar version in a different context is related in the memoirs of the Şeyh-ül Islam. See Cemalüddin, Mehmed, *Hatirat-i Siyasiyesi* [His] Political Memoirs] (Der Saadet [Istanbul], 1336/[1917–8]), p. 4 [in Ottoman Turkish]. On him see *İlmiyye Salnamesi* [The Yearbook of High Officials Holding Religious Duties] (Istanbul, 1334 [1915/6]), pp. 615–6 [in Ottoman Turkish].
49. See the biography by his son in n. 26, p.a.
50. Al-Tabba': *Ithaf al-A'izza*, vol. 4, pp. 400–405.
51. As in n. 26, p.b.
52. *Al-Muqtabas*, vol. 2 (1909), p. 136.
53. *Al-Muqtataf*, vol. 34 (June 1909), p. 599.
54. Al-'Alami, *A'zam tidhkar lil-'Uthmaniyyin al-Ahrar aw al-Hurriyya wal-Musawa wal-Mab'uthan min Ta'alim al-Qur'an* [The Most Significant Commemoration for the Free Ottomans, or Freedom, Equality and the Parliament are from the Precepts of the Qur'an] (Beirut, 1326/1908), pp. 47–62, especially p. 54 [in Arabic].
55. Ibid., p. 62.

56. Ibid., p. 63.
57. Ibid., pp. 63, 68–9.
58. Ibid., pp. 66–9.
59. Ibid., p. 72.
60. Ibid., pp. 2, 4, 6–27.
61. Ibid., pp. 11, 34.
62. Ibid., pp. 7–8 and 33–4.
63. Ibid., pp. 10, 24.
64. Ibid., pp. 30, 32.
65. Ibid., p. 31.
66. Ibid., p. 34.
67. Ibid., p. 45.
68. His son's biography in n. 26 and al-Tabba': *Ithaf al-A'izza,* vol.4, pp. 404–5.

CHAPTER 9

JEWS WRITING IN ARABIC: SHIMON MOYAL, NISSIM MALUL AND THE MIXED PALESTINIAN/ERETZ ISRAELI LOCALE

ABIGAIL JACOBSON

Introduction

On June 15 1915, a long eulogy appeared on the front page of the Hebrew newspaper *ha-Herut*,[1] mourning the passing of Dr. Shimon Moyal: 'Those who did not know Dr. Moyal personally, who did not talk with him about the Israeli people (*ha-'am ha-yisra'eli*), his wishes and dreams, those who did not know what a warm Hebrew heart (*lev 'ivri ham*) this man had – would not be able to understand the loss suffered by Palestinian Jews (*yahadut falestinit*) and in particular the Sephardi community', wrote the prominent Sephardi-Maghrebi activist Avraham Elmalech at the beginning of the eulogy. The eulogy continued to describe Moyal's life and career as a writer and physician who lived and studied in Beirut, Cairo and Jaffa, his writing in the Egyptian and Palestinian press, and his public work 'for the benefit of his people', as Elmalech put it.[2]

In this paper, I would like to focus on Shimon Moyal and his colleague, Nissim Malul, and examine, through their life and work, what

I view as the joint locale in late Ottoman Palestine/Eretz Israel. Moyal and Malul were both Ottoman Jewish subjects of Maghrebi origin, fluent in Arabic and well integrated and involved in the cultural and political life of the Arab *Mashriq*. They were both enthusiastic though critical Zionists, writers and activists in various organizations in Palestine and Greater Syria, who possessed a Mediterranean-Levantine multi-faceted cosmopolitan identity that challenged the growing political, linguistic and cultural divides between Jews and Arabs.[3] This is reflected to some extent in the terms Elmalech chose to describe Moyal: *Yisra'eli* (Israeli), *'ivri* (Hebrew), *yahadut falestinit* (Palestinian Jews), that all emphasize different geographic, national and cultural affiliations. By examining Moyal and Malul's writings, public activism and cultural involvement, I would like to argue that they represent a complex, somewhat ambivalent and nuanced identity that bridges the divides between Jews and Arabs. As this article demonstrates, Moyal and Malul's lives were intertwined in various circles – Arabic, Ottoman, Sephardi and Zionist – that coincided and overlapped, and formed their larger Levantine-Mediterranean identity. All of these circles blended and existed side by side during the vibrant period of the Young-Turk Revolution, in the mixed Palestinian/Eretz Israeli locale of pre-World War I Palestine. Among other things, it was the thriving press, the lively debates within it, the political discussions regarding the links between the Ottoman Empire and its provinces and the activities of various associations and organizations in Palestine and elsewhere that created an atmosphere that enabled the emergence of such personalities.

Cairo, Beirut and Jaffa – Levantine Biographies

The biographies of Moyal and Malul can in many ways account for their special position vis-à-vis the geo-political situation, the evolving national tensions between Jews and Arabs in Palestine, and their special place in the Arab *Mashriq*. It is also not surprising that they lived and worked in three of the most cosmopolitan cities of the Eastern Mediterranean at the time: Cairo, Beirut and Jaffa.

Dr. Shimon Moyal was born in Jaffa in 1866 to Yosef Moyal. His grandfather, Aharon Moyal, brought his family from Rabat to

Palestine in 1853 and settled in Jaffa. Moyal's education took him to Jaffa, Cairo and Beirut. He received a religious education through age sixteen, when he was sent to Beirut to study Arabic and French. He then moved to Cairo to study at al-Azhar University, where he became part of the intellectual milieu gravitating around Muhammad 'Abduh. He returned to Beirut to study medicine at the Jesuit College, and met a Jewish woman named Esther Azhari, a fascinating figure who was a writer, translator and feminist, active in various women and feminist organizations.[4]

Moyal and Azhari got engaged in 1893 and married in 1894. They moved to Istanbul where Moyal graduated from medical school. He then worked as a physician in Safed and Tiberias in northern Palestine for a while, but his real passion was in writing and intellectual pursuits. In 1899 the Moyals moved to Cairo, where their son 'Abdallah Nadim was born. They were integrated into the circle of Syrian intellectuals, and began writing in different Egyptian newspapers, preaching for a better understanding between the 'people of the east' and between Jews and Arabs. Moyal began to translate the Babylonian Talmud into Arabic, and Esther established a women's literary journal called *al-'A'ila* [The Family] and was also engaged in literary translations from French to Arabic, including some of Emile Zola's works.[5]

Motivated by the developing Jewish national effort in Palestine they moved back to Jaffa in 1908. Upon their return to Palestine the Moyals became integrated into the Sephardi intellectual milieu of Jaffa and Jerusalem. In 1909 Moyal finished translating excerpts from the Babylonian Talmud into Arabic, and in 1913 they fulfilled their dream and established a Jewish-Arab newspaper called *Sawt al-'Uthmaniyya* [The Voice of Ottomanism]. In an attempt to rebut Arab attacks on Zionism in the Palestinian Arabic press in the period before World War I, Shimon and Esther Moyal, together with some other Sephardi Jews, set up an organization called *ha-Magen* [The Shield] in 1913 whose goal was to respond to articles against Zionism published in the Arabic press, and to translate articles from Arabic into Hebrew. One of its goals was to promote a better understanding between Jews and Arabs in Palestine, and to encourage peaceful existence with the Arabs residing in the country.[6]

The biography of Nissim Malul's reads in many ways like that of Moyal. Nissim Ya'akov Malul was born in Safed in 1892 to a family that originally had come to Palestine from Tunisia some 200 years earlier. When he was a child the family moved to Egypt, where his father became Rabbi to the Jewish communities of Cairo and Tanta. Malul studied in Jewish schools in Cairo, and completed his higher education at the American College in Tanta, where he studied philosophy, Arabic literature and journalism. During this time he started publishing pieces in the Egyptian newspaper *al-Muqattam*, and tried to promote the status of Hebrew in Egyptian universities. Following a series of publications, he became the first Hebrew lecturer to be appointed to an Egyptian university.

In 1911 he returned to Palestine and started working for the *Eretz Israeli* Office, the Zionist office in Jaffa headed by Dr. Arthur Ruppin. His main role, as will be discussed below, was to respond to the anti-Zionist articles which were published mainly in the Palestinian newspapers *Filastin* and *al-Karmil*. He was fluent in Arabic, and his articles were published in other newspapers in Egypt and Lebanon as well. He was also involved in the publication of *Sawt al-'Uthmaniyya* and with the *ha-Magen* association. During World War I Malul was exiled to Damascus by the Ottomans, because of his suspected anti-Ottoman activities, as well as his involvement in *ha-Magen* and the *al-Lamarkaziyya* party.[7] He escaped to Egypt and remained there until the end of the war, where he became one of the officers of the Hebrew Battalion set up by the British, and served as a translator for the British Command. Following the British occupation of Palestine he returned there and founded two Arabic newspapers, *al-Akhbar* and later *al-Salam*, both funded by the Zionist movement with the aim of explaining the aims and activities of the movement, and preached in favor of Jewish-Arab understanding. Between 1922 and 1925 he became a member of the Zionist National Committee and later participated in the Arabic workers' newspaper *Ittihad al-'Ummal* [Union of Workers]. In 1927 he moved to Baghdad where he served as the principal of a Jewish school near Baghdad. He published various essays in Arabic, including two plays, and translated from Arabic to Hebrew. Malul passed away in 1959.[8]

Upon their return from Cairo in 1908 and 1911, Moyal and Malul respectively became part of several interrelated circles. The first was that of the *Eretz Israeli* Zionist office in Jaffa, the second was the Sephardi / Ottoman circle of the Sephardi young intelligentsia in Jaffa and Jerusalem, and the third was the Arab circle. All their activities at this period, right after the Young-Turk Revolution, can be characterized as an attempt to overcome the growing gaps and tensions between Jews and Arabs in the country, mainly (but not solely) by writing and publishing translated articles in the local Arabic and Hebrew newspapers such as *Filastin, ha-Herut, al-Manar* and *al-Muqattam*, among others.

The Sephardi-Ottoman Circle

Both Moyal and Malul viewed proficiency in Arabic among Jews in Palestine as *the* key to a better entente between Jews and Arabs. They emphasized the commonalities between Jews and Muslims, and viewed Christian Arabs as inciting national tension and hatred towards Jews and Zionists. Moyal, through the *ha-Magen* association, engaged in political activity that was opposed to the two Christian-owned newspapers published in Palestine at the time, *Filastin* and *al-Karmil*, all the while actively trying to expose the readers of these newspapers to the 'real intentions' of the Jews, and the possibility of working together for the advancement of Palestine. One of the major themes in his articles was the potential for cooperation between Palestinian Jews and Muslims. This was expressed in the framework of loyalty to the Ottoman homeland, *al-Watan*. Both Moyal and Malul viewed Sephardi Jews, who were familiar with the language and culture of the Arabs and lived among them, as go-betweens between Jews and Arabs, and as promoters of mutual understanding. The two of them worked in cooperation with the Zionist office in Jaffa, but also criticized some of the Zionists' policies towards the Arabs. Their ability to view both the Zionist and the Arab nationalist perspectives enabled them to operate between these two worlds, even though it is clear that their loyalty was always to the Jewish cause.

The issue of language was crucial for both Moyal and Malul. In the pages of the Sephardi newspaper *ha-Herut*, as well as in correspondence with the Zionist activists in Jaffa, they emphasized the importance of Arabic as a language that would connect the Jews to the land and its people. This went hand in hand with the call to express loyalty to the Ottoman homeland and learn the language of the country in order to demonstrate such loyalty and become actively part of its political framework.

Nissim Malul's three-part essay, published in June 1913 in *ha-Herut*, illustrates some of these issues.[9] Malul responded to a criticism against him in the Zionist workers' paper *ha-Po'el ha-Tza'ir*, and to some Ashkenazi Zionists' critics who feared that by learning Arabic and assimilating with the 'locals' (*anshei ha-aretz*), the Jews would lose their nationalist sentiments and fervor. In his article Malul argued that if the Jews wanted to settle in Palestine they had to learn Arabic, the language spoken in the country. He also argued that language is not a major component of one's national identity: 'There is no necessary condition for the nationalist to know his language [*sic*! The editor]. The nationalist is a nationalist in his national feeling, but not his language [*sic*! The editor], the nationalist is a nationalist by his national acts'.[10] Hence, national consciousness is demonstrated by actions, not by the language spoken by the people, according to Malul. Malul ends his third essay by claiming that 'We should know Arabic well and assimilate with the Arabs [*sic*! The editor][...] as a Semitic nation we should ground our Semitic nationalism and not blur it with European culture; with Arabic we will be able to create a real Hebrew culture'.[11]

This was a unique view, in complete contrast to most Zionist thinking of the time which considered that the revival of the Hebrew language was clearly connected to national revival. However, it also differed from *ha-Herut*'s own line as well. The newspaper's editor added a brief comment at the end of Malul's essay, stressing his belief that Arabic should be taught and used among the Jewish inhabitants of Palestine, but only as a second language.[12]

One of the issues that Moyal and Malul tried to promote the most, both in the pages of *ha-Herut* as well as in their correspondence with the Zionist leadership in Jaffa, was the idea of a Jewish-Arab newspaper, which would reach out to the Palestinian Arabs in their own language. The publication of such a newspaper was discussed often in *ha-Herut*. The editor of *ha-Herut*, Haim Ben-'Attar, suggested, for example, that such a newspaper would be published by a Muslim assisted by Nissim Malul. A Jewish-Arab newspaper, it was argued, would serve to prove the patriotism of the Jews toward the Ottoman Empire, the homeland: 'We should bring our Muslim neighbors closer to us by showing and proving to them how loyal and dedicated we are to our dear Ottoman homeland'. The Zionist leaders, however, apparently ignored the urgent need for the publication of such a paper.[13]

Moyal and Malul concretized their ideological beliefs in two main ways. The first was the publication of a daily Arabic newspaper, *Sawt al-'Uthmaniyya*, which was founded in Jaffa in 1913 and ceased to exist following the outbreak of World War I in 1914. The Moyals viewed this newspaper as a tool to respond to anti-Zionist criticism in the Arabic press and invested much money and energy in its publication. It also reflected their stand vis-à-vis the Ottoman Empire, and stressed their loyalty to it. According to Avraham Elmalech, *Sawt al-'Uthmaniyya* was distributed in Haifa and Jaffa, and Moyal also sent copies to Beirut and Syria.[14] Although *Sawt al-'Uthmaniyya* was a short-lived attempt to fulfill the dream of an Arab-Jewish newspaper, it was part of the larger and lively debate among Sephardi intellectuals regarding relations with the Arabs, the status of Arabic, and the response to the attacks on Zionism in the Arab press.[15]

The second practical manifestation of Moyal and Malul's ideology regarding relations with the Arabs was the founding in April 1914 of a new association called *ha-Magen*. This association was set up in Jaffa by representatives of prominent Sephardi and Maghrebi families such as Nissim Malul, Shimon and Esther Moyal, Avraham Elmalech, David Moyal, Yosef Amzalek, Yosef Eliyahu Chelouche, Ya'akov Chelouche, Moshe Matalon, David Hivan and Yehoshua Elkayam.[16]

Avraham Elmalech, the secretary of *ha-Magen*, described the background of the organization in its founding manifesto. It was established following attacks on the *yishuv* in the Arab press, which came despite Jewish attempts and hopes to work side by side with the Arabs for the advancement and development of Palestine, 'the shared homeland' (*ha-moledet ha-meshutefet*).[17] While realizing that something needed to be done against these attacks, wrote Elmalech:

> We, the Sephardim, who know the language of the country and who read this poisonous press daily, we who know the Arab people with whom we are living, who start feeling the change [in it] for the worst [...] we realized that we cannot sit silently while such a great danger threatens the entire *yishuv*.[18]

The overarching objective of *ha-Magen* was to 'defend by all kosher and legal means our status in the land'. More specifically, however, it had both internal and external goals. It aimed internally to strengthen the ties between Jews and the rest of the inhabitants of the country and the government primarily by targeting the Hebrew, Arabic and Turkish press. Here it planned to translate articles that focused on Jews into Hebrew, and encouraged people to respond to the articles that appeared in the Arabic and Turkish press and publish articles that could improve the relationship between Jews and Arabs in Palestine. *Ha-Magen* also wanted to influence the Arabic and Turkish press by increasing their readership and the numbers of their subscribers and improving their style and content.

Externally, the association aimed to secure full civic and political rights for Jews, including voting rights in municipalities and the Ottoman parliament. To achieve this goal, *ha-Magen* put forward the goal of translating all the governmental laws into Hebrew, so that everyone would know their rights and duties. The association hoped to bring Jews and Arabs together by establishing a joint literary club, and encouraged the publication of essays on Judaism and Islam to contribute to good relations between the two peoples.[19]

In many ways, *ha-Magen* exemplified the vision of the young Sephardi intelligentsia, including Malul and Moyal, as regards the Arabs in Palestine. Its platform was joint ownership of Palestine by both Jews and Arabs, and shared responsibility between them.[20] This emerges clearly from Elmalech's choice of words in the founding manifesto, 'their country – our country', and later 'the joint homeland'. The special role of the Sephardim is demonstrated here as well. They were viewed as those who could serve as the link between Jews and Arabs in Palestine, thanks to their knowledge of Arabic. The Sephardim truly felt they belonged to both worlds and could serve as a bridge between them.[21] The association, however, had limited power and influence. It operated only one branch, in Jaffa, and ceased its activity at the beginning of World War I.

The Zionist Circle

Although Moyal and Malul differed in their political orientations and connections to the Zionist movement, during the pre-War years they were both involved in its activities as writers and translators from Arabic. Moyal died in 1915, and much of Malul's political activity took place after World War I.

Nissim Malul started working in the Arab department of the Zionist office upon his return from Cairo in 1911, at the request of Dr. Arthur Ruppin. At a time when many articles opposing Zionist immigration and land purchase were being published in the Arabic press, mainly in the Palestinian newspapers *Filastin* and *al-Karmil*, but also in other newspapers in Damascus, Cairo and Beirut, Malul's main role was to respond to these articles and translate articles from Arabic to Hebrew. His job had two main objectives: first, to expose the Arabs to (what the Zionists viewed as) the advantages of Zionist activity to Palestine and secondly, to make the Zionists aware of what was written about them in the Arabic press. As a member of the Decentralist party in Egypt, he also brought news from the party to the attention of his Hebrew readers.

After returning to Palestine following World War I, Malul founded two Arabic newspapers, *al-Akhbar* and later *al-Salam*, both of which were funded by the Zionist movement, and published pro-Zionist articles in Arabic. *Al-Salam* was first published in Cairo, and then in Jaffa, Haifa and Jerusalem. The newspaper apparently suffered from constant lack of funding, as Malul kept requesting financial aid from the Zionist administration. In its heyday, the newspaper appeared twice or three times a week, and was sent free of charge to influential Arab figures in Palestine, Syria, Egypt, the Hejaz and Transjordan. Its annual budget was more than 1500 Liras. As proof of the newspaper's wide and influential circulation among Arab leaders, Malul mentioned the correspondence between the editorial board of the newspaper, and the Hashemite King Faisal and Emir 'Abdallah throughout the years.[22]

From 1922 to 1925 Malul was a member of the Zionist National Committee and later edited the Arabic newspaper *Ittihad al-'Ummal*, published by the *Histadrut*, the Jewish Workers' Union. His work on the newspaper, which represented the rights of Jewish and Arab workers alike, is considered the peak of his public and journalistic career.[23]

In addition to his journalistic work, Malul also reported to the Zionist leadership on the events taking place among the Arabs in Palestine. For example, in a report dated 27 February 1920, entitled 'the fake nationalist demonstration', he reported on a demonstration in Jaffa against the British policy toward the Zionist movement. He quoted from the speeches, including the Maronite priest Bulous 'Abud, the lawyer Sheikh Rajib al-Dajani, and others, who stirred up the public against the policies of the British government and the Zionists. The audience, claimed Malul, was led by the leaders of the Muslim-Christian Association in Jaffa, and was composed of many villagers (*fellahin*) who were brought to the demonstration by the Arab effendis. Malul's tone at the conclusion of his report was very grim and urgent. Such demonstrations may lead to disturbing outcomes regarding our relations with the Arabs and our status in the country, he wrote. He suggested that the British government should arrest some of the inciters against the British, but at the same time wanted the Zionist movement to publish newspapers in Arabic so that the Zionist movement could 'fight our battles when needed and expose the locals to the lies of the local newspapers'.[24] Malul thus urged the Zionist leadership to be aware of the negative atmosphere among Arab nationalist circles in Palestine, and to act against what he viewed as a danger to the relations between Jews and Arabs. As always, here too he promoted the idea of an Arabic newspaper.

Shimon Moyal was also engaged in responding to Arab accusations directed against the Zionist movement. Concomitantly, however, he is described as having close and complex ties with some of the Arab writers, nationalists and journalists of his time such as 'Issa and Hanna al-'Issa, the owners of *Filastin*, as well as Habib Hannania, the editor of *al-Quds*. He often wrote in the local Arabic papers, and explained the views of the Zionist movement to Arab readers.[25]

Despite the different nature of Malul and Moyal's political involvement, the core of their literary, intellectual and public activities in Palestine was their belief in the need to develop close relations between Jews and Arabs (especially Muslims) in the country, to expose the Jews who did not know Arabic to the Arabs and their culture, and to act as loyal Ottomans for the development of Palestine.

Nevertheless, despite their work for the Zionist movement, both Malul and Moyal took the 'activists from Jaffa' (*ha-'askanim mi-yafo*) to task for their lack of awareness of the growing tension between Jews and Arabs, and for not doing enough to ease this tension. Their criticism is very telling, and may derive from their special position and identity. The fact that they were Ottoman subjects (unlike many of the Zionist activists in Jaffa at the time who kept their European citizenships) was a central element in their identity, and made their voice a complex one that combined Zionism and Ottomanism, Jewishness and Arabness.

The Arab Circle

Moyal and Malul's ties to various Arab intellectual, political and literary circles and figures shed light on their position vis-à-vis the evolving national conflict and the situation in Palestine. The two of them were involved with the activities of *Hizb al-Lamarkaziyya*, the Decentralization Party, and brought news about its activities to the Hebrew readers in Palestine. The Decentralization party was founded in Cairo at the end of 1912 by Lebanese and Syrian immigrants, and was opposed to the centralization policies of the Committee of Union and Progress (CUP). Its president was Rafiq al-'Azm, a prominent figure in the pre-War Arabist movement. Among its leaders and founding members were Rashid Rida and Da'ud Barakat, the chief editor of *al-Ahram*. It sought administrative reforms and a decentralist regime within the Ottoman Empire, which would control domestic affairs in the Arab provinces in Greater Syria.[26] *Hizb al-Lamarkaziyya* was a small party, with very few Palestinian members active in it (a factor that may explain its quite tolerant views towards Jewish immigration to Palestine). It had Jewish, Muslim and Christian members, and branches in Syria, Lebanon and Palestine. In a special decision which was approved on 30 April 1913, it stressed its adherence to equality, regardless of national or religious origin, as well as the party's commitment and loyalty to the Ottoman nation. It assured Ottoman Jews of equal rights in a decentralist administration.[27]

Between 1912 and 1914, as part of the party's political struggle against the Young-Turks' policies of centralization, it was involved in attempts to reach an entente with the Zionist movement, in order to create a joint front against the CUP. Moyal and Malul, as the two Jewish members of the party active in its Jaffa branch, were involved in negotiations between Zionist leaders and the party's Arab leaders. The driving force behind this move was the impact of Zionist achievements in Palestine on some party members, and the assumption that the Jews, and especially the Zionists, could use their capital and international connections to develop Palestine, and work together, as two minority groups in the Empire, against the centralization tendencies of the CUP.[28] At the end of April 1913, following a series of negotiations between the leaders of the Decentralization Party and the Zionist movement, Rafiq al-'Azm published a statement supporting Jewish immigration, in which he said that *al-Lamarkaziyya* would support the rights of the Jewish nation, since the Jews could assist the Arab provinces with their capital, manpower and knowledge. The party agreed in principle to foster an understanding between the Zionists and the Arabs, leading perhaps to a true accord in the future.[29] Adopting Ottoman citizenship as well as the knowledge of Arabic were central principles of the Jewish-Arab understanding. These, as was discussed above, were elements that Malul and Moyal frequently emphasized as well.

Despite what seemed initially to be promising negotiations for a Zionist-Arab understanding which involved some prominent Zionist activists (such as Victor Jacobsohn and Sami Hochberg) and the leaders of the Decentralization party, attempts to reach an entente failed on the eve of World War I.[30] For our purposes, it is important to mention that as a last-ditch effort to save the negotiations and resolve the crisis between the two movements Nissim Malul was sent to Cairo in May–June 1914, where he met with some of the party leaders and tried to renew the connections between the two organizations and push forward an idea of a Zionist-Arab congress. He also tried to convince some local Egyptian newspapers to publish pro-Zionist articles which would stress the advantages of the Zionist movement to the Arabs and Palestine. However, his attempt to renew the negotiations failed, probably also because of the general suspicion among the leaders of the Decentralization Party towards the real intentions of the Zionist movement in Palestine, and due to failed attempts to secure any promises for reforms from the CUP.[31]

While Malul had various connections with Rashid Rida, as part of his activity in *Hizb al-Lamarkaziyya,* Shimon Moyal had earlier ties with two of the other prominent Muslim thinkers of the time, Muhammad 'Abduh and Jamal al-Din al-Afghani. Shimon and Esther Moyal first met Jamal al-Din al-Afghani when they lived in Istanbul. It is reported that Moyal was a member of *al-Ta'lif wal-Taqrib* movement, which was founded by Muhammad 'Abduh and Muhammad Mirza Baker in an attempt to bring together Jews, Muslims and Christians. Moyal also corresponded with Rashid Rida, through the pages of *al-Manar* that Rida edited, while commenting on Rida's accusations that the Jews supported Italy during the Ottoman-Italian war in Libya in 1911. In his response Moyal argued that the Jews were loyal to the Muslim (Ottoman) government, and claimed that the future of the Jews was closely related to that of Islam. Islam, he wrote, formed a large political unit and the Muslim and Jewish races were very close, both in language and in customs.[32]

The Mixed Palestinian/Eretz Israeli locale

What then defines this mixed Palestinian/Eretz Israeli locale that Moyal and Malul represented? The first element is the importance of Ottoman citizenship as a joint citizenship.[33] The concept of joint citizenship is strongly connected to the specific definition of Zionism embraced by Moyal, Malul, and other members of their Sephardi milieu. Both of these men were enthusiastic Zionists, though they also criticized the Zionist movement led, at the time, mainly by Ashkenazi foreign subjects (Ben-Gurion, Sharett, Ruppin). Their view of Zionism departed considerably from that of the 'second *aliya*' Zionists and can better be termed 'inclusive' Zionism, one which was attuned to local conditions in Palestine, the existence of two peoples in the country, and the need to live together in one locale. It was a more peaceful and realistic approach than that put forward by the 'second *aliya*' Zionism (which I term 'exclusive Zionism'), and considered the situation in Palestine in terms of future relations between the different inhabitants of the country. The notion of loyalty to the Ottoman Empire played a central role in the 'inclusive Zionism' approach, and enabled the young Sephardi intelligentsia to examine the reality in Palestine through a different lens from that of the European Zionists. Their loyalty to the Empire affected their perspective both toward the local Ottoman authorities as well as toward the Arabs living in the country.[34]

Second, the distinction between Muslims, who were viewed as possible partners and Christians is also important to emphasize in this context. This distinction can be related to the general trauma caused to the Ottoman Empire by the Balkan wars, and to the close proximity in which Sephardi Jews and Muslims lived in Jerusalem, for example.[35]

Moyal and Malul presented a unique perspective on the evolving national conflict during the years preceding World War I (and in the case of Malul, also during the Mandate), as well as toward the unfolding nature of Arab-Jewish (or, rather, Jewish-Muslim) relations in Palestine. In the close connections they had with the Arab world, and in their dual location – residing in Palestine and active in the Jewish community, but at the same time also very involved in Arab cultural, intellectual and political life – they illustrate the richness of a Mediterranean-Levantine identity that draws on different cultural, geographical and linguistic worlds. What stands out in much of their literature and intellectual activity in Palestine was a belief that close ties must be developed between Jews and Arabs (especially Muslims) in the country, that Jews who did not know Arabic must be exposed to Arabs and their culture, and finally, that it was important to act as loyal Ottomans in advancing and developing Palestine.

Malul and Moyal are examples of the multiple and complex set of identities and loyalties which were possible in the mixed Eretz Israeli/Palestine locale. They also suggest ways in which existing categories, such as 'Jews' and 'Arabs', which seem to be inherent to Palestinian history and historiography, may be challenged. This complex web of identities and manifestations of nationalism was possible especially at this moment in history, right after the Young-Turk Revolution and in the final years of the Ottoman Empire, before they were rigidified by foreign and local forces.

Notes

1. *Ha-Herut* was a Hebrew newspaper published in Jerusalem between 1909 and 1917. Among its writers were many of the young Sephardi and Maghrebi intelligentsia of the time, and it dealt with many issues, including relations between Jews and Arabs, the language debate in Palestine, as well as provided news from the Ottoman Empire and the world. It was the only Hebrew newspaper that continued to operate in Palestine during World War I, when the other newspapers, Hebrew and Arabic alike, were shut down by the Ottoman censorship.
2. *Ha-Herut*, June 15 1915, p. 1.
3. I have borrowed the concept 'Mediterranean Levantine Identity' from the writer and literary critic Jacqueline Kahanoff, who developed this concept to describe her own life and identity as an Egyptian-born Jew who immigrated to Israel. See Kahanoff, Jacqueline, *Mi-Mizrah Shemesh* [From the East the Sun] (Tel Aviv, 1978) [In Hebrew], especially the first part, 'The Levantine generation'; idem, *Between Two Worlds*, edited by Ohana, David (Jerusalem, 2005) [in Hebrew], especially the introduction.
4. On Esther Azhari Moyal, her life and literary work as an Arab-Jewish intellectual in the *Mashriq*, see Levy, Lital, *Jewish Writers in the Arab East: Literature, History, and the Politics of Enlightenment, 1863–1914* (Unpublished Ph.D. Dissertation, University of California Berkeley, 2007), pp. 227–75, as well as idem, 'Partitioned pasts: Arab Jewish intellectuals and the case of Esther Azhari Moyal (1873– 1948),' in Hamzah, D. (ed.), *The Making of the Arab Intellectual (1880–1960): Empire, Public Sphere, and the Colonial Coordinates of Selfhood* (New Jersey, forthcoming), ch. 6. Levy presents Azhari- Moyal as an example to reconstruct what she calls 'Arab Jewish modernity' during the late Ottoman period. See also Ben Hanania, Yehoshua, 'The writer Esther Moyal and her time', *Hed ha-Mizrah* 3 (September 17 1944), pp. 17–18.

5. Levy: *Jewish Writers in the Arab East*, pp. 246–67.
6. *Sawt al-'Uthmaniyya* and *ha-Magen* Association will be discussed in length below. On Shimon Moyal see, Central Zionist Archive (CZA) K13/91 (a file on the Moyal family); Tidhar, David (ed.), *Intziklopedya le-Halutzei ha-Yishuv u-Bonav* [Encyclopedia of the Pioneers and Builders of the Yishuv] (Tel Aviv, 1971), vol. 3, p. 1219 [in Hebrew]; Gaon, Moshe David, *Yehudei ha-Mizrah be-Eretz Yisra'el: 'Avar ve-Hove* [The Oriental Jews in Eretz Israel: Past and Present] (Jerusalem, 1937), vol. 2, p. 381 [in Hebrew]; Ben Hanania, Yehoshua, 'Dr. Shimon Moyal and the Jewish-Arab problem', *Hed ha-Mizrah* 3 (10 October 1944), pp. 7, 9 [in Hebrew]; Campos, Michelle, 'Between "beloved ottomania" and "the Land of Israel": The struggle over Ottomanism and Zionism among Palestine's Sephardi Jews, 1908–1913', *International Journal of Middle East Studies* 37 (2005), pp. 474–7; Jacobson, Abigail, 'Alternative voices in late Ottoman Palestine: Jews and Muslims on the evolving national conflict', *Jerusalem Quarterly File* 21 (August 2004), pp. 41–8; idem., *From Empire to Empire: Jerusalem in the Transition between Ottoman and British Rule, 1912–1920* (Ph. D. Dissertation, The University of Chicago, 2006), pp. 183–5.
7. The Decentralization Party was founded in Cairo in 1912 and was opposed to the centralist policies of the CUP. See more on the party below.
8. On Nissim Malul see, Tidhar: *Intziklopedya*, vol. 2, p. 696; Gaon: *Yehudei ha-Mizrah*, pp. 432–4; Ben Hanania, Yehoshua, 'The first Jewish-Arab journalist', *ha-Po'el ha-Tza'ir* 32 (1959), pp. 12–13 [in Hebrew]. On the newspaper *al-Salam* see CZA Z4/1250; Jerusalem Municipal Archive (JMA) Box 4622/2; Jacobson: *From Empire to Empire*, pp. 183–4.
9. 'Our situation in the country', ha-Herut, 221–3, 17–19 June 1913.
10. Ibid., 17 June 1913.
11. Ibid., 19 June 1913.
12. Ibid. Yosef Gorny, who analyzed Malul's essay, ascribes to him what he calls 'an assimilating- altruistic view regarding the Arab question'. See Gorny, Yosef, 'Shorasheha shel toda'at ha-'imut ha-le'umi ha-yehudi-'aravi ve-hishtakfuta ba-'itunut ha-'ivrit ba-shanim 1900–1918' [The Roots of the Consciousness of the Jewish-Arab National Conflict and its Reflection in the Hebrew Press during the Years 1900–1918], *Zionism* 4 (1975), pp. 81–2 [in Hebrew].
13. 'When? On the Rivalry of the Arabs with the Jews', *ha-Herut*, 17 December 1912.
14. An interview with Avraham Elmalech, the Institute of Contemporary Jewry, Project 28, Interview 2. It is reported that the Moyals invested around 4,000 French Francs in its publication.

15. Issues 77 and 78 of the newspaper, from 27 and 30 August 1914, were found in the Israel State Archive (ISA) in the files of the German consulate in Jaffa. These issues consist mainly of reports from the war front. One of the writers is Nadim ('Abdallah) Moyal, Shimon and Esther's son. See ISA, Record Group 67, Box Peh 533, File 1493. I would like to thank Michelle Campos for drawing my attention to this file. These are the only issues of the newspaper that I was able to locate. Ya'akov Yehoshua mentions the newspaper several times and claims that it is located in the National Library in Jerusalem. However, I failed to locate it there. Yehoshua states that the newspaper was first published on 28 January 1913, and that the last issue appeared in November 1914. See: Yehoshua, Ya'akov, 'Sahifat "Sawt al-'Uthmaniyya": Al-Sihafa al-'arabiyya fil-bilad fi matla' al-qarn al-hali' [Sawt al-'Uthmaniyya Newspaper: The Arabic Press in the Country at the Turn of the Present Century], *al-Sharq* 9/3 (1973), pp. 49–50 [in Arabic]. More on the debates taking place in *ha-Herut* see Jacobson: *From Empire to Empire*, pp. 124–88.
16. Campos, Michelle U., *A 'Shared Homeland' and its Boundaries: Empire, Citizenship and the Origins of Sectarianism in Late Ottoman Palestine, 1908–13* (Unpublished Ph.D. dissertation, Stanford University, 2003), p. 354. See Campos's discussion on the *ha-Magen* association on pages 353–6. The documents of the association were apparently burned by Nissim Malul, when he fled from Cemal Paşa during World War I. On the *ha-Magen* association see also the memoir of Yosef Eliyahu Chelouche, *Parashat Hayyai, 1870–1930* [The Story of My Life, 1870–1930] (Tel Aviv, 1931), pp. 166–70 [in Hebrew].
17. *Ha-Magen* founding manifesto, Tel Aviv Municipal Archive (TAMA), File 8, Folder 729/5235, p. 2.
18. Ibid., p. 3.
19. Ibid., pp. 4–5.
20. See also Campos: *A Shared Homeland*, p. 355.
21. An interview with Avraham Elmalech, the Institute of Contemporary Jewry, Project 28, Interview 2.
22. A letter from Nissim Malul to the Jewish City Council of Jerusalem (va'ad ha-'ir le-yehudei yerushalayim), 12 December 1929, JMA, box 4622/2; Nissim Malul, a letter to the president of the Jewish Congress, 25 August 1921, CZA Z4/1250.
23. Ben Ze'ev, Israel, *Mahberet* [Notebook], June–September 1959, pp. 146–8 [in Hebrew]. I thank Prof. Shmuel Moreh for providing me with this article.
24. Malul, Nissim, 'The fake nationalist demonstration', in CZA L4/999.
25. See for example, a series of translations from Moyal's articles published in *ha-Herut*, including Moyal's comments in *Filastin*, 16 September 1911, 20 September 1911 and 23 September 1911.

26. Mandel, Neville, *The Arabs and Zionism before World War I* (Berkeley, 1976), pp. 148–9; Khalidi, Rashid, *Palestinian Identity: The Construction of Modern National Consciousness* (New York, 1997), p. 249 fn. 36.
27. Malul, Nissim, 'The Arab movement and the Jews', *ha-Herut*, 18 May 1913; Mandel: *The Arabs and Zionism*, p. 158.
28. Tauber, Eliezer, 'The relations between the Syrian nationalists and the Zionist movement until the end of World War I', *Jewish History* 5/2 (Fall 1991), pp. 9–11 [in Hebrew].
29. Ibid., pp. 10–11.
30. For a detailed account of this attempt, as well as the reasons for its failure, see Ibid; Mandel: *The Arabs and Zionism*, pp. 141–164, and idem, 'Attempts at an Arab-Zionist entente: 1913–1914', *Middle Eastern Studies* 1/3 (April 1965), pp. 238–67.
31. Tauber: 'The relations', pp. 13–18.
32. Ben Hanania: 'Dr. Shimon Moyal', p. 7.
33. See on this also in Campos: *A Shared Homeland*.
34. Jacobson: *From Empire to Empire*, pp. 124–88.
35. Jacobson, Abigail, 'Sephardim, Ashkenazim and the "Arab Question" in pre-First World War Palestine: A reading of three Zionist newspapers', *Middle Eastern Studies* 39/2 (April 2003), pp. 105–30.

CHAPTER 10

THE YOUNG TURK REVOLUTION OF 1908 AS REFLECTED IN THE MEDIA OF THE JEWISH COMMUNITY IN PALESTINE

RUTH KARK AND NADAV SOLOMONOVICH

Introduction

The Young Turk Revolution in July 1908 aroused many expectations and hopes. Sultan Abdülhamid II was forced to reinstate the constitution, leading to the establishment in Istanbul of a parliament to which representatives of all the nations and ethnic groups in the Ottoman Empire were elected, including four Jews – though none of them came from Palestine.[1] Among other things, the Revolution had a great effect on the *yishuv*, the Jewish community in Palestine, and gave rise to diverse reactions. This chapter's purpose is to survey and analyze the immediate reactions of the Jews in Palestine to the Revolution. These reactions, which relate to both the immediate and more distant future, were studied on the basis of contemporary primary sources, particularly the Jewish press in Palestine and a few supplementary ones. They will be analyzed in three contexts: general reactions in the Ottoman Empire, those relating to Palestine as a whole, and others within a specific Jerusalem environment. A differentiation will be made between the internal Jewish sphere and the reactions of other, non-Jewish, segments of the population.

As has been noted, the reactions of the *yishuv* were diverse. From a positive standpoint, they included expectations for a better future, economic development, modernization, and greater freedom in Palestine. Negative reactions stemmed from fear that the spirit of freedom and equality would encourage the *yishuv* to undergo a process of Ottomanization that would undermine the status of Hebrew among its members and also lead to obligatory conscription of young Jews into the Ottoman armed forces.

Whether the reactions were positive or negative, a distinction should be made between spontaneous manifestations such as public celebrations and parades in the streets throughout the country, and responses based upon a meticulous analysis of the implications of the constitutional upheaval.

The chapter traces the coverage of and controversy about the Revolution in the various Hebrew newspapers in Palestine, and focuses on several main questions. Did the various Jewish ethnic groups react differently to the Revolution, and if so what form did this take? How did the Hebrew press relate to the new opportunities embodied in the reinstated constitution, such as participation in democratic processes in the Ottoman Empire, i.e., the possibility of having the right to vote and the right to stand for election to Parliament as representatives of the *yishuv*? Did the Hebrew-language press relate to the lifting of limitations and censorship formerly placed upon it, and if so, how? In addition, we discuss the coverage of the 'Jewish Ottoman Society', one of the societies established in several cities in Palestine to further Ottoman-Jewish friendship and promote Ottomanization. The Society called upon Ottoman Jews in Palestine to learn Turkish and become an integral part of the new Ottoman nation.

Methodological Comments

We chose to examine roughly the first three months after the promulgation of the constitution, i.e., from 24 July 1908 to the end of October.

The following Hebrew newspapers served as our sources: *Habazeleth* [*Havazzelet*] (1863; 1870–1911); *Ha-Or* / *Hazewi* [*ha-Tzvi*] / *Hashqafa* (1884–1914); *ha-Po'el ha-Tza'ir* (1907–1914; 1919–1970).[2]

Primary sources were examined to supplement the information gleaned from the newspapers. Among these were the letters written by the Jerusalem Jewish educator and public figure David Yellin, the correspondence in the archives of the Ottoman governor of Jerusalem between 1906 and 1908, 'Ali Ekrem Bey, and the yearbooks published in Jerusalem by the Jewish publisher Abraham Moshe Luncz (*Eretz-Israel Almanac* for 1909 to 1914). It is reasonable to assume that an even more comprehensive picture of this issue could be acquired by using newspapers in other languages, such as Ladino (Judeo-Spanish), and the diaries and memoirs of contemporaries.

Immediate Reactions in Several of Palestine's Major Cities

Unprecedented spontaneous mass celebrations took place in various cities throughout Palestine when news of the Revolution reached the country. In most cases the public consisted of members of all religions and ethnic groups who held joint meetings and processions. Our description of the celebrations will focus particularly on Jerusalem and Jaffa.

Celebrations in Jerusalem began on Friday, 7 August 1908, about two weeks after the Revolution, following an official announcement that the reinstated constitution would be read in public on Saturday. The festivities continued for several days with the participation of Arabs, Jews, and members of all religions and ethnic communities with no tension or controversy between them. The celebrations included processions, singing, dancing, and ceremonious displays of fencing. Speeches were made in Turkish, Hebrew and Arabic, praising the sultan and the constitution. *Hashqafa* reported:

> On Friday [7 August 1908] [...], after the noonday prayers of the Ishmaelites [Muslims] on the site of the Temple, a large crowd of about 5,000 persons began to sing and chant, carrying flags

before them and dancing with lances and firing pistols. And singing songs of joy and liberty, they marched from the site of the Temple until they reached the palace of the army [i.e., military barracks].[3]

In *Habazeleth* the same events were described as follows:

[...] members of different religions and of different nationalities, factions and sects [...] all came as one to celebrate the festival of liberty, and all called out as they marched: 'Long live the sultan!'[4]

The Jerusalem Municipality supported the celebrations and encouraged participation in them. It hung flags and decorations praising the sultan in the streets. The military band also participated in some of the festivities, having been dispatched by the commander of the Ottoman garrison in Jerusalem, Riza Bey. The Ottoman governor of the District of Jerusalem, 'Ali Ekrem Bey, in a report he sent on 28 July 1908, a few days after the Revolution, mentioned the heterogeneous composition of the celebrants:

The sounds of joy in the city of Jerusalem, to which there is no second in the world in the diversity of its religions, sects, and races, rose to the heavens in a thousand languages and styles. Speeches were delivered. Hands were shaken. Marches were played. In short, the appropriate things in honor of the liberty were done. After that the residents made the rounds of Jerusalem until evening, accompanied by the military band.[5]

In a special report sent by Thomas R. Wallace, the American consul in Jerusalem, to the US Assistant Secretary of State, he noted that the festivities took the governor by surprise: The clamoring of the people, and the demands of the hitherto hidden representatives of the Young Turkey Party, broke the inertia of the Governor, and he at last fixed a day, 8 August, (last Saturday) for the public reading of the Sultan's proclamation and declaration and illuminating the city.[6]

Similar to Jerusalem, Jaffa, the center of the new *yishuv*[7] – was also the scene of many mass celebrations marked by orations and sermons in various languages:

> The impressions of the day and the moment keep changing, you must hurry from meeting to meeting, from one assembly to another; new faces, various speeches in different languages, processions and melodies, hurrahs, the flags waving, with their multitude of embroidered patterns, from every corner and angle. The multitude of people, numbering tens of thousands, the different colors and tints of the oriental clothing and apparel unite into one shiny, noisy, and flowing sea.[8]

What was especially striking in Jaffa was the atmosphere of equality and fraternity between the various religions and nationalities:

> Overwhelmed by the joy engendered by His Majesty the Sultan's granting of the right to elect delegates to the parliament to all residents of Turkey irrespective of their religion, one resident from among the notables of our city [...] invited all the notable people of Jaffa of the various religions, and [...] also invite[ed] the Jews to take part in this celebration.[9]

In his report to the US consul, Wallace also referred to the sudden and surprising cooperation of Jews and Muslims in Jaffa:

> News came from Beyrout, where there has long been a deadly feud between Christians and Moslems [...] former differences being lost in the common rejoicings. This same result has been most marked here, where the bitterest enmity has prevailed, and in Jaffa, where not long since several people were wounded in a riot between Moslems and Jews, the two races came together quite oblivious of their differences.[10]

There were those among the Jewish population of Palestine who, upon hearing the news of the constitution, immediately began to think of its implications for the *yishuv* in the more distant future. We analyze and discuss the establishment of the Jewish Ottoman Society.[11]

General Expectations of the *Yishuv* from Implementation of the Constitution

After the promulgation of the constitution, the Hebrew press began to express various expectations, over and above the equal rights and obligations embodied in the constitution. These expectations primarily focused on several key spheres. First was the hope that it would lead to modernization and industrialization in Palestine that would bring economic development or even capitalism in their wake. In addition there were expectations for an improved status of the *yishuv* as a national minority within the Ottoman Empire.[12] Finally, there was anticipation as regards representation in the Ottoman parliament.

Modernization

Among the Jews of Palestine, the constitution engendered hopes for Westernization which would give rise to processes of modernization and the introduction of new technologies and industrialization. There were those, such as Abraham Moshe Luncz, who took this argument one step further, maintaining that economic development would encourage increased Jewish immigration, and eventually enable the Jews of Palestine to elect a representative to the Ottoman parliament:

> There is no doubt that in a short time Turkey, too, will be considered one of the enlightened countries, and our holy land, too, being part of Greater Turkey, will awake from its lowly state, and our brethren [...] will be able to cultivate its land and extract from it all the treasures it holds, to connect all ends [of the country] by roads and railways, and to establish within it factories [to produce] all the needed products and new inventions, until it returns to its ancient state and becomes a fertile land and the delight of all the nations.[13]

A further example of the anticipated outcomes of Palestine's economic development is mentioned in an article published in *Habazeleth*:

> At the end of their speeches [i.e., of the Pasha of Jerusalem and his senior officials] they said that now new schools will be opened in Jerusalem and its [i.e., the autonomous Jerusalem District's] cities, that the country's commerce will be uplifted, the status of manufacturing will be raised, steam power will take its rightful place, new railroads will be laid, and automobile wagons [term used in the original Hebrew], too, will be brought in.[14]

Two Jewish bankers were among the six Councilers in the mixed Board of the Joint Chamber of Commerce, Industry and Agriculture of Jerusalem, established in April 1909 as an outcome of the Young-Turk Revolution. With the aim of modernizing the country, it included the following among its objectives:

> The Chamber of Commerce [...] will propose to the Government in writing about the necessary measures for the development and progress of the crafts and industry, the creation of commercial schools, the modifications and reforms that should be introduced to the commercial laws and customary tariffs, the projects concerning the execution of public works, such as the construction of ports, inland navigation, extension of post and telegraph lines and railway tracks, opening and repair of bridges and roads, establishment of commercial markets, publication of commercial newspapers – in short, all that could contribute to the progress of commerce, manufacture and agriculture.[15]

The Status of the *Yishuv* as a National Minority

Jews were a minority group in Palestine, and were considered by some to be a national minority. Some believed that since this condition would not change in the foreseeable future national gains should be on the agenda, just as other national ethnic groups were attempting throughout the Empire. In other words, a demand must be made to the Ottoman parliament that in cities in which Jews constituted the majority of the population, they would be granted the governance of the city and its municipal institutions, and Hebrew would be the official language of those institutions:

> And then we [i.e., the *yishuv*] will be able to justify our demand that in Jerusalem, Safed, and Tiberias, in which the majority of the residents are Jewish, the leadership of the city and its [municipal] institutions be in our hands, and that the official language in the municipal offices and the courts of those cities be Hebrew.[16]

It should be borne in mind that the assumption upon which these national demands were based was that there was no contradiction between national and cultural autonomy, on the one hand, and loyal citizenship to the Empire, on the other.

The new constitution could at times have been mistakenly interpreted as the declaration of a republic. One example of such an interpretation is the following section from an article written by Eli'ezer Ben-Yehuda in his newspaper, *Hazewi*:

> Now there is no longer in the realm of Turkey a ruling nation and a subject nation. All nations are equal. And every nation, wherever it is the majority, has all the domestic liberty it needs [for the maintenance of] its national culture in all its components: rule of the city, local officials, its national language, liberty for all! And without any detriment to our nationalism, we can still be good, true Ottomans [...].[17]

Another example in the same spirit was expressed in the following passages from an article published in *ha-Po'el ha-Tza'ir* in anticipation of the decentralization of government throughout the Ottoman Empire:

> As can be anticipated [...] administrative decentralization, and we may look forward to more or less unfettered autonomy in

the vilayets of the state. This is especially true if we take into account that almost [the same] as the number of residents in Turkey [i.e., of Turks] is the number of [residents of] foreign nationalities, such as: Greeks, Arabs, Armenians, Macedonians, etc., and all these nations will undoubtedly side with the right to political, or at least administrative, decentralization.[18]

Election of a *Yishuv* Member to Parliament

Another important issue that received much attention in the Hebrew press was the new opportunity to elect a Jewish delegate from the *yishuv* to the parliament. One example of the importance attached to this possibility is an article published in Ben-Yehuda's newspaper *Hashqafa* only one week after the promulgation of the new constitution:

> His majesty the sultan issued an edict to elect a parliament that will convene in the capital Kushta.[19] And the right to elect and be elected has also been granted to the members of our nation. The honorable public should know that we must elect a loyal and honest man, a man of good attributes, wise and clever, and absolutely fluent in the language of the Turkish state. The elected person must be an 'emmisary of the public'[20] and speak in the name of the entire community [...] and that [he] will bring honor and glory to those who send him.[21]

Two weeks later, this same newspaper printed a detailed report of a meeting to which the *baladiyya* (i.e., the Municipality) invited all the *mukhtar*s[22] in Jerusalem to inform them how the elections to the parliament would be conducted. It was announced at that meeting that the right to vote and stand for election was granted to all male subjects of the empire, even residents of other cities if they had resided in Jerusalem during the previous year. The elections would be conducted in two stages: in the first, every 500 residents would elect one representative; in the second, these representatives would elect those who would represent Jerusalem in the parliament. By the end of the following week the *mukhtar*s were required to hand in two lists of all the men living in their neighborhood, one containing those up to the age of 25 and the other of men over 25 years of age. In a neighborhood, quarter, or street that had no *mukhtar* this assignment was entrusted to the neighborhood's elders.[23]

It is noteworthy that this important topic was the subject of relatively frequent reporting in most of the Hebrew newspapers at the time, as the public had to deal with three significant matters of principle: a) Is it worthwhile even trying to elect a Jewish member of parliament? b) If so, who should be elected? c) If not, to whom then should the Jewish population give its support? To some extent, public opinion on these issues can be ascertained from a report in *ha-Po'el ha-Tza'ir* of a meeting in Jaffa, also attended by representatives from Jerusalem, in which Ashkenazi and Sephardi Jews jointly tried to come to a decision about these issues.

Those present were not of one opinion about whether it was worthwhile to try to elect a *yishuv* member to the parliament. Some maintained that it would be wise to wait before doing so because the Ottoman parliament was as yet an unknown entity. Moreover, it was claimed that since Jews and Muslims in the Jerusalem District had not mutually agreed upon one candidate, if a candidate about whom agreement had not been reached fail to be elected, the *yishuv*'s weakness would be apparent to all. However, those present did concur that the *yishuv*'s Zionist aspirations should not be concealed, for were that to be done it was possible that its opponents – including the elected delegate – would depict them according to his own viewpoint. After much deliberation, the meeting concluded that it was important to send a delegate to parliament to defend the interests of the Jewish community. As for the fear that the Sultan might abrogate the parliament, those present at this meeting concluded that in any case the Jews should take part in the elections, since if parliament was suspended the fate of the Jewish community would be no different than that of the other 'Turkish nations' (i.e., ethnic minorities in the Ottoman Empire) who also sent delegates.

As for the identity of the delegate, the meeting decided that the Jews should join forces solely with the Muslim population of the country, not with the Christians: 'The meeting seriously discussed the second question – who should we support and with whom join forces. It decided that we must unite only with the Muslim Arabs, who treat us with honor and trust, and not with our perpetual enemies'.[24]

When it became known that a precondition for membership in the parliament was fluency in Turkish, the press showed clear signs of disappointment, and even recriminations against the authorities, claiming that this demand was a blow to the principle of free elections. It argued that limitations of language would not enable election of the most suitable representatives, but rather only of those fluent in Turkish, even if they were not the most qualified.[25] The problems posed by this latter condition led one correspondent to call upon the *yishuv* to prepare for the elections by training future candidates for the parliament. The writer, Menashe Ben-Zevi, claimed that this meant more than fluency in Turkish, but also cognizance of the laws of the empire and its economic condition. He recommended opening training centers in the cities and the larger Jewish agricultural settlements, and even teaching Arabic in the schools so that pupils would become accustomed to Arabic orthography.[26]

Even though – for obvious reasons – not mentioned in the press, there apparently were also expectations for a more just rule and an end to the regime of *baksheesh* (gratuities, bribes) that was prevalent throughout the Empire. An example of such feelings can be found in a personal letter from David Yellin to Dr. Eugen Mittwoch dated 10 June 1909, about a year after promulgation of the constitution, in which he gave vent to his disappointment with conditions in Palestine and with expectations that were never fulfilled:

> The matter of officials accepting baksheesh has not changed at all. Everything is as it was. And that is the essence of the decay, at least here in our county, Eretz-Israel. On the other hand, we see that the poorer masses understand nothing about liberty and act like hooligans, striking and at times even killing, while the government is still not firm, and the end result is the suffering of our brethren.[27]

At the same time, further on in this same letter, Yellin touched upon some positive aspects of the constitution, including freedom of speech and of the press, and the right to establish societies of various types. This leads us to another aspect worthy of note: the establishment of new societies following the promulgation of the constitution, and first and foremost the Jewish Ottoman Society.

Failure in the Jerusalem Elections to Parliament

During the period under study, i.e., the first three months after the Revolution, only *ha-Po'el ha-Tza'ir* was critical of the setback suffered by the *yishuv* in the elections to parliament held in Jerusalem. Although *Habazeleth* mentioned the elections in some short factual reports no real attempt was made to analyze why the effort to elect a Jewish member of parliament had proved unsuccessful.

Several reasons for the failure were outlined in an article in the Tishri 5669 (September–October 1908) issue of *ha-Po'el ha-Tza'ir*. Some were attributed to the Jewish population, while others put the blame on outside forces. Among the reasons for which the Jews were blamed, the first was the indifference exhibited by the Jerusalem community, both the educated classes and simpler folk: 'During the mass processions in the first period after the granting of liberty, one could not imagine that there would be such indifference to the first elections. Between the processions and the elections there was not even one public rally – even though there were no external interference'.[28] He then went on to claim that no one should be surprised by the election results, for only 60 per cent of the Jews exercised their right to vote on election day: 'Abstention in the elections was very great among the Jews. About 40 per cent did not exercise their right! [...] because they believed that in any case a Jew would not be elected as representative [...]'.[29]

As for external factors, the author puts the blame on the Young Turks' lack of organization and order that led to much uncertainty about who was eligible to vote. Roughly two weeks before the elections it turned out that only men who paid the land (*werko*) and commerce taxes would be allowed to vote, not those who paid the military exemption tax (*bedel-i 'askeri*). This announcement reduced the number of eligible voters in Jerusalem to ca. 4,000: about 1,100 Jews, 600 Christians, and the rest Muslims.[30]

Another complaint was that the elections were not conducted in a valid manner since in precincts with a Muslim or Christian majority the officials at the voting stations were of the majority religion and they prevented Jews from casting their votes: 'But in those areas in which the majority of residents are Muslims and Christians the officials supervising the elections were of these religions and they used their authority to prevent Jews from voting. For example: Mr. Valero fell short by only 5 votes to be elected, and when the official realized this he sealed the ballot box [...]'.[31]

Thus the Jewish press did not seriously take stock after the election failure, and did not draw lessons for the future. The only journal that did so was *ha-Po'el ha-Tza'ir* which did not hesitate to point an accusing finger at the indifference of Jerusalem's Jewish population. It should also be borne in mind that the readership of this journal was comprised of a very specific group within the population, namely the new *yishuv*, and only they read the analytical article, while other segments of the community had to make do with short informative reports lacking any in-depth analysis of what led to the results.

Reactions of Various Jewish Ethnic Groups in Jerusalem to the Constitution

Contrary to the intuitive assumption that news of the constitution would be received by all Jews in Palestine in a similar, positive manner, what emerges from a systematic survey of the Hebrew press of that period is a completely different picture. The Jewish community of Jerusalem reacted ambivalently; news of the constitutional change was received differently by members of the various ethnic groups. *Ha-Po'el ha-Tza'ir* divided the community into Sephardim, Ashkenazim, Yemenites, and 'young people and new laborers [i.e., the modern labor class]', and reported their reactions, as discussed below.

Sephardim

The Sephardim were those who looked most positively upon the new liberties because they had been local-born Jews for several generations and as such were best acquainted with the oppressive measures employed by the former regime. Moreover, the Sephardi educated classes took an interest in the Empire's economic condition, and some of them, in the Empire's capital, even joined the Young Turk movement. As a result, they were happier than others about the turn of events and had fewer doubts that the constitution would indeed be implemented. Sephardim even expressed their willingness to serve in the army: 'Among them [i.e., the Sephardim] there are fewer doubters, more pleased [persons]. And concerning the major question, "For they will take you to serve in the army", you hear voices, especially among the younger men, saying with confidence: "So what? Of course we will go!" They are also ready and willing to take advantage of liberty [...]'.[32]

Ashkenazim

Almost no ultra-Orthodox Ashkenazim participated in the celebrations. Since most of them were foreign citizens, they had become accustomed to viewing everything in the Ottoman Empire with distrust and relying solely on their own consuls stationed in Jerusalem. They feared both conscription to the army and that a new radical government would negatively influence the morals of their children and their religion: '[...] and among them you hear many doubts and fears: What will we gain from this? And what, God forbid, if our enemies become stronger? And perhaps liberty will cause people to stray from the straight and narrow path? And last and most terrible: Our sons will be taken [to serve in] the army!'[33]

Yemenites

Jerusalem's Yemenite Jewish community, comprised mostly of immigrants to Palestine, was portrayed as living in conditions reminiscent of the Middle Ages and as the object of years of oppression. According to writers in *ha-Po'el ha-Tza'ir*, the Yemenites completely ignored all expressions of joy over the promulgation of the constitution, such as processions and festivities. Like the Ashkenazim, the opportunities embodied in the new liberties did not interest them, but they were extremely concerned about the enforcement of compulsory military service: 'For thousands of years they have been in a state of servitude and demeaning degradation and did not consider the liberty granted as tidings of release from their unique state of captivity [...]. Their reaction is – silence [...]. Especially great is their fear of compulsory military service [...]'.³⁴

Young People and the Modern Labor Class

The attitude towards the constitution adopted by this sector of the population, mostly new immigrants from Russia, was totally different. Familiar with the severity of the former Ottoman and Russian regimes they therefore gave vent to their joy when the constitution was promulgated, though they expressed some doubts as to its implementation. The Hebrew press gives no clear indication as to their stand on the issue of conscription.³⁵

Various contemporary sources disagree with the picture presented by *ha-Po'el ha-Tza'ir* of the different attitudes of these Jewish ethnic and social groups towards the constitution and argue that there was more unity. The following report from Ben-Yehuda's *Hashqafa* illustrates this point: '[...] and the procession was excellent, all without division into factions. Sephardim, Yemenites, Ashkenazim, Hassidim, Perushim, yeshiva students, schoolchildren – all felt that this was a joyous day for them and all joined together to march in the procession'.³⁶

The more traditional Abraham Moshe Luncz, in his report of the events makes no mention of different attitudes:

This great and sudden transformation enacted in our country [...] has immediately led to changes in daily life and all its matters. All the various national groups have drawn closer one to another in love and amity, and all made speeches about liberty, fraternity, and equality, and all are also content with the two obligations imposed by the constitution, which are: compulsory education and compulsory military service. It has already been decided that after the parliament convenes military service will also be compulsory for Jews and Christians, who until now only paid the military [exemption] tax.³⁷

Hashqafa and Luncz may have been overly influenced by the scenes of rejoicing that followed promulgation of the constitution and the declaration of equality. Despite the conflicting versions presented by our sources, there is a consensus among them concerning the Sephardim's positive reaction to the constitution and their participation in the festivities.

Another important issue to which much attention was given was conscription of young Jewish men into the Ottoman army. Obviously there is a contradiction between Luncz's claim that *all* accepted conscription and the claim made by *ha-Po'el ha-Tza'ir*, that only the Sephardim saw it positively. A letter from David Yellin to Dr. Paul Nathan in Berlin, dated 31 May 1909, may be of some help in judging which report was closer to the truth. In his letter, Yellin voices an opinion directly opposed to that of Luncz, maintaining that there was much fear among the Jews concerning conscription. He wrote that 'the issue of conscription of non-Muslims into the Ottoman army also aroused fear among our brethren. Apparently, much time will elapse before our brethren understand that rights are not acquired without obligations'.[38]

On the basis of these three differing and conflicting opinions we cannot come to a categorical conclusion as to the Jewish reaction to the issue of conscription. We believe that Luncz's report is the least logical of the three and that his presentation of the facts is too idealized.

The Jewish Ottoman Society

The first report regarding the establishment of the *Jewish Ottoman Society* was published in *Hashqafa* on 21 August 1908. This report said that Dr. Yitzhak Levy, the director of the Anglo-Palestine Bank in Jerusalem and a well-known public figure who in the past had corresponded with Theodor Herzl and supported acquisition of landed property, founded the society in Jerusalem, with the aim of protecting Ottoman Jews. It also reported that an interim committee had been elected to manage the society's affairs and that its regulations and further information about it would be published in the next issue.[39] When the society's regulations were publicized, it became public knowledge that it called for equality and fraternity between Jews and Arabs, and was even criticized on this ground by Yosef Aharonovitz, the editor of *ha-Po'el ha-Tza'ir*.[40]

The next report about the society appeared three days later in *Habazeleth* and included a list of its objectives:

1. To spread knowledge of the government's laws and an understanding of the political situation in the country among all levels of Jews residing in Palestine.
2. To defend, on the basis of the laws, the civil and political rights of all Jews residing in Palestine.
3. To defend the individual rights of members of our society.
4. To try to also appoint Jewish representatives to all courts, in leadership [institutions] of the state such as *majlis idara* [administrataive council], *mahkama* [the *shari'a* court], the *baladiyya* [municipal council] etc. and in the parliament.
5. To increase the number of Jews who are subjects of our government and to bring those Jews who do not have the protection of another government under the protection of our government and to register them in the *nefus* books [census registers] according to the the laws of the government.[41]

In addition to its regulations, the Society published the means it intended to use to achieve them. These included engaging expert lawyers whose services would be available to Society members, publishing notices and information in the press, and submitting complaints and petitions to the authorities when necessary. Furthermore, the Society would make efforts to develop fluency in Turkish among all the Jews by means of evening classes, public readings, etc.[42]

The Society's founders emphasized that its mission would not be shaped by any faction or ethnic community, and that it was their intention to unite all the Jews residing in Palestine so as to enhance the power and status of the *yishuv*:

> In truth, the name 'society' has nothing to do with this, because this society will not be sectarian. The Ottoman Jewish subjects

of this country [i.e., empire], no matter who they are, no matter what their opinion about religion, or the internal leadership of the ethnic communites, these Ottoman Jews should come together, unite into one large force [...].[43]

Apparently the Society's efforts in Jerusalem were successful, and additional branches were established elsewhere. One paper reported about the establishment of a branch in Jaffa with 80 members.[44]

On 11 October 1908, in a letter to Mordecai Marcus Adler, the son of British Chief Rabbi Nathan Adler, David Yellin, who was a member of the Jerusalem branch of the Society, wrote that efforts to date had focused on the elections to the parliament. He reports the outcome of the elections in Jerusalem, in which three Muslims who tended to be favorable to Jews were elected.[45] Failure in this election campaign did not discourage the Society, which continued to play an active role in local politics and made an impressive gain in the next elections to the Jerusalem municipal council. Yellin, who was elected to that council as a representative of the Society, later described this achievement in a letter dated 26 May 1910 to Dr. Paul Nathan:

> Up to now there was not even one Jewish member on the municipal council, which is called upon to decide upon so many matters that are of primary concern to the Jewish population. Our society, the 'Jewish Ottoman Society', devoted its attention to this state of affairs and decided that this time it would rectify this anomaly. It mobilized all its strength and in the last elections successfully managed to vote in three Jewish candidates out of the five available seats. This is the greatest success to which one can aspire.[46]

Fear of Ottomanization in the *Yishuv*

In addition to outward expressions of joy engendered by the Revolution and the diverse expectations and reactions it aroused, another important feeling was present within the *yishuv* that was the very opposite of those surveyed to this point. This was fear that the process of

Ottomanization would undermine the unique character of the Jewish community, especially the status of the Hebrew language.

The major argument put forward was that the unique conditions in Palestine had led to the revitalization of Hebrew as a means of social cohesion, uniting the diverse groups in Jewish society. New newspapers in various languages might appear and do away with the need to turn to Hebrew. It was feared that the Ottoman government would establish schools in which the language of instruction would be Turkish, and that these would become an alternative to the private schools. This was most clearly expressed in an article published by Z. Kramarov in *ha-Po'el ha-Tza'ir*:

> When we assessed our condition in the Diaspora and fell into a state of utter despair, we always turned our eyes towards the East. There, in Eretz-Israel, foreign education does not weigh heavily upon us, a Hebrew [i.e., Jewish] life [i.e., milieu] is developing there, our language and culture is advancing, the Jews there do not fear assimilation, and we only have a secure future – a glorious future – in the wellspring of our lives, Eretz-Israel. Only freedom is lacking there, freedom of movement, freedom of speech, commerce, entrance [into the country] and so forth – [and if it is granted] our case will end well. Only let a constitution be granted [it is claimed], and we will come and occupy the country. But, our wise men, did not understand that what is an advantage for some is a disadvantage for others [...]. They completely forgot that if the Hebrew language has developed somewhat in Eretz-Israel, the main reason is precisely because the nation in which we live has barely developed: it has no literature to speak of, there are no state schools. [Therefore] the Jew, sometimes unwillingly, has to send his children to the schools of the various societies in which the language of instruction is Hebrew; when the Ashkenazi Jew does not speak Arabic, the Sephardi Jew must unwillingly talk to him in Hebrew. But it is a completely different state of affairs now in this period of freedom. Hundreds of schools will be opened by the government, education will be free, without payment, and perhaps compulsory.

> Arabic, too, will begin to spread, and Turkish will begin to be taught as the language of the government and the parliament; [the Jews] will start [to negotiate] relations with the Arab nation, which is also so close to us racially, and there is no doubt that what happened to Hebrew in European countries decades ago will now happen in Eretz-Israel. And more than a few parents will be in a situation in which, in accordance with the education laws, they will find it impossible to teach their young children three languages – and Arabic and Turkish are indispensable in the country [...].[47]

Ithamar Ben-Yehuda (later: Ben-Avi), the son of Eli'ezer Ben-Yehuda, came out against the decline in the status of Hebrew and was sharply critical of the establishment of Jewish newspapers in foreign languages such as Judeo-Spanish or Russian. He placed the blame for this development upon the new constitution and the abrogation of newspaper censorship, claiming that the new circumstances would bring about unprecedented disunity within the Jewish community in Eretz-Israel and might even lead to the creation of different 'nations':

> It may be that this new craze will cause great emotion, excitement the likes of which there has not been for days and years throughout our small country. And on the contrary: it will spread jargon [i.e., Yiddish] and Spanish [i.e., Judeo-Spanish] in Judea, in Ephraim, in the Galilee. On the contrary, it will continue to widen the breach that has already split us so greatly. Up to now we have been divided into sects, and [now] you come and create different nations among us. Each of these nations has its own language, literature, theater, schools.[48]

In a critical article, Yosef Aharonovitz – a member of the *ha-Po'el ha-Tza'ir* Party, sharply criticized Dr. Yitzhak Levy, one of the founders of the *Jewish Ottoman Society*. He came out against the ideals of religious and national fraternity and equality proposed by Dr. Levy, claiming that the Jewish community in Eretz-Israel should maintain its Jewish character and not view itself as part of the larger Ottoman nation:

> We Jews – you add [...] – should put aside our little concerns, there is now no difference between Jew, Christian, and Muslim! [...] But, sir, look how illogical you are: you preach, in the name of [our] nation's honor, that we should make every effort to specifically send a Jewish delegate to the parliament – what for? If truly there is no longer any difference between Jew, Christian, and Muslim, if we are all members of one nation, what is all the fuss about?[49]

Aharonovitz maintained that Zionism's only interest in the constitution must be how the latter could help in achieving the overriding Zionist vision, the establishment of an autonomous Jewish national entity in Eretz-Israel:

> And if you, sir, see that the entire Hebrew nation in all the lands of its dispersion takes an interest in the Turkish [granting of] liberty, then once more you must realize that it is not liberty per se that interests us, but rather liberty in relation to our great expectation – whether this liberty will provide us with the ability to become stronger in Eretz-Israel and at some time become the majority in the country. If this liberty will give us the ability to create in Eretz-Israel a national center for this wandering nation, then this liberty has great value for us. And if it does not give us that, then it has no value at all for us, for our numbers here are so small that when compared with the size of our nation they are considered as nothing.[50]

There were others who thought and spoke similarly. Even if this was the opinion of a minority in the community, it cannot be seen as marginal.

Anticipation of Freedom of the Press

Another issue dealt with by the Hebrew press was freedom of the press, one of the liberties inscribed in the new constitution.

However, the Hebrew newspapers were careful in reporting on this issue, preferring to quote from the Turkish press or to refer to articles published there rather than to express their own opinions on this matter. *Hashqafa*, for instance, summed up reports in the Turkish press: 'All the newspapers are filled with rejoicing, for print censorship has been abrogated, and the newspapers will now be able, in this country too, to properly fill their important role'.[51] The Hebrew newspapers emphasized the increased importance and status of the Turkish press, and carefully quoted from or summarized articles printed there on this topic:

> The Turkish-language press is developing. The editors express their opinions on all matters of state and show no pity in their judgment. They mounted an attack on the vezirs Tawfik and Razi Pasha, criticizing them sharply, and also called to order Sa'id Pasha, the former Grand Vizier.[52]

Despite the fact that they did not relate directly to the issue of freedom of the press, the Hebrew newspapers, too, were apprehensive that this right might be abrogated or limited:

> It is rumored that the Grand Vizier is considering proposing to parliament that it should introduce some limitations or prohibitions on freedom of the press, the reason being the arrogant statements published by some papers against the sultan himself and against the government.[53]

One of the issues of *ha-Po'el ha-Tza'ir* also reported on the establishment and publication by Christian Arabs of two periodicals in Arabic: the Jerusalem-based *al-Quds*, and *al-Asma'i*, a literary and political journal edited in Jaffa, but printed in Jerusalem.[54] These examples all show that the issue of freedom of the press was not disregarded in Palestine, and that this freedom to some degree even created and encouraged a free press that dealt with a diversity of topics, from state politics to local news.

Conclusion

In this chapter we have analyzed the immediate reactions of the Jewish community in Palestine, as reflected in the local Hebrew press of the time, to the Young Turk Revolution and the promulgation of the new constitution. The dominant picture that emerges from the Hebrew press is that of a multitude of responses to the constitution, responses that even sparked internal differences of opinion and conflicts in the *yishuv*. The surprising lack of any immediate discussion of issues such as new opportunities to acquire land and increase settlement efforts is particularly noteworthy.

During their regime the Young Turks tried to implement reforms in almost every sphere of life including the political, educational and judicial systems. They also tried to reshape society itself by borrowing from Western concepts of governance.[55] Nonetheless, there was a great deal of disappointment regarding the new regime in the *yishuv*, as demonstrated by the following quote from Luncz's *Eretz-Israel Almanac* for 1914, about six years after the Revolution: 'We hoped for much good from this change, but because of political events the central government could not consider the areas smaller than the capital and introduce reforms as it wished there, and [thus] everything has remained as it was [...]'.[56]

Notes

1. Luncz, Abraham Moshe, *Luah Eretz-Yisra'el {...} li-Shnat 5674, ha-Shanah ha-Tsha' 'Esreh* [Eretz-Israel Almanac [...] for 5674, the Nineteenth Year] (Jerusalem, 1914), p. 10 [in Hebrew].
2. For a background on these newspapers see Kressel, Getzel, *Toldot ha-'Itonut ha-'Ivrit be-Eretz-Yisra'el* [History of the Hebrew Press in Eretz-Israel] (Jerusalem, 1964) [in Hebrew]; Shapira, Yosef, *Ha-Po'el ha-Tza'ir ha-Ra'ayon veha-Ma'ase* [Ha-Po'el ha-Tza'ir in Theory and in Practice] (Tel Aviv, 1967) [in Hebrew]; Gilboa, Menuha, *Hebrew Periodicals in the 18th and 19th Centuries* (Jerusalem, 1992) [in Hebrew].
3. Kramer, Mendel, 'Hag ha-herut ha-'otmanit bi-Yerushalayim' [The Ottoman Festival of Freedom in Jerusalem], *Hashqafa*, 10 August 1908, p. 2 [in Hebrew].
4. 'Simhat netinei hod malkhuto ha-sultan ba-konstitutzion hanitna lahem me'et hodo' [The Rejoicing of the Subjects of His Majesty the Sultan in the

Constitution Granted by His Excellency], *Habazeleth*, 10 August 1908, p. 2 [in Hebrew].
5. Kushner, David, *A Governor in Jerusalem: The City and Province in the Eyes of Ali Ekrem Bey – 1906–1908* (Jerusalem, 1995), p. 191 [in Hebrew]. There is a contradiction regarding the date of the celebration between Ekrem Bey (28 July) and *Habazeleth* (7 August). Wallace's report (see note 6) validates *Habazeleth*'s claim regarding the date in which the celebration was held. Interestingly enough, soon afterwards, on 5 August, Ekrem Bey sent a letter to the Grand Vizier, asking to be relieved of his post, and indeed a few days later he left.
6. 'The present political situation in Turkey', Special Report by Thomas R. Wallace, US Consul, Jerusalem, to Assistant Secretary of State, Washington, D.C., 12 and 14 August 1908, United States National Archive, T471/10 (Fi 2477/10), p. 3.
7. The 'new *yishuv*' was the term used for the Zionist-oriented Jewish population of Palestine in the late nineteenth and early twentieth centuries to differentiate it from the 'old *yishuv*', comprising ultra-Orthodox elements.
8. 'Sword' [pseud.], 'Yafo' [Jaffa], *ha-Po'el ha-Tza'ir*, July–August 1908, p. 22 [in Hebrew].
9. 'Ehad ha-hogegim' [One of the Celebrants] [pseud.], 'Yafo' [Jaffa], *Hashqafa*, 14 August 1908, p. 3.
10. Wallace, p. 1. Wallace refers to what became known as the '*Purim* Riot'.
11. For further detailes on Ottomanization, see Ben-Bassat, Yuval, 'Rethinking the concept of ottomanization: The *Yishuv* in the aftermath of the Young Turk Revolution of 1908', *Middle Eastern Studies* 45/3 (2009), pp. 461–75.
12. On this subject, see Ibid.
13. Luncz, Abraham Moshe, [Untitled], *Luah Eretz-Yisra'el {...} li-Shnat 5669, ha-Shanah ha-Arba' 'Esreh* [Eretz-Israel Almanac [...] for 5669, the Fourteenth Year] (Jerusalem, 1908), p. 159 [in Hebrew].
14. 'Simhat netinei hod malkhuto ha-sultan' (n. 4. above), p. 2.
15. *Bulletin de la Chambre de Commerce d'Industrie et d'Agriculture de Palestine* 1/1 (Juillet 1909), pp. 1–3.
16. ''Al ha-perek' [On the Agenda], *ha-Po'el ha-Tza'ir*, July–August 1908, pp. 19–21. In Jerusalem, for example, there was a Jewish majority of 65 per cent in 1908. See Luncz, in Kark, Ruth and Oren-Nordheim, Michal, *Jerusalem and its Environs: Quarters, Neighborhoods, Villages, 1800–1948* (Jerusalem: The Hebrew University Magnes Press, 2001), p. 28.
17. Ben-Yehuda, Eliezer, 'Ha-Yom – im be-qoli tishme'u' [Today – If You Will Hear Me], *Hazewi*, 3 September 1908, p. 1 [in Hebrew].

18. 'Ma'aravi' [pseud.], 'Me-Hahayim ha-politim' [Political Matters], *ha-Po'el ha-Tza'ir*, September 1908, p. 14.
19. It was customary in Hebrew at this time to refer to the capital as 'Kushta' (i.e., Constantinople) instead of Istanbul.
20. The Hebrew term *shaliah tzibbur* is in quotation marks in the original, since the author borrowed it from the sphere of religious services, in which the cantor, who leads the congregation in prayer, is termed *shaliah tzibbur*, the emissary of the public or the congregation.
21. Kramer, Mendel, 'Ha-Shavu'a' [This Week], *Hashqafa*, 31 July 1908, p. 2.
22. A *mukhtar* was the head man of a village, or of a neighborhood in a city.
23. Kramer, Mendel, 'Ha-Shavu'a' [This Week], *Hashqafa*, 14 August 1908, p. 8.
24. 'Chronicle', *ha-Po'el ha-Tza'ir*, August–September 1908, p. 17. It is our understanding that 'perpetual enemies' relates to Christian Arabs.
25. M. P–N, "Irbuviya' [Confusion], *Hazewi*, 25 October 1908, p. 1.
26. Ben-Zevi, Menashe, 'Avodatenu' [Our work], *Hashqafa*, 25 September 1908, pp. 2–3.
27. Yellin, David, *The Works of David Yellin in Seven Volumes*, vol. 4: *Letters* (Jerusalem,1976), pp. 321–2 [in Hebrew].
28. 'A Citizen' [pseud.], 'Qorespondentziyot' [Correspondence], Jerusalem', *ha-Po'el ha-Tza'ir*, September–October 1908, p. 9.
29. Ibid., p. 10.
30. Ibid.
31. Ibid.
32. 'Yerushalayim' [Jerusalem], *ha-Po'el ha-Tza'ir*, July–August 1908, p. 18.
33. Ibid.
34. Ibid.
35. Ibid.
36. Bril, [A.], 'Chag ha-hofesh' [The Festival of Liberty], *Hashqafa*, 10 August 1908, p. 3. Bril, an agronomist from Jaffa, was later a corresponding member of the Jerusalem Chamber of Commerce, established in 1909.
37. Luncz: *Luah Eretz-Yisra'el {...} li-Shnat 5669*, p. 159.
38. Yellin: *Works* (n. 26 above), pp. 319–21.
39. 'Yerushalayim' [Jerusalem], *Hashqafa*, 21 August 1908, p. 2.
40. For details, see the next sub-section.
41. 'Agudat ha-Yehudim ha-'otomanim' [Jewish Ottoman Society], *Habazeleth*, 24 August 1908, p. 2.
42. Ibid.
43. Michlin, Haim Michal, 'Merkaz ha-Yehudim ha-'otomanim' [The Center of Ottoman Jews], *Habazeleth*, 4 September 1908, pp. 3–4.

44. 'Me-'Arey ha-Medina, Yafo' [Report] From the Cities of the State – Jaffa], *Hashqafa*, 23 September 1908; 'Hamevaser' [Bearer of Tidings], 'Yafo' [Jaffa], *Hashqafa*, 25 September 1908, p. 1; 'Khronika' [Chronicle], *ha-Po'el ha-Tza'ir*, August–September 1908, p. 17.
45. Yellin: *Works* (n. 26 above), p. 306.
46. Ibid., p. 328.
47. Kramarov, Z., 'Ha-Qonstityutzia veha-Yehudim' [The Constitution and the Jews], *ha-Po'el ha-Tza'ir*, July–August 1908, pp. 21–2.
48. Ben-Yehuda, Itamar, 'Mi yode'a?' [Who Knows?], *Hazewi*, 23 October 1908, p. 1.
49. Aharonovitz, Yosef, 'Mikhtav galuy le-Dr. Levi Menahel Anglo Palestine Company bi-Yerushalayim' [An Open Letter to Dr. Levy, Director of the Anglo-Palestine Company in Jerusalem – Editorial], *ha-Po'el ha-Tza'ir*, July–August 1908, pp. 24–5.
50. Ibid.
51. 'Ha-Me'ora'ot be-mamlakhtenu' [Events in Our Realm], *Hashqafa*, 4 August 1908, p. 1.
52. 'Ba-Mamlakha' [In the realm], *Hashqafa*, 28 August 1908, p. 2.
53. 'Ba-Mamlakha' [In the Realm], *Hazewi*, 2 October 1908, p. 3.
54. It is noteworthy that Khalil al-Sakakini, one of the outstanding Christian Arab intellectuals of the period, wrote in both these journals and was on the editorial board of *Al-Asma'i*. See al-Sakakini, Khalil, *'Such Am I, Oh World': From the Diaries of Khalil al-Sakakini*, translated, annotated, and introduced by Shilo, Gideon (Jerusalem, 1990), p. 11 [in Hebrew]. For more details about this journal, see Yehoshua, Ya'akov, *'Al-Munadi*: Ha-'Iton ha-Muslemi ha-rishon be-Eretz Yisra'el' [*Al-Munadi*: The First Muslim Newspaper in Eretz-Israel], *ha-Mizrah he-Hadash* 25/ 3 (1975), p. 215 [in Hebrew].
55. These reforms are beyond the scope of this paper. For further details and examples see Ahmad, Feroz, *The Making of Modern Turkey* (London, 1993); idem, *Turkey: The Quest for Identity* (Oxford, 2003); Tucker, Judith E., 'Revisiting reform: Women and the Ottoman Law of Family Rights 1917', *Arab Studies Journal* 4/2 (1996); Fortna, Benjamin C., *Imperial Classroom: Islam, the State and Education in the Late Ottoman Empire* (Oxford, 2002).
56. *Luncz: Luah Eretz-Yisrael li-Shnat 5674*, p. 10.

PART IV

INTER- AND INTRA-COMMUNAL RELATIONSHIPS

CHAPTER 11

ADMINISTRATING THE NON-MUSLIMS AND THE 'QUESTION OF JERUSALEM' AFTER THE YOUNG TURK REVOLUTION

BEDROSS DER MATOSSIAN

The historiography on the Young Turk Revolution of 1908 in general has mainly concentrated on the impact of the Revolution on the Ottoman Turkish society. Rarely do we see works that deal with the impact of the Revolution on the non-dominant groups in the Empire from a comparative perspective. How did the different ethnic groups view the Revolution? How did the Revolution influence the dynamics of power inside these groups? What were the relations between the Revolution and the religious groups within the Empire? How did the local/central government view the transformations taking place among the non-Muslim communities in the provinces? These and other questions still preoccupy historians of the Ottoman Empire and the modern Middle East. This article discusses the impact of the Young Turk Revolution on the different ethno-religious groups residing in one of the most contentious cities of the Ottoman Empire: the Old City of Jerusalem.[1]

The Young Turk Revolution of 1908 led to a radical upheaval in the dynamics of power within the ethnic groups in the Ottoman Empire.

Jerusalem, with its Armenian and Greek Patriarchates and the Chief Rabbinate, became a focal point of a political power struggle among Jews, Armenians, and Greeks. The importance that the ethno-religious and secular leadership in Istanbul gave to the crisis in Jerusalem demonstrates its centrality in the Empire's ethnic politics and shows how the question of Jerusalem became a source of conflict between the different political forces that emerged after the Revolution. The Revolution gave the dissatisfied elements within these communities an opportunity to reclaim what they thought had been usurped from them during the period of the *ancien régime*.

Hence, in all three cases studied in this article these communities internalized the Revolution by initiating their own micro-revolutions and constructing their own *ancien régimes*, new orders, and victories. This chapter illustrates the commonalities and the differences between the three cases and contends that post-Revolutionary ethnic politics in the Empire should not be viewed solely through the prism of political parties. Rather these ought to be examined in the light of ecclesiastic politics, which was a key factor in defining inter and intra-ethnic politics. While the Revolution aimed at the creation of a new Ottoman identity, which entailed that all the ethnic and religious groups be brothers and equal citizens, it also required that all the groups abandon their distinct religious privileges. This caused much anxiety among the ethnic groups whose communities enjoyed the religious privileges bestowed on them by the previous regimes. Thus, despite its proclaimed aim to undo ethno-religious representations, the Revolution nevertheless reinforced religious politics in Istanbul as well as in Jerusalem.

In the Jewish case, the center of power remained within the Chief Rabbinate (*hahambaşlık*). The election of Haim Nahum as the Empire's Chief Rabbi in 1909 strengthened the *hamambaşı*'s role as the ethno-religious representative of Ottoman Jewry, but this became increasingly difficult in a period where new actors entered the public sphere. In order to oppose the influence of the *Alliance Israélite Universelle* (AIU) in Istanbul, based on its extensive educational system, the Zionists founded their own institutions like the Maccabi gymnastic club branch, which became an important society that gained momentum in the post-revolutionary period.² The Zionists, who aimed at winning over the public opinion of the Sephardic Jewry for their activities, were considered an undesirable element by the Chief Rabbinate and by some other prominent Sephardic figures who feared that Zionist national activity in Palestine would enrage the Turkish and Arab populations. Haim Nahum, with the aid of David Fresko, the editor of *El Tiempo*, a Ladino daily published in Istanbul, became the main opponents of Zionist activities in the Empire. Fresko wrote a series of articles attacking Zionism, which were later published in a booklet.³ Concomitantly, however, the Chief Rabbinate's predisposition against the Zionists was also the result of the ongoing rivalry between various Jewish institutions such as the strife between the Zionists and graduates of the AIU schooling system.

In the Armenian case, the Revolution brought about a change of leadership and the transfer of power from the Armenian Patriarchate in Istanbul to the *Armenian National Assembly* (ANA), which became the representative of the Gregorian Armenians in the Empire.⁴ The downfall of Patriarch Maghakia Ormanian whose 'regime was nothing more but a miniature Ottoman *ancien régime* in the national arena',⁵ represented the beginning of a new era. This is because the Armenian *ancien régime* was embodied in one person: Patriarch Ormanian. The editor of the Armenian daily newspaper in Istanbul, *Puzantion* named after the editor's first name, described his dominance in the community this way: 'He was everything and as Louis XIV said *"l'état c'est moi"* Ormanian also could have declared more accurately that "I am the Patriarch, Patriarchate, Religious Council, Political Council, Economic committee, financial trustee, judicial committee, and educational committee"'.⁶ In fact, Ormanian was criticized by the Armenian revolutionary groups for his policies in general and his 'collaboration' with the Yıldız Palace. The Armenian Revolutionary Federation's official organ, *Droshak* [flag], hailed the collapse of Ormanian and heavily criticized him by calling him the 'Tatar Patriarch', who was mourning the Revolution like his superior, i.e. the Sultan.⁷ Thus, the Revolution became a milestone in defining intra-ethnic relationships in the Armenian *millet* of the Empire. It resulted in a micro-revolution, culminating with the reinstatement of the Armenian National Constitution, the (re)opening of the Armenian National Assembly, and the election of Madteos III Izmirilyan as Patriarch. Unlike the Jewish case, the ANA during the post-revolutionary period included representatives of most of the Armenian political currents (the Dashnaks, Hunchaks, and Ramgavars), and became a battleground between the different Armenian political groups. In addition, the Revolution also paved the way for the strengthening of Armenian political groups in the Empire, most prominently the Dashnaks, which, by propagating their significant role in the Revolution, attempted to strengthen their status in Armenian circles and claimed to be the representative of the Armenian ethnic group in the Empire.

Finally, the Revolution caused some erosion in political and social stability in the Empire's Arab provinces by challenging the politics of notables. In some areas it succeeded in changing the dynamics of power by creating new political actors, such as the *za'im*s of Beirut. In other geographical regions such as Damascus, however, it was unsuccessful, as local notables and the *'ulema* remained the most influential elements of society. In general, though, the Revolution seems to have had more impact on Arab Christians, specifically the Arab Orthodox community of Palestine, the third group examined in this chapter. In particular, it led to the emergence *al-Nahda al-Urthuduksiyya* [the Orthodox Revival] and led growing numbers among the Orthodox community to identify themselves with the Arab National movement. This Orthodox Revival would not have taken place without the existence of cultural nationalism among the Palestinian Christian elite at the end of the nineteenth century. This cultural nationalism was a by-product of the reforms in the nineteenth century specifically in the fields of law and education, missionary activities, and the development of print capitalism in Palestine that shaped 'an imagined community that came to describe itself as Palestinian'.[8]

The Revolution of 1908 and 'La Kestyon del Gran Rabino de Yeruśalayim'

The impact of the Revolution on the Jews of the Empire should be analyzed from two perspectives. One pertains to the micro-revolution that occurred inside the Jewish *millet*, whereas the other pertains to the increased Zionist activities in Istanbul after the Revolution. The Revolution paved the way for Jewish movements in the Empire to start not only reforming its own communities, but also to take an active part in the political and economic life of the Empire. However, unlike in the Armenian case, the transition of power in the Jewish case met with resistance by people loyal to the former regime of Moshe Halevi. It is worth noting here that the Chief Rabbinate of Istanbul was created in 1835 by the appointment of Avraham Levi as the Chief Rabbi. His position was recognized by the Ottoman government, making him both the temporal and the spiritual leader of the Jewish community. However, this newly created position remained marginal until 1860. In 1872 Moshe Halevi was appointed as the *kaymakam* [substitute] of the Chief Rabbinate. The historian Avraham Galanté argues that Halevi was not a person of initiative and action and that he did nothing, because his patrons kept him under their control, and that this ultimately resulted in disorder in the administration and recklessness in finances[9]. Moshe Halevi did not hold elections until the Young Turk revolution, thus demonstrating his reluctance to bring about change within the Jewish community of the Empire.

After the Revolution, Haim Nahum was appointed the *kaymakam* of the Chief Rabbinate in Istanbul.[10] This led to an uproar among those who remained loyal to the previous administration in the Jewish *millet*. The tensions emanating from this appointment should be viewed as the outcome of the tensions existing between the Zionists and the AIU. In one letter, while commenting on maneuvers by the German Orthodox Jews during the elections, Nahum clearly states: 'In any case, if I am elected, it will really be a victory for the Alliance, because a very strong campaign is being conducted against our society'.[11] This tension was fueled by the rivalry between Germany and France, which aligned with the Zionists and the Alliance respectively for influence over the Jews of the Empire.[12]

Shortly after the July Revolution, on 24 January, 1909 Haim Nahum was elected *hahambaşı* by 74 votes.[13] His opponents challenged the election arguing that only three quarters of the delegates had voted.[14] On the other hand, David Fresko's *El Tiempo* announced that the results were received with joy and happiness from all the provinces of the Empire, as evidenced by the numerous telegrams, letters and articles that the newspaper received.[15]

Immediately after his accession letters began to pour into the office of the *hahambaşı* from the provinces demanding the dismissal of their spiritual heads.[16] 'It is to be noted with regret', claimed *The Jewish Chronicle* from London, 'that, with the exception of Salonica, which has a worthy spiritual chief at its head in the person of Rabbi Ya'akov Meir, all the Jewish communities in Turkey are administered by Rabbis who are not cultured, and are imbued with ideas of the past'.[17] Rabbi Nahum mentions this in a letter addressed to Jacques Bigart the secretary general of the AIU in Paris:

> Feelings are still running very high, and I receive telegrams every day from the different communities in the Empire asking me for the immediate dismissals of their respective chief rabbis. Jerusalem, Damascus, and Saida [Sidon] are the towns that complain the most about their spiritual leaders. I am sending Rabbi Habib of Bursa to hold new elections in these places.[18]

Demonstrations against their respective rabbis were held in the Jewish communities of Damascus, Sidon, and Jerusalem.[19] In Damascus, the people demanded the removal of Rabbi Merkado Alfandari 'who has a mentality and an education that is not at all compatible with the new order of things'.[20] In Sidon the people demanded the removal of the Chief Rabbi under 'whose administrative tyranny the population suffered for many years'.[21] In Jerusalem, letters were sent to the Grand Vizierate and the Ministry of Interior demanding the removal of Rabbi Panigel who was only appointed provisionally.[22] The governors of these localities also telegraphed the Sublime Porte arguing in support of the demonstrators. In response, the Minister of Justice wrote to the *kaymakam* demanding that he take action without delay. On 3 September, 1908 the Secular Council (*meclis-i cismani*) convened under the presidency of the *kaymakam* Rabbi Haim Nahum and decided to dismiss these three Rabbis.[23] Of these dismissals, the question of the Chief Rabbinate of Jerusalem was the most important.

It is a good illustration of the ways the different factions within the Empire's Jewish community competed with each other after the Revolution.[24] The question of Jerusalem was high on the agenda of the Chief Rabbinate of Istanbul, not only because of its strategic position, but also because of the infighting there between those who supported the AIU and those who supported the Zionists.

The struggle over the position of the Chief Rabbinate of Jerusalem began after the death of Chief Rabbi Ya'akov Sha'ul Elyashar.[25] In 1906, the governor of Jerusalem, Reşid Paşa, appointed Rabbi Shlomo Mani as *kaymakam* and ordered him to hold elections for the post of *hahambaşı*. Two groups were in the running. One supported the candidacy of Haim Moshe Elyashar,[26] the son of the deceased, whereas the second backed the candidacy of Ya'akov Meir, a graduate of the AIU.[27] The latter group was composed of liberals such as Albert Antebi (the representative of the AIU in Palestine)[28] and Avraham Almaliach,[29] while the former was headed by well-established Sephardi families who wanted to maintain the status quo. Most of the other oriental Jewish groups (Yemenites, Bukharians, Persians) supported Rabbi Ya'akov Meir with the hope that if elected, their political status would improve. Local Jewish newspapers took opposing stances. *Habazeleth*, for instance, supported Elyashar, while *Hashqafa* supported the candidacy of Ya'akov Meir.

The elections were held and Rabbi Ya'akov Meir emerged as the winner. The Ashkenazi community did not participate in the elections and complained to the *kaymakam* in Istanbul Rabbi Moshe Halevi that Albert Antebi had influenced the governor and prevented them from casting ballots. Rabbi Moshe Halevi in turn annulled the elections and removed Rabbi Ya'akov Meir. However, as Rabbi Meir was on good terms with the incumbent governor of Jerusalem he did not leave his post until the arrival of the new governor 'Ali Ekrem Bey, after which he left for Salonica.[30] Rabbi Moshe Halevi then appointed Rabbi Eliyahu Moshe Panigel, Elyashar's father-in-law, to be the *kaymakam* of Jerusalem and oversee the elections for the new Chief Rabbi.[31] The *kaymakam* of the Istanbul Chief Rabbinate, Rabbi Moshe Halevi, along with the conservatives, backed Rabbi Panigel.[32]

With the appointment of Rabbi Panigel the struggles once more began between the two camps. The Ashkenazi community of Jerusalem supported Rabbi Panigel whereas the supporters of Rabbi Ya'akov Meir opposed him. Those who supported him presented his incumbency as an era when the community and its institutions had flourished. However, Rachel Sharaby notes that according to the newspaper *Habazeleth* he mismanaged the affairs of the community.[33] He raised the taxes of his opponents and marginalized the Yemenite Jews who were supporters of Rabbi Ya'akov Meir. Panigel became close to the German-Jewish *Ezra* society[34] in order to counteract the efforts of the AIU in Jerusalem.[35] However, the situation changed with the Revolution, the election of Haim Nahum as the *kaymakam* of the Chief Rabbinate of Empire and the appointment of a new governor of Jerusalem. This was a great boon for the opposing camp in Jerusalem, the supporters of Rabbi Ya'akov Meir. Rabbi Haim Nahum agreed to the demand of Albert Antebi and his movement to dismiss Rabbi Panigel and on the 4 November, 1908 he sent a telegram to Rabbi Panigel ordering him to resign and appoint a new *kaymakam* who would oversee the election of the Chief Rabbinate of Jerusalem.[36] This move caused much excitement in the city's Jewish community.

Haim Nahum appointed Hezkiya Shabatai, the Chief Rabbi of Aleppo as the *kaymakam* of Jerusalem and ordered him to hold elections.[37] However, he failed to do so because the Panigel camp refused to cooperate.[38] For their part, the Ashkenazi leadership refused to take any side, partly because of their disappointment with Panigel. Unable to hold elections, he returned to Aleppo and appointed his friend Rabbi Nahman Batito as the *locum tenens* in Jerusalem.[39] However, Batito as well was unable to hold elections, despite the fact that five candidates were nominated. Once more, the whole issue was stalemated because of the pro-Panigel and the anti-Panigel movements. This led Rabbi Haim Nahum to pay a special visit to Jerusalem to force a compromise in which Rabbi Ya'akov Meir would be appointed Chief Rabbi and Rabbi Panigel would be his deputy. However, the Jewish community of Salonica made sure that Rabbi Meir did not leave his position there. The situation stagnated until Rabbi Haim Nahum removed Batito from his position and appointed the Rabbi of Rhodes, Moshe Yosef Franco, as chief Rabbi of Jerusalem.[40]

To conclude, the Revolution led to a serious crisis within the Jewish community of Jerusalem. It resulted in the escalation of inter-communal tensions over the elections of the Chief Rabbi of Jerusalem. Unlike the Armenian case, however, the struggle within the Jewish community of Jerusalem divided the community into two camps: One camp (the liberals) supporting the candidacy of Ya'akov Meir and the other camp (the well-established Sephardi families) supporting the candidacy of Elyashar and Panigel. The battles between these two camps also reflected the struggle between different interest groups that intensified after the Revolution.

The Question of Jerusalem (Erusaghēmi khntirĕ) and Armenian Attempts of Centralization

The Armenian presence in Jerusalem dates back to the Byzantine period in the fourth century when an influx of Armenian pilgrims came to the city after the discovery of the Holy Places of Christianity, traditionally ascribed to Saint Helena, the mother of Emperor Constantine I.[41] The current Patriarchate came into existence in the first decade of the fourteenth century when the Brotherhood of St. James[42] proclaimed its head, Bishop Sargis, as patriarch. Eventually the Armenian Patriarchate of Jerusalem exercised its authority in Palestine, southern Syria, Lebanon, Cyprus and Egypt. During the Ottoman period and after the creation of the Armenian Patriarchate of Istanbul, the Ottoman state forced all the Armenian ecclesiastic centers in the Ottoman Empire to obey the newly created religious order in the capital. This subordination was mainly characterized by administrative affairs and did not encompass the recognition of the Patriarchate of Istanbul as a higher religious authority. The Armenian Patriarchate of Jerusalem had no choice but to adapt itself to the new situation. However, the Armenian Patriarchate of Jerusalem may have actually benefited from this situation because it received financial assistance from the Patriarchate of Istanbul as well as the support of the wealthy Armenian *Amira* class in its struggle to preserve its rights in the Holy Places.[43]

When the ANA was established following the promulgation of the Armenian National Constitution in 1863 [as part of the *Tanzimat* reforms], it took on the right to elect the Patriarch of Jerusalem from an initial list of seven candidates presented by the St. James Brotherhood. In addition, it had the right to supervise the finances of the Patriarchate. In the second half of the nineteenth century the Patriarchate of Jerusalem opposed these measures. Sultan Abdülhamid II seemed to have shared the same views as the Patriarchate of Jerusalem and in 1888 he issued an edict in which he confirmed the election of Patriarch Haroutiun Vehabedian and restored the autonomous status of the Patriarchate.[44]

In the pre-Revolutionary period, during Patriarch Haroutiun Vehabedian's reign (1889–1910), the Armenian Patriarchate of Jerusalem was in disarray. Some members of the Patriarchate's Brotherhood, taking advantage of the Patriarch's old age, ran the affairs of the Patriarchate by appropriating huge sums of money.[45] Prior to the 1908 Revolution, Patriarch Maghakia Ormanian (1841–1918) sent an investigative commission to Jerusalem to put things in order.[46] Though the commission did not achieve any substantial results, it led to the banishment of many members of the Brotherhood to areas outside Jerusalem. The disorder and chaos continued until the Revolution.

The Revolution brought with it hopes of freedom, equality and justice, and ushered in a new era by getting rid of the *ancien régime*. It was in this new era that the majority of the members of the Brotherhood of St. James saw the Revolution as the ultimate opportunity to reform the Patriarchate. In their quest for reform the members of the Brotherhood were also able to mobilize a segment of the Armenian community of Jerusalem. On 25 August 1908 the Brotherhood convened a Synod and decided to call back all the exiled priests of the Patriarchate to remedy the situation.[47] After several failed attempts to convince the Patriarch, the Brotherhood sent another letter, this time with the signatures of 23 priests from the Synod informing the Patriarch that the Synod has decided on the return of the exiled priests.[48]

However, when the third letter from the Synod also went unanswered, the Synod drafted a request for the dismissal of the Grand Sacristan [*Lusararpet*], father Tavit, who according to them was not qualified to fulfill his duties.[49] Members of the Synod argued in this letter that in addition to failing to protect some important Armenian rights in the Holy Places, he was the main reason for the banishment of many members of the Brotherhood.[50] When all these efforts failed, the Synod appealed to the ANA in Istanbul, and the 'question of Jerusalem' (*Erusaghēmi khntirě*) became one of the most important subjects of debate in this body, a fact which highlights its policy to centralize the administration, as will be seen below.

As tensions between the local lay community and the Patriarchate intensified, Avedis, the aid of the Patriarch, complained to the local government that members of the lay community were going to attack the Patriarchate. The local community, for its part, appealed to the governor of Jerusalem and requested the removal of Avedis.[51] As a result, the Patriarch's deputy, Father Yeghia, sent a letter to the *locum tenens*[52] in Istanbul, Yeghishe Tourian, the president of the ANA, in which he denounced the underhanded activities of Avedis and the Grand Sacristan Tavit. The governor of Jerusalem investigated the situation and, in order to mollify the local population, ordered the Patriarch to remove Avedis from his post.[53] In response the Patriarch banned two priests to Damascus, an act which led the members of the Brotherhood to send a letter of protest to the ANA. In addition, they demanded the expulsion of father Sarkis, Tavit, and Bedros who had exploited the administrative incompetence of Patriarch Haroutiun.[54]

The reading of the letter in the ANA fueled a heated debate among the deputies as to what needed to be done. Deputy Shahrigian Efendi explained that the issue was two-fold, the first pertaining to the reorganization and the second pertaining to finding a remedy for the deteriorating situation in the Patriarchate of Jerusalem. Deputy Djivanian answered that there were more essential issues to tackle than the Jerusalem problem and protested the interference of the local government in the affairs of the Brotherhood.[55] Meanwhile, the chairman stated that a letter had arrived from the Patriarch of Jerusalem arguing that members of the priesthood had attacked the Patriarchate and that he was resigning from his position.[56] Deputy Manougian responded that the National constitution obliged the Armenian National Assembly to exert its authority as regards the Jerusalem Question when the matter dealt with national jurisdiction and financial losses.

Archbishop Madteos Izmirilyan, who was presiding over the Assembly, proposed that a letter be sent to Patriarch Haroutiun indicating that the ANA would deal with the issue of Jerusalem.[57] After much debate,[58] the Assembly elected a Jerusalem Investigative Commission on 5 December, 1908.[59] The commission that left for Jerusalem was composed of three members, one priest and two lay people, a choice which reflects the extent to which laymen were able to play important roles in ecclesiastic politics in the aftermath of the Revolution.

However, the members of the Jerusalem Brotherhood opposed the recommendations of the commission. When the members of the commission felt that their lives were under threat from the Patriarch and his clique they returned to Jaffa. On 1 December 1908, Patriarch Haroutiun sent a letter to the ANA saying that the Synod had agreed on the return of all exiled priests.[60] In February 1909, the ANA received two letters from the Jerusalem Patriarchate. The first indicated that the investigative commission had not yet presented their recommendations to the Synod and had left for Jaffa. The second argued that there was no need for an investigative commission when peace and order prevailed in the cathedral.[61] These contradictory statements from Jerusalem elicited much agitated debate in the Assembly.[62]

On 22 May the Report of the Investigative Commission was read in the ANA after which Patriarch Izmirilyan gave his farewell speech.[63] The Commission criticized the Brotherhood, the Synod and Father Ghevont who was regarded as responsible for the appropriation of huge sums of money. In addition, the report found Archbishop Kevork Yeritsian, the former representative of Jerusalem in Istanbul, responsible for the deteriorating situation in Jerusalem, and considered him an agent of father Ghevont. On 5 July, the Political Council of the ANA decided to depose the Patriarch of Jerusalem Archbishop Haroutiun Vehabedian according to the nineteenth Article of the Armenian National Constitution and elect a *locum tenens* from the General Assembly.[64] A commission was formed which decided to remove the Patriarch from his position and replace him with a *locum tenens*.[65] The General Assembly supported the decision of the Political Council and decided to appoint Father Daniel Hagopian as a *locum tenens*. The position of the Patriarch in Jerusalem remained vacant from 1910 to1921.

In 1921 Yeghishe Tourian[66] was elected Patriarch under the regulations of the Constitution of 1888, except that confirmation was given by the British crown, not by the Sultan.[67]

The Revolution led to radical changes in the dynamics of power within the Armenian Quarter of Jerusalem. The micro-Revolution taking place in the Armenian community of Istanbul prompted the Armenian laity and the Armenian clergy of Jerusalem to initiate their own micro-Revolution by bringing down their own *ancien régime* and creating their own new order on the model of their counterpart in Istanbul. Thus, as a result of the transformations taking place in the Empire in general and in the Armenian community of Istanbul in particular, the Armenian community of Jerusalem (both laity and clergy) found the Revolution a valuable opportunity to root out those whom they accused of unjustly controlling the affairs of the local Armenian Patriarchate. When the efforts of the clergy failed they appealed to the ANA, demanding its intervention in the crisis. After the revolution, the ANA became the most important Armenian religious-political center in the Empire. However, when the ANA decided to take the matter into its own hands by sending an investigative commission to Jerusalem, the Jerusalem Patriarchate with its brotherhood, feeling that their autonomous status was endangered, immediately resolved their differences and opposed any such encroachments.

Patriarch Damianos, the Synod, and the 'Arabophone Question'

As of the early years of Christianity the Arab Orthodox community has existed in the region of Greater Syria. Throughout the course of history they have concentrated in such cities as Jerusalem, Bethlehem, Haifa, Jaffa, and Nazareth. In addition, they formed the majority of the Christians in the Arab villages of the Galilee. As a result of the Council of Chalcedon in 451 AD, the Patriarchate of Jerusalem was established, and given jurisdiction over Palestine and the east bank of the Jordan River. During the Byzantine period the Patriarchate of Jerusalem became the head of a hierarchy that included in it five metropolitans, sixty episcopacies, and hundreds of monasteries stretching all the way from the southern to the northern parts of Palestine. Thus, the Patriarchate of Jerusalem along with the other Orthodox Patriarchates (Constantinople, Alexandria and Antioch) became one of the most important spiritual centers for the Orthodox world. Though the Patriarch of Constantinople was an ecumenical patriarch, it had no spiritual domination over the other patriarchates. However, mainly due to its strategic position as the head of the Greek *millet* in the Ottoman Empire and its proximity to the central government, beginning in the sixteenth century the Patriarchate of Constantinople exerted its influence over the other patriarchates, including Jerusalem. Due to this influence, the Brotherhood of the Holy Sepulcher was exclusively made up of the Greek- speaking monks.[68]

When the Balkan states, starting from Greece, obtained their independence from the Ottoman Empire in the nineteenth century they established their own national churches as a response to growing Hellenism and the influence of the Patriarchate of Constantinople.[69] Concomitantly, the Arab Orthodox elements within the greater Syria area were influenced by these transformations and also voiced their discontent with Hellenism and the ways the Greek clergy were controlling the affairs of the Patriarchate. This came at a time when the Arab Orthodox elements argued that their congregations were neglected by the Greek Patriarchate, excluded from the administration of the patriarchate, and were prevented from taking any part in the Patriarchate's decision making processes.

The first manifestation of this discontent took place in 1872 with the deposition of Patriarch Cyril in the form of protests and demonstrations outside Jerusalem.[70] A council called the National Orthodox Association was set up to represent the grievances of the local population, but subsequently these tensions declined. The second phase of the struggle would continue after the Revolution. Interestingly, in the second half of the nineteenth century, the Orthodox Russians joined the fray and influenced the Arab Orthodox community through the Imperial Orthodox Palestine Society established by the Russian mission.[71] This Society was sympathetic to the Arab Orthodox contentions and aimed at improving their condition through education. By 1895, the Society had 18 schools with 50 teachers and more than 1,000 pupils in

Palestine. These schools were divided into three types: boarding school, day schools in which Russian was taught, and village schools under the control of an Arab teacher where studies were conducted in Arabic. It was from these institutions and other Western Missionary educational institutions, such as St. George's School (1899) and the Collège des Frères (1875) in Jerusalem, that a new generation of Arab orthodox intellectuals would emerge demanding reforms within their communities and a greater say in the affairs of the local Greek Patriarchate.

Hence, the situation regarding the Greek Patriarchate in Jerusalem was more complex than that of the Armenians or the Jews. The impact of the Revolution on the Greeks should be viewed from two perspectives: one involves the internal struggles within the Patriarchate between the Patriarch and the Synod, and the other to the resurfacing of the 'arabophone question' challenging the dominance of Hellenism.[72] To the Orthodox Arabs of Jerusalem the Revolution meant a greater share in the affairs of the Patriarchate. This was also the period in which young educated figures within the community such as Khalil al-Sakakini (1878–1953; an important Palestinian educator),[73] 'Isa al-'Isa and his cousin Yusuf al-'Isa (both editors of the influential newspaper *Filastin*),[74] and Khalil Beidas, played a dominant role in the formation of *al-Nahda al-Urthuduksiyya* by identifying themselves with the Arab National movement.

Al-Sakakini, for instance, was born into an Arab Orthodox family in Jerusalem on 23 January, 1878. After attending the Greek Orthodox School in Jerusalem, he continued his education at the Christian Mission Society (CMS) College founded by the Anglican Bishop Blyth, and at the Zion English College, both situated in Jerusalem. Later he travelled to the United Kingdom and from there to the United States where he stayed until the Revolution translating and writing for Arabic literary magazines on the East Coast and also doing translations for Professor Richard Gottheil at Columbia University. When the constitution was proclaimed in 1908, al-Sakakini along with some other intellectuals residing in exile returned to their hometowns. In Jerusalem, al-Sakakini worked as a journalist for the Jerusalem newspaper *al-Asma'i* [named after the famous Medieval scholar al-Asma'i] and taught Arabic at the *Salahiyya* school (Ste. Anne).

'Isa al-'Isa, born in 1878, was a close friend of al-Sakakini and was the editor of *Filastin* that was first published on 14 January, 1911 in Jaffa. He studied at the École des Frères in Jaffa and then graduated from the Greek Orthodox school and seminary in Kiftin in northern Lebanon in 1897.[75] In 1908 al-'Isa played an important role through his articles in the press that stressed the need to increase the role of the Arab Orthodox community in managing the affairs of the Greek Patriarchate.

Khalil Beidas, who was born in Nazareth in 1874 was one of Palestine's foremost intellectuals in the early twentieth century. He studied at the Russian Orthodox School and the Russian Teachers' Training center in Nazareth and graduated from there in 1892 and became a senior Arabic teacher at the Anglican St. George's School in Jerusalem. After travelling to Russia at the end of the nineteenth century he became influenced by the ideas of the major Russian cultural nationalists such as the writers Fyodor Dostoyevsky (1821–1881), Maxim Gorky (1868– 1936), and Leo Tolstoi (1828–1910). Upon his return to Palestine, he embarked on translating the works of major figures in Russian literature. Beidas had very strong connections with the Russian Orthodox Church and as a result he became a leading figure in the Arab Orthodox community of Palestine and represented their interests to the Greek Patriarchate. In addition, through his journal *al-Nafa'is al-'Asriyya* [Modern Treasures], Beidas became a key proponent of the Palestinian national movement. The Young Turk Revolution was a turning point for these intellectuals, who saw the period as one in which they could represent the interests of the Arab Orthodox community in a more active way.

The Constitution that was reinstated after the Revolution contained a provision which became the source of all subsequent tensions between the Arab Orthodox community and the Patriarchate on the one hand, and the Patriarch and the Synod on the other. It gave the Arab Orthodox community the opportunity to have a greater say in its own affairs as well as those of the Patriarchate, as attested in the diaries of Khalil al-Sakakini.[76] The provision found in Article 111 of the restored Ottoman Constitution stated that in each *qada* [district] there would be a council of each community residing in the area. The duties of this council included:

1) The administration of the revenues of immovable and capital sums subject to pious endowments (*waqf*) according to the stipulations of the founders and consistent with previous customs.
2) The use of properties designated for philanthropic aims complying with conditions prescribed in the endowment deeds relating thereto.
3) The administration of the properties of orphans in compliance with the special regulations on this subject.

On 15 September, 1908 six priests and fifteen lay notables of Jerusalem announced the election of a council of forty with the aim of carrying out the provisions of Article 111. On 25 September, 1908 the request was submitted to Patriarch Damianos[77] by father Khalil. Al-Sakakini explains in his memoirs:

> The Patriarch said: 'For four or five generations the Church has adhered to a well-a known policy necessitated by conditions and situations. Now that there is a new constitution this policy should be changed but we do not know what measures will be taken until the Parliament convenes. For that reason I cannot give you a positive or a negative response. It seems to me that you moved too quickly and it would be much better if you waited until Parliament convenes, since by then we might be able to initiate a gradual reform.'[78]

Al-Sakakini mentions that the deputation told the Patriarch that it was not its intention to undermine the rights of the Patriarchate, but rather to attempt to restore the usurped rights of the community.[79] The Patriarch explained to the deputation the legal position of the Patriarchate and proposed the appointment of a mixed committee to discuss it.[80] The committee met several times to discuss the implications of the provisions, but during the third meeting its lay members put forward eighteen demands. On 22 October, 1908 the

Patriarch rejected these demands but it was arranged that a mixed committee would look into the matter.[81] On 1 November the committee presented a demand to the Patriarch in the form of an ultimatum in which it called for the formation of a Mixed Council to be chosen annually. The Mixed Council would consist of six members of the clergy and six members of the lay community. This demand, which was based on the recently established model that existed in the Patriarchate of Istanbul, was rejected by the Patriarch, a situation leading to increased tensions within the community.[82] The Patriarch sent letters to the central government in Istanbul asking for their intervention. The church of St. James near the Holy Sepulcher, which was frequented by the Arab Orthodox clergy and community members of Jerusalem, was closed in order to avoid disturbances during the feast of St. James. On 24 November the local Arab Orthodox population organized a demonstration and it was decided to send a deputation to Constantinople.[83] The tensions between the lay Arab-Orthodox community and the Greek clergy rapidly spread to other cities of Palestine such as Jaffa and Bethlehem.[84] Some five thousand members of the community went on a religious strike, boycotting the churches. Due to the fact that St. James was closed they conducted their service in the Cemetery of Zion.[85] Meanwhile the Patriarch submitted a petition to the Grand Vizier in which he represented the position of the Patriarchate and further argued that the local community was already benefiting from the church's revenues and thus there was no need to form such a committee.

Members of the Synod of Jerusalem, mostly consisting of Greeks, were not happy with the way the Patriarch was handling the issue. They thought that he was sympathetic to the demands of the Arab laity and accused him of working without the approval of the Synod.[86] His decision to compromise rather than make a clear decision in favor of the Patriarchate was perceived as highly dangerous. In an official meeting the Synod decided unanimously that the Patriarch should resign and if he refused to do so he would be deposed. However, when the Patriarch refused to resign two members of the Fraternity were sent on the night of 26 December to the governor to announce his deposition. The Synod pronounced him incapable of assuming the burden of his office.[87] The deposition (*pavsis*) was approved at the general meeting of the Brotherhood the next day, and Archbishop Tiberias was elected as the *locum tenens* (*Topoteretes*).[88]

When the Brotherhood saw that the depositions did not work they resorted to *kathairesis* which implied that it 'altogether and permanently extinguishes the clerical character of the person affected'.[89] The Patriarch, nevertheless, did not relinquish his responsibilities and it was decided to postpone the *kathairesis* until after Orthodox Christmas. The main problem was that the *locum tenens* was recognized by the government only on 2 February, 1909. This in itself implied the deposition of Damianos. As a result the local Arab Orthodox population reacted negatively to the decision in the cities of Bethlehem (especially during Christmas), Jaffa and Ramle. Upon hearing the news in Jerusalem the community members occupied the Patriarchate in Jerusalem.[90] The Patriarch refused to comply with the deposition order and demanded that the central government send an investigative commission. The government consented and after some delay dispatched a committee of three members, under the presidency of Nazim Paşa, the Governor of Syria – a clear sign of the conflict's significance. On 8 February the committee reached Jerusalem and tried in vain to bring about a compromise.[91] This coincided with political changes in Istanbul when Hilmi Paşa became the Grand Vizier. He decided to summon both the Patriarch Damianos and the two Archimandrites who were responsible for the movement against him to Istanbul. The Patriarch, however, did not travel to Istanbul, claiming ill health. Things became worse when the *locum tenens* died, and the Synod elected a new *locum tenens* who was never recognized by the government. On 1 March, Nazim Paşa announced that 'he would not be responsible for the safety of anyone unless the Synod and the Brotherhood on that day recognized Damianos'.[92] The Synod thereupon capitulated and passed a resolution recognizing Patriarch Damianos. It was only on 25 July, 1909 that the Ecumenical Patriarch of Istanbul recognized him as Patriarch.[93]

On 8 March, 1909 the Synod reversed its previous decision to reduce the rental allowances of the Orthodox Community. On 26 July representatives of local lay community visited Istanbul to discuss the demands of the community. On 12 October the committee returned to Jerusalem. In November it became obvious that the government's response would be favorable to the Patriarchate, a fact which caused agitation. The substance of the decision was announced in December 1909, but it was not until 30 May 1910 that the full text was published.[94] The laity had six principal demands: to have a constitution for the communal councils in accordance with Article 111 of the Ottoman Constitution, a mixed council on the model of Istanbul, admission of native Arab Palestinians to the monasteries and their promotion to all ecclesiastic ranks, increased representation of local inhabitants in the election of patriarchs, bishops required to live in their Dioceses, and finally monks to be prohibited from engaging in secular occupations.

In general the government's decision was very favorable to the Brotherhood, as most of the demands of the community were rejected. These demands, which entailed greater participation of the laity in the affairs of the Patriarchate, were considered a threat to the Hellenic and ecclesiastic nature of the Brotherhood. However, one concession was made: the establishment of a Mixed Council for certain purposes and the assignment of one-third of the revenues of the Patriarchate to the Council. Some Christian Arabs viewed the report with dismay and cynicism. On the other hand others saw it as a source of hope that by means of their influence in the newly constituted Mixed Council the educational rights of their children might at last be recognized.[95] Subsequent controversies took place afterwards. It was only in 1913 that all the tensions were dissipated during a visit by Acmi Bey, the Ottoman Minister of Justice. In 1914 the Orthodox church of St. James was opened again to public service and the Patriarch celebrated mass there.

Conclusion

In an era of rising nationalisms, nation states, and increased global communication, ethnic politics in the Ottoman Empire intensified after the Revolution of 1908 and became one of the major catalysts in the precipitation of inter-ethnic tensions, culminating in the dissolution of the Empire. Despite the fact that the Revolution opened new horizons and new opportunities for the ethnic groups, it also created severe challenges both for the architects of the Revolution and the ethnic groups. The post-Revolutionary period became the litmus test for the endurance/sustainability of the main principle of the Revolution: the creation of an Ottoman identity based on equality, fraternity and liberty, whose allegiance would be to the Empire. Achieving this goal was extremely difficult in a period when all ethno-religious groups in the Empire began projecting their own perception of what it meant to be an Ottoman citizen. Many of these ethnic groups viewed the Young Turk Revolution as the beginning of a new era in which the emphasis was to be more on national identity, a byproduct of modernity. In this equation of modernity, it was hoped that ethnic groups would be represented based on their universal/national identity rather than on an ethno-religious basis. Ottomanism was to be the title of their book with their particular identities as the subtitles. However, as seen, the outcomes of the Revolution were contradictory in that it was not able to eliminate religious representation. On the contrary, the government's open support for all the religious leaders illustrates its reluctance to emphasize the separate national character of these communities.

The contested city of Jerusalem provides a good case study of the struggles and complexities of the post-Revolutionary period. In the confines of the old city walls the echoes of the Revolution brought hope to the disenchanted elements in these communities. In all the three cases discussed in this chapter the Revolution prompted major changes in the dynamics of power within these communities. The waves of micro-revolutions taking place within these communities in Istanbul echoed in Jerusalem. What followed was an internal struggle between the different elements of these communities, a struggle that can be best understood as one taking place between secularism/religion on the one hand and localism/nationalism on the other.

In the Armenian case, when the ANA of Istanbul, representing the Armenians of the Ottoman Empire decided to take the matter into its own hands, the Jerusalem Patriarchate with its brotherhood felt that their autonomous status was endangered and immediately resolved their differences and opposed any such external encroachments. In the Jewish case the struggle between the pro-Panigel and anti-Panigel factions became a microcosm of struggle between the different political and social trends emerging in the Empire. The case of the Greeks was unique in that unlike the Jews and Armenians, the community was ethnically different from that of the religious hierarchy. The Revolution thus proved to be a defining moment for the Arab-Orthodox communities in Palestine to achieve what they had aimed for, namely to abolish the Hellenism that had ruled the Patriarchate for centuries and to take on a dominant role in the affairs of the Patriarchate. The reluctance of the Ottoman government to support the Arab Orthodox laity and their open support for the established religious hierarchy reveals the contradictory dimension of the Revolution, which ostensibly sought to undermine religious representations and create a secular Ottoman citizenship. One explanation for this behavior is that the central government did not want to encourage the Arab-Orthodox community which was going through a process of national revival because of their direct involvement in the Arab national movement. It should be borne in mind that at the time members of this community played an important role in the rise of Arab nationalism in general, and Palestinian nationalism in particular. The growing national sentiments among the Arabs as well as other ethnic groups were considered by the Young Turks as a threat to the integrity of their vision of the Empire. In order to undermine the development of these identities they were apparently ready to jettison the major ideals of the Revolution.

Notes

1. Alexander Schölch estimated the number in 1914 to be 70,270 Muslims, 32,461 Christians, and 18,190 Jews. According to the British Mandate census of 1922 Jerusalem had 13, 300 Muslims, 14, 7000 Christians, and 34,100 Jews. See Schölch, Alexander, 'Jerusalem in the 19th century', in Asali. K.J., (ed.), *Jerusalem in History* (Brookline, N.Y., 1990), p. 232.
2. See Tziper, Daniel, *Ha-Degel ha-Tzioni Me'al ha-Bosphoros: Ha-Maccabi be-Kushta beyn Tzionut le-'Otmaniyut 1895–1923* [The Zionist Flag over the Bosphorus: the Maccabi in Istanbul between Zionism and Ottomanism 1895–1923] (Jerusalem, 2000) [in Hebrew].
3. Fresko, David, *Le Sionisme* (Istanbul, 1909).

4. In the second half of the nineteenth century, until the reign of the Armenian Patriarch of Istanbul Maghakia Ormanian (1896–1908), the Armenian National Assembly became an important political venue for the Armenians through which they discussed the social, political, and economic affairs pertaining to their community. Thus, the Assembly became the first nontraditional institution (a mini-parliament) in conventional politics was the rule, including elections, voting, hearings, debates, exchange of ideas, and decision-making process.
5. Aslanian, Dikran, 'Hosank'ner ew nerhosank'ner' [Currents and Undercurrents], *Puzantion*, 22 August , 1908, 3610, p. 1 [in Armenian].
6. Puzant Kecheyan, 'Ankum Pateriak' Ōrmaneani' [The Fall of Patriarch Ormanian], *Puzantion*, 30 July , 1908, 3591, p. 2.
7. 'Ōrmaneani Tapalumě' [The Collapse of Ormanian], *Droshak*, July 1908, No.7 (195), p. 105 [in Armenian]. By using the word 'supreme', Droshak is referring to the Sultan.
8. Khalidi, Rashid, *Palestinian Identity: the Construction of Modern National Consciousness* (New York, 1997), p. 88.
9. Galanté, Avraham, *Histoire des Juifs d'Istanbul* (Istanbul, 1985), Vol.1, pp. 258–9.
10. Benbassa, Esther (ed.), *Haim Nahum: A Sephardic Chief Rabbi in Politics, 1892–1923*, translated from French by Miriam Kochan (Tuscaloosa and London, 1995).
11. Nahum to J. Bigart (11 January, 1909) AAIU, Turkey, XXX E. in Benbassa: *Haim Nahum*, p. 154.
12. On the *Alliance Israélite Universelle* and their politics in the Ottoman Empire see Rodrigue, Aron, *French Jews, Turkish Jews: The Alliance Israélite Universelle and the Politics of Jewish Schooling in Turkey, 1860–1925* (Bloomington and Indianapolis, 1990).
13. Raphael Shimon received 9 votes, Moshe Haviv 2, and Avraham Danon 1. For detailed information on the elections see 'La Eleksyon del Gran Rabinato de Turkiya: La junta del ayer del Mejlis 'Umumi' [The Elections of the Cheif Rabbinate of Turkey: The Yesterday Gathering of the General Assembly], *El Tiempo*, 23 January 1908 [in Ladino]. For Haim Nahum's reaction to the election in the Ladino press in Palestine see 'Rabbi Haim Nahum Gran Rabino de Turkiya' [Rabbi Haim Nahum Chief Rabbi of Turkey], *El Liberal*, 29 January 1909 [in Ladino].
14. Eighty five delegates out of a hundred and twenty, from the provinces participated in the elections.
15. 'La Eleksyon del Gran Rabani de Turkiya: La Impresyon en el payis y en el estranyrro' [The Elections of the Cheif Rabbi of Turkey: The Impression in the Country and Abroad], *El Tiempo*, 3 February 1909 [in Ladino].

16. For the letters sent to the *hahambaşı* see HM2 8639; HM2 8640; HM2 8641 in The Central Archives for the History of the Jewish People in Jerusalem (CAHJP).
17. 'Turkey: The Chief Rabbinates in the Empire', *The Jewish Chronicle*, 4 September 1908.
18. Nahum to J. Bigart, (Constantinople, 6 September 1908) AAIU, Turkey, XXXE in Benbassa: *Haim Nahum*, p. 146.
19. On the struggles in Damascus before and after the Revolution see Harel, Yaron, *Between Intrigues and Revolution: The Appointment and Dismissal of Chief Rabbis in Baghdad, Damascus, and Aleppo 1744–1914* (Jerusalem, 2007), pp. 231–5 [in Hebrew]. On the situation of the Jews in Baghdad after the Revolution see ibid., pp. 306–327.
20. 'Las Komunidades Israelitas de la Provensya: Destitusyon de los grandes rabinos de Yeruśalayim, de Damasko i de Sayda' [The Jewish Communities of the Provinces: The Dismissal of the Chief Rabbis of Jerusalem, Damascus and Sidon]', *El Tiempo*, 2 September 1908.
21. Ibid.
22. Rabbi Panigel was appointed provisionally and charged with convening an assembly of the heads of the community to plan elections for the chief Rabbi within three months.
23. 'Las Komunidades Israelitas de la Provensya: Yeruśalayim, Damasko i Sayda' [The Jewish Communities of the Provinces: Jerusaelm, Damascus and Sidon], *El Tiempo*, 4 September 1908.
24. On the struggles over the Jerusalem Rabbinate in general see Sharaby, Rachel, 'The Chief Sephardic Rabbinate, 1906–1914: Conflicts and Personalities', *Cathedra* 37 (1985), pp. 106–112 [in Hebrew]; Haim, Abraham, 'The Hakham Bashi of Istanbul and the "Rabbinate Controversy" in Jerusalem', *Pe'amim* 12 (1982), pp. 105–113 [in Hebrew].
25. On Rabbi Elyashar, see Efrati, Nathan, *Mishpahat Elyashar be-Tokhekhey Yerushalayim: Prakim be-Toldot ha-Yishuv ha-Yehudi bi-Yerushalyim ba-Me'ot ha-Tesha'-'Esreh veha-'Esrim* [The Elyashar Family in Jerusalem: A Chapter in the History of the Jewish Community in Jerusalem in the Nineteenth and Twentieth Century] (Jerusalem, 1974) [in Hebrew]; see also Gaon, Moshe David, *Yehudei ha-Mizrah be-Eretz Yisra'el: 'Avar ve-Hove* [The Oriental Jews in Eretz Yisra'el-Past and Present] (Jerusalem, 1937), pp. 61–8 [in Hebrew].
26. On Haim Moshe Elyashar see ibid., pp. 59–60.
27. On Ya'akov Meir, see ibid., pp. 361–71; idem, 'Rabbi Jacob Meir', *Le Judaisme séphardi*, VIII (June, 1939), pp. 81–3.
28. On Antebi and the role of the AIU in Palestine during that period see Lazare, Lucien, 'L'Alliance Israélite Universelle en Palestine à l'époque de la

révolution des "Jeunes Turcs" et sa mission en Orient du 29 October 1908 au 19 Janvier 1909', *Revue des Études Juives* CXXXVIII/3–4 (juill.-déc. 1979), pp. 307–335.

29. Almaliach was the editor of the Ladino newspaper *El Liberal*, published in Palestine, which had an anti-Panigel policy. See for example, "Et la-davar: La Kestyon del Gran Rabino de Yeruśalayim' [The Time Arrived: The Question of the Chief Rabbi of Jerusalem], *El Liberal*, 19 March 1908.

30. On the 10 July 1907 Ekrem Bey, the governor of Jerusalem, sent a letter to the Grand Vizier in Istanbul expressing the opinion that Ya'akov Meir 'was not worthy of being appointed Rabbi through general elections given the seditious activities of the above mentioned Antebi'. Ekrem Bey to the Grand Vezir, 13 July 1907 document 13 in Kushner, David, *A Governor in Jerusalem: The City and Province in the Eyes of Ali Ekrem Bey, 1906–1908* (Jerusalem, 1995), p. 97 [in Hebrew]. On Ekrem's point of view on the elections of 1907; see document 14, pp. 98–100.

31. On Moshe Eliyahu Panigel, see Gaon: *Yehudei ha-Mizrah*, pp. 527–30.

32. See Friedman, Isaiah, 'The *Hilfsverein der Deutschen Juden*, The German Foreign Ministry, and the Controversy with the Zionists, 1901–1918', *Cathedra* 20 (July 1981), pp. 97–122 [in Hebrew].

33. Sharaby: 'The Chief Sephardic Rabbinate', p. 109.

34. Ezra Society was formed in Berlin in 1901 to promote Jewish education in Palestine and Eastern Europe.

35. On the relationship of Rabbi Panigel with Ezra see 'Li-Sh'elat behirat haham bashi li-Yerushalayim' [On the Question of Electing a Chief Rabbi for Jerusalem], *Habazeleth*, 28 December 1908 [in Hebrew].

36. See 'La Kestyon Rabinika en Yeruśalayim' [The Question of the Rabinnate in Jerusalem], *El Tiempo*, 11 November 1908.

37. 'Hezkiya Shabatai', *Hazewi*, 13 December 1908, 51, p. 2; 'Yeruśalayim' [Jerusalem], *Habazeleth*, 9 December 1908 [in Hebrew].

38. 'Yerushalayim' [Jerusalem], *Habazeleth*, 20 January 1909; 'Yerushalayim', *Habazeleth*, 25 January 1909.

39. 'Yerushalayim', *Habazeleth*, 17 February 1909; 'Yerushalayim', *El Liberal*, 19 February 1908. On his life see Gaon: *Yehudei ha-Mizrah be-Eretz Yisra'el*, pp. 141–2.

40. On Rabbi Franco see ibid., pp. 567–8.

41. Most of the historiography written about the Armenians of Jerusalem in the twentieth century is in Armenian. In English see Antreassian, Assadour, *Jerusalem and the Armenians* (Jerusalem, 1969); Hintlian, George, *History of the Armenians in the Holy Land* (Jerusalem, 1976); Azaria, Victor, *The Armenian Quarter of Jerusalem: Urban Life Behind Monastery Walls* (Berkley,

Calif., 1984); Rose, John H. Melkon, *Armenians of Jerusalem: Memoirs of Life in Palestine* (London and New York, 1993); Sanjian, Ara, 'The Armenian Church and community of Jerusalem', in O'Mahony, Anthony (ed.), *The Christian Communities of Jerusalem and the Holy Land: Studies in History, Religion and Politics* (Cardiff, 2003).

42. The Brotherhood is a monastic order of the Armenian Church in Jerusalem.
43. Sanjian: 'The Armenian Church', p. 63.
44. Ajamian, Shahe Bishop, 'Sultan Abdul Hamid and the Armenian Patriarchate of Jerusalem', in Ma'oz, Moshe (ed.), *Studies on Palestine during the Ottoman Period* (Jerusalem, 1975), pp. 344–7.
45. This included the steward of the Patriarchate, Father Ghevont, who had appropriated huge sums of money and the servant of the Patriarch, a layman called Avedis Tashjian.
46. On Ormanian's commission, see Maksoudian, Ghevont Father, *Erusaghemi Khndirĕ* [The Question of Jerusalem], Vol. I (Istanbul, 1908) [in Armenian].
47. A synod is a council of a church convened to decide on issues pertaining to doctrine, administration or application.
48. The twenty three members of the Synod to Patriarch Haroutiun Vehabedian, 28 August 1908. A copy of the letter appeared in the daily *Arevelk*, 3 October 1908 [in Armenian].
49. The Grand Sacristan is the second most powerful figure after the Patriarch. His duties include the administration of the entire Brotherhood.
50. Members of the Synod to Patriarch Haroutiun Vehabedian, 14 October 1908. A copy of the letter appears in M.D.S, *Erusaghēmi verjin dēpk'erĕ*, pp. 12–14.
51. 'Al-Quds al-Sharif' [Holy Jerusalem], *al-Muqattam*, 29 October 1908 [in Arabic].
52. Locum tenens is a Latin phrase which means place-holder. In the Church system the Locum tenens is a person who temporarily fulfills the duties of the Patriarch until the election of a new Patriarch.
53. 'Spasavor Avedis Erusaghēmi Vank'en Vedarwats' [Servant Avedis Expelled from the Monastery], *Jamanag*, 11 November 1908 [in Armenian]. 'Ba-mahane ha-armeni' [in the Armenian camp], *Hazewi*, 23 November 1908.
54. Father Vertanes and Father Karekin to the Chairman of the ANA Torkomian Efendi, 7 November 1908, a copy of the letter appears in the minutes of the ANA. See *Azgayin Ĕndhanur Zhoghov*, Nist Ē [Session VII], 7 November 1908, p. 79 [in Armenian].
55. Ibid.

56. 'Erusaghēmi Vichakě kě Tsanranay' [The Condition of Jerusalem Gets Worse], *Jamanag*, 20 November 1908.
57. See *Azgayin Ěndhanur Zhoghov*, Nist Ē [Session VII], 7 November 1908, p. 80.
58. Ibid., Nist T' [Session IX], 21 November 1908, pp. 121–27.
59. Ibid., Nist Zh [Session X], 5 December 1908.
60. From Patriarch Haroutiun to Madteos II Izmiriliyan Patriarch of Istanbul, 1 December 1908, 157. A copy of the letter appears in *Azgayin Ěndhanur Zhoghov*, Nist ZhG [Session XIII], 26 December 1908, p.183. This caused confusion in the meeting because in his previous letters Patriarch Haroutiun had expressed apprehension about Archbishop Kevork Yeritzian, but was now advocating his return.
61. On the letters see *Azgayin Ěndhanur Zhoghov*, Nist ZhZ [Session XVI], 13 February 1909, pp. 230–31.
62. Ibid., p. 231.
63. Archbishop Madteos Izmirilyan was reelected as Patriarch of Istanbul on 4 November 1908. 'Amen T.T. Matt'ēos Izmirliyan Verěntrwadz Patriark' T'urk'yo Hayots" [His Beatitude Madteos Izmirliyan Re-elected as Patriarch of Armenians of Turkey], *Arevelk*, 5 November 1908; *Azgayin Ěndhanur Zhoghov*, Nist E [Session V], October 22, 1908. For the report see *Teghekagir Erusaghēmi Hashuots' K'nnich' Khorhrdaranakan Handznazhoghovoy, matuts'uats Azgayin Eresp', Zhoghovin: 1909 Mayis 22i IA nistin* (K. Polis, 1909).
64. *Azgayin Ěndhanur Zhoghov*, Nist IB [Session XXII], 5 June 1909, p. 361.
65. See 'Teghekagir Erusaghēmi S. Patriark'in děm Eghadz Ambastanut'iants' K'nnich' Khorhrdaranakan Hants'nazhoghowoy', in *Azgayin Ěndhanur Zhoghov*, Nist IZ [Session XXVI], 17 July 1909, pp. 434–7.
66. For a complete biography of Patriarch Turian see Koushagian, Torkom Arch., *Eghishe Patriark` Durean* [Patriarch Yeghishe Turian] (Jerusalem, 1932).
67. In the Ottoman Empire it was the Sultan who confirmed the elections of the heads of the *millet*s.
68. The Brotherhood of the Holy Sepulcher is the Orthodox Monastic Fraternity that for centuries has guarded the Christian Holy places in the Holy Land.
69. Shea, John, *Macedonia and Greece: The Struggle to Define a New Balkan Nation* (Jefferson, N.C., 1997), p. 173.
70. Bertram, Anton Sir and Harry Charles Luke, *Report of the Commission Appointed by the Government of Palestine to Inquire into the Affairs of the Orthodox Patriarchate of Jerusalem* (Humphrey Milford, 1921), p. 72.
71. Hopwood, Derek, *The Russian Presence in Syria and Palestine 1843–1914: Church and Politics in the Near East* (Oxford, 1969).

72. Ibid; Bertram and Charles: *Report of the Commission*; Mahony, Anthony O., 'Palestinian-Arab Orthodox Christians: religion, politics, and church-state relations in Jerusalem, c. 1908–1925', *Chronos* 3 (2000), pp. 61–87; Katz, Itamar and Ruth Kark, 'The Greek Orthodox Patriarchate of Jerusalem and its congregation: dissent over real estate', *The International Journal of Middle East Studies* 37 (2005), pp. 509–534; Vatikiotis, P. J., 'The Greek Orthodox Patriarchate of Jerusalem between Hellenism and Arabism', *Middle Eastern Studies* 30/4 (1994), pp. 916–29; Clogg, Richard, 'The Greek Millet in the Ottoman Empire', in Braude, Benjamin and Bernard Lewis (eds.), *Christians and Jews in the Ottoman Empire: The Functioning of a Plural Society*, vol. I, p. 185 (New York, 1982).
73. See Al-Sakakni, Khalil, *The Diaries of Khalil Sakakini: New York, Sultana, Jerusalem, 1907–1912*, Volume I, edited by Musallam, Akram (Jerusalem, 2003) [in Arabic]. The diaries of Kahalil al-Sakakini are an important source for reconstructing the history of Palestine during the Late Ottoman and the British mandate periods. The diaries, an eight-volume series in Arabic began to be published in 2003. To date six volumes of the diaries have been published by the Khalil Skakakini Center (Ramallah) and the Institute of Palestine Studies (Beirut and Jerusalem).
74. See Ayalon, Ami, *Reading Palestine: Printing and Literacy* (Austin, 2004) and Khalidi: *Palestinian Identity*.
75. For a detailed study on 'Isa al-'Isa see Bracy, Michael *Building Palestine: 'Isa al-'Isa, Filastin, and the Textual Construction of a National Identity, 1911–1931* (Unpublished Ph.D. Dissertation: University of Arkansas, 2005).
76. Al-Sakakni, *The Diaries of Khalil Sakakini*, p. 291.
77. Damianos was the 132nd Patriarch of Jerusalem. He was born and educated in the Island of Samos, nowadays in Greece. In July 1897 he was elected Patriarch by the Holy Synod. Previously he had been the Titular Archbishop of Philadelphia (Amman). See Dowling, Archdeacon, *The Patriarchate of Jerusalem* (London, 1909), p. 17.
78. Al-Sakakni, *The Diaries of Khalil Sakakini*, p. 298. On these demands see Metaxakis, Meletios, *Les exigences des Orthodoxes Arabophones de Palestine* (Constantinople, 1909).
79. Al-Sakakni, *The Diaries of Khalil Sakakini*, p. 291.
80. Ibid., p. 304.
81. Bertram and Luke: *Report of the Commission*, p. 252; al-Sakakni, *The Diaries of Khalil Sakakini*, p. 320.
82. Bertram, Anton and J.W.A Young, *Report of the Commission* on Controversies between the Orthodox Patriarchate of Jerusalem and the Arab Orthodox Community (London, 1928), p. 252.
83. Al-Sakakni, *The Diaries of Khalil Sakakini*, p. 342.

84. Bertram and Young: *Report of the Commission*, p. 253.
85. Bliss, Frederick Jones, *The Religions of Modern Syria and Palestine* (New York, 1917), p. 70.
86. Ibid., p. 255.
87. Ibid.
88. Bertram and Young: *Report of the Commission*, p. 256.
89. Ibid., p. 257.
90. Ibid., p. 258.
91. Bertram and Young: *Report of the Commission*, p. 258.
92. Ibid., pp. 260–1.
93. Ibid., p. 264.
94. For the full demands and the response of the government see Ibid., pp. 265–9.
95. Bliss: *The Religions of Modern Syria and Palestine*, p. 72.

CHAPTER 12

THE ZIONIST STRUGGLE AS REFLECTED IN THE JEWISH PRESS IN ISTANBUL IN THE AFTERMATH OF THE YOUNG TURK REVOLUTION, 1908–18

YARON BEN NAEH*

'Who are those who fear?' was the title of a Hebrew article published on 19 Teveth 5671 (19 January 1911) under the pseudonym 'Ma'aravi'. In one passage the author wrote as follows:

> When the future historian of the Jews in Turkey will reach our period and deal with the development of the Zionist idea in Turkey and the intense opposition which that idea met in the land of the Ottomans, and when he asks himself: 'Who feared Zionism? Who waged the tremendous campaign against it?' – He will uncover a terrible state of affairs. The historian will be unable to locate materials for his study in the Turkish press, the archives of the various viziers, or in the record books of the political bodies and the legislatures. The Turkish press and Ottoman society a priori had nothing to say about Zionism, nor did they hold any suspicions against Jews in various countries, especially against Turkish citizens of Jewish descent. It was not

they who launched the campaign against the nationalist ideal in Israel [i.e., the Jewish nation][...]. The source of the evil was within Ottoman Jewry itself; it was from here that informing and slandering came, from here came anger and fear, and the Judeo-Spanish [Ladino] press and those foreign-language newspapers in which our Sephardic brethren wrote in order to mount an attack on Zionism – it is these that will supply the future historian will all the materials needed for his study [...].

Further on, the author denounces some Jewish periodicals for their irresponsible behavior and quotes from one journalistic source which hints at Jewish activity behind the scenes whose purpose was to intimidate the supporters of Zionism. His concluding statement reads:

Even in the camp of our opponents they have finally been forced to admit that informing has afflicted Ottoman Jewry and that the personal quarrels between certain Istanbuli journalists and leading personages among the Zionists created the entire controversy that may cause much trouble for all Jews and bring down mire and filth upon the Jewish nation [...].[1]

In this article I analyze the role played by the Jewish press in Istanbul in the Zionist effort to win the support of Jewish public opinion in the post-Hamidian period, from 1908 to the end of World War I.[2]

The Istanbul Jewish Community

Since 1860, the large Jewish community in Istanbul, numbering around 50,000 and continuously growing, was suffering social tensions and was grossly divided into two camps. The first was comprised of conservative elements, including most of the rabbis, while the other was a reform-seeking progressive faction led by the *Francos*, merchants of wealthy Judeo-Italian families who held influential offices in the communal leadership. The most famous of these was the banker Count Avraham Behor de Camondo (1829–89). In time, officials and supporters of the Alliance Israélite Universelle (AIU) would join forces with the progressives, gaining more influence as the number of graduates of AIU schools increased and joined the ranks of the middle and upper classes, and gained political strength in the communal leadership. Rabbi Ya'akov Avigdor (appointed *hahambaşı*, Chief Rabbi, in 1860) supported the ideas of the reformists, as did his successor Rabbi Yakir Giron (appointed in 1863, resigned and emigrated to Palestine in 1873). The organizational regulations of the community, adopted in 1865, known as *hahamhane nizamnamesi*, gave more power to the reformist circles, since they placed greater authority in the hands of the secular leadership.

The AIU, which began its activities in Istanbul in 1863, took root there in the following years, establishing a network of schools for boys and girls. It seemed that Ottoman Jewry was firmly moving forward into the modern age. Signs were evident of the beginnings of a process of secularization of Jewish life and a decline in importance and weakening of the *kehillah* – the organized Jewish community – and Jewish public opinion. Cultural life flourished as dozens of periodicals were published, mostly in French and Ladino, even in these years of censorship by the government. A growing reading public created a demand for belles-lettres, especially translations from French, and many novels were published serially, either independently or as supplements to newspapers.[3]

In 1872 Rabbi Moshe Halevi was appointed deputy *hahambaşı* (*kaymakam*, the locum tenens for the Chief Rabbi). During his long term in office the conservatives once again gained control of the *kehillah*, which had become afflicted with administrative anarchy, intrigue, and dispute. The condition of the Ottoman Empire under Abdülhamid II (r. 1876–1909) was somewhat paralleled by developments in the *kehillah*. Its condition became more severe at the turn of the twentieth century, when the elderly Moshe Halevi was still its *kaymakam*, and to all intents and purposes the head of the community. Communal institutions were practically paralyzed as the *kehillah* suffered from a lack of finances and was split by social and cultural tensions. The strongest and most influential external force among Istanbul's Jewish population at this time was the AIU, which maintained a large network of educational institutions and enjoyed the support of its graduates, who filled key roles in the community.

The Emergence of Zionism as a Visible Party

In the Revolution launched in July 1908, the Young Turks gained control of the Ottoman state and reinstated the constitution of 1876 which Sultan Abdülhamid II had abrogated shortly after he came to power. This was an event that generated many expectations. The Jewish press expressed joy at this dramatic development, stressing the participation of Jews in the festive mass demonstrations.

The Revolution, which greatly eased the Hamidian censorship, was also evident in the literary output of the printing shops in Istanbul. Within a short period of time a collection of poems on the independent nation in praise of freedom (*La Şarkı de Vatan Huürriyet*), a book about the rule of Sultan Abdülhamid: *Yildiz i sus sekretos i el Reyno de Abdul Hamid* [The Yıldız Palace and its Secrets, and the Reign of Abdülhamid], which even went into a second printing, and *Midhat Paşa, su vida i su ovra* [Medhat Pasha, His Life and His Career] were all published. Simultaneously, the Jewish press flourished as newspapers and journals, including many humorous periodicals were founded including *La Boz, El Burlon, El Jugeton, El Judio, El Grasiozo,* and *La Patriya*.[4] The swell of literary productions was also characteristic of other ethnic groups in the Ottoman Empire in the post-Revolutionary years.

In August 1908, Rabbi Moshe Halevi, who was identified with the old regime, was forced to resign. After much struggle, Rabbi Haim Nahum was elected to the office of *hahambaşı* (at first as *kaymakam*, and from March 1909 as the full-fledged Chief Rabbi).

Rabbi Hayim Nahum Efendi was one of the most interesting figures of the late Ottoman period. Born in Manisa (1873), he later received a modern education in Istanbul and from 1893 to 97 in Paris, where he also befriended members of the Young Turks movement. Upon his return to Istanbul he became the main associate and key figure of the AIU. After the coup of 1908 he was naturally the most influential person in the community, and a year later was appointed chief rabbi of the Empire. He served the regime and filled some diplomatic missions. Political changes brought about his downfall, and he fled to Paris (1920), later to become chief rabbi of Egypt (1925–60). Nahum was a supporter of Ottomanization, and thus opposed Zionism, though he was willing to assist some of their goals: allowing Jewish emigration to and settlement in Palestine and purchase of land there by non-citizens.

Nahum invested much effort in the restoration of communal institutions and in providing a firm basis for his authority. In addition to the support of the AIU, Rabbi Haim Nahum found a fervent advocate in the person of David Fresko, the editor of *El Tiempo*, who was one of the strongest critics of Rabbi Moshe Halevi and his close circle. Fresko, born in 1853, was one of the most talented and prolific writers in the local Jewish press. He was also a translator and a leading public figure for about fifty years. He co-edited *El Tiempo*, and had a share in the editing of a few others, among them *Journal Israélite*, *El Nacional*, *El Amigo dela Familia*, and *El Telegrafo*. He had been running *El Tiempo* since 1871 and used it to voice his ideas. At an advanced age he immigrated to France, where he died in 1933. When the Young Turks assumed power, the Zionists were filled with optimism about the official policy that would be adopted in relation to Jewish interests in Palestine; indeed, certain favorable statements by leading members of the Committee of Union and Progress (CUP) encouraged them to entertain such thoughts. Now began the Zionists' greatest hour. They began operating openly, initiating activities meant to enhance their status and influence in the Jewish community and in Turkish public affairs. The Zionist Organization opened an office in Istanbul directed by Victor Jacobsohn (1869–1935). Official Zionist policy at this time was to raise requests that would not be offensive to Turkish ears such as the lifting of restrictions on emigration to Palestine and the establishment of a Jewish cultural center there under Turkish sovereignty. They refrained from calling for autonomy or a Jewish state. They also stressed the importance of encouraging the use of Hebrew and the creation of a national consciousness.[5]

Zionism was a political movement whose *modus operandi* and objectives not only differed from those of the AIU, but were at odds with them. For some time it did cooperate with the German-Jewish Ezra organization (Hilfsverein der Deutschen Juden), and later, in 1911, with the Order of B'nai Brith. Zionist propaganda called upon the Jews to take their fate into their own hands, and act rather than wait passively for external support. Early Zionist criticism of the AIU in the press was targeted against the latter's alleged assimilatory tendencies, and the Zionists demanded that Hebrew become part of the schools' curriculum instead of Ladino. After 1910, confrontation between the two movements spread to additional issues and was waged openly.

There were several facets to the activities of the Zionist movement and its representatives in the imperial capital: a) political intercession with the Ottoman authorities; b) attempts to win over persons from among the Jewish elite and to encourage leading personages in the community to join its ranks; c) attempts to place candidates with Zionist leanings in communal leadership bodies; and d) vigorous efforts to persuade the Jewish masses in the city – who numbered tens of thousands – to support Zionist ideas and objectives. This they did primarily in two manners: through the establishment of recreational, cultural, and philanthropic organizations, and by directly or indirectly spreading the message of Zionism through the Jewish press.

The Jewish Press as a Battlefield

Zionist use of the press for propaganda purposes can only be understood by taking into account the important role of newspapers in the political – and to some degree also in the social-intellectual – life of Ottoman Jewry in the late nineteenth and early twentieth centuries.[6] Similar cases of utilization of the press, of course, were also true of other minorities and other countries.

Among the most important means of spreading Zionism, therefore, was the establishment – or, primarily, partial financial support – of periodicals in French, Ladino, and Hebrew that would back Zionism. This plan gave rise to internal disagreements within the executive of the Zionist Organization, and also between it and the branch in Istanbul. As early as 1908 Jacobsohn wanted to establish a Zionist journal with financial support from the Hovevei Zion [Lovers of Zion] movement in Odessa and the German Ezra organization, but David Wolffsohn (1855–1914), president of the Zionist Organization, rejected the proposal. Unwilling to abandon this initiative, Jacobsohn began to raise funds independently in Russia. Only after Wolffsohn's visit to Istanbul was permission granted to financially support journals in French and Ladino and establish one in Hebrew that would come out in favor of Zionist objectives. The members of the local press committee were Jacobsohn, Vladimir (Zeev) Jabotinsky (1880–1940, founder of Revisionist Zionism), and Sami Hochberg, who were in close contact with Menahem Ussishkin (1863–1941) and Nahum Sokolow (1859–1936).

In the capital, the Zionists supported several non-Jewish newspapers, first and foremost *Le Jeune Turc*, but also *Le Courrier d'Orient* which, most ironically, was owned by Ebüziyye Tevfik, who was known to have anti-Semitic leanings and was also the proprietor of the Turkish-language *Tesvir-i Efkar*. *Le Jeune Turc*, which supported the Committee of Union and Progress and called for loyalty to the Ottoman state. It also advocated permitting Jewish immigration to the Empire, particularly to Palestine where it argued for the founding of a center of Jewish culture under Ottoman patronage. Through the efforts of Jacobsohn and Jabotinsky, this paper met high standards and counted the Ottoman intellectual elite among its readers. Its circulation increased gradually, attaining 15,000 copies in 1910. Some leading members of the CUP party expressed their appreciation and helped get clearance again after it had been closed down by the authorities for publishing articles critical of Italy's policy of interference in the Balkans.

Despite its journalistic success, *Le Jeune Turc* was unable to influence official Ottoman policy towards Zionism. It is reasonable to assume that Henry Morgenthau (1856–1946), the American ambassador in Istanbul (1913–16), was in a better position to do so, due to his close relations with the ruling *triumvirate* – Talat Bey, Enver Bey, and Cemal Paşa, and later with Halil Bey. It is also known that Jacobsohn and his deputy, Richard Lichtheim (later to become one of the most important Zionist leaders in Germany), met with Morgenthau, who in time would come to oppose Zionism.[7]

Another periodical was the French-language *L'Aurore*, edited by Lucien Ceuto, himself a graduate of an AIU school, whose readership came from among Jewish educated circles who had turned their backs on Ladino. It conducted an ongoing polemical battle against Fresko's *El Tiempo*, which was identified with rabbinical circles, and was often critical of the AIU and the *hahambaşı*, Rabbi Haim Nahum. During this confrontation, Fresko filed suit against Ceuto, who in 1919 transferred his support, and that of his paper, to Rabbi Nahum. Additional journals supported by Zionist funds were *Le Bosphore*, and perhaps another one in French called *L'Orient*. Financial support was also tendered to the French-language *Le Journal de Salonique*, but was soon withdrawn because the journal did not continue to back Zionist policy, and to *al-Ittihad*, published in Arabic letters.[8]

In addition to these publications, most Zionist efforts were directed toward Jewish newspapers and journals in Ladino. The most important foothold they tried to gain was the veteran *El Tiempo*, whose editor, David Fresko, considered Ottoman citizenship and loyalty to the Ottoman state to be lofty values, and therefore rejected Zionism, whose final objectives he could foresee. He was opposed to the revival of Hebrew and believed that Jewish nationalism and Zionism were a dangerous form of false messianic expectations. For a short while he did agree to accept funds from the Zionists and publish their material, but the agreement between the two parties soon came to an end,[9] and Fresko became one of Zionism's severest critics.

One of the most important journals in Ladino that received financial aid from the Zionists was *El Judio*. Bearing the sub-title *Gazeta Judia Endepediente*, it was edited by David Elnecavé and began publication in 1909 in Istanbul. A decade later, in 1919, it appeared under the heading *Organo de la Federasion Sionista del Oriente* and three years later under its original sub-title – *Organo Zionista Independiente*. Elnecavé was active in public affairs, head of the B'nai Yisrael Society which in 1910 merged with the Society for the Ottoman Language, apparently a screen for Zionist activity. According to Yitzhak Bezalel, Elnecavé visited Palestine, was much impressed by what he saw, and recommended to Jews in the Balkans that they emigrate there. The manifesto he published in 1913 received much attention in the Jewish press of Palestine at the time.[10]

Other important Ladino journals in Istanbul to which the Zionists granted financial support were *El Nacional* (prior to 1873: *El Journal*

Israélite), and *El Telegrafo*, established in 1860 by Yehezkel Gabbay as *Journal Israélite*. The change of title of the latter (*Journal Israélite*) occurred in the 1870s when Yehezkel's son, Izak [Yitzhak], became its editor, serving in that capacity until his death in 1931. During the lengthy period in which Rabbi Moshe Halevi served as religious leader of Istanbul's Jews, the paper was closely identified with rabbinical circles and the communal leadership, from which it also received some monetary support.

The Zionist establishment also supported Jewish newspapers and journals in Salonica. *El Avenir*, established in 1897 and edited by David Florentin, propagated Zionist views until its closure in 1917. Another initially pro-Zionist journal was *La Epoka*, founded in 1875 and appearing twice weekly as of 1907 under the editorship of the sons of the printer Sa'adi Halevi. It changed orientation in 1911, maintaining the priority of Ladino over Hebrew and the Turkish homeland over Jewish nationalism. Other Salonican Jewish newspapers worthy of mention in this context are *El Pueblo*, *La Tribuna Libera*, and *La Esperansa*, the organ of the Zionist societies in Salonica that appeared from 1916 to 1920, with the sub-title *Organo Sionista*. Mention should also be made of *La Boz*, and perhaps also of *El Impartial*.

Zionism in the Izmir Jewish community was comparatively minor when viewed through the mirror of the press. The pro-Zionist *El Novelista* had to compete with the important *El Meseret* that had been appearing since 1898 and disseminated the anti-Zionist views of its editor, Alexander Ben Ghiat.[11]

The establishment of the only Hebrew Zionist periodical published in Istanbul, *ha-Mevasser*, was delayed until 1910, and it only continued to appear until 1912. Its publisher was Sami Hochberg, a member of the Zionist press committee, and the editor was Aharon Hermoni. The paper's editorial offices were located in Taksim Square. Its readership was not limited to Turkey; in fact, less than half the subscribers (whose number fluctuated between 100 and 400) lived within the borders of the Ottoman Empire. The ads, too, clearly showed that its readers were mostly of European origin. The publishers noted the price of a subscription in Istanbul 'in the other cities of Turkey and abroad', and in Russia – thus indicating the importance of this market. Moreover, they supplied addresses at which subscriptions could be taken out in Odessa, Vilna, Rohatin (in Austria), Antwerp, and New York, as well as three cities in Palestine: Jerusalem, Jaffa, and Haifa.

Ha-Mevasser was not very successful in Turkey, either because it was published in Hebrew, a language with which only rabbinical scholars and a few of the educated class were familiar, or because it only rarely dealt with controversies within the Jewish community, though it did take a stand on some current issues. While this editorial policy suited its foreign readers, it lessened any real influence *ha-Mevasser* could have had on the intra-communal discourse in Turkey.

Among the contributors to the first issue of *ha-Mevasser* were Nahum Sokolow and Zeev Jabotinsky. In the editorial, under the title 'Our objective', the founders of the journal pointed to the political changes in the Empire as the backdrop for an awakened Jewish national consciousness and called for its reinforcement through the study of Hebrew. The weekly, they wrote, 'will preach the renewal of Hebrew as a national [language] among Jews in the East' and 'will be a Hebrew-Oriental weekly for the dissemination of Jewish wisdom and its literature, and an informant about all that is happening and stirring within the Jewish ethnic groups in Turkey and Eretz Israel'. In his article, Sokolow openly used the term 'Zionism', maintaining that there was no contradiction between Turkish patriotism and Zionism, and that it was incumbent upon every Jew to be a Zionist and to assist in the establishment of a 'model state' in Palestine under the aegis of the progressive Ottoman state. He ended the article with the famous phrase: 'We have become Zionists; you were born Zionists'.[12]

In 1911, in one of the issues of *ha-Mevasser*, under the title 'Mosaic', Dr. Israel Auerbach published a selection of passages from 'the statements of the opposition in the Turkish parliament and with the pleasant [needless to say, used sarcastically – Y. B.-N.] participation of *El Tiempo, Parodos, Ekdam, Stamboul*, and others':

> Zionism is a dangerous movement. Every Zionist is an anarchist and a traitor. The dragnet of the Zionists is spread throughout all countries [...]. The Zionist movement is a dark cloud in the skies of Ottomanism [...]. Zionism is a gigantic organization that

has spread throughout all the countries of the world [...]. There is no finish and no end to the means of this organization [...] and above all these is the Jewish Colonial Bank[13] with cash assets of a billion that increase every month by means of the *shekel* (franc), the sum paid monthly by every Zionist. And to what ends are these means put! They buy all the Jewish newspapers, and the progressive newspapers of the Turks, and the Tanin, and the papers of the 'committee' in Salonica [...]. With monetary gain [for the recipients] they bought the entire Committee of Union and Progress in Salonica, which is completely under the control of the Dönme [descendants of the Sabbatean believers],[14] the Freemasons, and the disseminators of the Hebrew language in Salonica [...]. Only in one thing were they unsuccessful: [in their efforts] to buy, with their great assets, the integrity and conscience of David Fresko, and he is the guarantor of the existence of the Ottoman state [...]. That is the pure, unvarnished truth about Zionism, already attested by the central committee of the Alliance [Israélite Universelle] in Paris and of the [Jewish] communities of Izmir and Salonica and their rabbis. That is the true character of Zionism according to the opinions of antisemites, both Jewish and non-Jewish.[15]

In addition to clearly anti-Semitic opinions – some of which are still voiced and printed in present-day Turkey, these statements contain a reflection of actual Zionist activity, in this case 'buying' the support of certain newspapers for Zionist ideals, a fact discussed above and one that was openly obvious and known to contemporaries.

As noted, except for *ha-Mevasser* all the others were periodicals or journals that received some degree of financial support from the Zionists, whether for a consecutive period of time or intermittently. Only a few of them were edited by persons firmly committed to Zionism. At times their editors zigzagged between different political stances, whether according to their own inclinations or because it was financially worthwhile; i.e., due to political or economic motives. Only a few remained steadfast in their opinions throughout the entire period, and it would seem that during the decade under study the scales tipped toward the opponents of Zionism. Esther Benbassa has called for a new look at the small, private journals, those whose proprietor, editor, and author of the texts was often the same person, who was generally always in financial straits. These editors were in most cases graduates of AIU schools who were prepared to examine both Zionist ideals and new ideas in general with an open mind. She notes that the AIU rejected proposals by its graduates and supporters to publish a journal of its own, thus missing an important opportunity to spread its own ideas.[16]

Newspapers and journals that did receive monetary assistance from the Zionists had recourse to simple, popular language when writing for the masses – the Jewish community of Istanbul is estimated to have numbered about 75,000 at the time – and did not miss any opportunity to present themselves as a vigorous opposition to the Chief Rabbinate, the communal leadership, and the AIU. It should be borne in mind that in the absence of a strong socialist party, or even of workers' solidarity and organization, as in Salonica, the hostility between rich and poor was often manifested through identification with the Zionists. The latter attacked their opponents with every rhetorical means in their arsenal, at times even with curses. This atmosphere of harsh, outspoken, and aggressive journalism is clearly reflected in the sharply critical description by Avraham Elmaleh (1876–1967, a teacher, talented publicist, political figure, primarily a Sephardi activist, member of the General Assembly and later of the Israeli parliament), a resident of Palestine:

> What is especially characteristic of our youthful Ladino press is the manner in which it judges every new idea, or even an old one that has been revived [...]. It has a method different [from ours] to investigate the truth of any idea: it first of all mounts an attack against persons holding an idea that is displeasing to the editors. The important principle is to belittle those persons, and then the idea will disappear of itself. The direct path is the shortest. Why debate a lot? – The issues of the Ladino papers are first of all full of abuse and insults. Turn the pages of most of the Ladino papers that have appeared since the declaration

of political liberty in Turkey. You will search in vain for something serious, for something new from our so-called authors and poets; everywhere you will find only abuse and insults, vulgar attacks, informing, and gossip, the likes of which you can also find among idlers.[17]

The most consistent and strongest critic of Zionism was David Fresko and his paper, *El Tiempo*. After a short period of neutrality on this issue, when he was on the receiving end of Zionist financial support, Fresko sharply enunciated his beliefs, declared himself an Ottoman citizen and patriot, and repeatedly called upon the Jews to assimilate, learn Turkish, and openly display their patriotism. He discerned isolationist tendencies in Zionism that he considered damaging and forbidden.

Fresko attacked his opponents with much vulgarity. In one of the issues in 1911, for instance, he described Max Nordau[18] as a liar, cheat, traitor, and criminal, to quote but a few of the vicious epithets he used.[19] From time to time his articles engendered a round of angry replies, as both parties accused each other of being traitors, informing to the authorities, and causing damage to Jewish interests.[20] Fresko's fear was that the internal disputes among Jews would find their way into national politics, and his apprehensions of possible reaction of Muslims were not unfounded. In 1909 he published a booklet in French containing the thoughts of leading Jewish personages throughout the world on the connection between Zionism and patriotism. He sent it to the editors of Turkish newspapers and to members of the government administration, thus causing much harm to the Zionist movement. Fresko's actions also reverberated in Palestine and Europe. An anonymous author wrote the following in *El Tiempo*:

> The anti-Zionist paper of Constantinople did not find enough arrows to shoot at the Zionists in the pouch of Mr. David Fresko, so it turned to other parts of the world, to ask the opinion of well-known anti-Zionists, in order to print those views in Ladino, and later publish them [also] in Turkish, in order to defame 'the great deceit' [Zionism] in the eyes of the Turks.[21]

On the next page the author calls Fresko 'a devourer of Zionists, who calls for and demands to destroy, wipe out, and kill [!] all the Zionists'.

Thus overall, the periodical press proved to be a bad investment for the Zionist establishment. While the Jewish press aroused interest in Zionism and stimulated public debate, it did not tip the scales in its favor, and it is also doubtful whether its significant message reached the masses beyond the Jewish middle class. The press certainly did not improve the political standing of Zionism with the communal leadership or the authorities. Ottoman officials were increasingly apprehensive of reactionary nationalist movements, and also of the reaction of Palestine's Arabs, who were represented in the parliament in Istanbul. The primary contribution of the press was in making some of the Jewish public increasingly aware of Zionism.

Summary and Conclusions

Despite the opposition of the Chief Rabbi and his supporters, and even though Zionism's opponents included persons associated with the CUP, the movement succeeded in gaining a foothold among the Jews of Istanbul and Salonica, the largest and most important communities in the empire. This success, already evident on the eve of World War I, can be attributed to several factors. The first is the Jewish traditional religious consciousness and self-identity, which was reinforced by the communal framework and with the help of Zionism, was the basis for the rise of a new national consciousness. In addition was the influence of the growing number of Ashkenazi Jews in the Empire, refugees from Eastern Europe who brought with them firm opinions about, or at least an acquaintance with, active Zionism in its Eastern European form. The establishment of social frameworks in Istanbul such as various clubs (sport, theater, books), benevolent societies, and organizations after 1909, as well as B'nai Brith in 1911 provided opportunities for spending leisure time and directly or indirectly supported Zionism. These were foci par excellence for Zionist propaganda and mobilization. The objectives of some of these societies also included pro-Ottoman patriotism.

The second factor was the political, and especially economic, support of local Zionist activists by the World Zionist Organization, by contrast to the narrow-mindedness of the AIU leadership, which was blind to what was taking shape. Another favorable factor was the wide popular support within the Jewish masses. Zionist opposition to the communal establishment and its leaders led the Jewish masses to identify with the movement. Zionism responded to the needs of various social classes, providing them with cultural content and self-esteem. The last factor was the growing influence of Germany in the imperial capital on the eve of World War I, and concomitantly organizations and movements identified with Germany such as *Ezra* and Zionism.

Rabbi Nahum's partners – the communal leadership and the AIU – were unable to withstand the pressure from the Zionists, one of whose means was the Jewish press, and as time went on their weakness became evident. This situation reached its peak after the war, culminating in the resignation of Rabbi Nahum in 1920. But the victory of Zionism in Turkey was short-lived: when it was confronted Turkish nationalism and the Kemalist Republic, it was destined to disappear. The emigration to British Mandate Palestine and to the newly established State of Israel in the late 1940s was not a Zionist *'aliya* per se. Zionism might have had some long-lasting effect, and its members and activists [Mossad agents] aided those who chose Palestine as a destination, but I do not relate to it as a Zionist *'aliya*.

Notes

* This article is dedicated to my mentor Prof. Haim Gerber. I wish to thank my friend Mr. Yohai Goell for the translation and his remarks.

1. *Ha-Mevasser*, 19 January 1911, pp. 2–4 [in Hebrew]. On this short lived but important periodical, see Landau, Jacob M., 'Comments on the Jewish press in Istanbul: The Hebrew weekly *Hamevasser* (1909–1911)', in idem, *Jews, Arabs, Turks: Selected Essays* (Jerusalem, 1993), pp. 89–96.
2. My discussion is based on the detailed studies by Landau, Jacob M., 'The "Young Turks" movement and Zionism: Some comments', ibid.,

pp. 169–77; Benbassa, Esther, *Une diaspora sépharade en transition* (Paris, 1993), pp. 81–104, 157–80; as well as other studies, such as Eliav, Mordechai, *David Wolffsohn, the Man and His Times* (Jerusalem, 1977), chapters 7, 10 [in Hebrew]; and Farhi, David, 'The Jews of Salonica and the Young Turk Revolution', *Sefunot* XV (1971–81), pp. 137–52, especially pp. 141, 148–50 [in Hebrew]. The main primary source is the issues of *ha-Mevasser*. One might find Galante's discussion helpful: Galante, Avram, 'Abdul Hamit II et le sionisme', *Histoire des Juifs de Turquie* vol. IX (Istanbul, 1986), pp. 175–88. Interesting documents concerning Ottoman policy towards Jewish settlement and land purchase in Palestine were recently published: Başbakanlık Devlet Arşivleri Genel Müdürlüğü, *Osmanli Belgelerinde Filistin* [Palestine in Ottoman Documents] (Istanbul, 2009). For a general essay on the Istanbul Jewish community see Karmi, Ilan, *The Jewish Community of Istanbul in the Nineteenth Century* (Istanbul, 1996). See also Yeyni, Nathan, 'Zionist Activity', in Ben-Naeh, Yaron (ed.), *Jewish Communities in the East in the Nineteenth and Twentieth Centuries: Turkey* (Jerusalem, 2010), pp. 207–22 [in Hebrew].
3. Nassi, Gad (ed.), *Jewish Journalism and Printing Houses in the Ottoman Empire and Modern Turkey* (Istanbul, 2001); Stein Abrevaya, Sarah, *Making Jews Modern: The Yiddish and Ladino Press in the Russian and Ottoman Empires* (Bloomington, 2004); Borovaya, Olga, 'Jews of three colors: The path to modernity in the Ladino press at the turn of the twentieth century', *Jewish Social Studies* 15/1 (2008), pp. 110–30; Maggid, Moshe, 'Periodical Literature', in Ben-Naeh (ed.), *Jewish Communities*, pp. 123–36.
4. The best detailed work on Hebrew printing in Istanbul is still Yaari, Abraham, *Ha-Defus ha-'Ivri be-Kushta: Toldot ha-Defus ha-'Ivri be-Kushta me-Reshito {...} u-Reshimat ha-Sefarim she-Nidpesu ba* [Hebrew Printing at Constantinople: Its History and Bibliography] (Jerusalem, 1967) [in Hebrew]. Itzhak Bezalel noted seventy new Jewish newspapers and periodicals that appeared in Turkey, various regions in Greece, Salonica, and in Bulgraria. See Bezalel, Itzhak, *You Were Born Zionists: The Sephardim in Eretz Israel in Zionism and the Hebrew Revival during the Ottoman Period* (Jerusalem, 2007), p. 289, n. 29 [in Hebrew]. For information about the Judeo-Spanish newspapers noted, see Gaon, Moshe David, *A Bibliography* of the *The Judeo-Spanish (Ladino) Press* (Jerusalem, 1965) [in Hebrew].
5. For a one-sided description of Ottoman policy towards Zionism and Jewish settlement in Palestine, see Shaw, Stanford J., *The Jews of the Ottoman Empire and the Turkish Republic* (London, 1991), pp. 212–28, and more sources in his footnotes. See also Ortayli, I., *Ottomanism and Zionism during the Second Constitutional Period* (Istanbul, 2004), pp. 23–33.
6. For the development of a press-oriented culture among Ladino-speaking 'Sephardi' Jews, see Abrevaya Stein: *Making Jews Modern*, pp. 55–82.

7. Lowry, Heath W., 'The Young Turk triumvirate, ambassador Henry Morgenthau, and the future of Palestine, December 1913–January 1916', in Rozen, Minna (ed.), *The Last Ottoman Century and Beyond: The Jews in Turkey and the Balkans 1808–1945*, Vol. II (Tel Aviv, 2002), pp. 151–64.
8. See, for example Shaw, *Jews of the Ottoman Empire,* p. 224.
9. Elmaleh, Avraham, 'Akhen Noda' ha-Davar' [It has Become Known], *ha-Herut*, 1910, p. 26 [in Hebrew].
10. Bezalel: *You Were Born Zionists*, p. 188.
11. For Ben Ghiat and his lengthy dispute with Haim Ben-'Attar, editor of the Jerusalem Hebrew daily *ha-Herut*, see ibid., pp. 200–201.
12. Sokolow, Nahum, 'Yehudei Turkiya veha-Tziyonut' [The Jews of Turkey and Zionism], *ha-Mevasser*, 9 Tevet 5670 [21 December 1909], p. 7 [in Hebrew].
13. The Jewish Colonial Trust, the banking institution of the Zionist movement.
14. They converted to Islam in the last decades of the seventeenth century and were concentrated in Salonica until the 1920s.
15. 'Hatziyonut Kmot she-hi' [Zionism as it Truly is], *ha-Mevasser*, 5 Sivan 5671 [1 June 1911], pp. 221–2 [in Hebrew].
16. Benbassa: *Une diaspora sépharade*, pp. 102–4.
17. Elmaleh, Avraham, 'Ha-Safrut veha-'Itonut ha-Espanyolit' [The Ladino Literature and Press], *ha-Shiloach* 26 (1912), p. 258 [in Hebrew].
18. Max Nordau (1849–1923) who, in addition to his career as a physician and psychiatrist, became a leading Zionist figure and a capable ideologist, writer, and orator.
19. Abrevaya Stein: *Making Jews Modern*, p. 79.
20. Ibid., pp. 64–8.
21. 'Li-V'ayot ha-Sha'a' [As for Today's Questions], *ha-Mevasser*, 19 Tevet 5671 [19 January 1911], p. 4 [in Hebrew]. Yitzhak Bezalel found many reactions to Fresko's efforts in the pages of the Hebrew newspaper *ha-Herut*; see Bezalel: *You Were Born Zionists*, pp. 201–205.

CHAPTER 13

THE YOUNG TURKS AND THE BAHA'IS IN PALESTINE

NECATI ALKAN*

The Young Turk Revolution of 1908 was a turning point that opened up new prospects for Ottoman society and politics. It created a milieu in which new ideas could be shared in a relatively open manner. The case of the Baha'is in Palestine, even though they were seemingly a *quantité négligeable* among the religious communities, is a good example of the dissemination of reformist thoughts in that period. Based on unpublished letters of 'Abdu'l-Baha written in Ottoman Turkish, this chapter deals with the post-Revolutionary relations between the Baha'i leader 'Abdu'l-Baha ('Abbas Effendi, 1844–1921) in Ottoman Palestine and the Young Turk elite. It discusses the significance of Palestine to the development of the Baha'i community, the contributions of 'Abdu'l-Baha to the reform discourse in the Ottoman Empire, the tense relationship between 'Abdu'l-Baha and Sultan Abdülhamid II, 'Abdu'l-Baha's previously unknown connections with some leading Young Turks, and the Baha'i leader's attempt to infuse Baha'i thoughts into the CUP. The chapter rounds with an overview of the declining relationship between the CUP and 'Abdu'l-Baha during World War I.

The Baha'i Religion in Late Ottoman Palestine

Baha'u'llah (Mirza Husayn 'Ali Nuri, 1817–1892), the prophet-founder of the Baha'i religion, was expelled from his native country of Iran in

1853 due to his leading role in the revolutionary religious Babi movement.[1] With the approval of the Ottoman state, Baha'u'llah chose Baghdad as his place of exile. When tracing the life of Baha'u'llah from Baghdad – where he remained in exile for ten years and was given Ottoman citizenship to protect him from Iranian interference – to the Ottoman capital Istanbul, Edirne in Rumelia (1863–68) and finally to 'Akka [Acre] in Palestine, the development of the Baha'i religion needs to be situated in the wider context of late Ottoman reformism. It was largely due the tolerant attitude of the Sublime Porte in general that the Baha'i religion survived and took on its present form as the successor to the Babi faith that was nearly eradicated in Iran.[2]

Baha'u'llah died in Palestine as a prisoner of the Ottoman Empire. He was allowed to live outside the prison-city of 'Akka for the last fifteen years of his life. During these rather silent years when he was not under the spotlight of the Ottoman government, he composed many of his important writings that refer to the reformation of the world in general and to reforms in the Ottoman Empire and Iran in particular. His opus magnum, *al-Kitab al-Aqdas* [The Most Holy Book], which he composed in 'Akka, constitutes the core of his universal reforms. In Palestine he continued writing and sending letters to the political and religious leaders of his day in which he called upon them to establish world peace. He invited them to follow his religion as it offered solutions to the ills of the age and would, he claimed, usher in a 'Golden Age'.

Baha'u'llah also entrusted his son and successor 'Abdu'l-Baha with the external affairs of the community vis-à-vis the Ottoman authorities, and it was in this period until 1908 that 'Abdu'l-Baha was increasingly in the fore. The prestige of the Baha'is in Ottoman Palestine was enhanced through 'Abdu'l-Baha's friendly relations and connections with some Ottoman officials such as Midhat Paşa, and later liberal Young Turks. These contacts opened the gates of the citadel to Baha'u'llah after nine years of incarceration within the city walls, provided a safe environment for the development of the religion and paved the way for 'Abdu'l-Baha's release from his own confinement in 'Akka.

'Abdu'l-Baha on Reforms

The wave of reforms in the Young Turk period allowed for an exchange of ideas among diverse ethnic and religious groups. Education was regarded as the pivot of reform by the Young Turks, and this common feature linked them with Baha'i ideas. Baha'u'llah and 'Abdu'l-Baha were in contact with Ottoman reformers from the 1870s onwards. With a claim to a new religious faith, in many of his writings, Baha'u'llah, calling himself a 'World Reformer',[3] stressed the need for education as a means toward the spiritual regeneration and the material progress of humanity.[4] 'He repeatedly linked chiliastic concerns with democratic themes, showing the way in which he saw his appearance as a world messiah to have turned the world upside down'.[5]

The political climate during the reform period in the Ottoman Empire (*Tanzimat*, 1839–76) and Iran, are discussed in 'Abdu'l-Baha's *Risala-yi Madaniyya* [Treatise on Civilization, 1875] and *Risala-yi Siyasiyya* [Treatise on Politics/the Art of Governance], 1892).[6] In his first treatise 'Abdu'l-Baha deplores the backwardness and decadence of Iran and proposes reforms in all spheres of the state, affirms the need for a parliament and ethical and secular education and the employment of able statesmen to ensure just rule.[7] He calls the *Risala-yi Madaniyya* 'a tribute' to the 'high endeavor' of Nasiru'd-Din Shah (r. 1848–96), the incumbent Qajar ruler, to improving the conditions in Iranian society; 'a brief statement on certain urgent questions'.[8] The treatise was circulated anonymously and is said to have attracted wide readership among the Iranian intelligentsia, particularly after its printing in 1882. But later when it became known that its author was a Baha'i, no one would admit to having read it.[9] His *Risala-yi Siyasiyya*,[10] written as a response to the events during the Tobacco Revolt in Iran (1890–92), is a discussion of politics and society.[11] 'Abdu'l-Baha emphasizes that man-made laws are not enough to enable human progress and that divine law or religion is indispensable to educate the people. He adds that the interference of religious leaders (*'ulema*), especially ignorant ones, in political affairs is dangerous and cites the deposition of Ottoman Sultan Abdülaziz (r. 1861–76) as an example. In that 'greatest object lesson', students of religious schools revolted, demonstrating against the Bulgarian uprisings, the massacres of Muslims in the Balkans and the inability of the state to deal with the affair.[12] In a letter written during the Iranian Constitutional Revolution (*mashrutiyyat*, 1906–11) 'Abdu'l-Baha refers to his *Risala-yi Siyasiyya* and sums up the involvement of religious leaders and students in the fall of Abdülaziz. He says that in Istanbul on every corner and bazaar their cry 'We want war! We want war! (*harb isteriz, harb isteriz*)'[13] could be heard. After this conflict during which religion was abused for political ends and much blood was shed, the Ottomans lost most of their domains in Rumelia and Anatolia. He says that despite his advice and exhortations in the *Risala-yi Siyasiyya*, 'the ears were deaf and the eyes blind' and similar violent events occurred during the Constitutional Revolution.[14]

In one of his unpublished Turkish letters dealing with reform in the Ottoman Empire and Iran, 'Abdu'l-Baha once more advocates the non-involvement of *'ulema* in politics. This letter is also probably his only known direct reference to the *Tanzimat*. He speaks about Iran's worsening conditions caused by ignorant *'ulema* and the country's need for reform after the model of the Ottomans as inaugurated by Sultan Mahmud II. His emphasis is on secular reforms; clerics should only be concerned with spiritual and ethical matters; i.e., they should educate the people and guide their conduct. He furthermore commends the shah for having inaugurated reforms for the betterment of Iranian society.[15] Here reference is made either to the reform attempts of Nasiru'd-Din Shah in the 1870s[16] or the 'useful reforms of the just government' of Muzaffaru'd-Din Shah (1896–1906).[17]

'Abdu'l-Baha and Sultan Abdülhamid II

'Abdu'l-Baha actively disseminated Baha'i reformist thoughts and was in touch with leaders of the dissident 'Young Ottoman' movement such as Namık Kemal, Ziya Paşa and Midhat Paşa, either through letters or personally.[18] These contacts made him a political mischiefmaker in the eyes of Sultan Abdülhamid II. Moreover, he was accused by local Ottoman officials in Palestine of having harmful relations with foreigners and of buying land for the Zionists in Palestine in the 1890s. Some Arab local officials in Palestine reported false accusations to the sultan that the Iranian 'Abbas Efendi, who was in exile in 'Akka and able to obtain anything he wanted through his wealth and influence, had allied himself with like-minded officials to buy land at a cheap price from poor people, then to sell it to Jews and foreigners for profit.[19]

In addition, news of subversive religious activities in Lebanon and in 'Akka in 1905 reached Istanbul. It was claimed that committees under the supervision of Muhammad 'Abduh, then the grand *mufti* of Egypt, were attempting to spread the 'Babi [Baha'i]' and 'Wahhabi [Salafi] sects' by exploiting the laxity of Ottoman civil and military servants. Conservative Ottoman *'ulema* who opposed reformism made the Salafis and their leader Muhammad 'Abduh appear dangerous in the eyes of the sultan, by insinuating that the expansion of the superstitious and mischievous ideas of these 'sects', which contradicted the Islamic *shari'a*, along the Syrian coast, poison the people's minds. The argument went on that, foreign intrigues heightened the nefarious impact of the Baha'i and Salafi activities. Therefore, the propagandists of these heretical sects need to be monitored, their efforts in establishing committees prevented and the coastline constantly controlled; if necessary more troops should be sent there.[20] The Hamidian regime had also been concerned for some time that 'Abbas Efendi was maintaining good relations with Bedouin sheikhs, and this issue needed proper attention in order to prevent an Arab revolt.[21] Later the sultan sent a Commission of Inquiry (1905) to investigate the matter and 'Abdu'l-Baha was interrogated. As a result he was accused of mischief and almost exiled to Fizan in the Libyan Desert.[22]

Earlier, in 1901, Abdülhamid had renewed 'Abdu'l-Baha's confinement in 'Akka. The Ottoman authorities were observing the activities and development of the Baha'is inside and outside the Empire closely. 'Ali Ferruh Bey, the then Ottoman ambassador to Washington D.C., filed a report[23] on the strong influence of the Baha'i leader on people and his loyalty to the Sultan, and was convinced of the 'future power and importance' of the 'Babi sect'. He advised Abdülhamid to use 'Abdu'l-Baha as a 'spiritual weapon' (*manevi bir silah*) against Iran and its efforts to spread Shi'ism. This did not convince the Sultan. Neither was he persuaded by 'Abdu'l-Baha's own pledge of loyalty.

In a Turkish letter to Abdülhamid – to my knowledge the only letter directly addressed to the Sultan – the Baha'i leader talks about the imperial decree 'that has been issued recently' concerning his confinement in 'Akka.[24] 'Abdu'l-Baha most probably wrote his letter as a response to the renewal of his imprisonment in 1901.[25] He says that 'no dishonorable condition and act contrary to the imperial will has manifested itself on my behalf or our community' and assures the emperor that he and his followers are his loyal subjects who 'hesitate to meddle in the affairs of the government (*umur-i hükûmet*) and the transactions of the people (*muamelât-ı ahali*)', as required by Baha'i principles (non-involvement in partisan politics).

The motivation for the letter was 'Abdu'l-Baha's contacts with Americans and the report that they were joining the religious community he headed. Here and in other Turkish letters 'Abdu'l-Baha presents the Baha'i religion as a *tarikat* ['way', 'path' or 'religious order'] within Islam, and not as a new religion. Throughout their stay in Ottoman domains – until the death of 'Abdu'l-Baha in 1921 – the Baha'is presented themselves to outsiders in the Middle East as followers of Islam and as advised by Baha'u'llah and 'Abdu'l-Baha refrained from attracting Ottomans to the Baha'i faith. Any other course of action would have been disastrous because the Baha'is would have faced severe persecution. 'Abdu'l-Baha notes in his letter to Abdülhamid that 'nothing has been undertaken to attract and admit even a single individual from among the Ottoman subjects to join our *tarikat* during our lengthy stay in 'Akka for more than thirty years'. 'Abdu'l-Baha consequently states that the Americans were guided to Islam (*ihtida*) through the teachings of Baha'u'llah. Initially, American Protestant missionaries in Iran engaged in religious conversations with the Baha'is and joined the 'Baha'i *tarikat*'. The new converts returned to America, propagated the Baha'i teachings and won over many Americans in a short time. Later, some Americans who travelled to Palestine met 'Abdu'l-Baha, and this resulted in their belief in the 'manifest religion of Muhammad' and they recognized 'the unity of God, approved and confirmed the prophethood (*nübüvvet*) of His Holiness, the glory of the Messengers [Muhammad], and believed in the greatness (*ulviyet*) of my late father Baha'u'llah'.

These conversions prompted anger and enmity among the American Protestant community in Palestine, 'they gave the affair a different coloring and informed his Majesty'. This resulted in the renewal of 'Abdu'l-Baha's imprisonment. Nevertheless, he expressed the wish that the guidance of Americans to Islam would please Abdülhamid and his subjects.[26] He asks him to examine the appended Baha'i chronicles written during his father's time and so witness 'the affection (*ihlas*) and loyalty (*sadakat*)' of Baha'u'llah toward the Sultan.

After the Young Turk Revolution in 1908 'Abdu'l-Baha freely expressed his disapproval of Abdülhamid's injustices toward Baha'u'llah, himself and the Baha'is. Before this, notwithstanding the steps taken by the Sublime Porte against the Baha'is in that period, 'Abdu'l-Baha spoke with gratitude about Abdülhamid at that time and stressed the Sultan's impartiality towards the Baha'is. Owing to the atmosphere of censure and the tight network of spies working to identify subversive activities during the Hamidian reign, 'Abdu'l-Baha could not have done otherwise.[27]

Secret Connections and a Baha'i Paşa

In August 1908, immediately after the Young Turk Revolution, 'Abdu'l-Baha was released from imprisonment as a result of the amnesty for political prisoners.[28] A few years later, he was able to leave the 'Akka-Haifa area and travelled to Egypt, Europe and North America to spread the Baha'i teachings (1910–1913). Often in his talks he praised the CUP for releasing him and for their efforts to secure freedom. 'Abdu'l-Baha expressed his appreciation for his liberation before it was clear that the military wing of the CUP would take over with a *coup d'état* (1913) or what that would mean. Past research was unable to determine how and through whom 'Abdu'l-Baha was freed from imprisonment. In the light of Turkish letters that he wrote after his release, we know now that he had had secret contacts with the civilian, parliamentarian wing of the Young Turk circles in Istanbul and Salonica during the reign of Abdülhamid. In those letters 'Abdu'l-Baha praises the CUP and supports its goals.

'Abdu'l-Baha made contact with the leading Young Turk Bursalı Mehmed Tahir Bey (1861–1925). He was a military man, teacher, mystic and Ottoman writer, who had been assigned to different military and administrative posts including Salonica and Istanbul and was delegate for Bursa at the Ottoman Parliament from 1908–11.[29] Tahir Bey was also cofounder of the secret *Osmanlı Hürriyet Cemiyeti* [Ottoman Freedom Society] in Salonica (1906). Around that time Mustafa Kemal (Atatürk) founded a similar organization when he was stationed in Syria[30] and went secretly to Salonica in 1906 to make contact with the like-minded Mehmed Tahir, who had been his teacher at the military school there.[31] It is possible that as a well-known reformist figure in the Middle East 'Abdu'l-Baha made contact with Tahir Bey through reform-minded officers such as the young Mustafa Kemal during his postings in Syria and Palestine.

What is certain is that 'Abdu'l-Baha was in contact with Tahir Bey via a Baha'i in Istanbul by the name of Ahmed Şevki Efendi and through an Ottoman official named Bedri Paşa. The latter, Hasan Bedreddin (1851–1912),[32] was a military commander and writer who had been involved in the deposition of Sultan Abdülaziz in 1876.[33] Due to the repressive atmosphere during the reign of Abdülhamid, he was removed from Istanbul to Syria and Palestine where he served as colonel.[34] After the Young Turk Revolution, Bedri Paşa was governor general (*vali*) of the province of İşkodra [Shkodër, today in Albania], from 1909 until 1911.[35] In Persian Baha'i sources he is mentioned as Bedri Bey (Badri Beg), who was exiled to 'Akka before 1908, was translator of 'Abdu'l-Baha into French and a Baha'i.[36] The latter's other contact person, Giridî Ahmed Şevki Efendi, was a soap-maker/merchant (*sabuncu*) from Crete. He is not mentioned in available Baha'i sources but appears in a photograph of Baha'is of Istanbul, taken in April 1919.[37]

'Abdu'l-Baha must have come in contact with Bedri when he was deputy commander in 'Akka around 1898. Because of having been a Young Turk and the injustices he allegedly committed at that post, he was sent to another place.[38] According to the letters of 'Abdu'l-Baha, Bedri's next posts were in Beirut and then Damascus.[39] 'Abdu'l-Baha's more substantial letters to Bedri Paşa in terms of political matters were written during the latter's governorship in İşkodra and after his retirement. As military governor Bedri Paşa had to face uprisings by Albanian insurgents against the CUP and clashes between Christians and Muslims. He proclaimed 'holy war' against Christian rebels and tried to suppress them.[40] As the troops were insufficient, he used religion and appealed to the Muslims to accept arms from the government and defend their town and faith.[41] He wrote to Istanbul asking for permission to pursue a more aggressive policy toward the Albanian rebellion. Bedri wanted more control over the mountainous İşkodra region in the north and requested more troops. The Sublime Porte praised the governor for his initial reforms but encouraged him to proceed with caution.[42]

'Abdu'l-Baha refers to events in Albania during the governorship of Bedri Paşa and praises him for the 'exceptional administration' in view of the rebellions all over the Ottoman Balkans, particularly in Albania.[43] He adds that it is crucial to deliver the people from ignorance and inertia and bring them into the civilized world. 'Abdu'l-Baha encourages Bedri to establish unity based on Baha'i core beliefs by abolishing division and enmity among the diverse people of the province. The means for this 'foremost achievement' was the diffusion of knowledge and education, making it accessible to all, and so delivering the diverse sects from evils and foolish prejudices.[44] Through Bedri Paşa's 'divine confirmation', the people and tribes of İşkodra, 'who are the most fanatical in Albania, live in comfort and peace' and the province is 'different from other provinces as regards the perfect safety and peace in such a time of tumult and rebellion'.[45] According to 'Abdu'l-Baha a practical and beneficial step to be taken for the security of the country would be the construction of roads everywhere in the province.[46]

In another letter written after Bedri Paşa's retirement and his stay in Istanbul, 'Abdu'l-Baha states that in talks he held during his travels in Europe he always praised the CUP. When he was a prisoner during the time of Abdülhamid's 'despotism', he was freed by the 'resolute efforts' of the Committee as soon as liberty was proclaimed. When he came across some objections in newspapers towards the 'esteemed Committee', he 'candidly and justly defended it for the sake of seeking the truth'.[47] Referring to the war between the Ottomans and Italy in Libya in 1911–12 in the same letter 'Abdu'l-Baha warns the Turks against Italy's nationalistic and imperialistic ambitions: 'Detailed information about Italy's violent breaking of treaties, its utter oppression, injustice, and finally the harmful consequences of the sudden cruel and bloodthirsty attacks causing destruction, has been delivered with conclusive proof'. In line with Baha'i ideas, he adds though that 'inasmuch as there are many traitors in Europe, there are also faithful people who think beyond national lines and promulgate universal peace and expect the advent of the unity of mankind'. He wrote to Bedri Paşa that he was willing to present the ideals of the CUP in the United States where he was invited by leading public figures: 'If there are suitable thoughts that the esteemed Committee has and wants to present and promulgate there, I ask you to convey these to me through your Excellency'.[48]

In yet another letter to Bedri Paşa 'Abdu'l-Baha also talks about enemies and nay-sayers in the Ottoman Empire who want to cause chaos because of their selfish interests, and who, as part of their schemes, presented him as an enemy of Abdülhamid. He writes that 'it is evident and known to you and to the world that my secret connections with the Young Turks in the time of Abdülhamid have been always the cause of hardships'. After his release he was accused of being a supporter of despotism so as to instigate the CUP to turn against him. 'Since my conduct and manners are as manifest as the sun for your Excellency', he then asks Bedri Paşa, 'investigate the matter and inform the esteemed Committee of Union and Progress in Istanbul and Salonica, especially Tahir Bey, the Bursa delegate, of the truth'.[49]

From Palestine 'Abdu'l-Baha contacted Mehmed Tahir Bey through the Baha'i Ahmed Şevki Efendi in Istanbul, and sent two Baha'is to meet him.[50] After the meeting, 'Abdu'l-Baha expressed his gratitude. He wanted to convey to members of the CUP, especially to Mehmed Tahir Bey, that if the principles of 'the Baha'i *tarikat*, the teachings of his holiness Baha'u'llah, his exhortations and counsels are understood properly, it is impossible not to admit that it is the source of happiness to mankind'. 'Abdu'l-Baha thanked the CUP for having sent a person to meet him [i.e. 'Abdu'l-Baha] and asked for further meetings between a person appointed by the CUP with Baha'is he dispatched to Istanbul.[51] In still another letter to Ahmed Şevki Efendi, 'Abdu'l-Baha expresses his hope of meeting and talking with a figure from the CUP; specifically Mehmed Tahir Bey should visit him in Egypt.[52] He then talks about the Young Turks as 'the destroyer of the edifice of tyranny and the source of life for Turkey and Iran' and hopes that the 'righteous liberals of Iran may live long through the aid and grace of God' because 'since the day on which liberty (*hürriyet*) was proclaimed in Iran, the Baha'is live overall with joy and peace'. He adds that he prays that God may assist and confirm the CUP. As he was in prison for thirty years under Abdülhamid, after the Revolution the CUP 'took the chains and fetters' from his neck and placed them around the neck of the 'tyrannical and bloodthirsty' Abdülhamid. Thousands of oppressed victims were liberated from chains and fetters and from exile, and the 'rascal (*herif*)' himself was incarcerated.[53] Despite Abdülhamid's tyranny that surpassed that of Yazid,[54] foolish common people would still respect and love him; because they were blind and ignorant they despised the CUP.

'Abdu'l-Baha directed Ahmed Şevki to present his letter to Mehmed Tahir Bey.[55] Then, in his letter to Mehmed Tahir Bey himself, 'Abdu'l-Baha thanks the Committee for its 'zeal and justice (*himmet ve adalet*)' in liberating him and adds that through the Revolution 'the radiating light of the morn of liberty illumined the horizons of the country'.[56] 'Abdu'l-Baha calls Rumelia, were the Revolution started, 'the dayspring of the lights of freedom' and 'dawning-place of the lights of truth'.[57]

Young Turk and Baha'i Ideas

In another letter, written in Persian, 'Abdu'l-Baha underscores the similarity between the ideals and goals of the CUP those of the Baha'is.[58] He states that the 'Baha'is assist the Committee of Union and Progress with heart and soul. They are on the same path, have the same disposition, seek freedom and love liberty (*azadi-talab va hurriyyat-parvar*), hope for equality, are well-wishers of humanity and ready to sacrifice their lives to unite humanity (*vahdat-i bashari*)'.

Despite the laudable efforts of the CUP in striving for unity among the various groups in the Ottoman Empire, 'Abdu'l-Baha states that the aims of the CUP are only concerned with the physical world and those of the Baha'is are broader in that they seek the unity of humanity as a whole and are concerned with spiritual progress. He affirms that true progress comes from spiritual power, and the East is its source. But presently the East is the captive of the West; they are at war because Europe made it its policy to constantly attack defenseless Asia. A look at history reveals that throughout the ages and centuries the East has been victorious over Europe through its spiritual power (*quvvat-i ruhani*) and not through material power (*quvvat-i jismani*). There were times when troops of the East – the Umayyads, Tamerlane, Genghis Khan and Sultan Selim [Selim I, the Ottoman sultan] – were victorious over the West; however, this was not continuous and it was only through its spiritual powers that Asia subdued Europe and won immense victories. 'Abdu'l-Baha calls on the East, here represented by the CUP, to use its spiritual power once again to oppose Europe and shake its pillars, and so reveal the true splendor of Asia.

In line with this 'Abdu'l-Baha cautions the CUP not to rely on conventional politics and refers to Baha'u'llah's teachings which stress that however much human politics (*siyasat-i bashariyya*) shows progress (*taraqqi*), it is nothing compared to divine politics (*siyasat-i ilahiyya*), because 'divine politics is the light of the physical world and an immeasurable mercy that encompasses all peoples and nations. [...] Therefore we need to follow divine politics, especially in this glorious century and this age of the progress of humanity in which nothing but divine politics leads to success'. By conforming to divine politics Baha'u'llah bestowed a new spirit (*ruhi-yi jadid*) on Iran that has easily penetrated and influenced even the remotest places in America. 'Now all the peoples of the East must be content and happy with this politics, and delighted in the pervading influence of the teachings of Baha'u'llah in Europe and America'. Lastly, he calls on the Baha'is to do everything in their power to familiarize themselves with the 'benevolent aims' (*maqasid-i khayriyya*) of the CUP and respond to its just endeavors by assisting it.

This opportunity was afforded when 'Abdu'l-Baha visited Washington D.C. in April 1912 in the first week of his travels in the United States to present the Baha'i religion.[59] There he met Yusuf Ziya Paşa, the Ottoman ambassador to Washington. For the Sublime Porte 'Abdu'l-Baha's presence in the American capital was a sensitive political issue that could upset the balance with Iran and Russia. Hence, initially it did not want the ambassador to be contact in with him. In his memorandum to Istanbul Yusuf Ziya Paşa states that considering 'Abdu'l-Baha's positive reception by eminent people in America, his constant praises of the CUP that displayed justice and liberated him and the gathering held in his honor by the Iranian embassy[60] at which he was present, the Ottoman Embassy could not be indifferent toward him. Therefore 'Abdu'l-Baha and some of his followers were honored at a dinner. He adds that this was received positively and his followers (about 800) wrote and signed a letter of gratitude to be forwarded to the Young Turk government, hoping that the Baha'is could be of assistance to the CUP.[61]

'Abdu'l-Baha and Cemal Paşa in Palestine

Even though 'Abdu'l-Baha was shown due respect initially by the Young Turks, the tides turned against him once more after the militant nationalist Young Turks seized power in 1913 and Enver Paşa, Talat Paşa and Cemal Paşa took over as a dictatorial triumvirate.[62] The euphoria over the 'liberty', 'equality' and 'brotherhood' of the Young Turks did not last long. On the contrary, the rule of those three Paşas in particular proved to be me more repressive and bloodier than that of Abdülhamid and ended in the collapse of the Empire after World War I. Non-Turkish and non-Muslim minorities, especially Christians, suffered from the radical nationalistic ideology of the CUP which resulted in forced settlements, deportation and a 'Turkification' policy.[63] The Baha'is were not affected by this, but CUP antagonism manifested itself otherwise.

The attitude of General Cemal Paşa (1872–1922), Military Governor of the Ottoman troops in Syria (1914–17), towards 'Abdu'l-Baha was the opposite of the early and liberal Young Turk leaders.[64] Whereas the latter approached Baha'i ideas positively, Cemal was a sworn enemy of 'Abdu'l-Baha and the Baha'is. According to Baha'i sources due to false accusations the Paşa originally wanted to execute him. Later, when he met 'Abdu'l-Baha in Palestine, his anger subsided and he enjoyed the Baha'i leader's presence. Cemal Paşa, as reported by a Baha'i eyewitness, supposedly asked 'Abdu'l-Baha what the cause of the Ottoman Empire's weakness was and he responded, 'the existence of diverse religions'. And when Cemal asked what the remedy was, the Baha'i leader allegedly replied, 'that the leaders of all religions and denominations existing within the Ottoman Empire and Islamic lands gather in Constantinople and, after consultations, agree on a single and unifying religion'. Cemal Paşa is said to have approved these words and added: 'After my return [from the Suez campaign], I will take you to Constantinople. There I will gather the religious leaders and force them into unity and agreement on one religion'.[65]

After this positive encounter Cemal Paşa's attitude towards 'Abdu'l-Baha once again changed for the worse due to negative reports sent to him about 'Abdu'l-Baha. He promised to crucify the Baha'i leader when he returned victorious from his military campaigns in Sinai, but his troops were defeated by the British army and this did not take place. At the beginning of World War I, 'Abdu'l-Baha planned to take practical steps to intervene peacefully against belligerence. He intended to convene a gathering of leading Muslim and Christian leaders in Palestine where he hoped to advise them to cooperate to avoid disorder and chaos in the region. 'Abdu'l-Baha was prevented by opponents from doing so. Despite this he was occupied with local affairs and took over the task of providing food for the people in the region who suffered from the mismanagement of the Ottoman overlord.[66]

Conclusion

The attitude of the Ottoman government during the reign of Abdülhamid II towards the Baha'i leadership was generally hostile. Constant efforts by opponents of 'Abdu'l-Baha reinforced the Sultan's antagonistic policy. However, 'Abdu'l-Baha was able to ally himself with like-minded reformers within the Young Turk movement, and familiarize them with Baha'i reformist thoughts which resulted in his release. His vision of the West and modernity and his international ties may have been attractive and beneficial to the governors. On the whole, whereas the approach of the Young Turk reformers was embedded in the framework of a secular modernism and nationalism, the reforms of Baha'u'llah and 'Abdu'l-Baha were beyond the proposals of the reformers in the Ottoman Empire in that they were universalistic and emphasized not only material civilization but also moral and religious values.

The first years of the Young Turk rule were crucial for the development of the Baha'i faith as a religion independent of Islam. 'Abdu'l-Baha was free to travel outside the Ottoman domains and was given the opportunity to spread the Baha'i ideas in the West, which led to success and the positive reception he received from high and low alike was echoed in the Ottoman Empire. In Palestine the Baha'i religion was significantly consolidated by its founder and 'Abdu'l-Baha, and from there he organized its expansion in numbers and disseminated its ideas to other regions inside and outside the Ottoman domains. The Baha'is were spared by the aggressive minority policies of the CUP. After the initial positive reception of Baha'i ideas by early Young Turks and the improved conditions that prevailed for six years after 'Abdu'l-Baha's release by liberal members of the CUP, he again faced the enmity of the Ottoman government – this time led by the military wing of the Young Turks who apparently tried, in vain, to use him for their political goals.

Notes

* I would like to thank Prof. Houchang Chehabi (Boston University, USA) and Dr. Moojan Momen (independent scholar, England) for their valuable comments. I am also grateful to Dr. Momen for proofreading the text several times. In this chapter I used a simplified Arabic/Persian transliteration system without specific signs above and below letters. Ottoman names and words are rendered in the modern Turkish alphabet.

1. For the Babi and Baha'i religions, see e.g., Smith, Peter, *The Babi and Baha'i Religions: From Messianic Shi'ism to a World Religion* (Cambridge, 1987); Amanat, Abbas, *Resurrection and Renewal – The Making of the Babi Movement*

in Iran, 1844–1850 (Ithaca/London, 1989); Momen, Moojan, *The Babi and Baha'i Religions: Some Contemporary Western Accounts, 1844–1944* (Oxford, 1981); idem, *A Short Introduction to the Baha'i Faith* (Oxford, 1997); Cole, Juan R. I., *Modernity and the Millennium: The Genesis of the Baha'i Faith in the Nineteenth-Century Middle East* (New York, 1998).

2. Alkan, Necati, *Dissent and Heterodoxy in the Late Ottoman Empire: Reformers, Babis and Baha'is* (Istanbul, 2008).
3. Baha'u'llah, *The Summons of the Lord of Hosts* (Haifa, 2002), pp. 92, 161.
4. For a discussion, see Christopher Buck, 'Baha'u'llah as "world reformer"', *Journal of Baha'i Studies* 3/4 (1991), pp. 23–70; Cole: *Modernity;* Alkan: *Dissent.*
5. Cole: *Modernity*, p. 62.
6. All Baha'i writings in the original Arabic/Persian and those that are officially translated into English and used in this chapter, are available online at the Baha'i Reference Library (official digital library of the Baha'i World Centre, Haifa, Israel), http://reference.bahai.org
7. 'Abdu'l-Baha, *The Secret of Divine Civilization,* English translation by Gail, Marzieh (Wilmette/Ill., 1990; henceforth *SDC*), p. 118. For a discussion of *SDC*, see Momen, Moojan, 'The Baha'i influence on the reform movements of the Islamic world in the 1860s and 1870s', *Baha'i Studies Bulletin* 2/2 (1983), pp. 47–65; Saeidi, Nader, *Risala-yi Madaniyya va Mas'ala-i Tajaddud dar Khavar-i Miyana* [The Treatise on Civilization and the Issue of Modernization in the Middle East] (Dundas/Ontario, 1993) [in Persian]; McGlinn, Sen, 'Resala-ye madaniya' [Treatise on Civilization], online entry in *Encyclopaedia Iranica*, http://www.iranica.com/newsite /home/index.isc
8. 'Abdu'l-Baha: *SDC*, p. 6.
9. Momen: 'Baha'i influence', pp. 48–9.
10. 'Abdu'l-Baha, *Risala-yi Siyasiyya* [Treatise on the Art of Governance] (Tehran, BE 91/1933–4) [in Persian]. For provisional translations, i.e. individual translations of Baha'i scripture not made at and approved by the Baha'i World Centre in Haifa, see Cole, Juan R.I., ''Abdu'l-Baha's treatise on leadership', online at H-Bahai, Translations of Shaykhi, Babi and Baha'i Texts, vol. II/ 2 (May, 1998), http://www.h-net.org/~bahai/areprint/vol2/siyasi.htm and McGlinn, Sen, 'A sermon on the Art of Governance (Resale-ye siyasiyyah) by 'Abdu'l-Baha', H-Bahai, *Translations of Shaykhi, Babi and Baha'i Texts*, vol. XII/1 (March, 2003), http://www.h-net.org/~bahai/trans/vol7/govern.htm.
11. See also Baha'u'llah's 'Lawh-i Dunya' [Tablet of the World], *Tablets of Baha'u'llah Revealed After the Kitab-i-Aqdas* (Wilmette/Ill., 1988), pp. 83–97.

12. Cf. Shaw, Stanford and Ezel K. Shaw, *History of the Ottoman Empire and Turkey* (Cambridge, 1977), vol. II, pp. 162–3.
13. Ottoman Turkish in the original.
14. Provisional translation of a letter in Persian, *Makatib-i 'Abdu'l-Baha* [Letters of 'Abdu'l-Baha], vol. 5 (Tehran, 132 BE/1975–76), pp. 173–6 [in Persian].
15. Undated letter addressed to the Baha'is of Saysan in Iranian Azerbaijan, Baha'i International Archives (henceforth BIA), AC3/8/305. Certified copy of the original letter attached to the memorandum to the present writer, dated 22 June 2008. I am indebted to the Baha'i World Center (Haifa, Israel) for permission to quote from this and the following Turkish letters of 'Abdu'l-Baha; memorandum to the present writer, dated 12 June 2008. This and subsequent letters from the BIA are the author's translations.
16. Cf. 'Abdu'l-Baha: *SDC*, pp. 5, 16. At that time in Iran, there were many attempts to set up a 'Council of State'; see Nashat, Guity, *The Origins of Modern Reform in Iran, 1870–80* (Urbana, 1982), pp. 95–113, and Bakhash, Shaul, *Iran: Monarchy, Bureaucracy & Reform under the Qajars: 1858–1896* (Oxford, 1978), pp. 133–186.
17. 'Abdu'l-Baha, *Tablets of Abdu'lu'l-Baha Abbas* (Chicago, 1915 & 1919), vol. 2, p. 401. There were really no reforms of any great substance in Iran until the Constitutional Revolution. The major change was a more benevolent attitude by Muzaffaru'd-Din compared to his father. See Martin, Vanessa, *Islam and Modernism: the Iranian Revolution of 1906* (London, 1989); Bayat, Mangol, *Iran's First Revolution: Shi'ism and the Constitutional Revolution of 1905–1909* (Oxford/New York, 1991).
18. Alkan: *Dissent*, pp. 100–102, 109–114.
19. Başbakanlık Osmanlı Arşivi (BOA), Y.PRK.AZJ. 27/39, dated 3 Ağustos 1309 [15 August 1893]; quoted in Uçar, Ahmet, 'Filistini kim sattı?' [Who Sold Palestine?], *Tarih ve Düşünce* 29 (June 2002), pp. 20–23.
20. BOA, Y.PRK.ASK. 228/60, 26 Safer 1323 [2 May 1905].
21. BOA, DH.MKT. 438/43, dated 4 Rebiülevvel 1313 [25 August 1895].
22. For a discussion of these issues, see Alkan: *Dissent*, pp. 161–70.
23. 'Amerika'da Tarikat-ı Babiyye', BOA, Y.MTV. 214/176, 11 May 1901; Alkan: *Dissent*, pp. 155–9.
24. BIA, undated draft letter to Sultan Abdülhamid II, AA001/003/00249.
25. Balyuzi, Hasan M., *'Abdu'l-Baha: The Centre of the Covenant of Baha'u'llah* (Oxford, 1971), pp. 95–6.
26. On the issue of conversions of Christians in the Hamidian period, see Deringil, Selim, *The Well-Protected Domains: Ideology and the Legimation of Power in the Ottoman Empire, 1876–1909* (London/New York, 1999), pp. 84–91.

27. Alkan: *Dissent*, pp. 159–61.
28. Balyuzi: *'Abdu'l-Baha*, pp. 123–4. For the amnesty granted to political prisoners in the Ottoman legal code from 1908, see Biliotti, A. and Ahmed Sedad, *Législation Ottomane depuis le rétablissement de la constitution* 24 *Djemazi-ul-ahir 1326–10 Juillet 1324/1908* (Paris, 1912), p. 3, texte IV.
29. Vehbi, Muallim, *Brusalı Tahir Bey* (Istanbul, 1334/1915–6); Woodhead, Christine, 'Mehmed Tahir, Bursali (1861–1925)', *Encyclopaedia of Islam*, 2nd Edition (EI^2), vol. IX, p. 616. He later distanced himself from the Young Turks and politics.
30. Shaw, *History of the Ottoman Empire and Turkey*, vol. II, pp. 264–5. The Society was integrated in 1907 into the CUP.
31. Ramsaur, Ernest E., *The Young Turks: Prelude to the Revolution of 1908* (Princeton, 1957), p. 98; see further Baer, Marc David, *The Dönme: Jewish Converts, Muslim Revolutionaries, and Secular Turks* (Stanford, CA, 2010), p. 99.
32. Gövsa, İbrahim A., *Türk Meşhurları Ansiklopedisi* [Encyclopaedia of Famous Turks] (Ankara, 1946), p. 68 [in Turkish]; İnal, İbnülemin M. Kemal, *Son Asır Türk Şairleri* [Turkish Poets of the Last Century], 4 vols. (Ankara, 1969), vol. I, p. 157 [in Turkish]; Bursalı, Mehmet Tahir, *Osmanlı müellifleri* [Ottoman Writers] (Ankara, 2000), vol. I, p. 2 [in Turkish]; İz, Fahir, 'Hasan Bedr al-Din', EI^2, vol. 12 (Supplement) (Leiden, 2004), p. 359. Bedri Paşa was a playwright, producing plays such as one on abortion as a social ill in the Ottoman Empire: *Iskat-ı Cenîn: Facia* [Abortion: a Calamity] (Istanbul, 1290/1874–5) [in Ottoman Turkish]; he was moreover a military instructor at the Imperial Academy of War and specialized in explosives and cosmography. He composed and published plays together with his classmate and colleague Manastırlı Mehmed Rifat (1851–1907); they were also the first to translate European operas into Ottoman Turkish; Demirci, Tuba and Akşin Somel, 'Women's bodies, demography, and public health: Abortion policy and perspectives in the Ottoman Empire of the nineteenth century', *Journal of the History of Sexuality* 17/3 (September 2008), p. 417, n. 139.
33. Devereux, Robert, 'Süleyman Pasha's "The Feeling of the Revolution"', *Middle Eastern Studies* 15/1 (January 1979), pp. 22–4, 30. Mehmed Rifat was also among the soldiers who surrounded the palace the night that Sultan Abdülaziz was deposed. After Abdülhamid II came to power, Rifat was suspected of having plotted against Abdülaziz, consequently exiled to Syria and forbidden to return to Istanbul; on Rifat, see Gövsa: *Türk Meşhurları Ansiklopedisi*, p. 324; İz, Fahir, 'Manastırlı Mehmed Rıf'at', EI^2, vol. 6 (1991), pp. 372–3; Kahraman, Âlim, 'Mehmed Rifat, Manastırlı', *Türkiye Diyanet Vakfı İslam Ansiklopedisi*, vol. 28 (Ankara, 2003), pp. 519–20 [in Turkish]; see

also Devereux: 'Süleyman Paşa', p. 21. 'Abdu'l-Baha had secretly communicated with Mehmed Rifat; see Alkan: *Dissent*, p. 145, n. 3.
34. İz: 'Hasan Bedr al-Din', p. 359.
35. For his appointment and retirement, see BOA, DH.MKT. 2688/87, 28 Zilkade 1326 [22 December 1908] and BOA, İ.HB. 104/1330/M-041, 11 Muharrem 1330 [1 January 1912].
36. Mu'ayyad, Habib, *Khatirat-i Habib* [Memoirs of Habib] (Hofheim, 1998), vol. I, pp. 164–5 [in Persian]. For an annotated English translation see Rabbani, Ahang (trans.), *Eight Years Near 'Abdu'l-Baha: The Diary of Dr. Habib Mu'ayyad* (e-book at http://ahang.rabbani.googlepages.com/muayyad), pp. 239–40; Afroukhteh, Youness, *Khatirat-i Nuh Sala* [Memories of Nine Years] (Los Angeles, 1983), p. 354 [in Persian]. Here it is mentioned that Bedri Bey and two other Ottoman officials were removed from their office, without no reason given. It may have been due to their sympathy toward 'Abdu'l-Baha. For an English translation of Afroukhteh's memoirs see Mansour, Riaz (trans.), *Memoirs of Nine Years in 'Akka* (Oxford, 2007).
37. Photograph dated 22 April 1919 at the Baha'i Center in Fatih, Istanbul, with the names of mostly Iranian (Azerbaijani) Baha'is. As noted above, Baha'is were not allowed to attract Ottomans to their religion. Bedri and Ahmed Şevki are exceptions among others, such as Dr. Süleyman Rifat Bey, Hasan Hilmi Efendi and Emin Âli Bey who appear in the photograph. On the latter, see Alkan: *Dissent*, pp. 185–7.
38. BOA, Y.PRK.ASK. 228/60, 16 Rebiülevvel 1316 [4 August 1898].
39. BIA, undated draft letters to Bedri Paşa, AC006/434/00001 and AC005/254/00001.
40. Durham, Mary Edith, *The Struggle for Scutari* (London, 1914), pp. 19–20; Pearson, Owen, *Albania in the Twentieth Century: a History* (London, 2006), vol. I, p. 14.
41. Kondis, Basil, *Greece and Albania* (Thessaloniki, 1976), p. 51.
42. Gawrych, George Walter, *The Crescent and the Eagle: Ottoman Rule: Islam and the Albanians, 1874–1913* (London, 2006), pp. 160–61.
43. BIA, undated draft letter to Bedri Paşa, AC005/010/00012.
44. BIA, undated draft letter to Bedri Paşa, AC005/457/00009.
45. BIA, undated draft letter to Bedri Paşa, AC006/175/00006.
46. BIA, undated draft letter to Bedri Paşa, AC005/010/00012.
47. BIA, undated draft letter to Bedri Paşa (Samatya, Istanbul), AC005/261/00010.
48. Ibid.
49. BIA, undated draft letter to Bedri Paşa (Erenköy, Istanbul, at the Mansion of Sâdeddin Paşa), AC005/368/00012.

50. BIA, undated draft letter to Sabuncu Giridî Ahmed Şevki Efendi (Istanbul, Çakmakçılar, Sümbüllü Han, no. 38), AC005/352/00007.
51. BIA, undated draft letter, AC005/387/00002.
52. 'Abdu'l-Baha was in Egypt twice, in 1910 and in 1913 for longer periods before and after his journeys to the West.
53. BIA, undated draft letter, AC005/674/00001. Cf. 'Abdu'l-Baha: 'Abdu'l-Baha *in London* (London, 1982), p. 119; see also 'Abdu'l-Baha's interpretation of the verse in Baha'u'llah's *Kitab-i-Aqdas: The Most Holy Book* (Haifa, 1992), verse 89, referring to the ominous 'hooting of the owl' (*sawt al-bum*) and the 'throne of tyranny' (*kursi az-zulm*) concerning Istanbul that he associates with the oppression of Abdülhamid and his opposition to 'Abdu'l-Baha; see Ishraq-Khavari, 'Abdu'l-Hamid, *Ma'ida-i Asmani* [Heavenly Food], vol. V (Tehran, 129 B.E./1972), pp. 129–34 [in Persian and Arabic].
54. Yazid (r. 680–83), the second Umayyad caliph and son of Mu'awiya, whose troops killed Imam Husayn at Karbala and is hated in Islamic history, especially by the Shi'is.
55. BIA, undated draft letter, AC005/374/00007.
56. BIA, undated draft letter to Mehmed Tahir Efendi, through Giridî Ahmed Şevki Efendi, AC005/376/00004.
57. BIA, undated draft letter, AC006/092/00006.
58. BIA, AC006/595/00001, undated letter of 'Abdu'l-Baha in Persian, the addressee is not known but it may be a CUP official; 'Abdu'l-Baha mentions at the end that he is in Alexandria for a 'change of scene'; attached to the memorandum to the present writer, dated 12 August 2009.
59. Shoghi Effendi, *God Passes By* (Wilmette/Ill., 1944/1979), p. 289.
60. On the reception, see Gail, Marzieh, *Arches of the Years* (Oxford, 1991), pp. 80–81.
61. BOA, HR.SYS. 70/31, 1 July 1912; Alkan: *Dissent*, pp. 171–3.
62. Dyer, Gwynne, 'The origins of the "nationalist" group of officers in Turkey 1908–18', *Journal of Contemporary History* 8/4 (1973), pp. 121–64.
63. Hanioğlu, Şükrü, *Preparation for a Revolution: The Young Turks, 1902–1908* (Oxford, 2001), pp. 295–302; Kayalı, Hasan, *Arabs and Young Turks: Ottomanism, Arabism, and Islamism in the Ottoman Empire, 1908–1918* (Los Angeles, 1997), pp. 82–4.
64. Such as Abdullah Cevdet and other founding fathers of the Young Turk movement; see Alkan: *Dissent*, p. 188.
65. Mu'ayyad: *Khatirat-i Habib*, vol. 1, pp. 318–320 and pp. 451–2 (translation).
66. Balyuzi: *'Abdu'l-Baha*, pp. 413–15.

BIBLIOGRAPHY

Archives

- Abu Dis Archives
- Arab Studies Society (Orient House), Jerusalem
- Baha'i Centre (Fatih, Istanbul)
- Baha'i International Archives (The Baha'i World Centre, Haifa) (BIA)
- Başbakanlık Osmanlı Arşivi, Istanbul (BOA)
- Central Archives for the History of the Jewish People Jerusalem (CAHJP)
- Central Zionist Archive, Jerusalem (CZA)
- Israel State Archives, Jerusalem (ISA)
- Jerusalem Municipal Archive (JMA)
- Municipality of Nablus (MAN)
- Al-Najah University Archives, Nablus
- Public Records Office, Foreign Office, London (FO)
- Tel Aviv Municipal Archive (TAMA)
- United States National Archive

Newspapers, Bulletins, Journals

Altneuland: Monatsschrift für die wirtschaftliche Erschließung Palästinas
Arevelk
Basiret
Bulletin de la Chambre de Commerce d'Industrie et d'Agriculture de Palestine

Droshak
Filastin
Habazeleth
Hashqafa
Hazewi
Hed ha-Mizrah
Ha-Herut
Al-Hilal
Al-Ittihad al-'Uthmani
Jamanag
The Jewish Chronicle
Le Judaisme séphardi
Al-Karmil
Kudüs-i Şerif / al-Quds al-Sharif
El Liberal
Al-Manar
Al-Mashriq
Ha-Mevasser
Al-Muqattam
Al-Muqtabas
Al-Muqtataf
Al-Nafa'is al-'Asriyya
New York Times
Ha-Po'el ha-Tza'ir
Puzantion
Al-Quds
Al-Sharq
Ha-Shiloah
Tasvir-i Efkar
El Tiempo

Reports, Almanacs, Official Documents

Azgayin Ĕndhanur Zhoghov [Minutes of the Armenian National Assembly] (Constantinople, 1908–1909).

Başbakanlık Devlet Arşivleri Genel Müdürlüğü, *Osmanli Belgelerinde Filistin* [Palestine in Ottoman Documents] (Istanbul, 2009).

Bertram, Anton Sir and Harry Charles Luke, *Report of the Commission Appointed by the Government of Palestine to Inquire into the Affairs of the Orthodox Patriarchate of Jerusalem* (Humphrey Milford, 1921).

Bertram, Anton Sir and J.W.A Young, *Report of the Commission* on Controversies between the Orthodox Patriarchate of Jerusalem and the Arab Orthodox Community (London, 1928).

Al-Dustur [The Constitution], translated by Nawfal, Nawfal (Beirut, 1301 [1883/4]) [in Arabic].

İlmiyye Salnamesi [The Yearbook of High Officials Holding Religious Duties] (Istanbul, 1334 [1915/6]).

Kawtharani, Wajih (ed.), *Watha'iq al-Mu'tamar al-'Arabi al-Awwal 1913: Kitab al-Mu'tamar wal-Murasalat al-Diblumasiyya al-Faransiyya al-Muta'aliqa bihi* [The Documents of the First Arab Conference in 1913: The Book of the Conference and the French Diplomatic Correspondence Related to it] (Beirut, 1980) [in Arabic].

Luncz, Abraham Moshe, [Untitled], *Luah Eretz-Yisra'el {...} li-Shnat 5669, ha-Shanah ha-Arba' 'Esreh* [Eretz-Israel Almanac [...] for 5669, the Fourteenth Year] (Jerusalem, 1908) [in Hebrew].

———. *Luah Eretz-Yisra'el {...} li-Shnat 5674, ha-Shanah ha-Tsha' 'Esreh* [Eretz-Israel Almanac [...] for 5674, the Nineteenth Year] (Jerusalem, 1914) [in Hebrew].

Meclis-i Meb'usan Zabit Cerideleri [Minutes of the Ottoman Parliament] (Istanbul, 1911) [in Ottoman Turkish].

Ministère des Travaux Publics, *Concession de distribution publique d'énergie électrique et des tramways électriques dans la ville de Jérusalem et ses faubourgs*, (Istanbul, 1911).

Diaries, Letters and Autobiographies

'Abdu'l-Baha, *Tablets of Abdu'l-Baha Abbas*, vol. 2 (Chicago, 1915 & 1919).

———. *Risala-yi Siyasiyya* [Treatise on the Art of Governance] (Tehran, BE 91/1933–4) [in Persian].

———. *Makatib-i 'Abdu'l-Baha* [Letters of 'Abdu'l-Baha], vol. 5 (Tehran, 132 BE/1975–6) [in Persian].

———. *'Abdu'l-Baha in London* (London, 1982).

———. *Risala-yi Madaniyya* [Treatise on Civilization] (Hofheim, 1985) [in Persian].

———. *The Secret of Divine Civilization* (translated by Gail, Marzieh (Wilmette/Ill., 1990).

Afroukhteh, Youness, *Khatirat-i Nuh Sala* [Memoies of Nine Years] (Los Angeles, 1983) [in Persain]. For an English version see *Memoires of Nine Years in 'Akka*, translated by Mansour, Riaz (Oxford, 2007).

'Amr, Sami, *A Young Palestinian's Diary, 1941–1945: The Life of Sami 'Amr*, edited and translated by Katz, Kimberly (Austin, 2009).

Baha'u'llah, *Tablets of Baha'u'llah Revealed after the Kitab-i-Aqdas* (Wilmette/Ill., 1988).

———. *Kitab-i-Aqdas: The Most Holy Book* (Haifa, 1992).

———. *The Summons of the Lord of Hosts* (Haifa, 2002).

Al-Barghuthi, 'Umar al-Salih, *Al-Marahil* [Stages] (Amman/Beirut, 2001) [in Arabic].

Cemal'uddin, Mehmed, *Hatirat-i Siyasiyesi* [His Political Memoirs] (Der Saadet [Istanbul], 1336/[1917–8]) [in Ottoman Turkish].

Chelouche, Yosef Eliyahu, *Parashat Hayyai, 1870–1930* [The Story of My Life, 1870–1930] (Tel Aviv, 1931) [in Hebrew].

Djemal Pasha, *Memoirs of a Turkish Statesman, 1913–1919* (New York, 1922).

Al-Jawhariyya, Wasif, *Al-Quds al-'Uthmaniyya fil-Mudhakkirat al-Jawhariyya* [Ottoman Jerusalem in the Jawhariyya Memoirs], vol. 1, edited by Tamari, Salim and Issam Nassar (Jerusalem, 2003) [in Arabic].

Kohen, Moiz's Diaries, Rifat Bali's private archives, Istanbul [in French and Ottoman Turkish].

Mahsin, A., *Siyonizm Tehelikeleri* [The Dangers of Zionism] (Istanbul, 1329 [1911]) [in Ottoman Turkish].

Mu'ayyad, Habib, *Khatirat-i Habib* [Memories of Habib], vol. I (Hofheim, 1998) [in Persian]. For an English version see *Eight Years Near 'Abdu'l-Baha: The Diary of Dr. Habib Mu'ayyad*, translated by Rabbani, Ahang), ebook at http://ahang.rabbani.googlepages.com/muayyad

Al-Sakakini, Khalil, *'Such Am I, Oh World': From the Diaries of Khalil al-Sakakini*, translated, annotated, and introduced by Shilo, Gideon (Jerusalem, 1990) [in Hebrew].

———. *The Diaries of Khalil Sakakini: New York, Sultana, Jerusalem, 1907–1912*, Volume I, edited by Musallam, Akram (Jerusalem, 2003) [in Arabic].

———. Al-Sakakini, Khalil, *The Diaries of Khalil Sakakini: Orthodox Renaissance, World War I, Exile to Damascus*, Volume II, edited by Musallam, Akram (Jerusalem, 2004), p. 97 [in Arabic].

Tamari, Salim (ed.). *'Am al-Jarad: Al-Harb al-'Uzma wa-Mahw al-Madi al-'Uthmani min Filastin: Yawmiyyat Jundi Maqdisi 'Uthmani, 1915–1916* [The Year of the Locust: Diary of an Ottoman Soldier from Jerusalem] (Beirut, 2008) [in Arabic].

———. (ed.) *The Year of the Locust* (Berkeley, forthcoming).

Tevfik Bey, Mehmed, *Bir Devlet Adamının Mehmet Tevfik Bey'in (Biren) II. Abdülhamid, Meşrutiyet ve Mütareke Devri Hatıraları* [The Memoirs of the Statesman Mehmed Tevfik Bey (Biren) Concerning the Period of Abdülhamid II, the Constitution, and the Armistice], edited by Hürmen, Fatma Rezan, 2 vols. (Istanbul, 1993) [in Turkish].

Yellin, David *The Works of David Yellin in Seven Volumes*, vol. 4: *Letters* (Jerusalem,1976) [in Hebrew].

Secondary Sources

Abu Hanna, Hanna, *Tala'i' al-Nahda fi Filastin: Khirriju al-Madaris al-Rusiyya 1862–1914* [The Pioneers of the Revival [of Arabic Language and Culture] in Palestine: the Graduates of the Russian Schools] (Beirut, 2005) [in Arabic].

Abu-Manneh, Butrus, 'The Christians between Ottomanism and Syrian Nationalism: The ideas of Butrus al-Bustani', *International Journal of Middle East Studies* vol. 11 (1980), pp. 287–304.

———. 'The Islamic roots of the Gülhane Rescript', *Die Welt des Islams* 34/2 (1994), pp. 173–203.

———. 'Jerusalem in the Tanzimat period, the new Ottoman administration and the notables', *Die Welt des Islams* 30 (1999), pp. 1–44.

———. 'The later Tanzimat and the Ottoman legacy in the Near Eastern successor states', in Mansour, Camille and Leila Fawaz (eds.), *Transformed Landscape Essays{...} in Honour of Walid Khalidi* (Cairo, 2009), pp. 61–81.

Ahmad, Feroz, *The Making of Modern Turkey* (London, 1994).

———. *Turkey: The Quest for Identity* (Oxford, 2003).

Ajamian, Shahe Bishop, 'Sultan Abdul Hamid and the Armenian Patriarchate of Jerusalem', in Ma'oz, Moshe (ed.), *Studies on Palestine during the Ottoman Period* (Jerusalem, 1975), pp. 341–350.

Al-'Alami, 'Abdullah, *A'zam tidhkar lil-'Uthmaniyian al-Ahrar aw al-Hurriyya wal-Musawa wal-Mab'uthan min Ta'alim al-Qur'an* [The Most Significant Commemoration for the Free Ottomans, or Freedom, Equality and the Parliament are from the Precepts of the Qur'an] (Beirut, 1326/1908) [in Arabic].

———. *Salasil al-Munazarah al-Islamiyya al-Nasraniyya* [The Series of Islamic – Christian Disputation] (Damascus, 1390/1970) [in Arabic].

Alkan, Necati, *Dissent and Heterodoxy in the Late Ottoman Empire: Reformers, Babis and Baha'is* (Istanbul, 2008).

Amanat, Abbas, *Resurrection and Renewal – The Making of the Babi Movement in Iran, 1844–1850* (Ithaca/London, 1989).

Anderson, Benedict, *Imagined Communities* (London, 1991).

Antreassian, Assadour, *Jerusalem and the Armenians* (Jerusalem, 1969).

Ariès, Philippe, *Geschichte der Kindheit*, third edition, translated by Neubaur, Caroline and Karin Kersten (Munich and Vienna, 1976).

Arsalan, Shakib, *Sira Dhatiyya* (Autobiography) (Beirut, 1969) [in Arabic].

Al-Asad, Nasir al-Din, *Ruhi al-Khalidi Ra'id al-Bahth al-Ta'rikhi al-Hadith fi Filastin* [Ruhi al-Khalidi the Pioneer of Modern Historical Research in Palestine] (Cairo, 1970) [in Arabic].

Aubin-Boltanski, Emma, 'La Réinvention du *mawsim* de Nabî Sâlih: Les territoires palestiniens (1997–2000)', *Archives de sciences sociales des religions* 123 (2003), pp. 103–120.

Avcı, Yasemin, *Değişim Sürecinde Bir Osmanlı Kenti: Kudüs 1890–1914* [An Ottoman City in Transition: Jerusalem 1890–1914] (Ankara, 2004) [in Turkish].

———. 'Jerusalem in the age of the Ottoman reforms: The urban identity and institutional change', *Arab Historical Review for Ottoman Studies* 40 (December 2009), pp. 9–21.

Al-'Awdat, Ya'aqub, *Min A'lam al-Fikr wal-Adab fi Filastin* [Prominent Figures of Thought and Literature in Palestine], Third Impression (Jerusalem, 1992) [in Arabic].

Ayalon, Ami, *Reading Palestine: Printing and Literacy* (Austin, 2004).

Azaria, Victor, *The Armenian Quarter of Jerusalem: Urban Life Behind Monastery Walls* (Berkley, Calif., 1984).

Baer, Marc David, *The Dönme: Jewish Converts, Muslim Revolutionaries, and Secular Turks* (Stanford, CA., 2010).

Bakhash, Shaul, *Iran: Monarchy, Bureaucracy & Reform under the Qajars: 1858–1896* (Oxford, 1978).

Bali, Rifat, 'Bir Yahudi dayanışma ve yardımlaşma kurumu: B'nai B'rith XI. bölge büyük locası tarihçesi ve yayın organı HaMenora dergisi' [A Jewish Support and Assistance Foundation: The History of *B'nai Brith*'s 16th Division Grand Lodge and its Organ of Publication HaMenora], *Müteferrika* vol. 8–9 (Spring-Summer, 1996), pp. 41–60 [in Turkish].

Balyuzi, Hasan M., *'Abdu'l-Baha: The Centre of the Covenant of Baha'u'llah* (Oxford, 1971).

Al-Barghuthi, 'Umar al-Salih and Khalil Tutah, *Ta'rikh Filastin* [The History of Palestine] (Jerusalem, 1923) [in Arabic].

Barkey, Karen and Mark Von Hagen (eds.), *After Empire: Multi-Ethnic Societies and Nation-Building: The Soviet Union and the Russian, Ottoman, and Hapsburg Empires* (Boulder, 1997).

Barru, Tawfiq, *Al-Arab wal-Turk fil-'Ahd al-Dusturi al-'Uthmani 1908–1914* [The Arabs and Turks during the Ottoman Constitutional Period, 1908–1914] (Damascus, 1991) [in Arabic].

Bawardi, Basilius, 'First steps in writing Arabic narrative fiction: The case of Hadiqat al-Akhbar', *Die Welt des Islam* vol. 48 (2008), pp. 170–195.

Bayat, Mangol, *Iran's First Revolution: Shi'ism and the Constitutional Revolution of 1905–1909* (Oxford/New York, 1991).

Baz, Gorgi Niqola, 'Sulaiman al-Bustani', in de Tarrazi, Filip (ed.), *Ta'rikh al-Sahafah al-'Arabiyyah* [The History of Arab Press], vol. 2, (Beirut, 1913) [in Arabic].

Bedreddin, Hasan (Bedri Paşa), *Iskat-ı Cenîn: Facia* [Abortion: A Calamity] (Istanbul, 1290/1874–5) [in Ottoman Turkish].

Ben-Arieh, Yehoshua, 'Ha-Nof ha-yishuvi shel Eretz-Yisra'el 'erev ha-hityashvut ha-tziyonit' [The Settlement Landscape of Eretz-Israel on the Eve of Zionist Colonization], in Kolatt, Israel (ed.), *The History of the Jewish Community in Eretz Israel since 1882* (vol. I–The Ottoman Period) (Jerusalem, 1989), pp. 75–141 [in Hebrew].

Benbassa, Esther, *Une diaspora sépharade en transition* (Paris, 1993).

———. (ed.), *Haim Nahum: A Sephardic Chief Rabbi in Politics, 1892–1923*, translated from French by Miriam Kochan (Tuscaloosa and London, 1995).

Ben-Bassat, Yuval, 'Rethinking the concept of Ottomanization: The *Yishuv* in the aftermath of the Young Turk Revolution of 1908', *Middle Eastern Studies* 45/3 (2009), pp. 461–75.

de Benoist, Alain, 'The idea of empire', *Telos* 98–9 (1993–4), pp. 81–98.

Berger, Lutz, *Gesellschaft und Individuum in Damaskus, 1550–1791* (Würzburg, 2007).

Bezalel, Itzhak, *You Were Born Zionists: The Sephardim in Eretz Israel in Zionism and the Hebrew Revival during the Ottoman Period* (Jerusalem, 2007) [in Hebrew].

Biliotti, A. and Ahmed Sedad, *Législation Ottomane depuis le rétablissement de la constitution 24 Djemazi-ul-ahir 1326–10 Juillet 1324/1908* (Paris, 1912).

Binder, Gerhard, 'Age(s)', in Cancik, Hubert and Helmuth Schneider (eds.), *Brill's New Pauly*, Antiquity volumes, online edition 2009.

Blake, Corinne L., *Training Arab-Ottoman Bureaucrats: Syrian graduates of the Mülkiye Mektebi, 1890–1920* (Ph.D. Dissertation, Princeton University, 1991).

Bliss, Frederick Jones, *The Religions of Modern Syria and Palestine* (New York, 1917).

Bonine, Michael E., 'The introduction of railroads in the eastern Mediterranean: Economic and social impacts', in Philipp, Thomas and Birgit Schäbler (eds.), *The Syrian Land: Processes of Integration and Fragmentation: Bilad al-Sham from the 18th to the 20th Century* (Stuttgart, 1998), pp. 53–78.

Bora, Siren H., 'Alliance Israélite Universelle'in Osmanli Yahudi cemaatini tarım sektöründe kalkındırma çalışmaları ve Izmir yakınlarında kurulan bir çiftlik okul: "Or Yehuda"' [Development Efforts in the Agricultural Sector by the Ottoman Jewish Society Alliance Israélite Universelle and the Agricultural School Established Near Izmir: 'Or Yehuda'], *Çağdaş Türkiye Tarihi Araştırmaları Dergisi* 1/3 (1993), pp. 387–400.

Borchard, Edwin M., 'The Mavromattis concessions cases', *The American Journal of International Law* 19/4 (October 1925), pp. 728–38.

Borovaya, Olga, 'Jews of three colors: The path to modernity in the Ladino press at the turn of the twentieth century', *Jewish Social Studies* 15/1 (2008), pp. 110–30.

Bracy, Michael, *Building Palestine: 'Isa al-'Isa, Filastin, and the Textual Construction of a National Identity, 1911–1931* (Unpublished Ph.D. Dissertation: University of Arkansas, 2005).

Brummet, Palmira, *Image and Imperialism in the Ottoman Revolutionary Press, 1908–1911* (Albany, NY, 2000).

Buck, Christopher, 'Baha'u'llah as "world reformer"', *Journal of Baha'i Studies* 3/4 (1991), pp. 23–70.

Bursalı, Mehmet Tahir, *Osmanlı Müellifleri* [Ottoman Writers], 3 vols. (Ankara, 2000) [in Turkish].

Al-Bustani, Sulaiman, *Iliyadhat Humirus* [The Iliad of Homer] (Cairo, 1904) [in Arabic].

——. *'Ibra wa Dhikra, aw al-Dawla al-'Uthmaniyya Qabla al-Dustur wa- Ba'dahu* [A Lesson and Remembrance, or the Ottoman State before the Constitution and after it] (Cairo, 1908) [in Arabic].

Büssow, Johann, *Hamidian Palestine: Politics and Society in the District of Jerusalem, 1872–1908* (Unpublished Ph.D. Dissertation: Free University, Berlin, 2008).

Calhoun, Craig, 'Imagining solidarity: Cosmopolitanism, constitutional patriotism, and the public sphere', *Public Culture* 14/ 1 (2002), pp. 147–171.

Campos, Michelle U., *A 'Shared Homeland' and its Boundaries: Empire, Citizenship and the Origins of Sectarianism in Late Ottoman Palestine, 1908–13* (Unpublished Ph.D. dissertation, Stanford University, 2003).

——. 'Between "beloved ottomania" and "the Land of Israel": The struggle over Ottomanism and Zionism among Palestine's Sephardi Jews, 1908–1913', *International Journal of Middle East Studies* 37 (2005), pp. 461–83.

——. *Ottoman Brothers: Muslims, Christians and Jews in Early 20th Century Palestine* (Stanford University Press, 2010).

Clogg, Richard, 'The Greek Millet in the Ottoman Empire', in Braude, Benjamin and Bernard Lewis (eds.), *Christians and Jews in the Ottoman Empire: The Functioning of a Plural Society*, vol. I (New York, 1982), pp. 185–208.

Cole, Juan R. I., *Modernity and the Millennium: The Genesis of the Baha'i Faith in the Nineteenth- Century Middle East* (New York, 1998).

——. 'Abdu'l-Baha's treatise on leadership', online at H-Bahai, *Translations of Shaykhi, Babi and Baha'i Texts*, vol. 2, no. 2 (May, 1998), http://www.h-net.org/~bahai/areprint/vol2/siyasi.htm

Cuinet, Vital, *Syrie, Liban et Palestine: Géographie administrative, statistique, descriptive et raisonnée* (Paris, 1896).

Davison, Roderic H., *Reform in the Ottoman Empire 1856–1876* (Princeton, 1963).

Dawn, Ernest C., 'The origins of Arab nationalism', in Khalidi, Rashid, Lisa Anderson, Muhammad Muslih, and Reeva S. Simon (eds.), *The Origins of Arab Nationalism* (New York, 1991), pp. 3–30.

BIBLIOGRAPHY

Demirci, Tuba and Selçuk Akşin Somel, 'Women's bodies, demography, and public health: Abortion policy and perspectives in the Ottoman Empire of the nineteenth century', *Journal of the History of Sexuality* 17/3 (September 2008), pp. 377–420.

Deringil, Selim, *The Well-Protected Domains: Ideology and the Legitimation of Power in the Ottoman Empire, 1876–1909* (London, 1998).

Devereux, Robert, 'Süleyman Pasha's "The Feeling of the Revolution"', *Middle Eastern Studies* 15/1 (January 1979), pp. 3–35.

Doganalp-Votzi, Heidemarie, 'The state and its subjects according to the 1876 Ottoman constitution some lexicographic aspects', in Kieser, Hans-Lukas (ed.), *Aspects of the Political Language in Turkey, 19th-20th Century* (Istanbul, 2002), pp. 61–9.

Doumani, Beshara, 'Rediscovering Ottoman Palestine: Writing Palestinians into history', *Journal of Palestine Studies* vol. 21/2 (Winter 1992), pp. 5–28.

———. *Rediscovering Palestine: Merchants and Peasants in Jabal Nablus, 1700–1900* (Berkeley and Los Angeles, 1995).

Dowling, Archdeacon, *The Patriarchate of Jerusalem* (London, 1909).

Durham, Mary Edith, *The Struggle for Scutari* (London, 1914).

Dyer, Gwynne, 'The origins of the "nationalist" group of officers in Turkey 1908–18', *Journal of Contemporary History* 8/4 (1973), pp. 121–164.

Efrati, Nathan, *Mishpahat Elyashar be-Tokhekhey Yerushalayim: Prakim be-Toldot ha-Yishuv ha-Yehudi bi-Yerushalyim ba-Me'ot ha-Tsha'-'Esreh veha-'Esrim* [The Elyashar Family in Jerusalem: A Chapter in the History of the Jewish Community in Jerusalem in the Nineteenth and Twentieth Century] (Jerusalem, 1974) [in Hebrew].

Eisenman, Robert, 'The Young Turk legislation, 1913–17 and its application in Palestine/Israel', in Kushner, David (ed.), *Palestine in the Late Ottoman Period: Political, Social and Economic Transformation* (Jerusalem, 1986), pp. 59–73.

Eldem, Edhem, 'Ottoman financial integration with Europe: Foreign loans, the Ottoman Bank and the Ottoman public dept', *European Review* 13/3 (2005), pp. 431–45.

Eliav, Mordechai, *Britain and the Holy Land (1838–1914): Selected Documents from the British Consulate in Jerusalem* (Jerusalem, 1997).

———. *David Wolffsohn, the Man and His Times: The Zionist Movement between 1905–1914* (Jerusalem, 1977) [in Hebrew].

Ersanlı, Büşra, 'The Ottoman Empire in the historiography of the Kemalist era: A theory of fatal decline', in Adanır, Fikret and Suraiya Faroqhi (eds.), *The Ottomans and the Balkans* (Leiden, 2001), pp. 115–154.

Esherick, Joseph W., Hasan Kayalı, and Eric Van Young (eds.), *Empire to Nation: Historical Perspectives on the Making of the Modern World* (Lanham, MD, 2006).

Feroz, Ahmad, *The Making of Modern Turkey* (London, 1993).
———. *Turkey: The Quest for Identity* (Oxford, 2003).
Findley, Carter V., *Ottoman Civil Officialdom a Social History* (Princeton, 1989).
Fishman, Louis, 'The 1911 Haram al-Sharif incident: Palestinian notables versus the Ottoman administration', *Journal of Palestine Studies* vol. 33/34 (Spring 2005), pp. 6–22.
Foran, John (ed.), *Theorizing Revolutions* (London, 1997).
Fortna, Benjamin C., 'Education and autobiography at the end of the Ottoman Empire', *Die Welt des Islams* 41 (2001), pp. 1–31.
———. *Imperial Classroom: Islam, the State and Education in the Late Ottoman Empire* (Oxford, 2002).
Frangia, G., *Projet: Sur l'adduction des eaux d'Arroub* (Constantinople, 1912).
Fresko, David, *Le Sionisme* (Istanbul, 1909).
Friedman, Isaiah, 'The *Hilfsverein der Deutschen Juden*, the German Foreign Ministry, and the controversy with the Zionists, 1901–1918', *Cathedra* 20 (July 1981), pp. 97–122 [In Hebrew].
Frierson, Elizabeth Brown, *Unimagined Communities: State, Press, and Gender in the Hamidian Era* (Unpublished Ph.D. Dissertation, Princeton University, 1996).
Furlonge, Geoffrey, *Palestine is My Country: The Story of Musa Alami* (London, 1969).
Gail, Marzieh, *Arches of the Years* (Oxford, 1991).
Galanté, Avraham, *Histoire des Juifs d'Istanbul*, vol. I (Istanbul, 1985).
Gaon, Moshe David. *Yehudei ha-Mizrah be-Eretz Yisra'el: 'Avar ve-Hove* [The Oriental Jews in Eretz Israel: Past and Present], in two volumes (Jerusalem, 1928–1937) [in Hebrew].
———. *A Bibliography* of the *Judeo-Spanish (Ladino) Press* (Jerusalem, 1965).
Gawrych, George Walter, *The Crescent and the Eagle: Ottoman Rule: Islam and the Albanians, 1874–1913* (London, 2006).
Gelvin, James L., *Divided Loyalties: Nationalism and Mass Politics in Syria at the Close of Empire* (Berkeley, 1998).
———. *The Modern Middle East: A History*, Second Edition (New York and Oxford, 2005).
Georgeon, François, *Abdulhamid II: Le sultan calife* (Paris, 2003).
Georgeon, François and Klaus Kreiser (eds.), *Enfance et jeunesse dans le monde musulman / Childhood and Youth in the Muslim World* (Paris, 2007).
Gerber, Haim, *Ottoman Rule in Jerusalem, 1890–1914* (Berlin, 1985).
Gilbar, Gad G., 'The growing economic involvement of Palestine with the West, 1865–1914', in Kushner, David (ed.), *Palestine in the Late Ottoman Period: Political, Social and Economic Transformation* (Leiden, 1986), pp. 188–209.
Gilboa, Menuha, *Lexicon of the Hebrew Press in the Eighteenth and Nineteenth Centuries* (Jerusalem, 1992) [in Hebrew].

Gorny, Yosef, 'Shorasheha shel toda'at ha-'imut ha-le'umi ha-yehudi-'aravi ve-hishtakfuta ba-'itunut ha-'ivrit ba-shanim 1900–1918' [The Roots of the Consciousness of the Jewish-Arab National Conflict and its Reflection in the Hebrew Press during the Years 1900–1918], *Zionism* 4 (1975), pp. 72–113.

――. *Zionism and the Arabs, 1882–1948: A Study of Ideology* (Oxford, 1987).

Gövsa, İbrahim A., *Türk Meşhurları Ansiklopedisi* [Encyclopaedia of Famous Turks] (Ankara, 1946) [in Turkish].

Gür, Alim, *Ebüziyya Tevfik Hayatı: Dil, Edebiyat, Basın, Yayın, ve Matbaacılığa Katkılar* [The Life of Ebüziyya Tevfik: Language, Literature, Press, Publication, and Printing Supplements] (Ankara, 1998) [in Turkish].

Haddad, William W. and William Ochsenwald (eds.), *Nationalism in a Non-National State: The Dissolution of the Ottoman Empire* (Columbus, OH, 1977).

Haim, Abraham, 'The Hakham Bashi of Istanbul and the "Rabbinate Controversy" in Jerusalem', *Pe'amim* 12 (1982), pp. 105–113 [in Hebrew].

Al-Hanbali, Shakir, *Al-Ta'rikh al-'Uthmani al-Musawwar* [The Illustrated Ottoman History] (Damascus, 1331/[1913]) [in Arabic].

Hanioğlu, Şükrü M., 'Notes on the Young Turks and the Freemasons', *Middle Eastern Studies* 25 (1989), pp. 186–94.

――. *Preparation for a Revolution: The Young Turks, 1902–1908* (Oxford, 2001).

――. *A Brief History of the Late Ottoman Empire* (Princeton, 2008).

Hanssen, Jens, *Fin de Siècle Beirut: The Making of a Provincial Capital* (Oxford, 2005).

Harel, Yaron, *Between Intrigues and Revolution: The Appointment and Dismissal of Chief Rabbis in Baghdad, Damascus, and Aleppo 1744–1914* (Jerusalem, 2007) [in Hebrew].

al-Hawwari, 'Irfan Sa'id Abu Hamad, *A'lam min Ard al-Salam* [Notables from the Land of Peace] (Haifa, 1979) [in Arabic]

Hershlag, Zvi Yehuda, *Introduction to Modern Economic History of the Middle East* (Leiden, 1997).

Hintlian, George, *History of the Armenians in the Holy Land* (Jerusalem, 1976).

Hopwood, Derek, *Russian Presence in Syria and Palestine, 1843–1914: Church and Politics in the Near East* (Oxford, 1969).

Hourani, Albert, *Arabic Thought in the Liberal Age, 1798–1939*, second edition (Cambridge, 1983).

――. 'Sulayman al-Bustani (1856–1925)', in Seikaly, Samir, R. Baalbaki, and P. Dodd (eds.), *Quest for Understanding: Arabic and Islamic Studies in Memory of Malcolm H. Kerr* (Beirut, 1991), pp. 43–57.

Husni, Yusuf, *Al-Idahat al-Jaliyya fi Qawa'id al-Lugha al-'Uthmaniyya* [Plain Clarifications of the Rules of the Ottoman Language], second impression (Beirut, 1885) [in Arabic].

al-Husri, Sati', *Al-Bilad al-'Arabiyya wal-Dawla al-'Uthmaniyya* [The Arab Lands and the Ottoman Empire] (Beirut, 1965) [in Arabic].

Irwin, Robert, 'Futuwwa: Chivalry and gangsterism in medieval Cairo', *Muqarnas* 21 (2004), pp. 161–70.

Ishraq-Khavari, 'Abdu'l-Hamid, *Ma'ida-i Asmani* [Heavenly Food], vol. 5 (Tehran, 129 B.E./1972) [in Persian/Arabic].

Isin, Engin F. and Patricia K. Wood, *Citizenship and Identity* (London, 1999).

İnal, İbnülemin M. Kemal, *Son Asır Türk Şairleri* [Turkish Poets of the Last Century], 4 vols. (Ankara, 1969) [in Turkish].

İz, Fahir, 'Manastırlı Mehmed Rıf'at', *Encyclopaedia of Islam*, 2nd ed., vol. 6 (Leiden, 1991), pp. 372–3.

———. 'Hasan Bedr al-Din', *Encyclopaedia of Islam*, 2nd ed., vol. 12 – Supplement (Leiden, 2004), p. 359.

Jacobson, Abigail, 'Sephardim, Ashkenazim and the "Arab Question" in pre-First World War Palestine: A reading of three Zionist newspapers', *Middle Eastern Studies* 39/2 (April 2003), pp. 105–130.

———. 'Alternative voices in late Ottoman Palestine: Jews and Muslims on the evolving national conflict', *Jerusalem Quarterly File* 21 (August 2004), pp. 41–8.

———. *From Empire to Empire: Jerusalem in the Transition between Ottoman and British Rule, 1912–1920* (Unpublished Ph.D. Dissertation, The University of Chicago, 2006).

Jankowski, James and Israel Gershoni (eds.), *Rethinking Nationalism in the Arab Middle East* (New York, 1997).

Jeha, Michel, *Farah Anton* (Beirut, 1998) [in Arabic].

Al-Ju'beh, Nazmi, 'Maqam Nabi Salih', in Sharif, Walid et al (eds.), *Pilger, Sufis und Gelehrte: Islamische Kunst im Westjordanland und Gazastreifen* (Tübingen, 2004), pp. 154–5.

Kahanoff, Jacqueline, *Mi-Mizrah Shemesh* [From the East the Sun] (Tel Aviv, 1978) [in Hebrew].

———. *Between Two Worlds*, edited by Ohana, David (Jerusalem, 2005) [in Hebrew].

Kahraman, Âlim, 'Mehmed Rifat, Manastırlı', *Türkiye Diyanet Vakfı İslam Ansiklopedisi*, vol. 28 (Ankara, 2003), pp. 519–20 [in Turkish].

Kansu, Aykut, *The Revolution of 1908 in Turkey* (Leiden, 1997).

———. *Politics in Post-Revolutionary Turkey, 1908–1913* (Leiden, 2000).

Kappeler, Andreas, *The Russian Empire: A Multiethnic History* (Harlow, England, 2001).

Kark, Ruth, 'The Rise and decline of coastal towns in Palestine', in Gilbar, Gad G., (ed.), *Ottoman Palestine 1800–1914* (Leiden, 1990), pp. 69–90.

———. *Jaffa: A City in Evolution 1799–1917* (Jerusalem, 1990).

Kark, Ruth and Michal, Oren-Nordheim, *Jerusalem and Its Environs: Quarters, Neighborhoods, Villages, 1800–1948* (Jerusalem, 2001).

Karmi, Ilan, *The Jewish Community of Istanbul in the Nineteenth Century* (Istanbul, 1996).

Karpat, Kemal H., *The Politicization of Islam: Reconstructing Identity, State, Faith, and Community in the Late Ottoman State* (New York, 2001).

Katz, Itamar and Ruth Kark, 'The Greek Orthodox Patriarchate of Jerusalem and its congregation: Dissent over real estate', *International Journal of Middle East Studies* 37 (2005), pp. 509–534.

Kayalı, Hasan, 'Elections and the electoral process in the Ottoman Empire, 1876–1919', *International Journal of Middle East Studies* 27 (1995), pp. 265–86.

———. *Arabs and Young Turks: Ottomanism, Arabism, and Islamism in the Ottoman Empire, 1908–1918* (Berkeley, 1997).

Al-Kayyali, Sami, *Al-Adab al-'Arabi al-Mu'asir fi Suriyya 1850–1950* [The Contemporary Arab Literature in Syria 1850–1950] (Cairo, 1968) [in Arabic].

Kedourie, Elie, 'Young Turks, Freemasons and Jews', *Middle Eastern Studies* vol. 7/1 (1971), pp. 89–104.

———. 'The impact of the Young Turk Revolution in the Arabic speaking provinces of the Ottoman Empire', in Kedourie, Elie, *Arabic Political Memoirs and other Studies* (London, 1974), pp. 124–161.

Khalidi, Issam, 'Body and ideology: Early athletics in Palestine (1900–1948)', *Jerusalem Quarterly* 27 (2006), pp. 44–58.

Khalidi, Rashid, 'The 1912 election campaign in the cities of Bilad al-Sham', *International Journal of Middle East Studies* 16 (1984), pp. 461–74.

———. 'Social factors in the rise of the Arab movement in Syria', in Arjomand, Said Amir (ed.), *From Nationalism to Revolutionary Islam* (Albany, NY, 1984), pp. 53–70.

———. 'Ottomanism and Arabism in Syria before 1914: A reassessment', in Khalidi, Rashid, Lisa Anderson, Muhammad Muslih, and Reeva S. Simon (eds.), *The Origins of Arab Nationalism* (New-York, 1991), pp. 50–69.

———. *Palestinian Identity: The Construction of Modern National Consciousness* (New York, 1997).

———. *Palestinian Identity: The Construction of a Modern National Consciousness*, 2nd ed. (New York, 2009).

King, Jeremy, *Budweisers into Czechs and Germans: A Local History of Bohemian Politics, 1848–1948* (Princeton, 2002).

Kirli, Cengiz, *The Struggle over Space: Coffeehouses of Ottoman Istanbul, 1780–1845* (Ph.D. Dissertation, SUNY-Binghamton, 2000).

Kondis, Basil, *Greece and Albania* (Thessaloniki, 1976).

Koushagian, Torkom Arch., *Eghishe Patriark Durean* [Patriarch Yeghishe Turian] (Jerusalem, 1932) [in Armenian].

Krämer, Gudrun, *A History of Palestine: From the Ottoman Conquest to the Founding of the State of Israel* (Princeton, 2008).

Kressel, Getzel, *Toldot ha-'Itonut ha-'Ivrit be-Eretz Yisr'ael* [History of the Hebrew Press in Eretz-Israel] (Jerusalem, 1964) [in Hebrew].

Kurzman, Charles (ed.), *Modernist Islam, 1840–1940* (New York, 2002).

Kushner, David, 'Ha-Dor ha-aharon le-shilton ha-'othmanim be-Eretz Yisra'el, 1882–1914' [The Last Generation of Ottoman Rule in Eretz Israel, 1882–1914]', *The History of the New Jewish Community in Eretz-Israel since 1882*, pp. 1–74 [in Hebrew].

———. *A Governor in Jerusalem: The City and Province in the Eyes of Ali Ekrem Bey, 1906–1908* (Jerusalem, 1995) [in Hebrew].

———. 'Kuds-i Şerif/Al-Kuds al-Sharif – the official gazette of the District of Jerusalem at the end of the Ottoman period', *Cathedra* 129 (2008), pp. 67–84 [in Hebrew].

Landau, J.M., 'Remarks on the attitude of the "Young Turks" to Zionism', *Zionism* IX (1984), pp. 195–205.

———. *Tekinalp, Turkish Patriot 1883–1961* (Leiden, 1984).

———. 'Comments on the Jewish press in Istanbul: the Hebrew weekly *Hamevasser* (1909–1911)', in idem, *Jews, Arabs, Turks: Selected Essays* (Jerusalem, 1993), pp. 89–96.

———. 'The "Young Turks" movement and Zionism: Some comments', in idem, Ibid., pp. 169–77.

———. *Exploring Ottoman and Turkish History* (London, 2004).

Lazare, Lucien, 'L'Alliance Israélite Universelle en Palestine à l'époque de la révolution des "Jeunes Turcs" et sa mission en Orient du 29 October 1908 au 19 Janvier 1909', *Revue des Études Juives* CXXXVIII/3–4 (juill. –déc. 1979), pp. 307–335.

Lemire, Vincent, 'Water in Jerusalem at the end of the Ottoman period (1850–1920): Technical and political networks', *Bulletin du Centre de recherche français de Jérusalem* 7 (Autumn 2000), pp. 136–150.

Levy, Lital, *Jewish Writers in the Arab East: Literature, History, and the Politics of Enlightenment, 1863–1914* (Unpublished Ph.D. Dissertation, University of California Berkeley, 2007).

———. 'Partitioned pasts: Arab Jewish intellectuals and the case of Esther Azhari Moyal (1873–1948)', in Hamzah, D. (ed.), *The Making of the Arab Intellectual (1880–1960): Empire, Public Sphere, and the Colonial Coordinates of Selfhood* (New Jersey, forthcoming).

Lewis, Bernard, *The Emergence of Modern Turkey* (London, 1961).

——. 'The idea of freedom in modern Islamic political thought', in Lewis, Bernard, *Islam in History: Ideas, Men and Events in the Middle East* (London, 1973), pp. 267–81.

Lieven, Dominic, *Empire: The Russian Empire and Its Rivals* (New Haven, 2000).

Lowry, Heath W., 'The Young Turk triumvirate, ambassador Henry Morgenthau, and the future of Palestine, December 1913–January 1916', in Rozen, Minna (ed.), *The Last Ottoman Century and Beyond: The Jews in Turkey and the Balkans 1808–1945,* vol. 2, (Tel Aviv, 2002), pp. 151–64.

Maggid, Moshe, 'Periodical Literature', in Ben-Naeh, Yaron (ed.), *Jewish Communities in the East in the Nineteenth and Twentieth Centuries: Turkey* (Jerusalem, 2010), pp. 123–36 [in Hebrew].

Mahony, Anthony O., 'Palestinian-Arab Orthodox Christians: Religion, politics, and church-state relations in Jerusalem, c. 1908–1925', *Chronos* 3 (2000), pp. 61–87.

al-Maqdisi, Anis, *Al-Ittijahat al-Adabiyya fil-'Alam al-'Arabi al-Hadith* [The Literary Currents in the Modern Arab World], third edition (Beirut, 1963) [in Arabic].

McGlinn, Sen, 'A sermon on the art of governance (resale-ye siyasiyyah) by 'Abdu'l-Baha', H-Bahai, *Translations of Shaykhi, Babi and Baha'i Texts*, vol. 7/1 (March, 2003), http://www.h-net.org/~bahai/trans/vol7/govern.htm

Maksoudian, Ghevont Father, *Erusaghemi Khndirĕ* [The Question of Jerusalem], vol. I (Istanbul, 1908) [in Armenian].

Manna', 'Adil, *A'lam Filastin fi Awakhir al-'Ahd al-'Uthmani* [The Notables of Palestine during the Late Ottoman Period] second edition (Beirut, 1995) [in Arabic].

——. *Ta'rikh Filastin fi Awakhir al-'Ahd al-'Uthmani, 1700–1918: Qira'a Jadida* [History of Palestine at the End of the Ottoman Period: A New Reading] (Beirut, 1999) [in Arabic].

Mandel, Neville, 'Attempts at an Arab-Zionist entente: 1913–1914', *Middle Eastern Studies* 1/3 (April 1965), pp. 238–67.

——. *The Arabs and Zionism before World War I* (Berkeley, 1976).

Marcus, Amy D., *Jerusalem 1913: The Origins of the Arab-Israeli Conflict* (New York, 2008).

Mardin, Şerif, *The Genesis of Young Ottoman Thought: A Study in the Modernization of Turkish Political Ideas* (Princeton, 1962).

Martin, Vanessa, *Islam and Modernism: the Iranian Revolution of 1906* (London, 1989).

Masters, Bruce, *Christians and Jews in the Ottoman Arab World: The Roots of Sectarianism* (New York, 2001).

Mazza, Roberto, 'Antonio de la Cierva Lewita: The Spanish consul in Jerusalem 1914–1920', *Jerusalem Quarterly* no. 40 (Winter 2009/10), pp. 36–44.

McGlinn, Sen, 'Resala-ye madaniya' [Treatise on Civilization], online entry in *Encyclopaedia Iranica*, http://www.iranica.com/newsite/home/index.isc

Metaxakis, Meletios, *Les exigences des Orthodoxes Arabophones de Palestine* (Constantinople, 1909).

Michel, Ange, *Les Frères des Écoles Chrétiennes en Turquie, 1841–2003* (Istanbul, 2004).

Miller, Alexei and Alfred J. Rieber (eds.), *Imperial Rule* (Budapest, 2004).

Momen, Moojan, *The Babi and Baha'i Religions: Some Contemporary Western Accounts, 1844–1944* (Oxford, 1981).

———. 'The Baha'i influence on the reform movements of the Islamic world in the 1860s and 1870s', *Baha'i Studies Bulletin*, vol. 2/2 (1983), pp. 47–65.

———. *A Short Introduction to the Baha'i Faith* (Oxford, 1997).

———. *Baha'u'llah: A Short Biography* (Oxford, 2007).

Motyl, Alexander, 'Thinking about empire', in Barkey, Karen and Mark Von Hagen (eds.), *After Empire: Multi-Ethnic Societies and Nation-Building: The Soviet Union and the Russian, Ottoman, and Hapsburg Empires* (Boulder, 1997), pp. 19–29.

Muslih, Muhammad, *The Origins of Palestinian Nationalism* (New York, 1988).

Nashashibi, Nasser Eddin, *Jerusalem's Other Voice: Ragheb Nashashibi and Moderation in Palestinian Politics, 1920–1948* (Exeter, 1990).

Nashat, Guity, *The Origins of Modern Reform in Iran, 1870–80* (Urbana, 1982).

Nassi, Gad (ed.), *Jewish Journalism and Printing Houses in the Ottoman Empire and Modern Turkey* (Istanbul, 2001).

Niebuhr, Reinhold, *The Structure of Nations and Empires: A Study of the Recurring Patterns and Problems of the Political Order in Relation to the Unique Problems of the Nuclear Age* (New York, 1959).

Al-Nimr, Ihsan, *Ta'rikh Jabal Nablus wal-Balqa* [The History of Jabal Nablus and al-Balqa] (Nablus, undated), in four vols. [in Arabic].

Okyar, Osman, 'The role of the state in the economic life of the nineteenth-century Ottoman Empire', *Asian and African Studies* 14 (1980), pp. 143–64.

Ortaylı, İ., *Ottomanism and Zionism during the Second Constitutional Period* (Istanbul, 2004).

Özcan, Azmi, 'Osmanlıcılık' [Ottomanism], *TDV İslam Ansiklopedisi*, vol. 33 (2007), pp. 485–7 [in Turkish].

Özyüksel, Murat, *Hicaz Demiryolu* [The Hejaz Railway], (Istanbul, 2000) [in Turkish].

Pagis, Jonathan, *Ottoman Population Censuses in Palestine, 1875–1918* (Jerusalem, 1997) [in Hebrew].

Pakalın, Mehmed Z., *Osmanlı Tarih Deyimleri ve Terimleri Sözlüğü* [Dictionary of Ottoman Historical Idioms and Terms] (Istanbul, 1946–1953) [in Turkish].

BIBLIOGRAPHY 295

Pappé, Ilan, *History of Modern Palestine: One Land, Two Peoples* (Cambridge, 2004).

Pearson, Owen, *Albania in the Twentieth Century: A History*, in two volumes (London, 2006).

Qub'ayn, Salim, *Al-Dustur wal-Ahrar* [The Constitution and the Liberals] (Cairo, 1908) [in Arabic].

Ramsaur, Ernest E., *The Young Turks: Prelude to the Revolution of 1908* (Princeton, NJ, 1957).

Reid, D. M., *The Odyssey of Farah Anton* (Minneapolis and Chicago, 1975).

Reinkowski, Maurus, 'Late Ottoman rule over Palestine: Its evaluation in Arab, Turkish and Israeli histories, 1970–90', *Middle Eastern Studies* 35/1 (1999), pp. 66–97.

Rodrigue, Aron, *French Jews, Turkish Jews: The Alliance Israélite Universelle and the Politics of Jewish Schooling in Turkey, 1860–1925* (Bloomington and Indianapolis, 1990).

Rogan, Eugene, 'Aşiret Mektebi: Abdülhamid IIs school for tribes, 1892–1907', *International Journal of Middle East Studies* 28 (1996), pp. 83–107.

Rose, John H. Melkon, *Armenians of Jerusalem: Memoirs of Life in Palestine* (London and New York, 1993).

Sabunji, Lewis, *Al-Mir'a al-Saniyya fil-Qawa'id al-'Uthmaniyya* [The Exalted Mirror in Ottoman Grammar] (Beirut, 1867) [in Arabic].

Saeidi, Nader, *Risala-yi Madaniyya va Mas'ala-i Tajaddud dar Khavar-i Miyana* [The Treatise on Civilization and the Issue of Modernization in the Middle East] (Dundas/Ontario, 1993) [in Persian].

Salzmann, Ariel, 'Citizens in search of a state: The limits of political participation in the late Ottoman empire', in Hanagan, Michael and Charles Tilly (eds.), *Extending Citizenship, Reconfiguring States* (Lanham, MD, 1999), pp. 37–66.

Sanjian, Ara, 'The Armenian Church and community of Jerusalem', in O'Mahony, Anthony (ed.), *The Christian Communities of Jerusalem and the Holy Land: Studies in History, Religion and Politics* (Cardiff, 2003).

Sarkis, Yusuf I., *Mu'jam al-Matbu'at al-'Arabiyya wal-Mu'arraba* [Lexicon of Arab and Arabized Printed [Books]] (Cairo, 1928) [in Arabic].

Schölch, Alexander, 'Jerusalem in the 19th century', in Asali, K.J. (ed.), *Jerusalem in History* (Brookline, N.Y., 1990), pp. 228–48.

———. *Palestine in Transformation 1856–1882, Studies in Social, Economic and Political Development* (Washington D.C., 1993).

Schumann, Christoph, *Radikalnationalismus in Syrien und Libanon: Politische Sozialisation und Elitenbildung, 1930–1958* (Hamburg, 2001).

Şen, Leyla, 'Merkez-çevre ilişkilerinin önemli bir dinamiği olarak Osmanlı İmparatorluğu'nda ulaşım sistemleri' [Transportation Systems in the Ottoman Empire, as Dynamics of Center-Periphery Relations], *Kebikeç-İnsan Bilimleri İçin Kaynak Araştırma Dergisi* 11 (2001), pp. 95–124 [in Turkish].

Shabani, Omid A. Payrow, 'Who is afraid of constitutional patriotism? The binding source of citizenship in constitutional state', *Social Theory and Practice* 28/3 (2002), pp. 419–43.

Shafir, Gershon and Yoav Peled, *Being Israeli: The Dynamics of Multiple Citizenship* (Cambridge, 2002).

Shahvar, Soli, 'Concession Hunting in the Age of Reform: British Companies and the Search for Government Guarantees; Telegraph Concessions through Ottoman Territories, 1855–58', *Middle Eastern Studies* 38/4 (2002), pp. 169–93.

Shapira, Anita, *Land and Power: The Zionist Resort to Force, 1881–1948* (New York, 1992).

Shapira, Yosef, *Ha-Po'el ha-Tza'ir ha-Ra'ayon veha-Ma'ase* [*Ha-Po'el ha-Tza'ir in Theory and in Practice*] (Tel Aviv, 1967) [in Hebrew].

Sharaby, Rachel, 'The chief Sephardic Rabbinate, 1906–1914: Conflicts and personalities', *Cathedra* 37 (1985), pp. 106–112 [in Hebrew].

Shaw, Stanford J., *The Jews of the Ottoman Empire and the Turkish Republic* (London, 1991).

Shaw, Stanford and Ezel K. Shaw, *History of the Ottoman Empire and Modern Turkey, 1808–1975*, 2 vols. (Cambridge, 1977).

Shea, John, *Macedonia and Greece: The Struggle to Define a New Balkan Nation* (Jefferson, N.C., 1997).

Shoghi Effendi, *God Passes By* (Wilmette/Ill., 1944/1979).

Singer, Amy, *Palestinian Peasants and Ottoman Officials: Rural Administration around Sixteenth-century Jerusalem* (Cambridge, 1994).

Smith, Charles, *Palestine and the Arab-Israeli Conflict: A History with Documents*, Seventh Edition (Boston, 2009).

Smith, Peter, *The Babi and Baha'i Religions: From Messianic Shi'ism to a World Religion* (Cambridge, 1987).

Somel, Selçuk Akşin, 'Osmanlı reform çağında osmanlıcılık düşüncesi (1839–1913)' [Ottomanism Thought in the Ottoman Reform Period], in Alkan, Mehmet O. (ed.), *Tanzimat ve Meşrutiyet'in Birikimi* [The Formation of the Reforms and the Constitution] (Istanbul, 2001), pp. 1–23 [in Turkish].

——. *The Modernization of Public Education in the Ottoman Empire 1839–1908, Islamization, Autocracy and Discipline* (Leiden, 2001).

van Steenbergen, Bart (ed.), *The Condition of Citizenship* (London, 1994).

Stein, Sarah Abrevaya, *Making Jews Modern: The Yiddish and Ladino Press in the Russian and Ottoman Empires* (Bloomington, 2004).

Strohmeier, Martin, *Al-Kulliya al-Salahiya in Jerusalem: Arabismus, Osmanismus und Panislamismus im Ersten Weltkrieg* (Stuttgart, 1991).

Al-Sulh, 'Imad, *Ahmad Faris al-Shidyaq: Atharuhu wa 'Asruhu* [Ahmad Faris al-Shidyaq: His Work and his Period] (Beirut, 1980) [in Arabic].

Al-Tabba', 'Uthman, *Ithaf al-A'izza fi Ta'rikh Ghazza* [Presenting the Notables in the History of Gaza], edited by Abu-Hashim, 'Abdullatif Z., vol. 4 (Gaza, 1999) [in Arabic].

Tamari, Salim, 'The last feudal lord in Palestine', *Jerusalem Quarterly* 16 (2002), pp. 27–42.

——. 'Le café des manants: Khalil Sakakini, prince de l'oisiveté de Jérusalem', *Revue des Études Palestiniennes* 90 (2004), pp. 78–87.

Tauber, Eliezer, 'The relations between the Syrian nationalists and the Zionist movement until the end of World War I', *Jewish History* 5/2 (Fall 1991).

——. *The Emergence of the Arab Movements* (London, 1993).

Tekeli, İlhan and Selim İlkin, 'The public works program and the development of technology in the Ottoman Empire in the second half of the nineteenth century', *Turcica* 28 (1996), pp. 195–235.

Tidhar, David (ed.), *Intziklopedya le-Halutzei ha-Yishuv u-Bonav* [Encyclopedia of the Pioneers and Builders of the Yishuv] (Tel Aviv, 1971) [in Hebrew].

Tilly, Charles, 'How empires end', in Barkey, Karen and Mark Von Hagen (eds.), *After Empire: Multi-Ethnic Societies and Nation-Building: The Soviet Union and the Russian, Ottoman, and Hapsburg Empires* (Boulder, 1997), pp. 1–11.

Todorova, Maria, *Imagining the Balkans* (New York, 1997).

Toprak, Zafer, *Türkiye'de Ekonomi ve Toplum (1908–1950), Milli İktisat-Milli Burjuvazi* [*Economy and Society in Turkey (1908–1950), National Economy-National Bourgeoisie*] (Istanbul, 1995) [in Turkish].

Truesdell, Matthew, *Spectacular Politics: Louis-Napoleon Bonaparte, and the Fête Impériale, 1849–1870* (Oxford, 1997).

Tucker, Judith E., 'Revisiting reform: Women and the Ottoman Law of Family Rights 1917', *Arab Studies Journal* 4/2 (Fall 1996), pp. 4–18.

Turfan, Naim M., *Rise of the Young Turks: Politics, the Military and Ottoman Collapse* (London, 2000).

Turner, Bryan S., 'Contemporary problems in the theory of citizenship', in Turner, Bryan S. (ed.), *Citizenship and Social Theory* (London, 1993), pp. 1–18.

Tümertekin, Sıddık, *Türkiye'de Belediyeler: Tarihi Gelişim ve Bugünkü Durum* [The Municipalities in Turkey: Historical Development and Present Stiuation] (Istanbul, 1946) [in Turkish].

Tziper, Daniel, *Ha-Degel ha-Tzioni me'al ha-Bosphoros: Ha-Maccabi be-Kushta beyn Tzionut le-'Otmaniyut 1895–1923* [The Zionist Flag on the Bosphorus: The Maccabi in Istanbul between Zionism and Ottomanism 1895–1923] (Jerusalem, 2000) [in Hebrew].

Uçar, Ahmet, 'Filistin'i kim sattı?' (who sold Palestine?), *Tarih ve Düşünce* (June 2002), pp. 20–23 [in Turkish].

Vatikiotis, P. J., 'The Greek Orthodox Patriarchate of Jerusalem between Hellenism and Arabism', *Middle Eastern Studies* 30/4 (1994), pp. 916–929.

Vehbi, Muallim, *Bursalı Tahir Bey* (Istanbul, 1334/1915–6) [in Ottoman Turkish].

Watenpaugh, Keith, *Being Modern in the Middle East: Revolution, Nationalism, Colonialism, and the Arab Middle Class* (Princeton, 2006).

Whitty, John Irwine, *The Water Supply of Jerusalem, Ancient and Modern* (London, 1864).

Woodhead, Christine, 'Mehmed Tahir, Bursali (1861–1925)', *Encyclopaedia of Islam*, 2nd edition, vol. IX (Leiden, 1997), p. 616.

Yaari, Abraham, *Ha-Dfus ha-'Ivri be-Kushta: Toldot ha-Dfus ha-'Ivri be-Kushta me-Reshito {...} u-Reshimat ha-Sfarim she-Nidpesu ba* [Hebrew Printing at Constantinople: Its History and Bibliography] (Jerusalem, 1967) [in Hebrew].

Yazbak, Mahmoud, *Haifa in the Late Ottoman Period, 1864–1914: A Muslim Town in Transition* (Leiden, 1998).

——. 'The municipality of a Muslim town: Nablus 1868–1914', *Archiv Orientalni: Quarterly Journal of African and Asian Studies* 67 (1999), pp. 339–60.

——. 'Nabulsi Ulama in the late Ottoman period, 1864–1914', *International Journal of Middle East Studies* 29 (1997), pp. 71–91.

Yehoshua, Ya'akov, *Al-Sahafa al-'Arabiyya fi Filastin fil-'Ahd al-'Uthmani, 1908–1918* [The Arabic Press in Palestine during the Ottoman Period, 1908–1918], (Jerusalem, 1974) [in Arabic].

——. '*Al-Munadi*: Ha-'Iton ha-Muslemi ha-rishon be-Eretz Yisra'el' [*Al-Munadi*: the first Muslim newspaper in Eretz-Israel], *ha-Mizrah he-Hadash* 25/3 (1975), pp. 209–215 [in Hebrew].

Yerlikaya, Ilhan, *Basiret Gazetesi* [The Newspaper Basiret] (Van, 1994) [in Turkish].

Yeyni, Nathan, 'Zionist Activity', in Ben-Naeh, Yaron (ed.), *Jewish Communities in the East in the Nineteenth and Twentieth Centuries: Turkey* (Jerusalem, 2010), pp. 207–22.

Zachs, Fruma, *The Making of a Syrian Identity: Intellectuals and Merchants in Nineteenth Century Beirut* (Brill, 2005).

Zandi-Sayek, Sibel, *Public Space and Urban Citizens: Ottoman Izmir in the Remaking, 1840–1890* (Unpublished Ph. D. Dissertation, University of California, Berkeley, 2001).

Zeine, Zeine N., *The Emergence of Arab Nationalism* (Beirut, 1966).

Zürcher, Erik J. 'Muslim nationalism: the missing link in the genesis of modern Turkey', *ha-Mizrah he-Hadash* vol. 39 (1997–8), pp. 67–83 [in Hebrew].

——. 'The Ottoman conscription system in theory and practice 1844–1918', in idem (ed.), *Arming the State: Military Conscription in the Middle East and Central Asia, 1775–1925* (London, 1999), pp. 79–94.

——. *Turkey: A Modern History* (London, 2001).

INDEX

'Abbas Effendi, see 'Abdu'l-Baha
'Abd al-Hadi (family), 48
'Abdallah (Emir), 174
'Abduh Family (Nablus), 129
'Abduh, Muhammad, 263
Abdülaziz (Sultan), 146, 261–2, 266, 276
'Abdu'l-Baha, 259–78
Abdülhamid II (Sultan), 3–4, 9, 61–2, 69, 73, 81, 85, 91, 96, 103, 107–8, 115, 118, 126, 130, 145, 148, 151–3, 183, 220, 243–4, 259, 262, 264–78
Abu al-Su'ud, Ishaq, 44
'Abud, Bulous, 174
Abu Khadra, Sa'id, 6–7, 17–18, 23–8, 43–4, 47
Abu-Manneh, Butrus, 9
Acre, 5, 45, 48, 131, 260 (see also 'Akka)
adhan (Muslim call for prayer), 137
Adler, Mordecai Marcus, 200
Adler, Nathan (British Chief Rabbi), 200
al-Afghani, Jamal al-Din, 177
'Afule ('Afula), 93
Ahmad Faris (al-Shidyaq), 147
Ahmad, Feroz, 4
al-Ahram, 175
Aharonovitz, Yosef, 199–203, 208
al-Akhbar, 168, 173

'Akka, 260, 263–6, 277, 281 (see also Acre)
al-'Alami, 'Abdullah, 9, 151–3, 156–9, 162 (fn. 26)
Albania, 266–7
Alexandria, 224, 278 (fn. 58)
Alexandria, Greek Orthodox Patriarchate, 224
Alfandari, Merkado, 216
'Ali Ekrem Bey, 100 (fn. 27), 185–6, 206, 217, 235 (fn. 30)
'Ali Ferruh Bey, 263
'Ali Paşa (Grand Vizier), 146–8
Alkan, Necati, 11
Allenby, General Edmond, 138
Allepo, 45, 136; and Chief Rabbinate of, 218
Alliance Israélite Universelle (AIU), 43, 58, 75 (fn. 11), 212–3, 215, 217–8, 233 (fn. 12), 234 (fn. 28), 242–5, 247–8, 251, 255
America (USA), 264–5, 270–71
American College (Tanta), 168
American Protestants, 264–5
Amigo dela Familia (El), 245
amira class, 219
Amzalek, Yosef, 171
Anatolia, 8

Anglo-Palestine Bank, 198, 208
Antebi, Albert, 217–8, 234 (fn. 28)
al-Antaki, 'Abdulmasih, 152
Antioch, Greek Orthodox Patriarchate, 224
Anti-Semitism 104–112, 119–20, 122 (fn. 30), 247, 251
Anton, Farah, 148
Antonius, George, 151, 159
Antwerp, 250
Arab: Congress of 1913, 27–8; identity, 11; intelectualls, 9; nationalism 6, 23, 27–8, 45, 64–5, 73, 125, 139, 232; national movement, 225; Ottomanists, 9, 145, 154, 160; Arab-Turkish brotherhood, 9
Arabic, 185, 193, 201–202, 204
Arabophone question, 225
Arabs, 185, 191, 193, 199, 204, 207
Armenian *millet*, 213
Armenian National Assembly (ANA), 213–4, 219–23
Armenian Patriarchate (Jerusalem), 212, 219–23
Armenian Patriarchate (Istanbul), 212, 219, 222
Armenian question, 8, 115, (fn. 41)
Armenian Revolutionary Federation, 213
Armenian synod, 220–3
Armenians, 211–32
'Arub, 86, 88, 92
al-'Asali, Shukri, 116–8
Ashkenazi, 170, 178, 192, 201, 217–8
Ashkenazim, 195–7, 254; and leadership in Jerusalem, 218 (*see also* Jews)
Asitane (*Asitane-i Aliye*, *see also* Istanbul), 129, 140
al-*Asma'i*, 204, 208, 225
Avigdor, Ya'akov, 243
Auerbach, Israel Dr., 250
Aurore (L'), 247
Austro-Hungry, 126
autobiographical literature, 56–8, 60, 62, 64–5, 68

Avcı, Yasemin, 8
Avenir (El), 249
'Awja River (ha-Yarkon), 89
a'yan (notables), 129
'Ayn Farah, 87–8, 90
'Ayn Favar (Fawar), 87, 90
al-'Azem, Wasif Bey 137
al-Azhar, University 153, 157, 167
al-A'zm, Rafiq 175–6

Babis, 260, 263, 273
Baghdad, 44, 168, 234 (fn. 19), 260
Baha'i religious leadership, 11
Baha'is, 259–78
Baha'u'llah, 259–61, 264–5, 268, 270
Baker, Muhammad Mirza, 177
baladiyya (municipality), 191, 199
Balkan Problem, 45
Balkan states, 224
Balkan Wars, 3, 178
Balkans: 132, 262, 267; and Italian interference, 247
Barakat, Da'ud, 175
al-Barghuthi, 'Umar al-Salih, 56–60, 64–6, 72–3,
Basiret, 146–7
Basiretçi, 'Ali Efendi 146–7
Batito, Nahum, 218
al-Baytjali, Iskandar al-Khuri, 64
bedel-i 'askeri (military exemption tax), 194
Bedreddin, Hasan *see* Bedri Paşa
Bedri Paşa, 266–8, 276–7
Beidas, Khalil, 67, 225–6
Beirut, 57, 59–60, 63, 71, 89, 93–4, 100 (fn. 28), 117, 129, 133, 148–50, 153–4, 157, 165–7, 171, 173, 214, 266; and *zaim*s, 214
Ben-'Attar, Haim, 257 (fn. 11), 171
Benbassa, Esther, 252
Ben Ghiat, Alexander, 249
Ben-Gurion, David, 178
Ben-Naeh, Yaron, 11
Ben-Yehuda, Eli'ezer, 190–91, 197, 202, 206

Ben-Yehuda, Ithamar (Ben-Avi), 202, 208
Ben-Zvi, Menashe, 193, 207
Bethlehem, 90–91, 223
Bezalel, Yitzhak, 248
Bigart, Jacques, 216
Bilad al-Sham, 45, 126–7
B'nai B'rith, 245, 254
B'nai Yisrael society, 248
Bordeaux (Ottoman Consulate General in) 154
Bosphore (Le), 248
Bourdett-Coutts (Lady), p. 86
Boz (La), 244, 249
British: government, 174; Mandate (*see* Palestine under British Mandate); occupation of Palestine, 168; policies in Palestine, 174
al-Budayri, Ishak, 44
Bukharian Jews, 217
Burlon (El), 244
Bursa, 216, 266
Bursalı, Mehmed Tahir Bey, 266, 268–9, 276, 278
Büssow, Johann, 7
al-Bustani, Butrus, 26, 148, 153–4
al-Bustani, Salim, 154
al-Bustani, Sulaiman, 152–7, 162 (fn. 24)
Byzantine period, 223

Cairo, 27, 149, 152–4, 165–9, 173, 173, 177, 180 (fn. 7)
caliph, 148, 278
caliphate, 9
DeCamondo, Count Avraham Behor, 242
Campos, Michelle C., 6, 17
capitulations, 83
Cavid Bey, 109
Cemal Paşa (Jamal Pasha), 132–3, 137, 181 (fn. 16), 247, 271–2
Cemal'üddin, Mehmed (*Şeyh-ül Islam*), 156
censorship, 3, 56, 66
centralization, 8

Cevad Paşa, Ahmet, 155
Cevdet Paşa, Ahmet, 150
Ceuto, Lucien, 247–8
Chamber of Commerce (Jerusalem), 189, 207
Chelouche, Ya'akov, 171
Chelouche, Yosef Eliyahu, 62, 171
Cheif Rabbinate (Jerusalem), 212, 214–19
Cheif Rabbinate (Istanbul), 215
childhood, 7–8, 56–7, 66, 73, 135
Christian Mission Society, 225
Christians, 187, 192, 194–5, 197
la Cierva y Lewita, Antonio de, 134
Committee of Union and Progress (CUP), 1–2, 18, 42, 44, 49–50, 66, 104–6, 108–12, 120, 145–6, 151, 245, 251, 254, 259–78
compulsory draft, 9
confiscation, 9
conscription, 28–9, 57, 60–61, 76 (fn. 26), 137–8, 184, 196–8,
Constantinople, Greek Orthodox Patriarchate, 224
Constitution (Armenian National), 213, 220, 223
Constitution (Ottoman) 3, 9–10, 18, 20–21, 24–6, 37–8, 47, 64, 69, 71–2, 128, 131, 226, 244
Constitutional Revolution (Iran), 262, 275 (*see also mashrutiyyat*)
Constitutional School (*al-Madrasa al-Dusturiyya*), 46, 69–70, 72–3, 136
Council of State, 146, 275 (fn. 16)
coup d'état (1913), 4
Courrier d'Orient (Le), 247
Crete, 2
Cyril, Patriarch, 224

al-Dajani, Rajib, 174
Damascus, 44, 133, 137, 149, 159, 168, 173, 214, 216, 221, 266
Damascus-Beirut Railway line, 98
Da'irat al-Ma'arif, 154
Damascus Gate, 129

Darülfünun-ı Şahane (Imperial
  University), 59
Darwin, Charles, 63
Dashnaks, 214
Davison, Roderic H., 146
Dead Sea, 137
Decentralization Party (*Hizb al-
  Lamarkaziyya*), 168, 175–7,
  180 (fn. 7)
decentralization policy, 27
Der Matossian, Bedross, 10
despositin (*pavsis*), 229
despotism, 1, 62, 64, 69, 73
dhimmi, 27, 59, 126
diaries, 5
Diryese Paşa, 89
discipline, 58–9, 69
displacement, 9
Dizengoff, Meir, 89
Dönme, 251
Doumani, Beshara, 128, 140 (fn. 5)
Droshak, 213
Dustur: see constitution
al-Dusturiyya school (*see* schools)

Ebüziyye Tevfik 106–8, 112–3, 117, 119,
  121 (fn. 9), 247
Edirne, 260
education, 56–60, 62, 64, 66–71
educational system, 8, 59, 212
Egypt, 14 (fn. 16), 98 (fn. 9), 118, 133,
  151, 168, 173, 219, 244, 263, 265, 269,
  278 (fn. 52); Chief Rabbi of, 244
Electoral Law, 37–8
electric lighting, 82, 88, 90–91
electric tramway, 82, 89–92, 100–102
Elkayam, Yehoshua, 171
Elmalech, Avraham, 165–6, 171–2, 217,
  252
Elnecavé, David, 248
Elyashar, Haim Moshe, 217
Elyashar, Ya'akov Sha'ul, 217
Emin Âli Bey, 277 (fn. 37)
empires, theoretical literature on, 18–20

English: instruction in, 69; interests,
  96–7; study of, 137
Entente Libérale (*Hürriyet ve İtilâf*), 18,
  23, 42, 45–6
Enver Paşa (previously Bey), 129, 132,
  247, 271
Epoka (La), 249
Eretz-Israel Almanac, 185, 205–6, 208
Eretz Israeli Office / Palestine Office, 87,
  168–9
Eretz Israeli Locale, 9, 166, 177–9
Esperansa (La), 249
ethno-national independence
  movements, 18
Ezra organization (*Hilfsverein der Deutschen
  Juden*), 218, 245–6, 255

Faisal (emir later king), 133, 174
Falanga, J., 95
Filastin, 22, 24, 40–1, 43–7, 49–50, 63–4,
  69–72, 168–9, 173, 175, 181 (fn. 25),
  225–6, 238
Fizan, 263
Florentin, David, 249
France, 93, 215, 245
Franco, Yosef, 218
Francos, 242
Frangia Bey, 86–9, 99 (fn. 16)
Freemasonry, 23, 26, 112
Freemasons, 108–9, 111, 121 (fn. 13), 251
French: diplomatic pressure on the
  Ottoman Empire, 93, 139, 149;
  instruction in, 58, 68, 137, 167;
  language, 68, 90; periodicals, 243,
  246–8, 253; Revolution, 103; Second
  Empire, 3; translation into, 266
Frères des Écoles Chrétiennes School, 58–9,
  225–6
Fresko, David, 213, 215, 245, 248, 251, 253
Friends School, 69
Fu'ad Paşa (Grand Vizier), 147–8, 150

Gabbay, Izak, 249
Gabbay, Yehezkel, 249

Galanté, Avraham, 215
Galilee, Arab villages of, 223
Gaza, 6, 9, 17, 23, 40, 43–4, 47–48, 50–51, 152, 156–7, 159
Gelvin, James, 141
German: Consulate (Jaffa), 181 (fn. 15); essays, 66; entry to World War I, 126; growing influence in the Ottoman Empire, 255; interests, 97; Orthodox Jews, 215; political influence, 96
German Lutheran School (*al-Dabagha*), 69, 136
Germany, 114, 126, 215, 247, 255; and Rivalry with France, 215; and Zionist leaders in, 247
ghiaur, 132
Giridî, Ahmed Şevki Efendi, 266, 268–9, 277–8
Giron, Yakir, 243
Gottheil, Richard, 225
Grand Sacristan (*Lusararpet*), 220
Grasiozo (El), 244
Greece, 2, 132, 224, 238 (fn. 77), 256 (fn. 4)
Greek Orthodox, 1, 62, 67, 135, 212–32
Greek Orthodox *millet*, 224–32
Greek Orthodox Patriarchate (Jerusalem), 212, 223–30
Greek Orthodox Patriarchate School, 62
Greek Orthodox, synod, 225–31
Greek question, 8
Greek (s), 18, 103, 105, 115–6, 191, 212, 232

Habazeleth, 185–6, 189, 194, 199, 206–7, 217–8
Hadiqat al-Akhbar, 148, 160 (fn. 10)
Hafiye (secret police), 155
Hagopian, Daniel, 223
Hahambaşı (Cheif Rabbi; *see also* Cheif Rabbinate), 215, 243, 248; and organizational regulations, 243; and *kaymakam* (*locum tenes*) of, 215–9, 243–4
Haifa, 46, 82, 92, 171, 173, 223, 250, 265

Haifa Railway Line, 92
Halevi, Moshe, 215, 217, 243–5, 248
Halevi, Sa'adi, 249
Halil Bey (Menteşe), 247
Halki, Mustafa, 150
Hamidian (policy, regime, period, generation, cenzorship), 2, 5, 8, 66, 148–9, 156
Hammad family, 129
Hammad, Tawfiq, 48
Hannania, Habib, 175
al-Haram al-Sharif, 69, 129
Haremeyn (Mecca and Medina), 9
Hasan Fehmi Paşa, 93
Hasan Hilmi Efendi, 277
Hashqafa, 185, 191, 197–8, 204–208, 217
Hassidim, 197
Hatt-ı Hümayun, 127
Hazewi, 185, 190, 206–208
Hebrew: language, 184–185, 188, 190–92, 201; and disseminators in Salonica, 251; in schools' curriculum, 246, periodicals, 245–7; study of, 250
Hebron, 40, 50
Hejaz Railway line, 82, 92, 98, 101
Hellenism, 224, 232
ha-Herut, 165, 169–71, 179 (fn 1), 181 (fn. 15), 181 (fn. 25)
Herzl, Theodor, 198
Heyet-i Âyan (Ottoman Senate), 38
Heyet-i Meb'usan, *see* Parliament
Hermoni, Aharon, 249
al-Hilal, 152
Hilmi Paşa, 229
Histadrut (Jewish Worker's Union), 174
Historiography: of the Young Turk period, 3–4, 18, 211; Kemalist, 4, 13 (fn. 8); on the Ottoman Armenians, 239 (fn. 41); Palestinian, 179
Hivan, David, 171
Hochberg, Sami, 176, 247, 249
Holy Sepulcher, brotherhood of, 224, 229
Homer, 154
Hunchaks, 214

Hurriyya/Hürriyet (freedom), 67, 69, 118, 269
al-Husayni, Ahmad 'Arif, 23, 51
al-Husayni (al-Husseini), Husayn (Hussein) Salim, 62, 92, 134–5, 137–8
al-Husayni, Sa'id, 23, 49, 88, 111–12
al-Husayni, Shukri, 44
Husni, Yusuf, 150

identity: multiplicity of, 166, 179; Mediterranean-Levantine, 166, 178, 179 (fn. 3)
Ihtida (conversion to Islam), 264–5
İkdam, 250
Al-Ikha (Arab-Ottoman Brotherhood Society), 140 (fn. 9)
imam, 37
Impartial (El), 249
Imperial citizenship, 18, 20, 23–4, 27–9
Imperial Orthodox Palestine Society, 224
industry, 189
inter-communal relations, 166–9, 171–3, 175, 178–9
Iran, 259–64, 269–71, 275, 277
Iraq 104, 106–108, 117, 122 (fn. 38)
Al-'Isa, 'Isa, 49–50, 225–6
Al-'Isa, Yusuf, 63, 72, 225
Istanbul: 5, 7, 8, 11, 14 (fn. 16), 20, 35, 44–5, 49, 58–62, 83, 86–7, 89, 92–3, 95–6, 103–106, 108, 110–112, 118, 121, 125, 128–9, 134, 140 (fn. 11), 145, 147, 149–151, 154, 167, 177, 183, 207 (fn. 19), 212–13, 215, 217, 219, 221–223, 228–231, 232 (fn. 2), 233 (fn. 4), 234 (fn. 24), 237 (fn. 60), 242–250, 247, 252, 254, 256 (fn. 2, 4), 260, 262–3, 265–9, 271, 276 (fn. 33), 277 (fn. 37), 278 (fn. 53); Chief Rabbinate of, 215, 217; Armenian Community of, 223; Jewish community of, 242, 252, 254; modern education in, 244; publication of Jewish press, 11, 248–9
İşkodra (Shkodër), 266–7

Italy, 108, 177, 247, 268
al-Ittihad, 248
Ittihad-ı Osmani, 147
Ittihad al-'Umal, 168, 174
Ittihad ve-Terakki Cemiyeti, see CUP
Izmir, 249
Izmirilyan, Madteos, 214, 220, 222
Izmir-Kasaba Railway line, 83

Jabotinsky, Vladimir (Zeev), 247, 250
Jacobson, Abigail, 9, 135, 165
Jacobsohn, Victor, 176, 245–7
Ja'far Pasha, 45–6
Jaffa, 8, 22–4, 40, 43, 45–6, 48–51, 71, 81–97, 164–76, 185, 187, 192, 200, 204, 206–8, 220, 222–3, 226, 228–9, 250
Jaffa Gate, 1, 63, 91
Jaffa-Jerusalem Railway Line, 89, 91, 98
Jaffa Municipality, 94
Jaffa port, 22, 24, 46, 48–51, 63, 82, 93–6; and Disinfecting Station, 94; and Life Boat Station, 94
Jamal Pasha, *see* Cemal Paşa
Jam'iyya (league of families), 7, 48
al-Jam'iyya al-'Abbasiyya, 48
al-Jam'iyya al-Hamadiyya, 48
al-Jami'a (al-Jami'a al-'Uthmaniyya), 148
Jarallah, 'Ali, 70, 136
al-Jawa'ib, 147
Jawharieh, Tawfik, 135–6
Jawharieh, Wasif, 126, 129, 135–8
Jenin, 92–3
Jerusalem (*see also* al-Quds; Kudüs), 3, 8, 36, 39–40, 43–6, 48–51, 184–7, 189–92, 194–6, 198, 200, 204–8, 250; Arab Orthodox community of, 223–30
Jerusalem invistigative comission, 220
Jerusalem Municipality, 25, 86–8, 90–2, 95–6
Jerusalem, Old City, 211
Jesuit College (Beirut), 167
Jeune Turc (Le), 247

INDEX

Jewish Chronicle, 216
Jewish Colonial Bank, 251
Jewish Colonization Association (JCA), 107
Jewish: educated circles, 247; ethnic groups, 184, 195–8; humorous press, 244; immigration (*'aliya*), 5, 178; and debate in Ottoman parliament 8; relations with the Arabs, 178; *millet*, 214–19; nationalism, 249; newspapers, 248; press, 241, 244, 255; 'question', 8 (*see also* Ashkenazim, Sephardim, Zionism)
Jewish Ottoman Society, 184, 188, 194, 198–200, 202, 207
Jews, 183–5, 187–190, 192, 194–5, 197–203, 207–208, 211–232, 263; local 170; foreign, 178; of Istanbul, 249 (*see also* Ashkenzaim, citizenship, Sephardim)
al-Jinan, 148, 154
Jordan River, 223
Journal de Salonique, 248
Journal Israélite, 244, 247–8
Judio, (El) – Gazeta Judia Endepediente, 244, 248
Jugeton (El), 244

Kahanoff, Jacqueline, 179 (fn. 3)
Kamil Paşa (Grand Vizier), 153
Kanuni Sultan Süleyman (also known as Suleiman the Magnificent), 97
al-Karmil, 40, 42, 45–6, 168–9, 173
Karasso, Emanuel 108–9
al-Kawakibi, 'Abdulrahman, 152
Kavaid-i Osmaniye, 150
Kayalı, Hasan, 10, 140
Kemal, Mustafa (Atatürk), 266
Kemal, Namık, 26, 32 (fn. 10), 262
Kemalist Republic: *see* Turkish Republic
al-Khalidi, Jamil, 70, 136
al-Khalidi, Raghib, 59, 62
al-Khalidi, Ruhi, 22, 40, 43, 49, 51, 88, 111–16, 151–9, 162 (fn. 25)

al-Khalidi, Yasin, 154
al-Khalidi, Yusuf Diya' (Ziya), 49, 154, 163 (fn. 34)
al-Khammash, 'Abbas Shaykh, 48
al-Khammash, Ahmad Shaykh, 48
al-Khatib, Nasib, 43, 46
Khuri, Khalil, 148, 160 (fn. 10)
Kiftin, 226
Kindanyan Bey, 94
Kitab-i-Aqdas (al-Kitab al-Aqdas), 260, 274, 278
Kohen, Moiz 106–7, 109–110, 114, 119, 122 (fn. 23)
Kramarov, Z., 201
Kudüs-i Şerif / al-Quds al-Sharif, 1, 68
Kudüs *mutasarrıfı* (the district governor of Jerusalem), 86, 92, 95
Kudüs *mutasarrıflığı* (the province of Jerusalem), 89 add
Kurd 'Ali, Muhammad, 157
Kushta (Constantinople, *see also* Istanbul), 191, 207

Ladino (Judeo-Spanish): in school curriculum, 246; journals, 248, 252; periodaicals, 243, 246–7; priority over Hebrew, 249
Lebanon, 133
Levy, Yitzhak, Dr., 198, 202, 208 (fn. 49)
Libya, 3, 17, 177, 268
Libyan Desert, 163
Lichtheim, Richard, 247
liwa (sub-division of province; Turkish: *liva*), 43–4, 46–7, 49–51
Louis XIV (king of France), 213
Luncz, Abraham Moshe, 185, 188, 197–8, 205–208

Mabeyn, 89, 153, 155–6, 162 (fn. 29)
Maccabi, 212
Maccabi Tel-Aviv, 78 (fn. 68)
Macedonians, 191
al-Madrasa al-Wataniyya, 153

ha-Magen Association 167–9, 171–2, 180 (fn. 6), 181, (fn. 16–17)
Magnus, Max, 87
mahkama (Muslim court), 199
Mahmud II (Sultan), 262
majlis al-idara (administrataive council), 199 (fn. 4)
majlis al-ikhtiyariyya (council of elders), 35–6
majlis 'umumi / meclis-i umumî (provincial council), 23, 78 (fn. 60)
Maktab al-Sana'i (Beirut), 157
Malul, Nissim: 9–10; and Arabic language 169–70; biography 168; journalistic writing 168–9, 171, 173–4; political activism 168, 171, 174, 176
al-Manar, 27, 152, 158, 163 (fn. 44), 169, 177
Manastırlı, Mehmed Rifat, 276–7
Mani, Shlomo, 217
Manisa, 244
Mashrutiyyat (Iranian Constitutional Revolution), 262
Matalon, Moshe, 171
Matzliah, Nissim, 113–4
Mavromatis, Euripide 89, 92
Meclis-i Meb'usan see Parliament
Meir, Ya'akov, 216–9
Meissner Paşa, 92
Memoirs, 5
Meseret (El), 249
Ha-Mevasser, 249–51
Midhat Paşa, (Grand Vizier), 148, 153, 244, 260, 262
millet, 46, 62, 127, 146–7, 213, 215, 224, 237 (fn. 67) (*see also* Armenians, Greek Orthodox and Jews)
Ministry of Interior, 89, 95
Ministry of Post and Telegraph, 91
Ministry of Public Health, 94
Ministry of Public Works, 86, 91, 94
Mittwoch, Eugen, Dr., 193
Mixed Councils, 230

modernization, 6, 8, 11
Morgan, James, 88
Morgentau, Henry, 247
Mowashahat of Andalusia, 136
Moyal, family ('Abdallah Nadim; Aharon; David; Esther Azhari; Yosef and Shimon), 166–7
Moyal, Shimon, 9–10; and Arabic language 169–70; biography 166–7; connection with Arab intellectuals 177; journalistic writing 167, 169, 171; political activism 167, 171, 173, 176
Mudanya Railway line, 83
mufti, 35
Muhammad (Prophet), 264
Muhammad Rashad (Sultan), 130
mukhtar 35, 37, 191–2, 207, (fn. 22)
Mülkiye (College of Public Administration, Istanbul), 61, 154
al-Munadi, 24–5
Municipalities Law, 36
al-Muntada al-Adabi (The Arab Literary Club), 140
al-Muqattam, 168–9
al-Muqtabas, 157
al-Muqtataf, 157
Mushabbak, Aftim, 70, 136
Muslim-Christian Association, 174
Muslim Higher Court (Istanbul), 129
Muslims, 1, 185, 187, 192, 194–5, 198, 200, 253
mutasarrif (see also: mutasarrıf), 36, 86, 92, 95
Mutasarrifiyya (see also mutasarrıflık), 39–40, 48–50
Mutasarrıflık 5, 89
Muzaffaru'd-Din Shah (Iran), 262, 275

Nablus, 5, 36, 38–9, 47–8, 92, 131
Nabulsi family, 129
Nacional (El), 245, 248
al-Nafa'is al-'Asriyya, 64, 67, 226
nahiya (sub-district) 38–9

INDEX

Nahum, Haim, 212–3, 215–6, 218, 244–5, 248, 255
al-Nashashibi, Is'af, 62–3, 70, 73
al-Nashashibi, 'Uthman, 23, 40, 51, 62
Nasiru'd-Din Shah (Iran), 261–2
Nassar, Issam, 9
Nassar, Najib, 42
Nathan, Paul, Dr., 198, 200
Nationality Law (1869), 146
National Orthodox Association, 224
Navon, Joseph, 89
Nazareth, 153, 223, 226
Nazim Paşa, 229
nefus books (census registers), 199
newspapers: *see* press and under specific titles of papers
New York, 250
Nimr, 48
Niyazi Paşa, 129
nizam (order), 67, 70
Nordau, Max, 253
Notre Dame de France, 129
Novelista (El), 249

Odessa (Odesa), 246, 250
Organo de la Federasion Sionista del Oriente (later known as *Organo Zionista Independiente*), 248
Orient (L'), 248
Ormanian, Maghakia, 213, 220
Osmanlı Hürriyet Cemiyeti, 266
Ottoman: Commission of the Hamidiye-Hejaz Railway, 92; Jewry, 8, 11, 242–3, 246; imperial project, 6; Language, 149–150, 156; Language, Society for, 248; and loyalty, 169–71, 177–8; navy, 1; official documents, 5; Red Crescent society, 134, 137; perceptions of, 3, 145–59, 230
Ottomanization (adoption of Ottoman citizenship), 245, 248

Palestine (*see also* Eretz Israel, Holy Land): 1–11; and Arab population, 6, 254; and 'civilizing mission', 6; immigration to, 243; and civil society, 6; and infrastracture projects; and Jewish interests, 245; and Jewish-Arab conflict, 6; Jewish community of, 10; Jewish local press, 10; and Jewish settlment, 8; late Ottoman period in, 6–7; and Muslim notables, 6; and Zionist activity 8; under British Mandate, 6, 5, 14 (fn. 13), 51, 92, 232 (fn. 1), 238 (fn. 73), 255
Palestine Chamber of Commerce, 92
Palestinian: identity, 11; intelectuals, 7, 55, 61–3, 69–70; locale, 9; urban population, 7; youth, 6–7, 55–7, 61, 64, 66, 72–3
Panigel, Eliyahu Moshe, 216–19
Pan-Turanianism, 132
Paris, 244
Parliament, Ottoman (*Meclis-i Meb'usan*), 17, 21, 25, 151, 153–4, 159, 250; elections for, 6–7; and 1908 elections, 21–2; and 1912 elections, 22
Parodos, 250
Patria (El), 244
Persian Jews, 217
Perushim, 197
Ha-Po'el ha-Tza'ir, 170, 185, 190, 192, 194–9, 201, 204
Ha-Po'el ha-Tza'ir (party), 202
politics of notables, 214
Porte *see* Sublime Porte
preparatory schools, 1
press 21–2, 24; post-revolutionary press, 10; Arabic 55, 66–7, 69–71, 73, 172; French, 243, 246–7; Hebrew 172, 184, 188, 191–2, 195, 197, 203, 205; Ladino, 243, 246–8, 252; Turkish, 172, 204, *see also* names of specific newspapers
Provincial Law (1871), 89
Provincial Municipal Law (1877), 86
public celebrations, 3
Pueblo (El), 249
Puzantion, 213

qada (kaza), 35–6, 38, 40, 42, 44, 47–8, 51 (fn. 1, 11), 52 (fn. 12), 226
qadi, 35
qaimaqam (kaymakam) 35, 95,
Qub'ayn, Salim, 151–3, 155, 161 (fn. 23)
al-Quds (newspaper), 204

Rabat, 166
Ramadan, 135
Ramgavars, 214
Rashid Pasha, Mehmed, 154
Rawdat al-Ma'arif School, 69
Razi Paşa, 204
Reform Edict (1856), 127, 146
Reşid Paşa, 217
Rhodes, Rabbi of, 218
Rida, Rashid, 163 (ft 44), 175, 177
Risala-yi Madaniyya, 261, 274
Risala-yi Siyasiyya, 261–2, 274
Riza Bey, 186
Rohatyn, 250
Rumelia, 260, 262, 269
Ruppin, Arthur, 87, 168, 173, 178
Russia, 197, 247, 249, 271
Russian: Consulate (Jerusalem), 100 (fn. 27); Empire, emmigration of Jews from, 106, 121 (fn. 6); Empire, historhiography of, 18; influence on Arab Orthodox community, 224–6; instruction in, 225; interference, 139; interests, 97; language, 202; literature, 226; Orthodox school (Nazereth), 226; school, graduates of, 64; Teachers Training center (Nazereth), 153, 226

Sabaheddin (Prince), 61
Sabunji, Lewis, 150
al-Sa'di, 'Abdel Fattah, 131
Sa'diya quarter (Jerusalem), 135
Safed 167–8, 190; District of, 116
al-Sa'id, Hafiz, 23–4, 49
Sa'id Paşa/Pasha, 153, 204

al-Sakakini, Khalil, 46, 62–3, 66–7, 70, 72, 126, 131, 134, 136–7, 140–41, 225–7
salaf, salafi, 157, 263
salafis, 263
al-Salahiyya School, 225
al-Salam, 168, 173
al-Saleh, Muhammad Sheikh, 135
Salonica, 108, 132, 216, 218, 249, 251, 252, 254, 265–6, 268
sanjaq (district; Turkish: sancak), 5, 38–9, 47
Sawt al-'Uthmaniyya, 167–8, 171, 180 (fn. 6)
Saysan, 275 (fn. 15)
Schneller, Johann Ludwig, 67
school(s), 56–60, 62, 64, 66, 68–71, 73 (see also under specific names)
secular council (meclis-i cismani), 216
Sephardi(c): intellectuals, 10, 165–182, 192, 195–8, 201; families, 217
Sephardim (also Oriental Jews/ Maghrebim): community; and national approach, 172–3; and relations with the Arabs 172–3, 178; and relations with the Ashkenazim, 178
Shabtai, Hezkiya, 218
Shahada, Bulus, 69
Sharaby, Rachel, 218
Sharet, Moshe, 178
shari'a, 9, 127
Sharif Hussein, 133
Sheikh Jarrah (Jerusalem), 135–6
Sheikh Rihan, 135
shekel, 251
Shi'ism, 263, 273, 275, 278
Shumayyil, Shibli, 63
Shuqayri, As'ad Shaykh, 45, 131
Sidon (Sida), 216
Smith, Charles, 140
Sokolow, Nahum, 247, 250
Solomon's Pools, 87
Sorbonne (The University of), 154
Sports, 71–3
St. George's School, 59, 225–6
St. James, brotherhood of, 219

INDEX 309

Stamboul, 250
Sublime Porte, 35, 105, 119, 140 (fn. 11), 146, 153, 162 (fn. 29), 216, 260, 265, 267, 271
Şükrü, Hanioğlu M., 140
Süleyman Rifat Bey, 277
Sultaniye (al-*Sultaniyya*) High School (*Mekteb-i Sultani*), 59, 150
Suphi Bey, 92
Syria/Syrian, 45, 132–3, 149–50
Syrian Orphanage, 67
Syrian Protestant College, 71

al-Ta'lif wal-Taqrib movement, 177
Talat Paşa, 132, 247, 271
Tanin, 251
Tamimi family, 129
Tanta, 168
Tanzimat, 8, 20, 61, 81–2, 84, 90, 96, 99 (fn. 14), 127–8, 146–7, 154–5, 220, 261–2
Tasvir-i Efkâr 106–7, 247
Tawfik Pasha, 204
Telegrafo (El), 245, 248
telephone communication, 90–2, 100
Tellioğlu, Atnaş Efendi, 94
Tibawi, A. L, 141
Tiberias, 167, 190, 229; District of, 116
Tiempo (El), 213, 215, 245, 248, 250, 253
Tobacco Revolt (Iran), 261
Tourian, Yeghishe, 221
Transjordan, 173
Tribuna Libera (La), 249
Tripoli (Libya), 132
Truesdell, Matthew, 3
Tunisia, 168
Tuqan family, 48, 129
Tuqan, Haydar, 48, 131
Turfan, Naim, 127, 140
Turgenev, Ivan Sergeyevich, 63
Turjman, Ihasam, 130, 133
Turkey, 4, 249, 251
Turkification Policies, 18, 45, 126, 132, 271

Turkish: language, 184–5, 191, 193, 199, 201–204; press, 241, 253; homeland, 249; patriotism, 250; Republic, 255

'ulema, 214, 261–3
Ussishkin, Menahem, 247

Valero (family), 195
Vartkes Efendi 114–5
Vehabedian, Haroutiun, 220–2
Verité Theater, 1
Vilayet Law (Law of Provincial Administration), 35–6
Vilna, 250

*Wahhabi*s (*salafi*s), 263
wali (governor), 36 (*see also Mutasarrıf*)
Wallace, Thomas, R., 186–7, 206
waqf (Muslim pious endowment), 47, 87, 128, 227
watan (homeland), 23, 27
werko (*wirko*, land and property tax), 36, 194
wilaya, 45, 47, 52 (fn. 39)
Witty, John Irwine, 86
Wolffsohn, David, 246–7
World War I, 3, 6–8, 92, 98, 242, 254–5, 259, 271–2

Yazid (Ummayyad caliph), 269, 278
Yellin, David, 185, 193, 198, 200, 207–208
Yemenite Jews, 195–7, 217
Yeritsion, Kevork, 222
Yiddish, 202
Yıldız Palace, 213
yishuv (the Jewish community in Palestine), 117, 171–2, 183–4, 187–195, 199–200, 205–6
yishuv, 'old *yishuv*', 206 (fn. 7)
yishuv, 'new *yishuv*', 187, 195, 206 (fn. 7)
Young Turk: 'civilizing mission', legacy, 3; perceptions of Palestine, 5; Revolution, 3, 6, 244, 259, 265–6, 269, 276, 278

Young Turks, 4, 8–9, 11, 12 (fn. 5), 32 (fn. 11), 37–8, 61, 82–3, 85, 108, 125, 129–130, 132, 139, 145–6, 149–151, 153, 159, 176, 194, 205, 232, 244–5, 259–61, 268–9, 271, 273, 276 (fn. 29)
youth (*see* Palestinian youth)
Yusuf Ziya Paşa, 262, 271

Zeine N. Zeine, 132, 151, 159
zikr, 135, 140
Zion English College, 225
Zionism, 6, 8, 103–120, 125, 167, 203, 213, 241–2, 244–255, 256 (fn. 5), Anti-Zionism 111; and Arabic press, 169, 171, 173; and debate in Ottoman parlament, 8; and patriotism, 253; and political movement, 245, and Relations with the Arabs, 176; critic of, 253; in Eastern Europe, 254; in Izmir, 249; interpretations of, 177–8; oppozition to, 245, 247, 252; Revisionist Zionism, 247; spreading of, 246
Zionist establishment, 249
Zionist movement, 11, 45, 168, 173–8, 246, 250, 253, 257 (fn. 13)
Zionist organization: 87, 106, 255; and branch in Istanbul, 245–6; and leaders in Germany, 247
Zionists, 25, 87, 111, 114, 116–7, 166, 169–70, 173–4, 176–8, 212–13, 215, 217, 242, 245–8, 250–55, 262; Anti-Zionist(s), 111–12, 168, 171, 253
Zionist World Organization, 255
Ziya, Halid, 61
Zola, Emile, 167